Rebel Music in the Triumphant Empire

Rebel Music in the Triumphant Empire

Punk Rock in the 1990s United States

David Pearson

OXFORD

UNIVERSITY PRESS

Oxford University Press is a department of the University of Oxford. It furthers
the University's objective of excellence in research, scholarship, and education
by publishing worldwide. Oxford is a registered trade mark of Oxford University
Press in the UK and certain other countries.

Published in the United States of America by Oxford University Press
198 Madison Avenue, New York, NY 10016, United States of America.

Library of Congress Cataloging-in-Publication Data
Names: Pearson, David (David M.) author.
Title: Rebel music in the triumphant empire : punk rock in the 1990s
United States / David Pearson.
Description: New York : Oxford University Press, 2021. |
Includes bibliographical references and index. |
Identifiers: LCCN 2020027714 (print) | LCCN 2020027715 (ebook) |
ISBN 9780197534885 (hardback) | ISBN 9780197534892 (paperback) |
ISBN 9780197534915 (epub) | ISBN 9780197534922 (oso)
Subjects: LCSH: Punk rock music—United States—History and criticism. |
Rock music—United States—1991-2000—History and criticism.
Classification: LCC ML3534.3 .P43 2020 (print) | LCC ML3534.3 (ebook) |
DDC 781.660973/09049—dc23
LC record available at https://lccn.loc.gov/2020027714
LC ebook record available at https://lccn.loc.gov/2020027715

DOI: 10.1093/oso/9780197534885.001.0001

Hardback printed by Bridgeport National Bindery, Inc., United States of America

Contents

Acknowledgments

First off, some prior publication credits. Part 1 of chapter 5 is based on my article "Punk's Popularity Anxieties and DIY Institutions as Ideological (Anti-)State Apparatuses" in *Punk and Post-Punk* 7, no. 1 (2018). Parts of the Introduction and chapter 3 are based on my article "Extreme Hardcore Punk and the Analytical Challenges of Rhythm, Riffs, and Timbre in Punk Music," first published in *Music Theory Online* 25, no. 1 (2019), https://mtosmt.org/issues/mto.19.25.1/mto.19.25.1.pearson.html.

This book has been a long time in coming, so let me go mostly in chronological order with the acknowledgments. To mum and dad, thanks for supporting me in my musical endeavors from those first saxophone lessons through the more abrasive guitar playing, and then even more abrasive saxophone playing. Dad gets credit for those dope beats on the steering wheel when a punk cassette was in the car stereo, and mum gets credit for instilling in me the desire to explore and understand the world around me ("did you do your reading?"). To Richie, Raphi, and the whole RM Crew: on a personal level, this book started with you in band practices, 35-cent cans of pop on Coventry, and going to shows.

With my sense of humor, sometimes abrasive attitude, political conscience and consciousness, and general refusal to make peace with oppressive institutions, it's been quite a challenge figuring out how to work within, through, and around the elitist institution that is academia. The late Richard Burke, my music history professor at Hunter College, modeled a way of keeping your soul intact while working in academia and letting his love for music shine as he shared, with tremendous generosity, intelligence, and humor, his incredibly wide-ranging knowledge of music with so many students. I miss you and I continue to draw on all I have learned from you.

I began my scholarly writing on punk at Hunter College, with Mark Spicer as my MA thesis advisor, and later a part of my dissertation committee. Thanks for the rigorous editing and feedback, for engaging with the music analysis on such a high level, and for steering me into greater dialogue with popular and rock music scholarship. I also have to send a shout-out to all those who I made music and friendships with at Hunter College: Thomas, Diana, Kate, John, Mindy, Amanda, Eliza, Rosie, Alicia, and everyone else.

This book grew out of my PhD dissertation at the Graduate Center of the City University of New York. Jane Sugarman, my dissertation advisor, always found the time to give thoughtful and very detailed feedback despite having so many other advisees. Thanks especially for helping work through the best ways to draw on the viewpoints and experiences of the people this book is about, and for always insisting each sentence say what I meant with clarity. And to the rest of my dissertation committee—Janette Tilley and Scott Burnham—your encouragement and feedback, including catching some errors that I hadn't, is much appreciated.

I also thank CUNY Graduate Center itself for awarding me a Doctoral Student Research Grant that enabled me to spend a month in San Francisco delving through the *MaximumRockNRoll* archives, interviewing a couple musicians, and getting to know about the punk scene out west. And even more importantly for having that handy hot-water spout in the library kitchenette that I must have used to make hundreds of cups of tea while working on what became this book. My years in the PhD program, and navigating the world of academia, were made much more tolerable (and sometimes pleasant) by the friends who shared my discomfort with elitism and my love for keeping it real, especially Elise, Aaron, Serena, and Elizabeth.

This book greatly benefited from the fact that the punk scene is among the most self-documented musical cultures in the world. From its beginnings, participants in punk have documented their scene in the zines (short for fanzines) they produced, interviewing bands, reviewing recordings, and reporting on local scenes. These zines made for excellent primary sources in my research, providing crucial information and wonderful quotes as well as helping me to narrate a history of 1990s punk. The Fales Library and Special Collections of New York University, the Music Library at Bowling Green State University, and the University of Michigan-Ann Arbor Library Special Collections provided me with access to a number of the zines quoted in this book. But the most extensive collections of punk zines are not located in academic libraries, but in DIY (do-it-yourself) punk archives. My deep gratitude goes out to Grace Ambrose and Eli Wald at *MaximumRockNRoll*, who allowed me access to their office in San Francisco to go through every issue of *MaximumRockNRoll* from the 1990s. In addition, a grateful thanks goes out to everyone who contributed to creating and maintaining the Zine Library at ABC No Rio on the Lower East Side of New York City, as well as all those who have fought to keep ABC No Rio open in the face of numerous eviction attempts by the city government. ABC No Rio's zine library enabled me to fill in the gaps of zines not found at any academic library.

The other greatest resource for this book was the musicians who agreed to be interviewed. They provided thoughtful answers to some difficult questions, shared their personal experiences, and helped shape my conception of this work. I thank Taína Asili, Bill Chamberlain, Michelle Gonzales, Kirsten Patches, Al Pist, and Martín Sorrondeguy for their time and ideas.

Finally, a big thanks to Suzanne Ryan at Oxford University Press for immediately seeing the value of this book and helping me navigate through the publication process, and especially for appreciating scholarly writing aimed at reaching beyond specialists.

***

I dedicate this book to my brother Matthew, who passed away while I was doing the research for this book. During my childhood, our house was filled with his beautiful singing and the songs he invented. It is doubtful that I would have become a musician without this early inspiration. More importantly, it was my bond and interactions with Matthew when we were little that taught me how to love and care for people, and I hope to carry that love into everything I do.

Introduction

> The [first] Gulf War was why I started doing punk in the nineties. [At the] University of Wisconsin[-Madison], we were classical music players. I was a French horn major and my late husband Phil [Suchomel] was a classical guitar player. We were the few in the music department who were really against the war. We started protesting a lot and getting into all sorts of trouble at protests. We decided to start a band with the Gulf War looming because we wanted to speak out against that. I think Phil wanted to direct my anger outbursts and emotional issues into—he thought that I would make a great punk singer. And that's what we started doing.
>
> —Kirsten Patches, singer of Naked Aggression[1]

Naked Aggression got its start as a punk band in late 1990, as the United States was preparing to bomb Iraq. The band was driven by the anger and political sentiments of two indignant music majors, who eventually dropped out of the University of Wisconsin-Madison, moved to California, and dedicated the 1990s to touring, re-cording, and projecting their political message. Naked Aggression's music brazenly protested the New World Order being constructed as the United States ascended to the position of sole superpower following the Cold War. Its lyrics took aim at US military aggression, the Christian Right and restrictions on women's reproductive rights, "corporate globalization" (the dominance of multinational corporations in the world economy), and the ignorance, apathy, and conformity of much of the American population. Its music drew on the fast tempos and irate guitar riffs of 1980s hardcore punk but developed this foundation in its own direction, with Kirsten Patches' voice offering a combination of melody and abrasive yells. Tragically, guitarist Phil Suchomel passed away from an asthma attack on 25 April 1998, bringing the band to a temporary halt. Today, Naked Aggression has reconstituted itself and continues to tour throughout the United States and around the world.[2]

Most punk band members were not also music majors at a university, making Naked Aggression something of an anomaly, yet their story is in many ways a microcosm of what this book is about. In the 1990s United States, a wave of punk bands emerged that defiantly rejected American empire—that is, the economic, military, political, and cultural dominance of the United States throughout much of the world. Furthermore, these punk bands refused to buy into the notion that democratic capitalism was the best of all possible worlds. Their lyrics provided trenchant analysis as

Rebel Music in the Triumphant Empire. David Pearson, Oxford University Press (2021). © Oxford University Press.
DOI: 10.1093/oso/9780197534885.003.0001.

well as a plethora of slogans for protesting the state of the world around them, and these lyrics reverberated with an irreverence that spoke powerfully to a segment of youth. These bands constructed musical styles that viscerally expressed the social critiques in their lyrics and pushed punk music in new directions while staying rooted in 1980s hardcore punk. Their social critiques and musical styles circulated within, and were buttressed by, a DIY (do-it-yourself) mode of cultural production that enabled punk bands to retain substantial control over their message, music, and practices, and facilitated direct and intimate contact with their audiences. This DIY mode of production involved independent record labels and "zines" (short for fanzines), as well as informal performance venues that allowed punk bands to flourish outside of the mainstream music industry. Through their initiative and the support of a segment of the punk scene, this wave of political punk bands brought together a small but significant number of American youth determined to resist US empire both in their daily lives and through involvement in protests and political organizations.

At the core of this book is an examination of why and how the music created by these political punk bands served as a motivating factor and a spiritual glue for tens of thousands of rebellious youth. As I argue, punk musical style can viscerally provoke people to confront the oppressive conditions of the world around them and transform their lives and practices in an attempt to resist and/or live outside of those conditions. Alongside an exposition of musical style, this book also addresses a range of issues relating to punk music, including genre distinctions, propaganda aesthetics, participation in punk by Latinos[3] and women, overcoming right-wing and macho elements within the punk scene, and the always controversial question of "selling out."

I have chosen to focus on the 1990s for two reasons. First, internal to the US punk scene, several important developments took place that reshaped punk from the inside out. In the late 1980s, the punk scene was plagued by musical stagnation and violent confrontations with right-wing and hypermasculine elements in its midst. Through struggle, these problems were overcome with the emergence of what is sometimes referred to as the 1990s underground punk renaissance. Stylistically, the subgenres of crust-punk/dis-core, extreme hardcore punk, and So-Cal punk cohered as expressions of different political positions and social critiques. Demographically, Latinos began to enter the US punk scene in greater numbers and with a more assertive presence. Alongside Spanish-language Latino bands were other assertions of subjectivities that had been previously more marginalized within 1980s punk, such as those of women and gay[4] bands and band members. Finally, the mid-1990s witnessed the mainstream music industry's second great awakening to punk, with several bands garnering commercial success, which in turn provoked a protectionist reaction from the underground punk scene.

Second, external to the punk scene, the 1990s was a period of economic, political, and social transition in the United States that placed punk in a different historical context than its late 1970s and early 1980s incarnations. The Cold War was over and the United States emerged as the sole superpower—and thus could project its military might around the world virtually unchecked. What is now referred to as neoliberalism—the assertion of unbridled free market forces as economic policy and the dismantling of social safety nets within a global framework in which the United States occupied a commanding position—was fast becoming the dominant economic arrangement. Beginning in the 1970s and 1980s, Structural Adjustment Programs dictated by the International Monetary Fund (IMF) and World Bank—two institutions fundamental to the functioning of global capitalism—wreaked havoc on Third World countries and opened the door to more intense forms of exploitation of labor and the environment by multinational corporations.[5]

Domestically, the Clinton presidency highlighted the contradictions (or concordances) between professed liberal multiculturalism and the realities of white supremacy structuring economic and social relations,[6] patriarchy, and other forms of oppression. While colorblindness became unofficial ideology, Black people and other targeted populations were increasingly locked away in prisons, and the 1992 Los Angeles rebellion betrayed the continued police violence Black people faced daily. Immigrants were increasingly the targets of scapegoating and repression, particularly as the number of Mexican immigrants—documented and undocumented—dramatically expanded. The Christian Right, both inside Congress and outside the halls of power, diligently fought to restrict women's reproductive rights and LGBT rights, and the Clinton administration often conciliated with its values and demands. Bill Clinton, after all, signed the 1996 Defense of Marriage of Act, which defined marriage as between a man and a woman and allowed states to refuse marriage to same-sex couples.[7]

The 1990s was also a moment of economic and social transition, with the rise of digital technology and the Internet, and the continuation of the process that began in the 1960s of the replacement of many previously stable forms of employment with the uncertainty of the service industry. The general sense of instability amid transition was an important dilemma for punk. This is in part because this dilemma was not just encountered by the most oppressed in society, but also, albeit in a different way, by middle-class suburban youth whose ability to pursue the American dream was now far less certain than in the past, provoking an existential postmodern crisis.

This context of a triumphalist US empire imposing its will abroad, domestic conflicts over patriarchy, the oppression of Black people, immigration, and other social questions, and a postmodern crisis of uncertainty provoked the punk scene to reshape its politics of rebellion. While Reagan, Thatcher, and the Cold War had informed punk's previous politics of rebellion, in the 1990s United States, the punk scene had to offer a deeper critique of liberal democratic capitalism, corporate globalization, US military power in a unipolar world, and the intricacies—rather than just the most blatant expressions—of white supremacy and patriarchy if it was to remain relevant. In the course of rising to this challenge, political punk bands developed new ways of speaking and sounding, raised the alarm about social questions that were then far less popularly understood than they are today, and stumbled into their own limitations and weaknesses. However much it succeeded or failed in its ambitions, 1990s "political punk"[8] stands out as a rejection of living blissfully ignorant in the triumphant empire. Moreover, while it would be easy to dismiss as naïve the idealism of its participants, many of whom sincerely believed that the punk scene could radically change the world, it is worth embracing this idealism for its beauty and resilience and seeing what we can learn from it about the transformative potential of music.

What Is Punk?

Punk began in late 1970s London and New York and fast became a media spectacle due to its capacity to shock respectable society with its sounds, fashion, behavior, and attitude. After this initial shockwave was over, punk music became an underground cultural phenomenon, mostly out of the media spotlight. In the 1980s United States, a nationwide network of performance venues, record labels, and zines connected the "hardcore" punk bands of the 1980s to a dedicated audience. This network continued into the 1990s as punk bands diverged in various musical directions. From its inception, rebellion against authority has been at the heart of punk, though this rebellious ethos has been defined in radically different ways by different bands and participants. Some embraced various shades of Leftist politics, while a small but vocal minority took up neo-Nazi ideology, and still others eschewed overt politics in favor of disorderly behavior aimed at offending propriety. Before elucidating punk's history and musical style in greater detail, it is necessary to address some of the debates among scholars over how to interpret punk.

The early incarnations of punk sparked immediate scholarly interest, which has increased exponentially in the new millennium. To account for this spike in punk scholarship, punk folklorist David Ensminger suggests that "By 2015, punk seems like a perfect postmodern storm to many academics, for it evokes the ripe intersection of bricolage, pastiche, feminism, queer and post-colonial theory, detournement, Situationism, and disintermediation."[9] I would add that an emphasis on change at the local level in both academia and activist circles, especially in the United States, has also made scholarship on the DIY aspect of punk particularly popular in recent years.

At its best, this new wave of scholarship on punk has provided empirical documentation of how DIY record labels and bands function and of the existence of a thriving underground punk scene over the last several decades. This is a welcome contrast to scholarship on punk that defined the meaning of punk based on Cultural Studies theory or focused only on the small handful of commercially successful punk bands, often failing to engage the punk scene's own robust discourse about itself. However, what has also emerged in the new wave of scholarship on punk is a romanticization of DIY, an uncritical celebration of the small-scale independent producer, a dualistic opposition between local and nonlocal culture and political activity, a lack of and even opposition to engaging questions of musical style and genre, and the assumption that distance from the mainstream via DIY automatically portends radical political opposition. I will have more to say about the romanticization of DIY in chapter 5, but for now it is worth pointing out that DIY has been effectively used by musicians—punk and nonpunk—from a variety of political persuasions, from revolutionary anarchists to neo-Nazis. Undoubtedly DIY practices have been crucial to the functioning of punk and provide bands with substantial control over the means of cultural production and a closer connection to their audiences, but scholars have a responsibility to provide nuanced analysis rather than romanticization. On dualistic opposition between local and nonlocal, this book will demonstrate that political punk bands of the 1990s, even if deeply rooted in local practices and espousing lifestyle or local change as the preferred form of political engagement, spoke to national and global issues, and that their music circulated within a larger than local context.[10]

The relationship between (radical) politics and punk has been addressed in one way or another by virtually all studies of punk. But as Michelle Phillipov argues,

> Almost from the start, punk scholars have tended to assume that the genre's politics are definitionally progressive and emancipatory. Despite enormous changes to the demographic make-up of the punk fanbase and significant generic and subcultural developments within the movement, academic approaches to punk have changed very little in over two decades of scholarship.[11]

To this I would add that the present trend of romanticizing DIY in punk scholarship has continued this problem by simply asserting that DIY practices are inherently politically radical rather than interrogating their content and effectiveness. David Ensminger's *The Politics of Punk: Protest and Revolt from the Streets* (2016) provides a welcome contrast to this trend, using benefit concerts—performances in which the financial proceeds went toward a political cause or organization—as a concrete means by which to gauge punk's political activities and effects. Furthermore, Ensminger rejects rigid distinctions such as DIY versus commercial punk, local versus nonlocal, and politics in daily life versus mass political movements, thus providing a broad portrait of various punk practices rather than only those which conform to a more narrow definition of punk or radical politics.

At issue in the different approaches scholarship on punk has taken is the question: What is punk? Scholars debate whether it is a subculture, a style, an attitude, a fashion, a social group, a political movement, or a network of cultural production. This academic debate in some ways mirrors contention within the punk scene over how to define itself, with different factions taking different positions.

Rather than confining punk to one particular definition or insisting that we focus on one particular aspect of it, I think it is most helpful to view punk as a three-dimensional object that we can look at from many different angles, be it fashion, personal relations, musical sounds, media, record production and distribution, venues, or any other angle we choose. To best understand punk, we will have to look at it from many angles. It is likely impossible for any one study to do justice to all of these angles, so it is best to acknowledge the three-dimensional nature of punk, rather than insist that it be viewed from any one author's framework, and write the best scholarship we can from whatever angles we have expertise in.

Before explaining the angles from which I will be looking at punk, it is worth adding a couple of points to my definition of punk. First, punk has a history, which every new wave of participants in punk engages with in some way or another. Second, punk is shaped by the activities and ideas of those who participate in it. These may seem like obvious points, but the desire to define punk has too often obfuscated or distorted rather than elucidated both its history and the activities and ideas of its participants.

On its history, while the word "punk" was used to describe some music going back to at least the 1960s, punk became a distinct musical and cultural phenomenon in the second half of the 1970s. A constellation of musical and social factors contributed to the emergence of punk. On the musical end were simplified 1960s garage-rock style, the increasingly shocking stage tactics and fashion sensibilities of Iggy Pop, David Bowie, and others, and a growing rejection of the spectacle and virtuosity of 1970s arena rock. On the social end, high youth unemployment in deindustrializing 1970s England has been widely recognized as a prime reason for the appeal of the Sex Pistols' bleak and irate declaration of "no future."

There is some debate as to whether punk music started in New York or London, but in any event both places were crucial birthing grounds of the first wave of punk bands. Arguably, punk's foundations came from the United States, especially New York, but punk became a genre and a social phenomenon in London. Malcolm McLaren, something of a punk rock impresario, heard the emerging punk sounds of bands such as Television, and the fashion and visual aesthetics of bassist/singer Richard Hell, in New York at the club CBGB's in the Lower East Side in the mid-1970s, and briefly managed the band the New York Dolls. McLaren acted as a bridge between the New York scene and his native England. Upon returning to London in 1975, he played a significant role in orchestrating the spectacle of the Sex Pistols, a band he managed, in its abrasive antics that shocked bourgeois sensibilities. These antics included, among other things, using foul language on a live primetime television appearance with Bill Grundy on 1 December 1976, and performing their antimonarchist tirade "God Save the Queen" (which, despite being banned by the BBC, reached #1 on the UK singles charts in July 1977) on the River Thames amid the Queen's jubilee. However accurately or inaccurately, 1977 has become the official year of punk's birth largely because it was the year the Sex Pistols barged into the public spotlight, and references to "'77" in punk culture continue down to the present day. While the Sex Pistols received the most media and historical attention, a plethora of British bands were part of the 1977 punk explosion, including the Clash, the Damned, the Buzzcocks, Sham 69, and X-Ray Spex.[12]

The caustic sounds, flamboyant fashion, and vulgar behavior of punk became a media sensation, first in England and then in the United States, and captured the imaginations of rebellious youth on both sides of the Atlantic. Though it would be impossible to pin down a unitary political position within the punk scene, its early participants reveled in shocking bourgeois respectability with dyed hair, defiant attitudes, theatrics, and an abrasive musical style of fast rock tempos, distorted guitars, simple riffs, and snarled vocals unconcerned with pitch precision. Furthermore, punk bands and zines—the latter springing up with the inception of punk music in

New York with the zine *Punk* and in London with *Sniffin' Glue*—encouraged direct modes of participation, from interaction between bands and audiences, to fans creating media on punk (zines), to forming bands with little or no musical training.

While this first wave made its way into the media spotlight and several bands signed to major record labels, the initial spectacle did not last longer than a few years. Several punk or punk-inflected bands, notably the Clash, continued into the 1980s with popular commercial success on both sides of the Atlantic. In Britain, some punk bands, such as the UK Subs and the Exploited, made their way onto the UK indie charts while a few underground bands such as Crass sold large quantities of records through DIY methods. But in the United States, with a few exceptions, for the most part punk became an underground cultural phenomenon by 1980. No longer receiving much mainstream attention, especially in the United States, punk youth increasingly had to organize their own concerts and record, produce, and disseminate their own music. The impetus for DIY record production was thus mainly necessity rather than choice. Nevertheless, these practices became a badge of pride and the preferred mode of operating, eventually even becoming a matter of ideological principle.

Simultaneous with this move underground was the transition from late 1970s punk style to hardcore punk. The latter was mainly a product of US bands, such as the Middle Class and the Bags, with the Bad Brains and those who followed in their wake in the Washington, DC, scene such as Minor Threat often popularly associated with the turn to hardcore. Black Flag's early recordings straddled the divide between '77 style and hardcore, while their base of operations in the Los Angeles suburbs heralded the social transformations bound up with hardcore style. Britain was not without its contributors to hardcore punk style, notably Discharge, whose music will be discussed in chapter 2. Hardcore bands increased tempos in punk from around 200 beats per minute (BPM) to over 300 BPM, featured faster-moving guitar riffs and more minor-mode material, and yelled their lyrics rather than singing them in a snotty snarl. Hardcore was a purification of musical style which stripped away many of the diverse musical references of late-1970s punk. In the United States, the transition to hardcore coincided with a move from the cities to the suburbs and the foregrounding of a more white, male subjectivity.[13]

Aside from the transition to hardcore, punk in the 1980s also witnessed the transition from the more inchoate politics of rebellion espoused by '77 punk to a number of bands that staked out coherent radical political, and in some cases ideological, positions, and encouraged direct participation in political movements. In England, the band Crass spearheaded the adoption of anarchism as a political philosophy and way of life, rather than anarchy as an embrace of chaos against the established order. Following Crass's lead, a number of UK bands developed the styles and subgenres of anarcho-punk and peace-punk. While peace-punk tended to be slower in tempo (by punk standards) and more melodic, anarcho-punk included bands playing a more hardcore style, such as Doom.

In the United States, hardcore bands such as the Dead Kennedys and M.D.C. used their music to critique the policies of the Reagan administration, among other perceived social ills. Punk and hardcore became intimately connected to political causes such as antiracism, solidarity with revolutions in Central America and the antiapartheid movement in South Africa, and protests against the potential of nuclear war. While this political turn was by no means universal in punk, a general anti-Reagan ethos permeated US punk, and the political bands of the 1980s established a foundation for future waves of political punk, as will be discussed more thoroughly in chapter 2.

While London and New York stand out as crucial sites of punk's beginnings, since 1977 punk has spread around the globe, first to Western and Eastern Europe, Latin America, and Japan, and subsequently to Australia, East and Southeast Asia, and other parts of the world. Raymond Patton's *Punk Crisis: The Global Punk Rock Revolution* (2018) documents the connections between punk bands and politics in the Western and Eastern blocs, how they took inspiration from the Third World, especially Jamaican reggae and Rastafarianism, and had a substantial impact on the political crises enveloping both sides of the Cold War divide.[14]

As punk proliferated around the world, various styles and subgenres emerged throughout the 1980s, and bands used punk for various political purposes, from Rock Against Racism to Nazi skinhead recruitment. Some styles of punk that emerged in the 1980s included thrash, a more ferocious style of hardcore prominent in Europe, Brazil, and Japan; NYHC, a metal-inflected style of hardcore ideologically associated with "straight-edge" (abstaining from alcohol, drugs, and promiscuous sex); grindcore, which pushed tempos to extreme new heights; and pop-punk, a melodic, catchy style associated with the Berkeley, California, scene in the late 1980s. Some musicians with roots in punk branched out in new directions that substantially departed from punk, such as new wave and indie-rock. Especially given the multilinear development of punk in the 1980s, it is far beyond the scope of this brief historical summary to analyze even all the most prominent incarnations of punk prior to 1990, and those most relevant to punk in the 1990s United States are addressed in greater detail in the following chapters.

Though local punk scenes differ depending on their context, there have been strong international connections forged through zines, record distribution across borders, and touring bands (though it is mostly bands from the First World rather than the Third World that are able to tour internationally). Finally, though I have avoided giving a concise definition to punk, most participants would agree that there is a general though somewhat ineffable ethos that is recognizable in punks across the globe, which includes—perhaps as its most defining feature—a posture of rebellion, defiance, and irreverence to authorities.

Punk Musical Style

Of all the angles from which to examine punk, musical style has received the least attention from scholars. Only David Easley's work on early 1980s hardcore has attempted to analyze punk music with the empirical evidence of musical transcription.[15] With the recent trend of DIY romanticization, several scholars have outright dismissed the notion that punk has a musical style and have argued against any musical analysis in punk scholarship. For example, in his otherwise impressive book documenting DIY punk practices around the globe, Kevin Dunn argues that "To define punk in musical terms is an impossible feat. Which isn't to say that people don't try. Or, more significantly, that major corporations haven't constructed a 'punk sound' that they can market."[16]

Phillipov, in her trenchant critique of the state of punk scholarship, comments on the dearth of discussion of punk's musical style:

> [T]he problem is not so much one of too few close readings of individual musical texts but one of subordinating musical meanings to wider concerns about political investments. Too often music is treated as subsidiary to other institutional and ideological practices, as simply a vehicle for the expression of politics rather than something which is embedded in a variety of meanings and affects in its own right and interplays with politics in complex ways.... The specific pleasures of snotty vocals, heavily distorted guitars, or rapid-fire, three-chord structures are simply streamlined into one-dimensional platitudes about "politics," "resistance" and "subversion."[17]

To this I would add that, in studies that romanticize DIY, a form of economic determinism has emerged that reduces questions of musical style to attempts to resist co-optation. While certainly underground punk bands have sought to resist co-optation in a variety of ways, choices of and preferences in musical style have had as much (if not more) to do with the joy of experiencing the music, the desire to continue innovating within the punk tradition, and the sonic delivery of lyrical messages. Furthermore, the narrative of style choices made to resist co-optation does not, for the most part, fit the historical record provided by record reviews in zines. Early 1980s US hardcore punk bands by and large began to release records independently because they could not find any other means to disseminate their music—major record labels would not sign them—rather than because they adhered to an ideological principle.[18] Pop-punk, as exemplified by the band Green Day, was a more palatable and melodic style of punk that garnered mainstream commercial success beginning in 1994. It existed as an underground phenomenon beginning in the late 1980s based around the DIY label Lookout! Records and the underground punk venue 924 Gilman Street in Berkeley, California, thus making any claims that pop-punk began as an attempt to covet commercial success dubious at best.[19]

On a more basic level, there are two ways in which the rejection of the very notion that punk is a musical style is out of sync with what we can learn by listening to punk music and reading punk zines. First, this rejection is in stark contrast to discourse within the punk scene, in which participants are capable of and often deeply vested in evaluating bands on musical grounds and delineating various subgenres of punk. Record reviews are a standard feature of punk zines and offer direct evidence of the punk scene's ardent dedication to, if not obsession with, discussing intricate questions of musical style with a relatively coherent set of conventions guiding that discussion.

Second, listening to the diverse musical output of punk over its well over forty-year history makes clear that there are musical conventions that run through this history, as well as moments of stylistic change and the continual emergence of new subgenres of punk that engage with and transform those conventions. Recognizing and enumerating these conventions by no means erases the tremendous musical diversity within punk. Conventions in punk, I would argue, have emerged due to common impulses among multiple bands during the same time period that were then crystallized by one or a few bands setting standards that were then codified by virtue of their impact on the punk scene. Though it may be uncomfortable for many to acknowledge the existence of conventions in punk, it should be understood that conventions are simply common ways of doing things, not rules that must be followed or a whitewash of the diverse expressions that depart from (and, in doing so, confirm the existence of) those conventions.

'77 Punk Style

So what are these conventions? Dunn is correct to point out the diversity of early punk sounds,[20] but the '77 punk explosion also contributed to codifying punk musical style, with the Sex Pistols in England and the Ramones in the United States arguably the most important bands in this regard. Both these bands featured a standard rock ensemble of guitar, bass, drums, and vocals. The guitar was heavily distorted, and for the most part the guitarist played power chords—root, fifth, and octave without any third to delineate major or minor harmony or any additional chord tone. In punk, heavily distorted power chords play more the role of timbre than harmony, offering a full, powerful, and abrasive sound. The bassist in punk bands usually plays the root of the power chords played by the guitarist, with minor variations and inflections. The guitarist and bassist usually play what could more properly be called riffs—in this case short, simple, fast-moving, and rhythmically emphatic melodic statements—rather than extended chord progressions. In this conception, riffs were melodic rather than harmonic statements, though there are certainly moments of more extended chord progressions in punk that function as underlying harmonies. The emphasis on riffs over chord progressions contributes to the feeling of speed and the abrasive quality of punk music, as do the relatively constant, fast strumming patterns of guitarists and bassists.

A common ornamentation on the riff played by the bassist, or by both guitarist and bassist, as part of the riff itself is what Mark Spicer has whimsically dubbed the "safety-pin gesture."[21] In its standard presentation in '77 punk, the safety-pin gesture comes in a stream of eighth notes repeating the same pitch in which, for each group of four or eight eighth notes, a lower neighbor a tone or semitone below the repeated pitch is played as an accented appoggiatura on the downbeat (see figure I.1). It can be

Figure I.1 Sex Pistols, "Bodies," bassline on first verse and first chorus

played by bass alone while the guitar sticks to the repeated pitch/power chord, or by bass with guitar. The safety-pin gesture has its roots in earlier rock and, prior to rock, blues riffs, but was reasserted in '77-style punk and has remained a standard musical gesture in the punk tradition, appearing in various permutations.

Punk riffs are constructed from a collection of pitches that can be defined by the roots of the power chords of each riff. Throughout this book, while at times I will refer to pitch letter names (E, B♭, etc.), for analytical purposes, I describe the pitch collections of riffs by arbitrarily starting from 0, as though all power chord roots were played on one string and are identified by finger placement on the guitar fretboard. Thus a riff built on E, A, and B power chords is built from the pitch collection [057]. A riff built on A, B, and C power chords would be built from the pitch collection [023]. This approach helps to identify commonalities between different punk riffs and relates pitch content to hand placement on the guitar fretboard.[22]

The most common pitch collections of '77-style punk riffs are [027] and [057], both subsets of [0257], another common pitch collection. In performance, the collection [0257] outlines a box on the E and A strings of the guitar and bass. The collection [057] suggests the I, IV, and V chords so ubiquitous in rock and drawn from blues harmonies. Representative examples of '77-style punk riffs and the safety-pin gesture can be heard on the Sex Pistols' "Bodies" (see figure I.1).[23] The pitch collection for each of its riffs fits within the [0257] collection.

My transcriptions of riffs usually only provide the root of power chords, and the reader can assume that both the guitars and bass play that root together (an octave apart), with the guitar(s) playing a power chord based on the root. Furthermore, it should be assumed that there might be slight rhythmic variations in the strumming pattern of each iteration of the riff, and what I have transcribed is merely its most normal performance pattern in the song. The purpose of my transcriptions is not to capture every musical detail, but to provide a departure point for discussing the music. I am under no illusion that musical sounds can ever be represented accurately or fully with visual depictions.

Drummers in '77-style punk generally played a fast rock beat, with strong snare-drum hits on beats two and four—the "backbeat" of rock. Kick-drum hits were more variable, centering on beats one and three but often adding syncopation or double hits. Punk drummers usually kept time with splashy hits on the edge of the hi-hat either every beat or twice per beat, with loud accents on the crash cymbal or ride cymbal added to emphasize arrival points in the riffs and song structure. The tempo of late 1970s punk was usually under 200 BPM, with the Sex Pistols favoring tempos around 150 BPM and the Ramones opting for slightly faster tempos around 180 BPM. Early punk was not a qualitative increase in tempo beyond previous rock, but perhaps the feeling of speed was intensified due to the relentless energy of riffs, heavy hits on the drums, and the frantic style of singing. I refer to a drum beat in punk around or below 200 BPM with a splashy hi-hat as a *standard punk rock beat*, several examples of which are shown in figure I.2.

Sex Pistols' vocalist Johnny Rotten's sardonic snarl has become representative of the abrasive vocal approach of '77-style punk, with the lyrics somewhat slurred and the vocalist lacking concern for absolute precision in pitch. Vocal melodies in punk, when they exist, mostly follow the roots of power chords, thus staying within a limited range and without much variance in pitch. Similar to the way guitar chords in punk are about timbre more than harmony, punk vocals are about timbre and emotional intensity over pitch and melody. Song structures in '77-style punk follow the verse-chorus format standard in rock, with intros and bridges added to individual songs depending on the band and particular song. Punk song lengths are kept brief, with '77-style punk tracks generally around two or three minutes.

Finally, a few words on musical technique are in order. '77-style punk certainly embraced amateurism and an "anyone can do it" attitude, with little musical training necessary to start a band. While this amateurism and the low bar for participation are central to punk, I would argue that performing punk nevertheless required the development of specific musical techniques—such as fast strumming and rapidly shifting

Figure I.2 Some typical drumbeats in '77-style punk (i.e., standard punk rock beats)

from one power chord to the next for the guitarist; fast, heavily accented playing and hitting the hi-hat in just the right place for the drummer; and just the right sneer for the vocalist—that were mastered aurally by punk musicians, even if in a short period of time. The "sloppiness" some hear in punk music is not just or even mainly a matter of amateurishness, but the cultivation of musical techniques, such as a way of strumming and the location of hits on the hi-hat, that deliberately create a seemingly sloppy sound. Many early punk bands were renowned for their ability to strum power chords and play rock drumbeats at such fast speeds and with so much intensity, and in many cases this was a result of hours of practice to achieve that effect. The Ramones, for example, were notorious for drilling their songs at band practices.

Betraying the cultivation of techniques necessary for (im)proper punk musicianship is the fact that when musicians trained, including formally, in other styles of music attempt to play punk, they must unlearn their previous technique and adopt a new approach to playing their instrument. Two guitarists with experience in non-punk styles of music and highly developed technical skill who joined the punk band NOFX attest to this fact. Steve Kidwiler, a metal guitarist who studied at the Guitar Institute of Technology (GIT) in Los Angeles, confesses, "I struggled with [NOFX's] unorthodox strum patterns—theirs was not a technique covered in the GIT curriculum."[24] El Hefe, NOFX's guitarist from 1991 to the present, who assiduously studied a variety of styles of music at college and is highly competent as a guitarist, singer, and trumpet player, describes his difficult transition to playing punk in this way:

> I went to see [punk band] TSOL once, but I was more familiar with mariachi and barbershop than I was with the bands that influenced NOFX. It was a struggle to distinguish the rhythm patterns on [NOFX's album] *Ribbed*, and it took me a while to figure out how the hell they were strumming. I studied blues and jazz. Even the metal songs I knew were based on stuff we'd covered in my junior college music classes. I had to unlearn everything about proper guitar playing technique in order to play punk.[25]

Punk Goes Hardcore

Since the late 1970s, punk style and technique have undergone various transformations. It is beyond the scope of this book to analyze the myriad of pre-1990 punk styles, but the transition to hardcore in the early 1980s merits attention here because it impacted virtually all subsequent punk. The Bad Brains, an all-Black band from Washington, DC, along with California's the Middle Class, are often recognized as among the first bands to speed up punk to the tempos of hardcore—between 300 and 400 BPM, with some hardcore songs reaching around or above 400 BPM. Herein resides what is perhaps the most significant musical innovation punk has made to rock music. Once a rock beat approaches close to 300 BPM, a qualitative shift occurs in which it is no longer possible to "feel" the beat as being four beats within a quadruple meter, with the snare drum providing the backbeat on beats two and four. It becomes physically difficult, if not impossible, to tap your feet to the "beat," and though the number of "beats" you tap your foot to may change, the feeling of speed remains. The alternation between kick and snare drum becomes a whirlwind of abrasive accents. For this reason, I do not use BPM to measure tempo in punk, but instead what I call KSA—kick-snare alternation—as this captures the feeling of speed but is no longer audible as a "beat." The kick drum is not always played in alternation with the snare drum, but remains, in my view, a "felt" presence that may be replaced by a cymbal hit (most often a hi-hat). In transcriptions, I indicate KSA=XXX with the note value I am counting as the pulse in parenthesis.

With this quantitative increase in tempo resulting in a qualitative change in rhythmic feel, or groove, hardcore music required some means to outline larger accent patterns within the blur of fast kick-snare alternation in order to be rhythmically audible. Early 1980s hardcore drummers thus provided occasional accents on a cymbal, most often the crash cymbal, within the pulse stream, as well as kick-drum accent patterns other than only alternation with the snare drum. These accents usually match arrival points or accents in the guitar riff. Given the lack of a standard quadruple rock meter, riffs in hardcore function as metric units, and for this reason in transcription I group the music into bars based on riffs—often one riff as one bar, but sometimes half a riff or two riffs—and do not include a time signature, as this would contradict the rhythmic feel of fast kick-snare alternation. In transcriptions and discussion of musical examples, I refer to the fast KSA drumbeat of hardcore as a standard hardcore drumbeat. Examples of two common hardcore drumbeats are shown in figure I.3. Hardcore drumbeats and guitar strumming patterns often use the rhythm given in figure I.4, with the kick drum and a heavier hit on the hi-hat or crash cymbal struck on the first of each group of four sixteenth notes.

Alongside this change in tempo and groove, 1980s hardcore riffs were usually shorter and shifted from one power chord to the next more rapidly than in '77-style punk. In addition, 1980s hardcore riffs made greater use of pitch collections in the minor mode, with emphasis on motion by minor third (i.e., 0 to 3), though [057], [027], and [0257] pitch structures remained common. It is worth pointing out here that in both late 1970s punk and early 1980s hardcore, diatonic pitch collections prevailed and dissonant melodic material was quite rare.[26] Vocalists in 1980s hardcore moved away from not only the sardonic snarl of Johnny Rotten but also any attempt to sing melodies, and yelled with a far more distorted vocal timbre and more punctuated accents. A fitting example of hardcore style is Minor Threat's 1981 song "Straight Edge" (figure I.5).[27] It betrays one last feature of hardcore style: while song structures

Figure I.3 Two standard hardcore drumbeats

Figure I.4 Standard hardcore rhythm

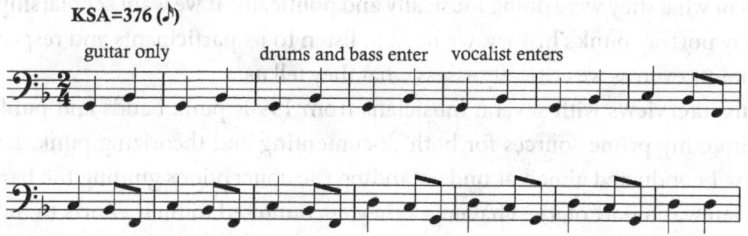

Figure I.5 Riffs from Minor Threat, "Straight Edge," intro, first verse, and refrain

remained in verse-chorus format, song lengths decreased to around and sometimes less than one minute, with two minutes being the upper limit of hardcore song length (of course there are exceptions). Between the speed, short song length, yelled vocals, and more emphatic and faster-moving riffs, hardcore was and is a music of direct communication unencumbered by any musical excess.

The musical features of hardcore described thus far amounted to a qualitative change in punk style such that it is possible to speak of punk and hardcore as two different but related subgenres. Punk remains the umbrella category under which I group hardcore, though it is important to emphasize that after the early 1980s, punk bands had to engage with hardcore's innovations, even if by rejecting them in favor of '77 style. Besides '77 style and hardcore, there were and are, of course, many other subgenres and stylistic innovations within punk music. The relevant historical developments will be discussed as needed to understand 1990s punk styles in subsequent chapters of this study.

A final note on transcriptions is that I have used accent markings to indicate cymbal accents and staccato markings to indicate palm-muting in some transcriptions. Palm-muting is a guitar technique in which the pinky-side of the strumming hand is held down on the strings near the bridge of the guitar while the guitar strings are picked, producing a muted sound. I also sometimes refer to "left guitar" and "right guitar" to differentiate two guitar tracks in a recording based on which speaker they are coming out of.

Sources and Use of Sources

My approach to theorizing 1990s US punk is to start from the conceptions and explanations of participants in the punk scene rather than theories developed in academia, applying the latter whenever it is helpful in explaining a particular facet of this study. This method is a necessary corrective to the still too rare use of ethnographic approaches in popular music studies. Moreover, I do not believe that professional intellectuals—academics—have a monopoly on theory and thinking. Musicians and participants in the punk scene often have highly developed conceptions and assessments of what they were doing musically and politically. If we want scholarship to accurately portray punk's history, we need to listen to its participants and respect their viewpoints even as we critically assess what they tell us.

Thus interviews with several musicians from 1990s punk bands and punk zines constitute my prime sources for both documenting and theorizing punk. Each interview I conducted aimed at understanding the conceptions guiding the bands the musician was a part of, the challenges they encountered in their efforts to move the punk scene in the direction of radical politics and action, and how they assessed their experience in the 1990s punk scene. I should note that punk musicians generally eschew the label "musician" because it can imply professionalism and elitism. In this book I intend the word musician to simply mean anyone who makes music rather than only a formally trained, professional musician.

Zines, originally short for fanzines, range from photocopied, self-published, small-run publications created by one individual to professionally printed, collectively produced, but independent publications with larger print runs up to the tens of thousands. What distinguishes a zine from a magazine, more than anything, is that the former is not principally driven by commercial considerations.[28] From its inception, punk music fostered the creation of numerous zines that documented recordings, performances, and social activities. Some zines were short-lived and locally based, and had minimal distribution, while other punk zines endured as ongoing institutions with national or international distribution and a small staff. For this book, I only consulted zines in the latter category, as my aim is to document larger, national trends within the US punk scene. I consulted all issues published in the 1990s of four of the most prominent punk zines: *MaximumRockNRoll*, *Profane Existence*, *Punk Planet*, and *HeartattaCk*. Each of these zines features record reviews, interviews with bands, columns by prominent participants in the punk scene, letters, and a variety of news, from political commentary to reports of local punk scenes. Each zine differs in its political positions, definition of punk, and emphasis on what styles of punk it covers.

Throughout this book, I favor using the terminology the punk scene uses to describe itself. The word "scene" is the standard term within punk used to describe the constellation of bands, performance venues, record stores, places to hang out, and social networks at local, national, and international levels. The preferred term for a punk musical performance or concert is "show," as in "punk show."[29] Other punk terminology will be explained as it appears throughout this book. When I quote from zines, I eschew the academic practice of inserting [sic] to acknowledge grammatical and spelling mistakes in quoted sources, as punk writing does not necessarily strive to follow academic standards of writing, and in some cases deliberately uses "incorrect" grammar and spelling. When referring to punk scene participants and musicians, I generally use the name they use to represent themselves, which may not be their real name. Sometimes this means using only a first name, or the common punk practice of using a band name as a last name and identification, such as Al Pist of the band The Pist. Where punk musicians or scene participants have gone on to play a public role using their full real name, I use that, as with Martín Sorrondeguy, who was better known as Martín Crudo during his tenure as singer of the band Los Crudos, as well as with Michelle Gonzales, who went by Todd Spitboy while she was the drummer in the band Spitboy.

A word is in order about my own participation in the punk scene, as this provided me with a crucial starting point for research and undoubtedly impacted how I wrote this book. Entering my teenage years in the mid-1990s in Cleveland, Ohio, I discovered punk first through some of the more commercially successful punk bands and then sought out more underground punk bands. I went to many punk shows throughout my teenage years—probably one per week—and played guitar and saxophone in several short-lived punk bands. While I participated in the local punk scene, my social life never entirely centered on punk, and my musical preferences and activities ranged from punk to rap to jazz to modernist classical music. Punk and rap were important inspirations toward my own adoption of radical politics, and I became increasingly involved in several protest movements and organizations. As my political consciousness and involvement developed, I became frustrated with the punk scene for its whiteness and my perception of the gap between political proclamations and commitment within it. Furthermore, there was substantial opposition to and cynicism toward radical politics within the punk and hardcore scenes in Cleveland in the late 1990s. By the early 2000s, my involvement in the punk scene was limited to listening to the music and going to the occasional show, and I am, for all intents and purposes, disconnected from the punk scene today. I hope this limited participation in and distance from the punk scene has provided me with both an ability to understand the workings of an underground culture often difficult for outsiders to discern and a critical vantage point from which to assess punk without too much personal investment.

The Shape of Things to Come

This book is ultimately a cultural history of the political wing of 1990s punk in the United States that foregrounds musical style while also addressing the most pertinent issues political punk confronted. The result is that many aspects of 1990s punk have been left out, and transnational connections are only made when they are necessary to understand the US punk scene. In the chapters that follow, there is little discussion of many styles of punk, such as drunk punk, straight-edge hardcore, and ska-punk, simply because they are far less relevant to the narrative. The Riot Grrrl movement and the band Fugazi, though fascinating subjects of 1990s US music and politics that were related to punk, were substantial departures from punk both in style and social scene, and thus are too far afield to be adequately addressed in this book. That so many academics consider Riot Grrrl and Fugazi to be the epitome of 1990s punk is indicative of widespread scholarly misunderstanding of punk.[30]

This book also focuses on national trends rather than local scenes, exploring the latter when they are relevant as concentration points of national trends. Reading through ten years of zines as well as my interviews with musicians enabled me to identify, with considerable certainty, which issues were most central to punk's history in the 1990s. Furthermore, musical style constitutes an excellent marker of national trends, as it circulates across space. While punk musical style has always been locally inflected, the coherence of specific styles that transcend geography indicates that local inflection has largely been a variation on national and international trends. Local scenes are, of course, fascinating objects of study that shed a different light on the topics addressed here, but they are not the point of this book.

Chapter 1 offers a historical account of the changes taking place within and outside of the US punk scene in the late 1980s and early 1990s. The rising wave of political punk had to contend with Nazi skinheads within the punk scene, the macho violence surrounding straight-edge hardcore, and dramatic political changes in the United States more broadly. The struggles political punk went through in its ascendance indicate that punk is by no means automatically a fountain of radical politics and activity, but a contested cultural space shaped by its participants. Musical style was an important part of these struggles. Through analysis of the music of the seminal Latino, Spanish-singing hardcore band Los Crudos, I examine how punk bands in the early 1990s increased the levels of musical intensity beyond what previous incarnations of punk had achieved. These new levels of hardcore intensity broke out of the musical stagnation that gripped late-1980s punk and challenged apathetic attitudes within the punk scene.

Chapter 2 delves into the propaganda aesthetics that guided much 1990s political punk. I examine the historical process by which crust-punk/dis-core style became intricately linked to radical politics, so much so that its sounds in and of themselves immediately signified a band's political perspective to anyone familiar with punk conventions. I develop a theory of propaganda music and identify musical traits, such as the use of familiar conventions, the distillation of message, and reiteration, as criteria by which to evaluate the effectiveness of propaganda music at viscerally impacting its listeners. Close analysis and reception history of Aus-Rotten's *The System Works . . . For Them* LP applies this theory of propaganda music to crust-punk/dis-core. The dangers of stagnation and routine in propaganda aesthetics are then addressed through reception history, and the continual reinvigoration and diversity of punk music is elucidated through analysis of political bands that departed from crust-punk/dis-core style.

Chapter 3 provides an analysis of extreme hardcore punk, a style that projected dystopian warnings of humanity's and the planet's destruction through dissonant riffs, rapid or extremely slow tempos, and screamed or growled vocals, with analysis of music by the bands Dropdead, Hellnation, Capitalist Casualties, and His Hero Is Gone. This exposition of extreme hardcore style reveals the limitations of academic declarations on punk music as merely three-chord, abrasive rock that any amateur can perform, and demonstrates how musical meaning in punk is intimately connected to stylistic and expressive choices.

Chapter 4 examines the struggles within 1990s punk to foreground the subjectivities and identities of Latinos and women. Los Crudos pioneered an assertive Latino presence in punk by singing in Spanish and forming a scene in their mostly Latino neighborhood of Pilsen, Chicago. Los Crudos went on to forge links among Latino punks by touring the country and releasing records by Latino bands on the Lengua Armada record label. Demographic changes in the United States, especially as a result of Mexican immigration, and political battles over the place of immigrants in US society created the context for the new influx of Latinos into the US punk scene beginning in the 1990s. Women and feminist politics became an assertive if embattled presence in 1990s punk, with the all-women band Spitboy pioneering this trend in the early 1990s. This assertive presence transformed style and expressive power in punk by bringing personal experience with oppression into enunciations of radical politics and creating songs in which a lyrical trajectory of despair to rage to empowerment guided form and expressive nuance.

Chapter 5 addresses the controversy over "selling out" that raged within the underground punk scene as the mainstream music industry turned to pop-punk music as a profitable product following the rise of alternative culture in the early 1990s. This chapter provides a history of the debate over DIY versus commercial success as it played out in the pages of punk zines, reaching fever pitch by 1994. After detailing this debate, I examine the So-Cal punk style that, second to pop-punk, was the most numerically popular and commercially successful style of punk in the 1990s. While So-Cal punk diverged from the underground political punk bands at the core of this book, it nevertheless provides an important musical and social contrast that addressed the postmodern existential crisis gripping the 1990s generation. A close analysis of NOFX's *The Decline*, an eighteen-minute punk epic, elucidates how So-Cal punk style and NOFX's expressive devices sonically portrayed a US empire in the spiral of social decline.

Ultimately the purpose of this book is to consider the effectiveness of a musical culture as a fountain of political rebellion, and the Conclusion attempts to make some limited assessment of 1990s punk's successes and shortcomings in this regard. However we gauge that effectiveness, the stories, sounds, and struggles documented in this book provide crucial lessons that I hope future generations of rebellious youth and musicians can learn from and adapt to their own circumstances.

1
Out of the "Dregs of the Eighties" and Screaming at the New World Order

In an interview with Martín Sorrondeguy, singer of Los Crudos, I asked him what he thought was different about punk in the 1990s. He responded by describing the process of ridding the punk scene of "the dregs of the eighties and really this leftover violent element from eighties punk that was still hanging on."[1] Indeed, the pages of punk zines in the early 1990s were littered with descriptions of the previous domination of the scene by the violent elements Sorrondeguy labeled the "dregs of the eighties," as well as and overlapping with Nazi skinheads, the male-dominated straight-edge hardcore scene, and apathy or hostility toward politics in punk. Such a situation made it difficult for those who wanted punk to be about fostering a radical critique of society and a movement for social change to get a hearing or even just not risk getting beat up. But it also created an impetus for transforming the situation by drawing lines of demarcation and consciously constructing a section within the punk scene that was unapologetically devoted to the music as a vehicle for radical change.

In a 1998 interview in the zine *HeartattaCk*, Kelly Halliburton, bass player in Detestation and a number of other Portland punk bands, reflected on both the worst of the 1980s and the conscious action to overcome it:

> In the early eighties at shows the whole place would be full of punks but there would be a small circle of skinheads in the middle of the floor that no one could fuck with.... All of it came to a head in '88 when three nazi skins that were in the punk scene beat an Ethiopian student to death. That sort of polarized the Portland punk scene, either you were a total nazi, which a lot of people were, or you were totally anti-racist. That was about the time the Portland anarcho-punk scene got going.... [When Nazis came to shows] they would have thirty, forty punks kicking their ass out the door. They got the hint really fast they weren't welcome at our shows.[2]

In the introduction to an interview with the band Civil Disobedience, Martial Flaw wrote:

> Although at one point Michigan had a fairly strong and thriving scene, it failed miserably and fell apart by the mid 80's (approximately 1986–87) due to a massive influx of fascists, fakes, fashion mongers, and generally ignorant attitudes. Since then a few truly revolutionary bands have risen from the ashes of the old and

Rebel Music in the Triumphant Empire. David Pearson, Oxford University Press (2021). © Oxford University Press.
DOI: 10.1093/oso/9780197534885.003.0002.

began rebuilding the Punk movement there. CIVIL DISOBEDIENCE are one of those bands and should be credited with standing strong and keeping their ideals despite overwhelming odds.[3]

Most writing on punk has associated the music with left-wing politics, but from early in punk's history the far Right, including Nazi skinheads, have used it as a ground for recruiting disaffected white youth.[4] Skrewdriver, a British punk band that started in 1976 and went on to ally itself with the far Right National Front political party, was the most prominent example of this trend. In the late 1980s United States, Tom Metzger, leader of the White Aryan Resistance (WAR), began recruiting skinheads connected to the punk scene after a visit to Britain, during which he learned of the National Front's effectiveness in doing the same. Several bands touring in the underground punk circuit subsequently noticed a marked increase in the presence of Nazi skinheads at their performances across the country.[5] In response, a determined effort to purge punk of what many perceived as the white-supremacist scourge continued into the 1990s via organized boycotts of any record store that carried Skrewdriver records.[6] What is crucial for our purposes in understanding the burgeoning of brazenly (leftist) political punk in the 1990s was the real, and often physical, battles that took place within punk to eliminate Nazis from the scene. Descriptions in zines make it clear that through the conscious activity of an increasingly unified, unequivocally anti-Nazi segment of the punk scene, the eradication effort had made substantial progress by the early 1990s.

A local scene report in a 1990 issue of *Profane Existence* cautiously celebrated that "the racist skins have been booted out of Denver. Unfortunately only as far as the suburbs of Englewood and Westminster."[7] Also in 1990, an article by the anarchist organization Love and Rage titled "Bay-Area Boneheads Bashed with Bottles, Boots, Brains and Brawn" published in *Profane Existence* described how, during a Nazi rally in San Francisco, "the unsuspecting Nazis marched into the park [Union Square] and were met with fists, boots and bottles and chants of 'Nazi Scum Fuck Off!' "[8] In a 1990 interview with Lance Hahn of the band Cringer, *Profane Existence* asked, "It seems that the gay-punk community is making a strong stance out there [in San Francisco]—do you think that the past history of 'fag-bashing' justifies sending out decoys and then ambushing 'fag-bashers'?"[9] The determined efforts of punks to confront organized white supremacists and fascistic violence inside and outside the punk scene and their willingness to use force when necessary were exemplified in the organization Anti-Racist Action (ARA), started in 1988. ARA recruited out of the punk scene, with a consistent presence of literature tables at shows. Its activities, including arrests for demonstrations against and fights with Nazis, were consistently reported in punk zines.[10]

"The Lack of Pro-Thought Music"

While organized fascistic violence may have been the most horrendous problem plaguing the punk scene in the late 1980s, it was by no means the only impediment to radical politics. The social atmosphere was fraught with hostility to using punk as a vehicle for social critique. Sorrondeguy explained to me that "in the eighties you couldn't just be like, 'I want to talk about queer politics at this show,' you would have gotten bottles thrown at you, and people would go 'get the fuck out of here.'"[11] Besides overt hostility, the lack of political bands had a stultifying effect that ensconced the scene in apathy. In the previously cited interview, Kelly Halliburton described how in the late 1980s,

[T]he only thing going on in Portland were bands that sung about fucking people and drinking a lot of beer and having fun. We looked at that and thought these bands were just dumb rock star bands anyway and they're singing about things we couldn't relate to. We were really pissed about a lot of things and figured that Portland punk should have a little more substance.[12]

Al of The Pist, a political punk band from Connecticut founded in 1992, similarly described the abundance of apolitical pop-punk and NYHC (the latter will be discussed further in what follows) as the prime motivation for starting his band:

That's really the reason we started The Pist. We really saw that there weren't a lot of bands playing that we wanted to see. Like we would go see M.D.C. and there was a bunch of pop-punk bands opening for them, and we were like, what's going on here? Where are all these political bands that should be on this bill? There just aren't any. So we were like let's start a band that takes the ideas of the Dead Kennedys and the Subhumans, bands like that, Crass, and put it to the type of music we liked and go from there.[13]

While it would be an exaggeration to say there were not any political punk bands in the late 1980s and early 1990s, striking in zine discourse is the identification of a small number of bands that bucked the trend of apathy at that time. On the East Coast, a mere three bands were consistently mentioned as the harbingers of the 1990s wave of political punk: New York's Nausea and Born Against and South Carolina's Antischism. *MaximumRockNRoll* provided the following description of Born Against in 1990:

Sick of recent destruction of independent punk/underground music in New York, the lack of bands with any semblance of a real message (besides "hate", "revenge", or "straightedge"), and not being able to give birth, BORN AGAINST came into existence as a direct result of the lack of pro-thought music, a miscarriage of a bloated, disfigured "scene."[14]

A review of a retrospective discography of Antischism's music demonstrated the reviewer's appraisal of the band's role: "the sheer absence of bands of this nature makes me reflect fondly on their brand of charging political thrash powered with scathing male and female vocals, doused in an occasionally moody dirge."[15]

Most striking about these and numerous other passages in zines was the rather consistent history they presented: a handful of identifiable political bands stuck their necks out at a time of hostility toward radical politics in punk and opened up space for subsequent bands. Nausea and Antischism would play important roles in the development of musical style by helping to establish crust-punk as the most prominent form for propagandistic punk to take. Along with Born Against, they continued to have their records advertised and their music used as a reference point in zines throughout the 1990s.

"We've got better things to do than get our heads kicked in by you"

Perhaps the most powerful aspect of punk music is its sonic ability to pierce any complacency. With its blazing drumbeats, distorted guitars blasting short, power-chord-based riffs, and yelled vocals, it commands the attention of anyone within earshot. Amy of Nausea contrasted the power of punk music to challenge people's thinking with political pop music, which "makes it more palatable so people swallow it but what do they do, they shit it right back out. They [the musicians] may have good intentions in mind but they stay within such conservative limits."[16] Throughout punk's history, one way to deal with any perceived placated audience was to ratchet up the abrasive quality of the music to new extremes. But bands seeking to confront the apathy within the scene in the late 1980s faced an aesthetic problem: the branch of punk in the United States that had the strongest hold on heaviness in style was what is often called New York Hardcore (NYHC), Second Wave Straight Edge, Youth Crew, Pos[i]-Core, or, disparagingly, Tough-Guy Hardcore.

This style, which for convenience I shall refer to as NYHC, emerged in 1986 and adopted the banner of "straight edge," originally espoused by the band Minor Threat as personal abstinence from the drugs, alcohol, and promiscuous sex that pervaded mainstream American youth culture and that had led to myriad problems in the punk scene. But for NYHC, straight edge became an increasingly puritanical code that justified violence against those deviating from it. Drawing crowds mostly from the suburbs of New York—Connecticut, New Jersey, and Long Island—NYHC was a substantial departure from previous punk on multiple levels. As Stacy Thompson explains, NYHC bands "kept the short hair of the First Wave [of straight edge] but performed in hooded Champion brand sweatshirts ('hoodies'), athletic footwear, and muscle tees." Beyond a jock-oriented clothing style, "an abundance of NYHC lyrics deal with male physical strength, and the whole scene celebrated the fit male body that it pictured as young, muscular, broad-shouldered, small-waisted, and free of body and facial hair." The NYHC scene functioned through "crews," often representing the suburb they came from. This act of male-bonding was reinforced with one of the most common lyrical themes in NYHC: loyalty and betrayal among male friends. All this made NYHC "probably the most male-dominated subgenre of punk rock thus far."[17]

At punk shows, the area in front of the stage where people dance wildly, often frantically running around in a circle and/or slamming their bodies into each other, is referred to as the "pit." While early-1980s hardcore had already pushed pits in a more violent and male-dominated direction, NYHC crews cultivated dance moves such as the windmill that featured flailing fists, jabbing elbows, and even karate kicks. Thus the pit was no longer just a site of bodies being flung against one another, but also one of limbs performing martial arts moves. William Tsitsos identifies this as the transition from slamdancing, in which pit participants ran together in a counterclockwise circle, to moshing, in which participants performed their more violent dance moves in relatively stationary positions. For Tsitsos, this change in dancing style fit with the value that the NYHC scene placed on control, including over the physical body, rather than the chaotic aesthetic of slamdancing. Moreover, "the fundamental body movements of moshing, such as the more violent swinging of the arms, the more violent body contact, and the lack of group motion place[d] even greater emphasis on individual territoriality over (comm)unity."[18] CBGB's, the legendary New York club associated with the rise of punk, hosted Sunday afternoon all-ages hardcore matinees in the late 1980s. But the venue dealt with so many injuries at the matinees that they had to hire bouncers to prevent stage diving and eventually ceased the matinees when they became too violent to contain.[19] Moreover, this new type of moshing effectively banished most women from the pit, as average height differentials between men and women meant that when elbows flew backward, women were the ones who disproportionately wound up with broken noses.[20]

The critique within the punk scene of the macho violence surrounding the NYHC style and its 1990s descendants is captured well in lyrics from the song "New School" by The Pist:

> We've got better things to do than get our heads kicked in by you
> Your aim is to ruin all our fun, you're picking fights with everyone
> Your anger's just a fucking front, an ego boosting macho stunt
> You fucked with us and all our friends, it's time to put it to an end.
>
> We're sick of your tough guy stance
> We're sick of the way that you dance
> We're sick of your baggy pants
> So leave now while you still got the chance
>
> We want no part of your war, there's better things worth fighting for
> So what, you kick ass in the pit? You worthless jock, you piece of shit
> New jack with a flailing fist, a dying breed that won't be missed
>
> So pass this message to your crew
> We want nothing to do with you[21]

Since styles within punk become signifiers of the culture around their respective subgenre, NYHC's metal-inflected guitars, crash-cymbal accent patterns, particular vocal timbres, and chorus "gang vocals" (in which a whole crew of men sang along on at least a part of the chorus) came to represent a more macho variant of hardcore. The breakdown—a song section in early 1980s hardcore in which the intensity level changed or subsided, the tempo decreased, and the instruments and vocalist usually performed in a more subdued manner until increasing the intensity at the end of the breakdown—was transformed in NYHC.[22] Fitting with the new body movements of the NYHC scene, breakdowns became characterized by the churning of palm-muted guitars and tom-tom drum patterns as well as the use of heavy accents on the crash cymbal and gang-vocal shouts.

Key elements of NYHC style can be heard on Youth of Today's 1986 "Make a Change."[23] As shown in figure 1.1, the verse riffs, with their thick-toned guitar power chords, demonstrate the crash-cymbal accents (notated with accent markings in the example) that sonically suggest the value of (physical) power. The chorus (figure 1.2), in contrast to the rapid pace of the verse, is musically akin to a breakdown. The drums beat away on tom-toms with hits on the crash cymbal at the start of each bar, gang vocals can be heard on the second bar of the chorus, and the guitarist plays feedback-drenched harmonics by muting the strings with the fret-hand starting after beat three of each bar. Furthermore, the guitar riff on this breakdown betrays the metal affinities of NYHC with its Phrygian melodic gesture.[24]

Youth of Today's "Break Down the Walls," with a breakdown musical style throughout, is a prime example of the kind of music that went alongside the more violent moshing of NYHC—it would be difficult to imagine the chaotic energy of slam dancing in a circle to the deliberate musical gestures and slower tempo of this song. The verse riff (see figure 1.3) is a salient example of the predilection for minor-mode riffs in 1980s hardcore and the more metal-tinged flavor of some NYHC riffs that have the faster melodic motion of lead guitar parts. That this verse riff is occasionally played by one guitar like a lead guitar part—as single notes an octave higher than the

Figure 1.1 Verse riffs from Youth of Today, "Make a Change"

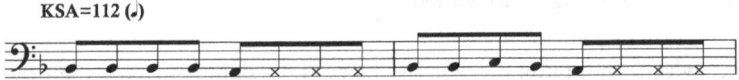

Figure 1.2 Chorus riff from Youth of Today, "Make a Change"

KSA=140 (♩)

Figure 1.3 Verse riff from Youth of Today, "Break Down the Walls"

(1)Break
(2)Down
(3)the Walls

KSA=140 (♩)   (4)We'll break down the walls

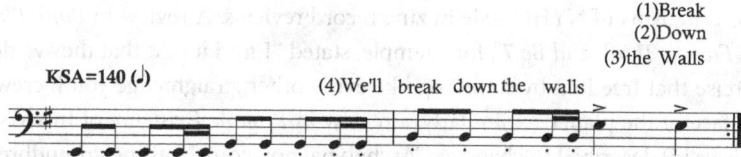

Figure 1.4 Chorus riff and vocals from Youth of Today, "Break Down the Walls"

roots of the power chords—is a further indication of NYHC's borrowings from metal. The tresillo rhythm—accents on beat one, the "and" of beat two, and beat four within a quadruple meter—and heavy accents of the guitar strumming pattern and drumbeat are examples of the more deliberate and precise, and thus controlled and "powerful," musical gestures of NYHC. The chorus (see figure 1.4) demonstrates the use of palm-muted guitars and gang vocals in the NYHC breakdown, in this case with a build-up to the intense accents that punctuate, with crash-cymbal hits and no longer palm-muted guitars, the ending of each iteration of the riff. Also noteworthy are the sixteenth notes in the guitar picking of both verse and chorus riffs that provide forward momentum and render the accented arrivals more powerful.

As the sound first cultivated by NYHC pioneers Youth of Today was embraced and codified by subsequent bands, musical style became inseparably linked to social content. For those seeking to take punk in a decidedly radical political direction, including eschewing macho displays of male physical power, this meant distancing themselves stylistically and socially from NYHC. This distancing took place in part through a discourse in punk zines that decried the stagnation of musical style in late-1980s punk, especially but not only brought on by the numerous bands imitating NYHC style.

In an interview by *Profane Existence* in 1990, Joe from the band Citizens Arrest pointed out, in answer to a question about the uniqueness of their sound, that:

> Aside from the stuff NYC kids listen to, we listen to a lot of stuff that's harder to find like European thrash type and a wide range of other things, while most of the kids in NY listen to the same 20 bands over and over again and that's how you get the genericness of the scene today.[25]

"Genericness" constitutes one of the most powerful criticisms of bands in the pages of punk zines. On the one hand, it points to real problems of staleness and imitation in punk, which any established musical style deals with if models become imitated rather than being used as the departure point for innovation. Stagnation after the initial wave of hardcore in the early 1980s was a widely acknowledged problem in punk discourse. NOFX's Fat Mike summed up the problem in a 1991 *MaximumRockNRoll* interview with strident simplicity: "I guess there was 5 or 6 years where the bands just got worse. They started getting faster but not good. Maybe '84–'88 bands were getting worse."[26]

On the other hand, the "generic" label also served to devalue styles deemed in antagonism to the use of punk as a conduit for radical politics. This is evident in the numerous criticisms of NYHC style in zine record reviews. A review in *Punk Planet* of Bone's *Free to Think and Be 7*", for example, stated "I find it odd that they've decided to exercise that freedom by sounding like every other straightedge youth crew band on the face of the planet."[27] Similarly, a review in *Profane Existence* of Insted's *What We Believe* LP described the band as: "Archetypal pos-core. Nothing groundbreaking; you have to be a fanatic of this kind of music to tell these guys apart from 1000 other SE [straight-edge] bands."[28] Whatever the truth of such criticisms of NYHC-style bands, the "generic" label was deployed politically against punk styles perceived as lacking in or opposed to the politics of the reviewers, and styles deemed politically appropriate received greater leeway, though not a free pass, when it came to lack of originality.

Into the New World Order

At the onset of the 1990s, punk confronted ubiquitous violence, Nazi infestation, the macho culture of NYHC, apathy in the face of as well as outright hostility to the enunciation of radical politics, and stagnation in musical style. As important as these internal dynamics were, it would be wrong, as many studies of punk have done, to take the fact that punk is a consciously underground culture as license to ignore the way in which the larger dynamics of society impacted punk. Indeed, phenomena like the strong white supremacist presence were likely linked to the rightward turn in US politics throughout the 1980s—fringe fascistic elements flourished in part because of the climate created under the Reagan presidency. Moreover, for punk to stay relevant as a music of rebellion, it had to speak compellingly to the contemporary political situation. And as that situation dramatically changed with the onset of the 1990s, it demanded a substantial reinvention of punk's politics.

In the 1980s, Reagan functioned as a convenient target for the punk rebellion. As Dewar MacLeod puts it, "Ronald Reagan's victory in the 1980 presidential election may have done more than any other event to revitalize punk and ensure its longevity—not only because punks opposed his conservative politics, but because here was an enemy with a face."[29] MacLeod goes on to suggest that as Cold War tensions heightened and the threat of nuclear war became more palpable, punk changed to direct its social critique not at hippies but at Reagan:

This transformation was illustrated most starkly in the song "California Über Alles" by San Francisco's Dead Kennedys. The song was originally an ironic stab at the "zen fascism" [*sic*] of California Governor Jerry Brown, but after Reagan's election, singer Jello Biafra rewrote the lyrics to remove the irony, believing that Reagan's America represented a real threat.[30]

Furthermore, Reagan brought right-wing politics together with "middle-class values" as the voice of Christian morality from the sunshine state of suburban expansion. Since the "hardcore kids" of the 1980s were largely white suburban youth disaffected with their preordained place as respectable middle-class citizens, Reagan could easily function as a symbol for all the authorities and institutions that provoked their anger, be they the church, the rigid school system, cops, or their parents.

In this context, "Lyrics aimed at Reagan, and at the omnipresent specter of World War III, dominated the protest songs of hardcore punk."[31] One of the main musical forms for projecting this alarmist critique of the march toward fascism and nuclear disaster was the "hardcore anthem," of which Reagan Youth's song "Reagan Youth" is a prime example.[32] Its simple verse riff (see figure 1.5), alternating between two power chords, accelerates in rhythmic motion before the chorus, halving the duration of the E and D power-chords, adding extra and syncopated strumming on the E power chord, and with the drums switching to a tom-tom pattern punctuated by three accented hits on the snare drum. The B power chord at the last bar of each verse marks a rarity in punk: a V–I cadential gesture into the E power chord that begins the chorus. This chorus, shown in figure 1.6, gives the song its anthemic attribute with the simple,

Figure 1.5 Verse riff from Reagan Youth, "Reagan Youth"

Figure 1.6 Chorus riff and vocals from Reagan Youth, "Reagan Youth"

two-word encapsulation of the song's message, a call-and-response with the group background vocals that emphatically punctuate each incantation of "Reagan Youth," and overall catchy, chant-like character.

The directness and simplicity of message and the invitation to participation through singing along during the chorus were what made the hardcore anthem a powerful musical form capable of spiritually unifying its audience. In live performances, this unity was often given participatory form when the microphone was held out to the crowd around the stage. The lyrics to Reagan Youth's "Reagan Youth," provide a good example of just what politically captivated 1980s hardcore kids:

> We are the sons of Reagan heil
> We're gonna kill all pagans heil
> The right's our sacred mission
> We'll start an inquisition
> We're gonna purge the heathen kind
>
> Cause we are
> Reagan youth, heil, heil, heil
> Reagan youth, heil, heil, heil
> Reagan youth seig heil
>
> We are the sons of Reagan heil
> We are the godforsaken heil
> The right is our religion
> We all watch television
> Drugs have fried our brainwashed minds
>
> We are the sons of Reagan heil
> We are the unawakened heil
> We want another war
> Forward to El Salvador
> We're gonna kill some communists[33]

The hardcore anthem relied on a politics that could be boiled down to a simple chorus that didn't seem too far-fetched, at least to hardcore kids. In the 1980s this was easy to do by symbolically linking Reagan with fascism (hence the "Sieg Heil" in the chorus to "Reagan Youth"), and an anecdotal story exemplifies this practice. In a 1984 performance that took place in San Francisco at the same time as the Democratic National Convention, the Dead Kennedys entered the stage wearing Ku Klux Klan hoods, took them off, and "revealed Reagan masks underneath."[34] Given that Reagan had given an important 1980 campaign speech ardently defending states' rights at the Neshoba County Fair, just seven miles from where Civil Rights activists were murdered in Philadelphia, Mississippi, on 21 June 1964,[35] such symbolism on the part of the Dead Kennedys cannot easily be written off as Leftist extremism. But would such a performance resonate if it were done in 1996 with Bill Clinton masks under the Klan hoods?

This rhetorical question points to the lack, certainly after George H.W. Bush's presidency, of a convenient figurehead in the 1990s to stand for the different facets of society the punk rebellion was targeted against. Though Clinton presided over the largest expansion of the prison population of any US president and targeted Black men for incarceration at alarming rates, signed the death warrant of a mentally impaired Black man in Arkansas during his 1992 presidential campaign, and vowed to "eliminate welfare as we know it" with the not-so-subtle stereotyped demonization of poor Black women as lazy free-loaders, he also played saxophone on the Arsenio Hall show.[36] While Reagan could do, and, in the case of incarceration, did similar things to Clinton with disastrous effects for Black people, it is difficult to imagine him making a gesture intended to assure the population that he could converse with Black culture and by extension Black people. Thus the answer to the earlier rhetorical question is no.

While this example illustrates the more open white supremacy under Ronald Reagan versus the public display of multiculturalism and oppressive policies for Black people under Bill Clinton, the ability of a Democratic administration to put on a smile and stifle opposition with co-optation was by no means the only change or greatest challenge facing the punk rebellion. The onset of the 1990s marked a drastic transformation from the Cold War world to the triumph of the United States as sole superpower with seemingly unchallengeable military strength and domination over the world economy. This transformation was announced with great fanfare in the First Persian Gulf War, which pulverized Iraq through overwhelming aerial bombardment and ensured the United States a privileged position over the flow of oil. Saddam Hussein, a former ally of the United States presiding over a powerful military, proved incapable of challenging the New World Order.

In the January 1990 issue of *Maximum RockNRoll*, as the Eastern bloc was collapsing, the zine's founder Tim Yohannan addressed the reality of social life and culture in the Western bloc:

> It is ironic that here in the West we live in a situation of much less possibility, of ongoing boredom/stagnation, and much more subtle repression. The levels of political sense are much lower here, and we have no leadership that shows the capacity for the imagination we need to recreate our side of the world. I don't know if those in the East will be able to see just how fucked our society is before they begin retooling theirs. Beneath the glitz and glitter, and beneath the technology of VCRs and computers, lies a population lulled into apathy and ignorance. Morals are out, and greed is in. Hate and mistrust are the rage. Hard drugs are the most visible signs of our depression and desperation. And short-sightedness and short-cuts are the political paths we tread. Superficiality reigns supreme.[37]

Yohannan here pointed to what would become powerful defenses against any opposition to the triumphant empire: the notion that there is no alternative to the New World Order,[38] and the power of American culture to lull its population into submission through mass media, individualism as moral principle, and the provision of numerous escapes from the drudgery of everyday life, be they entertainment or drugs. Therein lies the significance and beauty of 1990s punk in the United States: it developed a coherent challenge to the morality and legitimacy of the triumphant empire and sought to make some semblance of a material reality of the idea that there could be a better alternative. How it did so and what role music played in that process is what this book seeks to understand.

Strategies for a Musical Culture of Rebellion

In an interview conducted in 1989, Al of Nausea commented:

> I was just talking with Vinny from [the band] A.P.P.L.E., and he put it great, he said the problem with Marxist/Leninist philosophy is that they said eventually the poor are gonna say, "Hey, we can't take this anymore," and then they'll overthrow the government. Well, America's a little bit smarter than that. They're not gonna push them to the point where they're gonna do it, they're gonna throw them little tidbits. "Yo, here's some Medicaid, here's some welfare programs" etc., and they pacify the people for a generation and then the next one they slowly start to take it away. They never give them solutions, they just give them appeasements. Once these are gone or the people start settling down, then they start pulling back; it's a big cycle. As long as they're thrown the continual thought of the American Dream, when they're down to their last thread of sanity left, they give 'em basic charity. This will continue until new generations are educated into *not* buying into it. That's what alternative culture is supposed to be all about, not buying into it.[39]

Corroborating Al's argument is the fact that the power of capitalism to bribe off or pacify opposition through concessions and co-optation and the persistent hold of bourgeois ideology over the people have been central problems addressed by post-Lenin Marxist-Leninist philosophers from Gramsci (hegemony), to Mao (cultural revolution), to Althusser (ideological state apparatus). Al posed a solution grounded in anarchist political thought but taking shape through cultural creation—a punk culture that maintains a distance from the dominant economic, political, and cultural institutions and fosters in its scene an alternative way of thinking and living. What punk possessed that other political strategies lacked was a ferocious musical style that connected with the energy of disaffected youth and inducted those youth into a scene that served as a thriving social network, enabling the active participation of many who joined it.

Sorrondeguy described to me how, in contrast to today, "there was a period [when youth activism] seemed really dead" in the late 1980s. He went on to explain:

> What a lot of political movements were unable to do was to reach young people. When you look at a lot of the activist movements of the time it was older people, people who were not tied to music. They didn't have access. What Los Crudos and

other bands did was we were the access. We're going to take this issue that is going on and we want to put it out.[40]

A striking example of this disconnect between existing political organizations and radical-minded youth comes from Kirsten Patches, singer of Naked Aggression. As she described, while a student at the University of Wisconsin-Madison,

> I was kicked out of the International Socialist Organization [ISO] for being in Naked Aggression. They said I hung out with too many punk anarchists and I had to choose either [to] stay in the ISO and dump my boyfriend and my band, or they were gonna dump me. Of course I just said "bye, it was nice knowing you."[41]

She described the decision to use Naked Aggression as a tool for political change in this way:

> Let's throw away any materialistic aspirations and any opportunity we might have because of our middle-class status and just go for the ideals. We can make this happen, we can spread these ideas. It has something to do with this philosophy of . . . through music you can break down divisions and walls and unify people at that show in that one moment. With political groups there's a lot of arguing and it's a lot more tedious. People want to start running elections. With music you can just directly affect people one on one and change minds. So maybe you're not affecting the ballot box, but you're affecting people to have a life-long change.[42]

Aside from the direct connection afforded by the power of a punk band's performance and its long-term transformative effect on those listening, the mixture of pleasure and politics was perceived as an asset by many within the punk scene. *Profane Existence* columnist Dan wrote, "I think many anarchists get especially annoyed when we [punks] mix such concepts as partying and having fun with politics and not be ashamed of it!"[43] Moreover, while there has been an abundance of wishful thinking in academia about music's political power without adequate research into its effect, the utopian spirit of 1990s political punk that held music in a central position to social transformation should not be easily dismissed. Taína Asili, singer of Anti-Product, captured that utopian spirit when she described the purpose of punk as not secondary to or serving as a cheerleader for political organizing:

> [It was] not about a conference, not about a festival, but just for the simple idea of a music scene that's focused on social justice and seeing the power of music as a vehicle for transforming our communities and our world. And just that. Without any other agenda. We were doing it with this really genuine feeling of wanting to make a better world and feeling like music and the punk scene was a powerful space to make that happen in. And it was.[44]

Creating such a powerful space, however, depended on particular strategies developed by political punk bands in the 1990s. Martín Sorrondeguy described one of the most effective ways for putting radical politics at the heart of the scene and getting rid of "the dregs of the eighties":

> I'm being a little facetious and funny in saying this, but we basically bored them away. Some of these people were coming around and wanting to fuckin' slam and fight and beat up people and whatever. It was a time when punk was revolutionizing itself, politically and ideologically. People were startin' to fuckin' bring things out into the open that were kind of being touched on in the eighties but not really full on. A lot of queer stuff was happening, women's stuff was happening. These dudes didn't want to hear that shit. They wanted to thrash or slam or get rough at a show. They kinda got bored and left. And I think a lot people were happy about that.[45]

Boring out those who did not want to listen was accomplished by the following tactic:

> Instead of allowing the message to be buried under the music, the fact that we talked about what we were doing in between songs and all that was a huge help. If we would have just played straight through, people would have been like, "Oh, it's a hardcore band. Oh, they play fast, short songs." Some people would have been way into that. But the fact that we were getting into things, people were going, "oh, shit," linking it to a story. And then just like boom boom boom boom, just playing, people were like "uuaaahhh." It was just a recipe for a very different experience at a show. I think that's what helped the band. People going, "you know what, I might not be into that sound so much, but the fact that the song's about this," . . . I think that spoke to people. And there's people who wanted both, and there's people who would love it if we just played a set straight through. But it was a little bit of both. I think that approach helped the band because it made people realize that we weren't *just* a hardcore band.[46]

Making performances points of departure for opening up conversation and finding ways to ensure the message did not get lost in the blare of hardcore songs became a common strategy for many bands. Taína Asili described how Anti-Product would "not only talk about our politics [between songs] but we would also bring with us a lot of literature and be able to talk with people after shows."[47] Michelle Gonzales of the pioneering all-women feminist punk band Spitboy told me that "we always passed out lyric sheets so you knew what we were saying."[48] As she explains in her memoir of the Spitboy experience, "I loved seeing women at our shows at the front of the stage scanning the lyric sheet for the next song, nodding their heads and smiling as they read. In the end, reaching them and seeing their approval was what mattered most."[49]

As these 1990s punk veterans describe it, one of the most powerful effects of the atmosphere created by this emphasis on message was to turn punk shows into a forum for discussion. Such a forum was crucial for navigating the 1990s political terrain, as the discussion had to get much deeper in the absence of a symbolic figure like Reagan providing a target that could unify punk as an oppositional force. Sorrondeguy summarizes the importance of going beyond the politics of proclamation:

> I think we were putting out there that there was purpose behind what we were doing. I'm gonna do this forty-second punk song, it's gonna be fast and loud, but there's much more attached to it and you're gonna hear us tell you why. It really broke down and contextualized the song. Here's a thirty-second song, and it's just gonna sound like a racket to you, but this is really what it's about. Which I think is what made it beyond the sloganeering of smash the state or whatever. It took [it] a little deeper. And I think that's what made the impact for people. It wasn't just a fast band or a hardcore band.[50]

Taína Asili fondly looks back on the atmosphere thereby created at punk shows: "I loved walking into a room and there were CDs and there were patches and there was literature and people having conversations about politics, bands having conversations with audiences about politics between songs, whether they agreed or not."[51]

These deliberately lengthy quotes demonstrate that political punk bands in the 1990s were quite conscious of what they were doing, situated themselves within a larger history of punk, drew on political philosophy and anarchism in particular, and both understood the particularities of the punk scene and the larger world they were confronting and developed strategies for transforming them. Thus the politically rebellious quality of punk, while undoubtedly spurred by larger social conditions, was by no means spontaneous, but consciously crafted. Put another way, it was not inevitable that a wave of political punk would emerge in the 1990s, but rather it was the result of struggle and transformation. I will wait until the Conclusion to assess the successes and failures of this wave. For now, it is worth closing this section with a salient example of political punk's self-conscious advocacy of a struggle to transform the scene and the world, written by Joel in the pages of *Profane Existence*:

> For the most part, punks have historically been interested in shocking society. In North America, at least, punk's political practice has been to reject the middle class values being shoved down our throat. Being a largely white, middle class youth movement . . . punk's relations with the outside world have been concentrated on shocking and rejecting that world [. . .]
>
> This rejection of our roots, our middle class backgrounds, is important, for (theoretically, at least) we are the inheritors of the white supremacist, patriarchal, capitalist world order. A prime position as defenders of the capital of the ruling class and the overseers of the underclass has been set aside for us by our parents, our upbringing, our culture, our history, and yet we have the moral gumption to reject it. As punks we reject our inherited race and class positions because we know they

are bullshit. We want no part in oppressing others and we certainly want no part of Suburbia, our promised land.

However, as important as it is for us to reject our somewhat privileged backgrounds, it is also not enough. Our goal needs to be not to merely reject society, but to recreate it as well. Punk's effectiveness up until now has primarily been negative in the sense that its primary political activity has been to criticize and reject America and everything it stands for. Now it is time to take positive action. *We need to turn our anger and disgust with middle class America and creatively channel it into mass-based political action.*[52]

The Flourishing 1990s DIY Scene and Its Politicized Institutions

For the emerging wave of political punk bands to get a hearing and put the above political strategies into practice, a set of institutions and local scenes would be necessary. While, by the 1990s, punk had a well-established DIY network of venues, zines, and record labels, this network was in a constant flux of high points and low points, and local scenes went through periods of strength and dissolution. Moreover, simply because a record label, venue, or zine maintained distance from the mainstream music industry did not mean it took on a politically rebellious character. Indeed, DIY principles and networks were also used to spread the music and social scene of NYHC, Nazi skinheads, and apathetic strands of punk. It has been to the great detriment of scholarship on punk that political rebellion has often been equated with the degree to which punk bands adhere to DIY principles without critically examining the content that filled those forms, even while those forms were crucial to enabling the political content.

In what follows, I will argue that the mid-1990s was a high point for DIY punk in general, and that significant unity within the overall scene prevailed that enabled political punk bands to reach a broad (in underground terms) audience throughout the United States. Furthermore, a number of particular zines, venues, and record labels emerged beginning in the late 1980s that directly served the mission of bringing radical politics to the punk scene. The first point can best be illustrated by the words of several of my interviewees. Kirsten Patches described the experiences of Naked Aggression:

We were really underground. Nirvana got big, Green Day got big, but there's this huge underground punk movement. We had *Book Your Own Fucking Life* with *Profane Existence*. We could organize massive tours around the United States with no booking agent. It was before the internet so it was amazing what could be done with just print as far as organizing shows. There was a really big underground scene. We could play for two hundred kids in Amarillo, Texas. Right now if we played there we'd probably get fifty people, maybe one hundred. In the nineties we could play these small towns and have two, three hundred people.... There was all this networking going on that was a really exciting underground period of time. It was amazing how in every small town . . . you could have these shows with other like-minded political things. It was pretty incredible.[53]

Taína Asili offered a similar summation of Anti-Product:

We didn't have booking agents, we didn't have social media, we didn't even have email. We had a network of people who trusted in people to come to their venue or sometimes their basement and create a space for us to make music in. You would be fed, you would be housed, and you would have powerful conversations with folks in their living rooms through the night and into the morning. However imperfect it was I felt a sense of community. I barely ever talked about money. I don't even know how much money we made. We were a successful punk band but I think the money just usually filtered right back into the work we were doing. It just wasn't about that. It was about the experience. And creating all these different experiences.... Whether you were in New Haven, Connecticut, or Baltimore, or L.A., or the Bay Area, there were these scenes where people were interacting and working together on a regular basis face to face. There was often a space in that city for that, that people would fight for, whether it was a squatted venue or a DIY basement space or a church that would regularly take enough shows. There was some sort of space that people would fight for to have this work going on at—both music work and activist work.[54]

Bill Chamberlain of The Pist described how, by virtue of the thriving underground network, not a weekend went by when he was not playing a show:

When these bands were going on I remember there was that show *The X-Files*, and someone asked if I had ever seen it, and I hadn't. Because for years I played every Friday night. That was the nature of the scene. One weekend you'd play in Buffalo and Pittsburgh, then the next weekend you'd play shows in Connecticut and bands from Buffalo and Pittsburgh would play.[55]

Political punk was but one wing of that underground network. But its wider exposure hinged on the fact that political punk bands would regularly perform alongside drunk-punk, ska, straight-edge hardcore, and other styles of punk without facing as much hostility or indifference as they might have in the late 1980s. Several of my interviewees heralded the unity in the 1990s scene. Al Pist noted:

We played tons of shows with Blanks 77—bands like that that were just kind of goofy punk bands that had their place in the scene for sure but we really didn't have much in common with them outside of the style of music we played. But we all got along. Everybody supported each other.[56]

This is all the more significant considering that Blanks 77 was perhaps the epitome of drunk-punk in the 1990s—as the designation suggests, the prime concern of its audience was alcohol, not anarchism.

Kirsten Patches substantiated Al Pist's contention with Naked Aggression's experience:

> We would play with tons of people, Voodoo Glowskulls, who are awesome people, Swinging Utters. We played with a lot of bands repeatedly that really weren't political, but we were in that touring circuit so we were all playing together. NOFX was huge. They stayed at our house once in Madison in the early nineties.... We used to play with the Bouncing Souls all the time. A lot of [those] bands went on to get really big.[57]

Along with the wide geographic reach of the underground punk scene and the relative lack of divisions in the scene that enabled political bands to reach a wider audience, the touring circuit described above also enabled decidedly political bands to find one another as they crisscrossed the country. These direct links made the political punk wave a force larger than the sum of bands that were part of it and facilitated mutual support by setting up gigs for comrades on tour. Al described the coming together of like-minded bands on The Pist's first tour:

> I think once it [political punk] started to catch on, like we went out on tour, and we're like, "Oh my God, there's other bands out here too that are playing this sort of thing." Our first stop on tour was outside of Pittsburgh. We played with Destroy! and Aus-Rotten in some hall out in the middle of nowhere. And we were like "Wow this is great. There's some other bands out here that are singing about the same things we are."[58]

But the general strength of the DIY scene would not have facilitated the 1990s wave of political punk without specific DIY institutions being created for that purpose. It is no coincidence that *Profane Existence*, the most politically focused zine that articulated an explicitly anarchist point of view, began publication at the end of 1989. In its choices of bands to interview and records to review, *Profane Existence* gave clear preference to those espousing similar politics to its own. Its record review section contained a disproportionately higher amount of crust-punk, the style most associated with anarchist politics, than other zines. *Profane Existence* functioned more as a tool of political education than music journalism. Its interviews provided a forum for bands to articulate their political views, often without much emphasis on their musical sounds. Moreover, political commentary outweighed band interviews and record reviews in the pages of the zine, with ample coverage of the squatter movement in Europe, struggles to free political prisoners in the United States, an ongoing series on the history of anarchism, an ongoing series by Alicia non Grata titled "Take Back Your Life: A Womyn's Guide to Alternative and Natural Health," and commentary on major political events from the 1992 Los Angeles rebellion to the presidential elections. Since most of the writing in *Profane Existence* came from an anarchist viewpoint and the zine was upfront about the anarchist principles guiding its work, it served to train a generation of punk youth in anarchist philosophy. With its slogan "From a profane existence to a unified resistance," *Profane Existence* was always open in declaring its mission to be transforming punk from a rebellious musical culture into a political movement, albeit one with lots of music, fun, and alcohol too.

While *Profane Existence* was distributed and had its impact felt throughout the United States and around the world through the underground punk network, the zine is also indicative of the importance of some local scenes that anchored and functioned as sites of innovation for the broader wave of political punk. Minneapolis, the home of *Profane Existence*, was clearly such a center during the 1990s, and a two-page spread in a 1992 issue of the zine demonstrated how. While decrying the lack of local all-ages venues, Criterion T noted the number of outstanding political bands of varying styles, from "local grindgods" Misery to "those goofballs of crust," Destroy! Making up for the lack of show venues were the many coffee shops and co-ops and the fact that "you can go to quite a few of the local record and bookstores and find a shelf-full of cool, local zines." Criterion T also cited the many radical political organizations and activities with punk participation, from the Twin Cities Anarchist Federation and Anti-Racist Action, to a recent Take Back the Night rally with a punk edge. Indicating the transformative effect of the city's punk scene, Criterion T wrote:

> What I feel is one of the most significant aspects of the Minneapolis underground community is the number of people willing to actually get off their butts and fuck some shit up. There have been quite a few protests lately where punx and skins have made an impressive showing and usually display the most enthusiasm (and anger!).[59]

In 1994, a number of dedicated punk participants came together to open Extreme Noise, a collectively run record store that also served as a drop-in center where one could find info on area shows and political events.[60] While local scenes come and go, scenes such as Minneapolis in the 1990s reached a critical mass of people and institutions fostering political punk that reverberated around the country, providing inspiration to outsiders, some of whom would even make pilgrimages to learn from it first-hand.

MaximumRockNRoll and *Punk Planet*, though less ideologically unified around anarchism, also provided often quite rigorous political commentary and analysis. Started first as a radio show and then established as a zine in 1982, *MaximumRockNRoll* was founded by Tim Yohannan with the express purpose of making punk a politicized culture of rebellion. Yohannan viewed the hippie movement as failing because it did not distance itself from the (capitalist) institutions of the mainstream music industry and thus could be easily co-opted and turned into a vehicle for profit-producing commercial products. Consequently, for *MaximumRockNRoll*, rebellious politics were intrinsically linked to the DIY practices of punk, and the zine refused to do record reviews of any band on, or accept advertisements from, a major record label.[61] Consolidating and spreading this adherence to DIY practices, *MaximumRockNRoll* and *Profane Existence* teamed up in the 1990s to produce what was perhaps the most important resource for the underground punk scene: *Book Your Own Fucking Life* (*BYOFL*). With its vast listing of punk venues across the country—some simply basements whose occupants opened them up for performances—*BYOFL* enabled punk bands to tour without any booking agent and with few resources, and is a testament to the strength of the 1990s DIY underground punk scene.

While punk venues came in many shapes and sizes, certain venues were associated with political punk by virtue of the bands that played there, the consistent presence of political literature, and use of the space for benefit concerts for a variety of political organizations. Several such venues emerged across the country in the 1990s, such as Epicenter in San Francisco, but ABC No Rio in the Lower East Side of Manhattan was perhaps the epitome of this trend. The building that houses ABC No Rio was taken over by artists and musicians in the 1980s after its owners abandoned it, and the squatters successfully petitioned the city for official recognition and ongoing use of the space. As described by Jim Testa in a 1994 issue of *Punk Planet*, when ABC No Rio was battling eviction, the first punk show there took place in "1990, shortly after CBGB stopped its famous Sunday hardcore matinees." Mike Bullshit, the organizer of the first punk performances at ABC No Rio, did so in order for there to be shows "without the macho, confrontational violence that ruined the CBGB shows." He "made it a policy not to advertise the shows in newspapers or magazines, but to use word of mouth and flyers to attract bands and punks who wanted to have shows, not beat people up." Thus the very formation of ABC No Rio was bound up with the process of ridding the scene of the "dregs of the eighties." As Testa celebrates,

> Soon, ABC No Rio had created an entirely new scene in New York, with bands like Born Against, Rorschach, Go!, Citizens Arrest, and many more whose non-violent, non-sexist, non-homophobic attitude was miles removed from the ugly, violent, NY/HC scene of the late 1980's.[62]

ABC No Rio flourished during the 1990s with weekly Saturday matinee shows and hosted most, if not all, of the political punk bands discussed in this study at one point or another. It has continued in this vein over the years, with an explicit policy of no racist, sexist, or homophobic bands, insisting on viewing lyric sheets before booking a performance.[63]

Besides zines and venues, certain record labels garnered the reputation of releasing only political punk music. In his study of punk record labels, Alan O'Connor lists Lengua Armada, Sound Pollution, Havoc, and Profane Existence, which was a record label in addition to a zine, as standouts in this regard.[64] I shall leave it to the interested reader to consult O'Connor's excellent study for more on this aspect, but suffice it to say that in the mail-order world of punk vinyl records, one could expect that anything from the catalog of these and other labels like them would project a radical critique of American capitalism and related social ills in one way or another. Festivals in which several days of musical performances were combined with political workshops were also increasingly common in the 1990s, with the More Than Music festival in Columbus, Ohio, indicating in its title the political aims of its progenitors. Thus what emerged in 1990s punk were physical locations, print media, and record labels widely identified as being sites of the new wave of political punk. That so many of these institutions began in the late 1980s or early 1990s is indicative of the conscious activity of different pockets of people across the country to change the direction of punk.

While local scenes and DIY institutions would come and go throughout the decade in question, the transformative effects of the efforts described so far were celebrated in a number of local scene reports published in zines. A 1995 issue of *MaximumRockNRoll* provides a telling example of the synergy between musical creativity, venues, zines, and empowerment in Chicago:

> Chicago today is a fully functional punk rock Babylon (are you laughing yet?), not just because of the increasing turnouts at local shows, but because of the increasing quality in the bands, fanzines, places to play, and the opportunities to be involved. While some might believe that you should be a card carrying member of the punk rock lineage to even step up to bat, the politics around here are thankfully at a minimum. There isn't complete harmony; bands are still fiercely competitive, but it seems that the success of one band forces the others to step up their game a bit. And as a result, there's plenty of good performing bands…. Violence at shows and general dick attitudes are all but gone, most shows are run without "security" barriers, waivers, or pressures to stay within someone else's rules. And thankfully, there's no Biohazard tributes…. The big success story is **The Fireside Bowl** (2648 W. Fullerton), which literally IS a bowling alley where shows are put on every weekend night.[65]

In a 1991 issue of *Profane Existence*, columnist Joel provided a summation of the achievements of the underground punk scene that makes a fitting conclusion for this section:

> Face it, punk rock is possibly the only genuine outlet for resistance white middle class suburban youth have…. We punks can organize gigs, organize and attend demos [political demonstrations], put out records, publish books and fanzines, set up mailorder distributions for our products, run record stores, distribute literature, encourage boycotts, participate in political activities, and get completely drunk off our fucking heads. Can any other youth-based counterculture of the 80's and 90's claim so much?[66]

"Freaks for Hardcore"

Within the radical politics and DIY practices of the 1990s underground punk renaissance, music was the spiritual glue that held it all together. Overcoming the dregs of the eighties was in part achieved by constructing musical styles that sonically shocked people out of apathy, disavowed links with NYHC, and came to be aurally associated with a political message. An excellent starting point for understanding the role of musical style in the 1990s underground punk renaissance is with the music of Los Crudos. Started in Chicago in 1991, they were an all-Latino band who sang in Spanish and took lyrical aim at US-backed military dictatorships in Latin America, the repression and exploitation of immigrants in the United States, and other forms of oppression. In chapter 4, I discuss Los Crudos's role in pioneering the greater participation of Latinos in US punk. In what follows, I focus on Los Crudos's musical style, showing how they ratcheted up the levels of intensity in hardcore beyond its 1980s incarnations, thereby becoming one of the most popular 1990s underground punk bands. Los Crudos constitutes a perfect entry point for an exposition of musical style because they were considered "straight-ahead hardcore" rather than a new, more specialized subgenre of punk, such as crust-punk or extreme hardcore, which are discussed in subsequent chapters. Thus, analysis of Los Crudos's music illustrates the more general, overarching issues that the various subgenres of punk confronted.

Central to these overarching musical issues was the question of visceral intensity. In my interview with Martín Sorrondeguy, singer of Los Crudos, he explained the aesthetic behind their sound, illuminated the crossroads faced by bands seeking to retain and amplify the ferocious urgency of punk music to project their radical politics, and the musical resources they drew on to do so:

> We were *freaks* for hardcore punk. If you would have got a Los Crudos mixtape at the time we started, it would have been just peppered in, Italian hardcore, European stuff, early US stuff, all mixed in there. We were into, "1234!," we were into *that*.... When I met the [other] guys [in the band], they knew some stuff, but I was the record nerd, and I was like, "check this out, check this out, check this out," and playing this stuff. Next thing you know we'd go to More Than Music fest in Columbus, [Ohio] and [guitarist] José's sitting there with his shirt off smoking a cigarette with a boom-box blasting Wretched and people were like, "what *is* that?" Because everybody was kind of emo and emo-ing out. Sit[ting] on the floor. And we were like, "okay, people want to sit on the floor." There was this time of like, "oh wow, okay, people wanna sit, okay, cool."
>
> And then it was like, "no man, this is *music*." There's an art. If you play, let's say, Bad Brains' "Pay to Cum," any given time in my lifetime, I don't wanna sit, I wanna fucking just start dancing and bouncing off the walls. I just fucking love that song. I wanted to make punk that just made people go "aaahhh!" We were all on board with that as far as musically and what we wanted to play. So we were kind of an

oddball band for the time. There were other bands who were playing fast, in different places, and we just kind of knew each other, because we were like, "oh you're playing fast; we play fast." We were into that; that was our thing. And other people were just doing different styles of stuff. Not that it was bad or anything. I wasn't into all of it, but we would play together.[67]

As explained earlier in this chapter, the preeminent style of hardcore punk in the late-1980s United States was NYHC, and, given its associations with macho violence, it was not a stylistic option for political punk. One response, indicated by the people sitting on the floor emo-ing out[68] at the More Than Music fest, was to depart from hardcore in the direction of indie-rock.

Exemplary of this trend was the band Fugazi. Formed in 1987 in Washington, DC, the "post-hardcore" generic label often given to Fugazi is fitting given the impetus and history behind the band. Ian MacKaye, vocalist and guitarist of Fugazi, previously fronted Minor Threat, widely acknowledged to be pivotal in the process of moving punk in the direction of hardcore. As the DC hardcore scene grew increasingly violent in the mid-1980s, MacKaye distanced himself from its excesses and sought out a sound that was less confrontational. Fugazi cultivated a different following than the punk scene proper, and dropped the directness and ferocity of hardcore in favor of a more personal, emotional, and multidimensional lyrical and sonic approach. MacKaye was so distraught by the violence that had engulfed the DC hardcore scene he had helped create that when a mosh pit broke out at a Fugazi show, he would stop the music and admonish the crowd to cease anything verging on violence.[69] Fugazi's style featured much slower tempos than hardcore, with a kick-snare alternation (KSA) more akin to typical rock music; drew on reggae and funk-rock for its rhythms, basslines, and musical foundation; sang rather than yelled its vocal lines and favored much more melodic lead guitar parts and basslines; and achieved an "art-rock" sensibility through its more complicated forms and the fact that, unlike in hardcore, the guitars and bass had their own distinct individual parts. For Fugazi, this formula served the political critiques of its lyrics, which, rather than the anthemic or declarative style of most political hardcore lyrics, often came in more oblique or personalized forms.[70]

Fugazi's politics and its adherence to DIY ethics—its records were all independently released and it sought to keep its shows all-ages with a cheap admission charge—were generally respected by the punk scene. Some, however, found its tamer sound to be lacking in the urgency and anger that was so crucial to punk, and even a detriment to projecting a radical political critique. Felix von Havoc, singer in Destroy! and Code 13, columnist for a number of zines, "owner" of Havoc Records, and something of a historian of punk, would go so far as to write, "I would rather hear a real hardcore band with nothing relevant to say . . . than wimpy college rock with something relevant to say (Fugazi, Chumbawumba)."[71] This willingness to overlook political relevance in favor of hardcore musical style is all the more striking considering that Havoc was the author of the history of anarchism series in *Profane Existence* and was clearly dedicated to putting radical politics at the center of punk. Perhaps what best explains the view of Havoc, Sorrondeguy, and others that a strident political message required a strident sound is the visceral, physical reaction hardcore can provoke.

Kirsten Patches described the sound ideal of Naked Aggression:

> [Guitarist] Phil definitely had tones [in mind], and he wanted aggressive pick-ing, and he pretended to be chopping off people's heads with his guitar tone. We wanted it to be really aggressive and in people's faces so they couldn't look the other way. So they had to listen. You sort of bash them over the head with these ideas against corporate globalization and anti-war.[72]

In a not atypical statement for a positive record review in a punk zine, a *Punk Planet* reviewer wrote about Resist's *Ignorance Is Bliss* LP that the "melodic bass and an-themic vocals make you want to scream and smash things."[73]

Discussions of musical aesthetics have suffered from ignoring the role of body movement in favor of intellectual response largely due to the impact of nineteenth-century German canonic views on constructing aesthetic values in music scholar-ship. In his "Prolegomena to Any Aesthetics of Rock Music," Bruce Baugh argues that any aesthetics of rock must take into account that what he calls the "matter" of the music, including "materiality of tone," loudness, and rhythm, is far more important in provoking a response from listeners than are the formal structure and composition. Moreover, these "material or 'visceral' properties of rock are registered in the body core, in the gut, and in the muscles and sinews of the arms and legs, rather than in any intellectual faculty of judgment, which is why traditional aesthetics of music either neglects them or derides them as having no musical value."[74] It is exactly these vis-ceral properties and the physical responses these properties provoke that are valued in the previous quotes from punk musicians and zines.

If the physical response to NYHC was karate kicks, flailing fists, and elbow jabs, which hardcore provided the appropriate musical resources for the wave of 1990s political punk? For Los Crudos, the answer is indicated in Sorrondeguy's refer-ences to Bad Brains and Wretched. The former was an early harbinger of hardcore in Washington, DC, before the perception that the scene was ruined by violence. Thus early US hardcore was one resource, and explains why Los Crudos is often referred to simply as "hardcore" in record reviews. Wretched, by contrast, was an Italian hard-core band from the early and mid-1980s. The musical lineage from Wretched to Los Crudos is corroborated by a *MaximumRockNRoll* reviewer, who wrote, "Chicago's Los Crudos three songs again fuel on simplicity and sincerity, totally blasting like Italy's WRETCHED in abrasive intensity."[75] Politically, Wretched, along with other European, Japanese, and Brazilian 1980s hardcore bands were at minimum free from association with macho violence or the far Right, and in many cases such bands espoused radical Leftist politics.

Musically, these bands, often identified as "thrash,"[76] played a particularly ferocious style of hardcore, with vocals screamed in a frantic manner; a relentlessly fast-paced

KSA with little divergence from a constant pulse; a guitar timbre dripping with fuzzy distortion without the bass-heavy low tone common to more metal-inflected punk; and short, often fast-moving riff structures that usually stayed within diatonic modality. "Manic" is perhaps the adjective most frequently used to describe thrash in the pages of punk zines. The musical features described above add up to an out-of-control feeling and a cultivated sense of sloppiness different than the higher degree of precision in much metal-inflected punk.

More Wretched and aLärming than 1980s Hardcore

What is it about Los Crudos's music that made the band not an imitation of thrash's past but a fresh, invigorating take on hardcore that, if anything, elevated the level of intensity as compared with their 1980s stylistic predecessors? Why would reviewers consistently ecstatically acclaim the band's recordings with such descriptions as "Los Crudos' eleven songs absolutely rip from the very beginning with totally overwhelming energy, stripped down hardcore and caustic Spanish-sung vocals"?[77] A close examination of their riffs, rhythms, and vocal delivery provides some answers to these questions. Before digging into details, it is worth noting that tempos on most Los Crudos songs, not including breakdowns (of which there are few), are for the most part above 400 KSA, usually with a standard fast hardcore drumbeat. Furthermore, most songs on their collected discography last around or less than one minute, and all but one are under two minutes long.

As shown in figure 1.7, the verse and chorus riffs on "Achicados" ("Cowards") demonstrate one salient feature in Los Crudos's music: the predilection for melodic tritones, either as stand-alone intervals or as part of a [056] pitch collection.[78] Within the context of a hardcore riff, the A to D♯ tritone in the verse riff is not "resolved" to the G♯ at the end of the riff, but rather the G♯ functions more as an anacrusis into the functional tonic, A, and the D♯ functions as the secondary pitch of prominence. Thus the dissonant tritone defines the pitch structure of the riff.

Figure 1.7 Verse and chorus riffs from Los Crudos, "Achicados" ("Cowards")

Here a correction to commonplace ways of discussing punk in music scholarship and journalism is in order before we move forward with analysis. Punk is often casually referred to as dissonant, but in truth most punk music from its origins through the 1980s was harmonically and melodically consonant. Vocalists tended to deliberately eschew singing perfectly on pitch, though they did generally follow a melodic contour that matched the guitar chords and, as punk turned to hardcore, incorporated greater degrees of timbral distortion through yelling the lyrics. Punk riffs almost always used power chords, which consist of a root and pitches a perfect fifth and an octave above that root. These intervals above the root are, respectively, the second most and most consonant intervals possible. Melodically, most punk riffs up until the 1990s stayed within the bounds of diatonic modality.[79] They did so either by employing what Walter Everett calls the "power-chord minor-pentatonic" system that uses the power chords I, ♭III, IV, V, and ♭VII,[80] or, in riffs with more expansive pitch collections, by what could be called power-chord major or minor systems. The latter use pitches of the Aeolian, Dorian, Ionian, or Mixolydian modes as the roots of their power chords.

Punk riffs were played with distortion on the guitars, which does create a kind of harmonic dissonance by bringing out multiple overtones that clash with the pitches of the power chord. But even with all that distortion, the three pitches of the power chord remain the only ones audible as distinct pitches. Moreover, I would argue that the almost always present distortion on guitars in punk is *functionally* timbral distortion rather than harmonic dissonance. To put it another way: if you took almost any hardcore song from the 1980s, played the guitar riffs without distortion, and matched the pitch of the vocals with the root of each power chord, the result would be entirely harmonically and melodically consonant. (It would, however, no longer sound like hardcore, which proves Baugh's point about the importance of the "matter" of the music.)

Far from a quibble over the technicalities of musical terminology, this correction to declarations of punk music's dissonance is crucial for understanding how Los Crudos furthered the ferocity of hardcore in the 1990s. By constructing riffs based on dissonant intervals, especially tritones, Los Crudos transformed hardcore by making it melodically dissonant and nondiatonic.[81] As if to emphasize this quality, the chorus riff for "Achicados" starts by alternating between F♯ and C, two pitches a tritone apart. The second half of this chorus, however, switches to melodically consonant pitch material, moving from D down to B and then up to E. While this change from the first half to the second half of the chorus can be made using the pitches of one mode—F♯ Locrian—it is not a "normal" resolution of the F♯-C tritone and sounds more like a sudden shift to new pitch material with a newly felt tonic (E following the prior F♯ tonic). The abrupt quality of this change is made more clear by the fact that the verse riff, with its D♯ and G♯, could not possibly be constructed using the same diatonic mode as the chorus riff.

In the case of "Achicados," these riff changes aid in more powerfully delivering the lyrical structure. The verse lyrics ask a question or make a negative statement with each iteration of the verse riff, starting each line with rhythmic density and ending by holding out the last syllable, usually for over four KSA pulses, on a scream that makes more palpable the question or negative observation of the lyrics as the riff lands on the D♯ or G♯ power chord. The chorus vocals, by contrast, are declaimed with less rhythmic density and strong arrivals on the C and E power chords, the highest pitches of their respective halves of the chorus riff, making clear the admonishment given in the lyrics to those who fail to stand up against repression directed toward immigrants.

The swift switch to different pitch material in the riffs of "Achicados" points to another "dissonant" feature of Los Crudos's music beyond the predilection for tritones and other melodic dissonances. Within songs, different riffs are often constructed from different modes or pitch material.[82] An aside on the history of hardcore style is necessary to understand the significance of this musical feature. 1980s hardcore songs generally stuck to one mode or set of pitches to construct different riffs.[83] This can be seen in the song "Straight Edge" (see Introduction), in which the three riffs can all be derived from the G Dorian mode. Harmonic motion was achieved not by changing modes but by moving further away from the tonic and up the fretboard until reaching the D power chord, which is repeated until the end of the refrain, where the music returns to the G power chord and opening riff.[84] At their simplest, hardcore songs used the same set of pitches for all riffs of a song and simply transformed the order and rhythm of the power chords. Thus there was little variation in mode or pitch material in 1980s hardcore.

Los Crudos, by contrast, often moved from one riff to another with little or no relationship in mode or pitch material between the two and no harmonic transition to finesse the change. A salient example is the two riffs for "Tomando los golpes" ("Taking the Beatings"), shown in figure 1.8.[85] While the verse riff power-chord roots outline an E♭-minor triad, the chorus riff makes a spasmodic shift to outline an F♭ to C♭ power-chord alternation (and the fact that I felt the need to spell these pitches this way says something about the shift to different pitch material). There is no easy way to reconcile these two riffs within the same diatonic mode given their context,[86] and the clear shift in tonal center and pitch material makes for a jarring arrival of the chorus. This effect is heightened by the shift in vocal delivery from the more linear, drawn out, syncopated lines of the verse[87] and slow harmonic rhythm of the riff to the exasperated sounding quick bursts of syllables and faster harmonic rhythm of the riff on the chorus. This shift in vocal delivery serves the semantic meaning well, as the exasperated bursts of the chorus scream "Affirmation not assimilation / We do not seek

Figure 1.8 Verse and chorus riffs from Los Crudos, "Tomando los golpes" ("Taking the Beatings")

KSA=422 (♪)

Figure 1.9 Riffs from Los Crudos, "Victorias y ganancias" ("Gains and Victories")

asylum / We seek liberation" (translation), whereas the verse lyrics focus more on the daily suffering and mental and physical beatings facing Latino immigrants.

Another example of this shift in pitch material or mode from one riff to another is in "Victorias y ganancias" ("Gains and Victories"), as shown in figure 1.9. While its first riff uses power chords with roots based on the pitches of the A-major triad (though in the hardcore context C♯ may be heard as the tonic or primary power chord of the riff), its second riff uses a pitch collection that implies a whole-tone scale, and in any event departs from the mode of the first riff by using an F power chord. Other examples abound in Los Crudos's music of this type of procedure, and its effect is one of disruption—the shift to a riff based on a different mode or pitch material from the riff prior to it comes as an unpredictable surprise.

Unlike 1980s hardcore, in which choices in riffs usually had a certain degree of predictability to anyone familiar with the music and in any event did not usually shift to a new mode, the heightened intensity of Los Crudos's music is brought about in part by the aural rupture we experience. Having just grown accustomed to the modal or pitch material of one riff, we are suddenly taken into a disparate sonic realm by the arrival of the next one. This explains why even those familiar with the screams and speed of 1980s hardcore—and perhaps even the record collectors with foreign thrash on their turntables—were still astounded by the new levels of intensity emanating from Los Crudos records. For 1990s political hardcore not to be a mere nostalgic reiteration of the past but an innovative and powerful marker of the present, it had to somehow increase the abrasive quality so prized in punk aesthetics and do so in a different way. Disruption of the musical surface has been a crucial strategy in punk songs that has taken myriad forms, as shall become clear in subsequent examples. Los Crudos's variant of disruption through sudden shifts in modal or pitch material, however, is a substantial innovation in punk style.

After all this talk of melodic dissonance, it is worth pointing out that Los Crudos could also create raging thrash using solely diatonic pitch material, and often did so using riffs built from major triads. A salient example is the song "Poco a poco" ("Bit by Bit"), shown in figure 1.10, with its verse riff constructed from the pitches of the A-major triad and its chorus riff built from the [027] pitch collection. The latter riff in particular would be a perfect fit in late-1970s punk were it not for the speed with which it is performed (462 KSA) and the screamed vocals that it underpins. Thus the almost absurd contrast between the consonantly melodic—catchy, even—riffs and the distortion, speed, and screams are what makes "Poco a poco," and other songs with riffs of similar pitch material, still sound like raging thrash.

KSA=462 (♪)

Figure 1.10 Verse and chorus riffs from Los Crudos, "Poco a poco" ("Bit by Bit")

KSA=310 (♩)

Figure 1.11 Riff from second chorus of Los Crudos, "Sin caras" ("Faceless")

One final feature of Los Crudos's music merits attention: the use of accents, especially in such a way that allows the vocal lines to resonate more powerfully or be punctuated by the whole band. A cogent example is the chorus of "Sin caras" ("Faceless"), shown in figure 1.11, with its syncopated accents right before the downbeat of each bar occurring as the riff briefly moves up the fretboard from its reiterated B power chords, with this syncopation accompanied by hits on the crash cymbal. The energetic pull of this accented and syncopated power-chord shift in the riff structure powerfully renders the declaration in the lyrics of refusal, by immigrants, to be treated as less than human.

These musical features of Los Crudos's songs—melodically dissonant riffs, especially with tritones; strictly diatonic riffs using pitches of the major mode; disruption of the mode or pitch material from one riff to another; poignant rhythmic accents; speed; and "caustic" screams delivered in a wide variety of rhythms—are all well-represented on the song "La caída de Latino America" ("The Fall of Latino America"). In the song's intro, shown in figure 1.12, starts solely with Sorrondeguy's screams. The opening lyrics decrying the divisions among Latino immigrants are delivered with each line but the last in the same rhythm, an anacrusis into an elongated scream that begins on the syncopated side of beat one. The drums join, playing a typical slower-tempo hardcore beat with syncopated snare hits before and after beat three, adding to this familiar pattern a snare hit or roll on the "and" of beat four to go with the rhythm of the vocals. When the bass enters shrouded in fuzzy distortion, it reiterates the pitch E—in standard tuning, this is the lowest pitch the bass can play—with brief hints of F on the "and" of beat four that, in a Phrygian cadential enclosure of E, support the rhythm of the vocals together with the drums. This introduction is brought to an

Figure 1.12 Intro from Los Crudos, "La caída de Latino America" ("The Fall of Latino America")

Figure 1.12 Continued

intense close that primes the listener for the raging thrash to come by simplifying the rhythm down to a series of singular hits on kick drum and hi-hat.

As the first riff following the intro takes us into the terrain of blazing-tempo hard-core, the bassline introduction retrospectively becomes a large-scale harmonic an-acrusis full of nervous energy and anticipation to the F power chord that begins the verse, shown in figure 1.13. In "La caída de Latino America," the various traits of Los Crudos's riffs described earlier coalesce. The opening riff simply alternates at a slow harmonic pace, yet with a frantic drumbeat, between F and A power chords, making a melodically consonant major third. The second and third riffs, in contrast, outline tritones and employ pitch sets with semitones, but with those semitones in different places in the pitch collection ([016] and [056] respectively). These riffs all require entirely different modes or pitch collections, thus giving us the jarring effect of disruption of the sonic realm as the music moves from one riff to another. In "La caída de Latino America," this disruption is made all the more strident by the fact that each time, before the second and third riffs begin, the band plays an F power chord for a bar, giving us the expectation of a return to the initial riff but subverting that expectation. Perhaps the disruption of mode that marks each riff entrance is a mu-sical analogue for the social divisions among Latino immigrants that the lyrics are anguishing over.

Figure 1.13 Riffs and song structure (after intro) of Los Crudos, "La caída de Latino America" ("The Fall of Latin America")

The musical surface and visceral feel of the music are given added abrasion by the variety of rhythms in the riffs and drumbeats. While the first riff features a standard fast hardcore drumbeat and strumming pattern on the F power chord, the A power chord is given different strumming patterns with each iteration (which I have not notated in the example), and the drums play a blast beat[88] on its first, second, and fourth appearances. The third iteration of the A power chord, by contrast, is accompanied by a hardcore drumbeat without any cymbals. Even the blast beats are given variety, played on the top of the ride cymbal with a tingy sound the second time through the riff and on the snare drum the first and fourth times through the riff. Furthermore, in these first and fourth times through the riff, the drummer stops the blast beat on the thirteenth hit and then gives an accented snare hit at half the speed of the prior ones, harking back to the drum pattern of the song's intro.

The riffs also add to this rhythmic variation, with the first one in the slowest harmonic rhythm and the second one in the fastest harmonic rhythm. The second riff contains an example of the safety-pin gesture in punk,[89] with an appoggiatura in a short-long dotted rhythm with an A to D power chord. While this interval between power chords is wider than the normal tone or semitone of the safety-pin gesture, it is nevertheless somewhat guitar-friendly given the perfect-fourth tuning of most guitar strings. Here its function is to provide the music with an explosive quality through the rapid rhythmic accent and change in power chords before leaping down a tritone. It is during this second riff that Sorrondeguy's vocals are at their most frantic, usually delivered in short, disjointed rhythmic bursts. The third riff, while also outlining a tritone, does so in a straightforward hardcore rhythm in both the drums and strumming pattern, with the vocals declaimed usually in a short-long dotted rhythm that emphasizes the arrival of each power chord. The vocal delivery over the first riff, by contrast, is far more varied, ranging from a rhythmically dense opening that lands on a held scream, to declaimed, short and pointed shouts of each syllable every four KSA pulses over the A power chord.

What musical transcription and analysis fail to explain, however, is the power of Sorrondeguy's voice. The distorted vocal timbre and frantic energy emanating from these screams are an eminent example of what Baugh refers to as the "materiality of tone," and go a long way toward explaining the popularity of Los Crudos. These screams required Sorrondeguy to engage his abdominal cavity—to scream from the gut. They connect to the listener viscerally rather than intellectually, and, for many zine record reviewers, indicate the "sincerity" and "genuineness" of the band.[90] While these are loaded words in music journalism and scholarship, their usage betrays the importance of the voice in provoking us to feel the emotions behind the message.

The Record Collector as Stylistic Innovator

Despite the rise of cassettes, compact discs, and digital music files, the underground punk scene, especially in the United States, continued to use vinyl records as its preferred medium of music dissemination into the 1990s, and even continues this practice, though to a lesser extent, today. 7" records, also referred to as EPs, were the preferred format, as their shorter length than the 12" LP was more fitting for the brevity of punk music. For many, vinyl records were part and parcel of staying DIY through all the technological changes of the 1990s, with the compact disc considered suspect due to its high sales price and association with the corporate music industry. The circulation of vinyl records throughout the underground punk scene, nationally and internationally, also fostered personal connections between buyers, sellers, and traders and spawned a number of obsessive record collectors whose vast acquisitions made them deeply knowledgeable of punk musical style.

For US bands to cultivate a thrash-oriented style, they had to be familiar with the music of 1980s Scandinavian, Italian, Japanese, and Brazilian thrash. As Sorrondeguy described, in the early 1990s,

> There were very few people who would have known about international punk as far as bands go. Wedge would have known. He's a record collector. Felix von Havoc. I was one of those people. There were a few of us who were way into international stuff. You can link that back to some of the eighties people like Chris BCT. Pushead

was in on Japanese [bands] but he knew about other stuff. Very few people knew. We're talking pre-internet. Places like *MaximumRockNRoll* and specific people who collected. So I knew about bands in Peru and Mexico, but not a lot of people knew about that.[91]

That Sorrondeguy referenced specific individuals is telling of the specialized knowledge of this small cohort.[92] He went on to contrast today's easy access to obscure music through the internet with the prior effort it took to find such music:

I know this kid in Philadelphia who's obsessed with Latin American and obscure punk from all over the globe. He had a shirt that was handmade and it said "Phili Violators" [Philippine Violators]. It's a Filipino punk band. That's a mind blower, 'cuz that's freaking obscure. Now he might have found [the music] online and downloaded it. Prior to that, that's not how punk worked. Someone had to go, "check this out." And they'd pass this cassette to you. And you're like, "what *is* this?" It was a very different sort of journey to find things. It was really complicated. It was really hard to come upon a lot of this stuff that was happening all over the globe. You had to write to people and take trade. That's how we all found stuff. Even in the nineties, even then, people didn't know about a lot of that stuff. Some of us did, but not everybody. And then over time it just became more accessible, and then when the internet came, forget it. You can access everything. You just have to hear the name and look.[93]

Thus in the evolution of punk style, the record collector was not an antiquarian but an active agent in stylistic innovation. There are certainly examples of punk bands that are imitative copies of the past. But drawing on punk's history, including by taking inspiration from obscure records from faraway countries with small-press runs—sometimes only in the hundreds—was a crucial means by which to reinvigorate punk style and position a band aesthetically and politically within a changing musical tradition. For Los Crudos and others, this meant drawing on and taking in their own directions the punk subgenre of thrash as it had been developed by Italian bands like Wretched, Scandinavian bands like Totalitär, and Japanese bands such as Gauze.

Many academic treatments have failed to recognize the changing nature of punk music and the specific meanings stylistic variations take on within the punk scene, instead sticking to a narrative that emphasizes the simplicity of punk or viewing it as a postmodernist recycling of the past (of early rock and garage rock in particular). As Steve Waksman reminds us, "genre is such a potentially powerful tool for understanding popular music because it stands at the nexus of musical form, social organization, and cultural identity." Moreover, "Genres are continually changing from within, giving rise to new formations that retain some connection to established rules but seem to stretch those rules to their limits."[94] In punk, finite distinctions between different subgenres become deeply relevant for their aesthetic value, especially to move a crowd by their "musical matter," and for what politics they signify within the punk scene. As is evident from zine record reviews, aesthetic judgments within the punk scene displayed a keen sense of stylistic distinction, an ability to coordinate political meaning with musical style, and value on musical innovation. While the thrash of obscure overseas bands was fodder for Los Crudos's brand of political hardcore, the musical style codified as the preeminent form for espousing radical politics and anarchism in particular in 1990s punk was what is referred to as crust-punk or dis-core, the subject of chapter 2.

2
Crust-Punk/Dis-Core and the Codification of Propaganda Music

While a general impulse to push hardcore punk to greater intensities gripped most of the political wing of 1990s punk, certain subgenres emerged as symbolic representations of their political enunciations. Extreme hardcore, the subject of chapter 3, projected dystopia through specific musical techniques. The conventions of crust-punk/dis-core, by contrast, had little in the way of direct symbolic representation of extra-musical content.[1] Instead, crust-punk/dis-core relied on a selective engagement with punk music's history, drawing specific features from previous waves of political punk, and a propagandistic approach to composition and expressive nuance. In this chapter, I examine the history behind the construction of the crust-punk/dis-core style and theorize what techniques make for effective propaganda music. I present an analysis of the music of Aus-Rotten, particularly its 1996 *The System Works . . . For Them* LP, as an epitome of effective propaganda music in the crust-punk/dis-core style. Following this analysis, I point out the problems of routinization and staleness brought about by the ubiquity of bands in crust-punk/dis-core, as well as pathways out of this staleness. Finally, I examine several 1990s political punk bands that played styles other than crust-punk/dis-core to point out stylistic alternatives that relied on formulaic conventions but did so in creative, innovative ways. Before beginning this exposition of crust-punk/dis-core's style and history, however, it is necessary to explain its politics.

"You Guys Are Alarmist Nutballs"

In the lyrics of crust-punk/dis-core bands, several common themes emerged as central concerns. The United States was derided as a military aggressor that used its armed might to impose its will on other countries. The 1990s wave of political punk emerged just as the First Persian Gulf War rained down bombs on Iraq when former US ally Saddam Hussein stepped out of line and threatened the order of the oil economy. In addition, the political punk tradition meant an awareness of US intervention in Central America in the 1980s, a common theme in Reagan-era punk. For crust-punk/dis-core bands, US military aggression was not an aberration, mistake, or misguided policy, but a systematic function of imperialism, expressed in overt forms, such as the First Persian Gulf War, as well as more covert machinations such as CIA-sponsored coups.

Rebel Music in the Triumphant Empire. David Pearson, Oxford University Press (2021). © Oxford University Press.
DOI: 10.1093/oso/9780197534885.003.0003.

Crust-punk/dis-core bands considered the American way of life, and in particular the high standard of living and widespread availability of consumer goods, to be
predicated on the exploitation of and extraction of wealth from "Third World" countries. While this was not considered something radically new to the 1990s, political
punk bands demonstrated a growing awareness of the process of what was then often
called "corporate globalization"—the increasing dominance of multinational corporations over the world economy. Furthermore, the neoliberal reforms and structural
adjustment policies dictated by institutions such as the World Bank and IMF were
called out by political punk bands as destroying rather than developing the well-being
of people in "Third World" countries.[2]

The growing threat of environmental devastation as a consequence of industriali-
zation, heightened by the process of corporate globalization, was another topic of dire
concern to crust-punk/dis-core bands. Vegetarianism, veganism, and animal rights
as moral choices of not harming living creatures and as a means to combat the economic and social consequences of a society structured around meat production were
also common topics in lyrics. Finally, the growth of Christian fundamentalism in
the 1990s United States became an increasing cause for alarm among political punk
bands. Numerous song lyrics were devoted to exposing particular Christian fundamentalist organizations, such as Operation Rescue, a group that organized attempts
to shut down abortion clinics through street protests. Furthermore, political punk
bands recognized the growing strength of Christian fundamentalism within the halls
of political power, and the threats this posed to reproductive and LGBT rights.

While the preceding list by no means covers all the lyrical topics of crust-punk/
dis-core, it does point out the main lyrical themes. Aus-Rotten, one of the preeminent
crust-punk/dis-core bands of the 1990s, stood out in part for the specificity and mili-
tancy with which it addressed these themes. The lyrics from the first verse to the title
track to its 1996 *The System Works . . . For Them* LP provide one salient example:

> You know the system kills so you try to take a stance
> You speak up for the people who will never get their own chance
> But are your views sincere? Do you practice that what you preach?
> Or are you just fooling yourself, the truth just out of your reach?
> You're helping to enhance the rich while fucking over the poor
> You don't support your enemy when you are at war
> You've heard it all before and you know just what I'm saying
> You hate these corporate killers but you fucking keep on paying
> For the products you don't need, you share with them their fucking greed
> And responsibility for those who died, their exploitation and genocide
> All the shit you fucking hate, too blind to see that you helped create[3]

To the list of issues that were the familiar lyrical fodder of crust-punk/dis-core,
Aus-Rotten added a particular focus on the questions of political prisoners, the
prison system in general, and the way in which both these questions demonstrated

the continued oppression of Black people in the United States. Aus-Rotten did this not just with songs focused on these issues, such as "No Justice, No Peace," but also by inserting a "flexi" record of political commentary by Mumia Abu-Jamal—a former Black Panther and radio journalist known in Philadelphia as the "voice of the voiceless" who was on death row in Pennsylvania for allegedly killing a police officer— into their *The System Work . . . For Them* LP.[4] Punk has a checkered history when it comes to white supremacy, and opposition to white supremacy by punk was often limited to sloganeering and actions aimed at fringe far Right elements rather than the deeper institutional and daily functioning of white supremacy. Aus-Rotten's spotlight on the prison system and political repression against the Black liberation movement thus marked a more specific critique of the oppression of Black people. Moreover, the band's continued involvement in the movement to free Mumia Abu-Jamal and other political prisoners spelled a more concrete commitment to combatting white supremacy other than fighting Nazi skinheads.

What is perhaps more significant than the particular issues Aus-Rotten in particular and crust-punk/dis-core bands more generally concerned themselves with was, first, that they viewed these issues not as separate self-contained problems but as adding up to a system of oppression. Second was the enunciation of urgency and even alarmism around each of these issues. Third, the punk culture these bands sought to construct offered a means of individual transformation through abstention from contributing to the problems it identified, such as by eschewing consumerism, going vegan/vegetarian, or by dumpster-diving for food, and that lifestyle change could be reinforced by the collective culture of punk. The first point is made clear by the album title *The System Works . . . For Them* and the fact that crust-punk/dis-core bands wove these issues into a totality full of interconnections. Politically, this involved taking many of the ideas of prior political punk bands such as Crass and the Dead Kennedys and applying them to contemporary realities. As Kirsten Patches explained about her own band, "We were analyzing and synthesizing those ideas [of prior bands] and seeing how it could apply to what was going on with the Gulf War and big oil and the plotting of corporate globalization coming to life."[5] One result was that those listening to this propaganda music were given a means to see and reject not just particular horrifying problems but also the structures that gave rise to them.

On the second point, punk enunciations of these issues were generally filled with a sense of urgency, sometimes suggesting doomsday scenarios of an earth destroyed by pollution or war and the ascendance of fascism to power. Kirsten Patches made clear that this alarmism was far from paranoia:

There's always these weird conspiracy theory people, like the Illuminati or whatever. [But] the threat of corporate globalization—it was real. And at the end of the Clinton era we saw the ramifications: NAFTA, the insurance companies were allowed to merge with banks. Everything we had been yelling about in the early nineties as a punk rock band, it started to become more of a blatant reality for a lot of people across the world as the nineties progressed. So we were continuing to sound those alarm bells and now it's like our worst nightmare came true.[6]

Patches noted the backlash Naked Aggression and other bands received for their projection of urgency, as a common response was "you guys are alarmist nutballs."[7] The doomsday scenario in some crust-punk/dis-core lyrics may not have come fully true—at least not for the privileged classes in the United States, as those who bore the brunt of structural adjustment programs faced a different reality. Nevertheless, it is noteworthy that many of the issues political punk took up, such as environmental devastation, were not as widely acknowledged by mainstream media or even larger oppositional political movements in the 1990s as they are today. Thus political punk was one of the early voices addressing these topics, and its alarmism often seems warranted in retrospect given what we now know.

On the third point, 1990s political punk advocated more a culture of abstention and the construction of an alternative lifestyle rather than a political protest movement, though it did also generate involvement in protests and political organizations. In this regard it sought to fulfill what a *Profane Existence* columnist quoted in chapter 1 explained about punk:

> This rejection of our roots, our middle class backgrounds, is important, for (theoretically, at least) we are the inheritors of the white supremacist, patriarchal, capitalist world order. A prime position as defenders of the capital of the ruling class and the overseers of the underclass has been set aside for us by our parents, our upbringing, our culture, our history, and yet we have the moral gumption to reject it. As punks we reject our inherited race and class positions because we know they are bullshit. We want no part in oppressing others and we certainly want no part of Suburbia, our promised land.[8]

That crust-punk/dis-core generally advocated an anti-imperialist position in which it viewed the United States as an empire exploiting the rest of the world is thus significant as a further conscious rejection of being beneficiaries of this exploitation. Furthermore, that one of the principal actions advocated in Aus-Rotten's lyrics was boycotting corporations perceived to be exploitative and environmentally destructive is indicative of the centrality of abstention to crust-punk/dis-core politics. Finally, the construction of an alternative lifestyle involving veganism and avoiding the typical American pursuit of conspicuous consumption through the acquisition of consumer products fit in with the refusal to accommodate oneself to the appeasements continually offered to opposition movements in the form of the promise of the American dream. As Al from Nausea characterized it in an interview quoted in chapter 1, "That's what alternative culture is supposed to be all about, not buying into it."[9] Thus crust-punk/dis-core was the propaganda music that spearheaded the practical activity of a culture of "not buying into it."

Across the Atlantic and Back

How did the crust-punk/dis-core style come to be the predominant form of 1990s political punk and what musical conventions did it draw on? From its beginnings, punk music in general developed through a cross-Atlantic dialogue of style first centered in London and New York. This cross-Atlantic dialogue did not stop in 1977, however, but has continued throughout punk's history and expanded to include continental European countries, a cross-Pacific dialogue with Japanese bands, connections south of the US-Mexico border, and an increasingly globalized international punk scene. To understand the crust-punk/dis-core style that came to be codified as the foremost stylistic indicator of radical politics in 1990s punk, we must first take an excursion across the Atlantic and interrogate the development of anarcho-punk in the British Isles in the 1980s.

As the punk explosion of 1977 burned out and diverged in different directions, a band by the name of Crass centered in a farmhouse called the Dial House several miles outside of London saw an opportunity to give "the ephemeral rebellion hinted at by the [Sex] Pistols specific shape and form."[10] The band's drummer, Penny Rimbaud, who was then a 35-year-old former art teacher with an intellectual background in anarchism and avant-garde art, and its initial singer, Steve Ignorant, a then working-class teenager, brought together the raw anger of punk with a more sophisticated political critique and aesthetic strategy. When band members realized that the stridency and intelligence of their lyrics were starting to substantially impact punk audiences who wanted more than vague rebellion, they developed a serious artistic and political strategy for punk and put their prior drunken stage performances in the past.[11]

As Stacy Thompson notes, "in Crass songs the instrumentation serves as a vehicle for the lyrics, and the lyrics are so copious that the song structures seem incapable of containing them."[12] Indeed, Crass songs are more like poetically written political essays, giving their listeners an education in everything from the arms race, patriarchy, the fallacies of Christian doctrine, and justifications for living on the dole, to Britain's war in the Falklands. Their political interventions, especially in opposition to the war in the Falklands, led to the tapping of their phones by MI5. The "Thatchergate" tape, in which Crass spliced together recordings of Reagan and Thatcher to create a fictional conversation between the two about nuclear war and the Falklands, led to public investigations of the band by the Thatcher government. These actions made Crass have a definite—and to those in power, dangerous—impact on the political sphere.[13]

Crass's musical style, however, was worlds apart from the ferocious hardcore developing in the early 1980s. As Ian Glasper describes it in his comprehensive history of British anarcho-punk, "Built upon the fierce staccato rhythms of Penny [Rimbaud]'s militaristic drumming and Pete Wright's ruthlessly tight, incisive bass work, the truly unique Crass sound revolved around Andy and Phil's incredibly trebly, distorted guitar tones, weaving jaggedly in and around the thumping rhythm section, and Steve [Ignorant]'s raw, earthy, 'no frills' vocal delivery."[14] This sound, called "peace-punk" due to Crass's espousal of pacifism, was taken up and developed by a plethora of British anarcho-punk bands in the early 1980s. Though some bands in the United States employed this style from the early 1980s on, most notably "O.C. [Orange County] Peace Punk," they were but a small fraction of 1990s political punk. Several specific elements, however, were drawn on by some 1990s crust-punk/dis-core bands to greater or lesser degrees, particularly the militaristic drumming, treble-heavy guitar tones, and essay-like lyrics with syllabically packed vocal delivery. The latter is evident in Aus-Rotten's "The System Works . . . For Them," as discussed previously. The band Anti-Product's 1996 self-titled 7" record showcases Crass-style treble-heavy guitar tones. And Mankind?'s song "Find Your Future," which satirizes military recruitment, includes an example of militaristic drumming on the snare drum in its breakdown, transcribed in figure 2.1.

In crust-punk/dis-core, these elements were separated from the peace-punk stylistic framework as individual musical techniques and re-inscribed within the more hardcore crust-punk/dis-core style. While separated from their peace-punk framework, these elements were not entirely divorced from their origins, but rather used as signifiers of ideological and aesthetic affinity with Crass. Thus in punk, as with any genre, individual stylistic elements can be divorced from their original musical context and redeployed in a new musical context in such a way that listeners with knowledge of the genre's history will hear them as signaling the politics of their original incarnation.[15]

While Crass did not set the precedent for the overall musical style of 1990s crust-punk/dis-core, it did initiate a number of nonmusical aesthetic elements crucial to it. First, Crass album covers and packaging were veritable works of visual art in their own right, with the band's distinct font usually covering the borders of the album cover, striking images depicting the horrors of capitalism, and posters with similar depictions often inserted inside. Iconography also played an important role for Crass, with the band's symbol a blatant affront to Christianity. Artist Gee Vaucher was the driving force behind the visual dimension, and she played a role as important as that of any of the musicians in the band.[16] The horrific images, specific font, overall use of text on album covers, insertion of posters into albums, and use of specific symbols to represent individual bands were all carried into 1990s political punk.

Second, with regard to fashion Crass eschewed the flamboyancy typically associated with punk attire in favor of wearing all black on stage. This served two purposes: it

Figure 2.1 Mankind?, "Find Your Future," snare drum during breakdown

was a protest of the then-trendy punk fashion being sold on the King's Road, and it gave the band a collective anonymity that diffused the focus on individual members, especially the lead vocalist, as rock stars. As Penny Rimbaud accurately remarks, this all-black attire has "since become synonymous with the whole crusty anarcho-punk thing."[17] Third, besides music, Crass also employed "tape collages" on its albums, in which various audio clips, often from the news, were thrown together and suggested some sort of political meaning.[18] Fourth, Crass included women members, such as Eve Libertine, who functioned as a lead vocalist and, as Glasper notes, brought feminist politics into Crass's public persona. It was common practice in the late 1970s and early 1980s for British punk bands to use the word "cunt" as a term of derision and profanity, but Libertine ended the casual use of the word cunt in Crass's lyrics given that it could, intentionally or not, demean women.[19] Having a woman singer was viewed as an asset, politically and aesthetically, in 1990s political punk, as indicated by the numerous record reviews in zines that pointed out and praised "female vocals." Finally, Crass's adherence to DIY through the creation of its own record label, Crass Records, and the fact that the band continued to book its own shows and do its own promotion even as it garnered significant popularity, made it a model for subsequent DIY punk bands who viewed DIY as not just a necessity but an ideological commitment.[20]

There's Metal in Dis Punk

Crass laid an ideological (anarchist), political, and aesthetic foundation for subsequent bands that sought to make punk a conscious political rebellion. But its peace-punk style would soon be usurped by a crucial development in punk's history: its crossover with heavy metal. As Steve Waksman argues, writings on punk have usually erased metal from its history. While in 1977, British punk was an "all-or-nothing proposition, and metal was its adversary," this was no longer the case by 1979.[21] Waksman cites British band Motörhead, whose *Overkill* album was released in that year, as the first punk/metal crossover to be recognized as such, largely because audiences at its performances were drawn from fans of the two genres.[22] He notes several musical features indicating punk inflections in Motörhead's metal, including faster tempos, lack of virtuosic display, two-chord riffs, lack of sustained (held-out) power chords in favor of greater rhythmic propulsion brought about by constant strumming, and sonic density by virtue of the collapsed space between bass and guitar—the intervallic distance between the two instruments was much smaller than in metal.[23] Confirming Waksman's argument, Motörhead and its bassist/vocalist Lemmy Kilmister in particular were among the few metal bands/icons consistently showered with respect in punk zines.

While Motörhead's sound would constitute an important musical resource for political punk, its politics, perhaps best described as embracing the aura of the biker loser,[24] had little to offer. But punk/metal crossover would continue through

Figure 2.2 Riffs from Discharge, "The Possibility of Life's Destruction"

1980s Britain in various bands, many of which adopted the politics of Crass without its musical style. Perhaps the most significant band in this regard was Discharge, whose 1982 album *Hear Nothing See Nothing Say Nothing* became one of the most important reference points for 1990s political punk. The following commentary is based on that album rather than the band's later, more full-on metal, style. In contrast to the cultivated sloppiness, effect of disruption, and frantic energy typical of punk, the sonic force of Discharge was more akin to a consistent wall of sound.[25] A thicker guitar presence was achieved by recording two guitar tracks and using a bass-heavy guitar tone. Discharge's metal-inflected riffs, often outlining a tritone with an [0356] pitch collection (see figure 2.2), had a rhythmic consistency, using a standard hardcore rhythm, a "D-beat" rhythm (explained below), or repeated palm-muting. There was little variation in riff structures, with the chorus riff often simpler and having the effect of suspending—or at least slowing down—the forward momentum by little harmonic movement, sometimes even sticking to one power chord.[26] What kept these riffs punk was the ubiquity of the safety-pin gesture within them.

Another indicator of the crossover nature of Discharge was that tempos in its music—usually just a bit over 300 KSA—rarely reached a pace that sounded as if the drummer was nearly overwhelmed, thus suggesting an aesthetic of control more akin to metal than the cultivated chaos of punk. The vocals on Discharge songs were the opposite of the lyrical density of Crass—lyrics tended to be sparsely yelled over the expansive repetition of riffs, leaving plenty of space for pure riffage with no voice. Discharge's quite short lyrics were more a series of slogans than political essays, with the choruses often just one-line refrains. While they maintained the basic ideological inclinations of Crass lyrics, they were far more simplistic—not seeking to convince, but meant to make a direct point.

Two more traits are crucial to defining Discharge's style: the so-called D-beat and guitar solos. The D-beat pattern, transcribed in figure 2.3, takes a standard hardcore drumbeat and adds the syncopation of a tresillo rhythm[27] to the kick drum, which rhythmically matches the guitar strumming pattern and rhythmic motion of power chord arrivals on many Discharge riffs. The kick-snare pattern of the D-beat existed within punk prior to and after Discharge, and thus the identity of the D-beat proper is based not only on its rhythmic pattern, but also on the heavy thump and thud of the kick drum. This thump and thud is a visceral property particular to dis-core, felt in the gut by virtue of its sonic bass boom. Thus, within punk discourse, at times people

Figure 2.3 D-beat drum pattern (kick and snare drums only)

identify music as "D-beat hardcore" not so much by virtue of the D-beat rhythmic pattern, but by virtue of the audible and felt presence of the kick drum.

The mere presence of guitar solos in punk immediately suggests metal. Discharge, however, "punkified" virtuosic guitar solos by making them sound *dis-functional* through pitch bends, a meandering melodic quality with no grand musical climax, and a bass-heavy tone and timbre that distorts melodic clarity, as can be heard in the guitar solo following the second chorus on "The Possibility of Life's Destruction." The bass-heavy guitar tone, and the fact that the solos were not in the foreground of the recording mix but more a part of the overall texture, fly in the face of the archetypal metal guitar solo, in which a more trebly tone and front and center presence in the mix texturally and timbrally separate the guitar from the rest of the band. Moreover, in metal solos, the guitar plays a sonic and dramatic role equivalent to that of the lead singer, who is absent during the guitar solo.[28] The stylistic qualities heard on *Hear Nothing See Nothing Say Nothing*—metal-inflected riffs, bass-heavy guitar tones, repetitive and simple riff structures, sparse sloganeering vocals, D-beat rhythms in both drumbeat and riffs, and dis-functional guitar solos—all came to be crucial components of the formula for 1990s crust-punk/dis-core.

The Rise of Crust

Discharge would signal the beginning of a wider trend among British punk bands throughout the 1980s of drawing on metal and pushing hardcore to further extremes. Such bands were frequently identified with the generic labels crust, crust-punk, and crust-core. As punk historian Felix von Havoc explained,

> Undeniably Crust started in England. It took much of its politics, lifestyle and ethics from the early 80's peace punk / anarcho punk movement. But musically it borrowed heavily from both American and British Metal, US hardcore, Brazilian, Scandinavian and Japanese hardcore.[29]

Describing the band Hellbastard's early releases, Havoc identified the stylistic elements of crust as "gruff, usually reverb-drenched vocals, grinding, churning metal edged riffs, pounding bass, and wicked but brief leads."[30] To this we can add greater use of the tom-tom drums, usually in combination with palm-muted guitars, especially in slower crust songs. Note that the metal traits of crust were usually given qualifications that allow them to exist within a punk framework, as with the "wicked *but brief* leads" (emphasis added). Havoc considered Amebix's 1985 *Arise* LP to have codified crust style. The album's overall dark sonic atmosphere was achieved through the greater use of palm-muting by the guitars, sneeringly gruff vocals, and the overall lower tone of the recording—the guitar tone emphasizes the low end, the bass and kick drum are prominent in the mix, and even the snare drum sounds much lower in pitch than normal, likely due to adjusting the tension of the drum head.

This emphasis on a "dark" sound in crust was thus achieved through the tone knobs on guitar pedals and amps, a sound mix that emphasizes the lower-pitched instruments of the band and makes the higher-pitched instruments sound more bass-heavy, and "down-tuning" the guitars and bass. The latter technique was borrowed from metal, where the strings of the bass and guitar(s) were sometimes all tuned down by a semitone or whole tone, making the lowest open string on all instruments tuned to an E♭ or D, respectively, instead of the usual E. Besides creating the ability to play lower pitches, down-tuning also affects the timbre of bass and guitar, as the looser string tension results in a darkened sound. The importance of down-tuning to crust style is corroborated by Havoc's description of the evolution of punk/metal crossover: "[the band] Doom took the Dis Core style and tuned it down even lower and made it more brutal, then threw in sick thrash parts and gruff vocals for the ultimate crust brutality."[31]

Unlike obscure thrash bands known only to punk record collector aficionados in the United States, dis-core and crust were fairly widely known in the US punk scene. Discharge continued to be a stylistic reference point in the pages of punk zines—hence the "dis-core" generic label—and their albums were even available in some mainstream record stores. Amebix's *Arise* LP was released on Jello Biafra's Alternative Tentacles record label, a well-known and well-distributed DIY label centered in San Francisco. And Doom's *Police Bastard* EP and the *Extinction* LP by Nausea, one of the first crust bands on this side of the Atlantic, were among the most consistently advertised records in punk zines in the early 1990s. As Havoc put it,

> There was an eager audience for this new stuff in the USA. You could argue that [US] bands like Nausea, Disrupt, Apocalypse, Glycine Max, A//solution, Antischism, Confrontation, and Destroy were imitating the UK sound of the time, or that the music was developing simultaneously on both continents.[32]

What was the impetus behind such an eager audience for crust in the United States in the late 1980s/early 1990s? While undoubtedly musical tastes were part of the equation, to understand the rise of crust-punk/dis-core, we must appreciate the way generic boundaries and the intricacies of musical style took on political meaning. As Waksman puts it, "In popular music, genres influence not only how music sounds and how it is played, but also what that music is believed to signify, what values it is heard to transmit, and what codes of style best suit the sonic codes that mark the difference between one genre and another."[33] Complementing this theoretical formulation,

Havoc made clear that while punk/metal crossover was also common in the United States during the 1980s, "One principal difference [between US and UK crossover] was the political stance went with the UK bands while the American bands dropped most of their politics and embraced the music industry."[34] To this we can add that dis-core in particular was aesthetically designed to support the political slogans of the vocals, and its predilection for repetition without much variation aided in reiterating its message.

What emerged as the predominant style for political punk in the 1990s United States was what I broadly label crust-punk/dis-core,[35] which used the relentless repetitive power of Discharge-styled riffs to reiterate the political message of its lyrics, especially as boiled down to slogans. Crust-punk/dis-core shrouded itself in the dark sonic atmosphere of crust to aurally project its perception of the horrors emanating from the emerging neoliberal capitalist New World Order. It drew on aesthetic elements of Crass to enunciate a deeper intellectual critique and provoke its audiences to action (hence the use of Crass's "militaristic drumming" could both evoke the enemy and rally the punk masses). And it added the frantic ferocity and fast pace of American hardcore to underscore the urgency of its message. If there was one band from the 1990s that best concentrated these qualities, it was Aus-Rotten, and for that reason we shall now turn to an analysis of its music. From there, I will present evidence from zines that supports my assertion that crust-punk/dis-core was the foremost style of choice for political punk in the 1990s United States and point out the problem of stylistic staleness this resulted in, as well as bands that were perceived to have solved this problem. But before we move through this discussion of style, I will attempt to fill a significant void in the theory of musical aesthetics: a theory of propaganda music.[36]

Propaganda Aesthetics

In US culture, the word "propaganda" is generally used in a pejorative way, as we like to believe we are all free individuals who make our own independent decisions despite the ubiquity of advertisements in our daily life, the profound limits of acceptable discourse in official politics, and the crushing of creativity, questioning, and intellectual curiosity that occurs in a school system saturated with standardized testing. Moreover, the very definition of propaganda has been equated with misinforming, misleading, or manipulating to underhandedly brainwash someone into going along with the propagandist's nefarious intentions. When I use the term "propaganda music," I simply mean music intended to convince its audience of a particular (political) viewpoint and move them to act on that viewpoint. In propaganda music, as opposed to simply a propaganda text, this effect is achieved both intellectually and emotionally (or perhaps more accurately, viscerally), with the latter just as if not more important than the former. But to understand what makes effective propaganda music and appreciate crust-punk/dis-core, we must be willing to at least consider aesthetic values different from those of Western musicology that privilege originality, complexity, indirectness, or ephemeral feelings. In what follows, I attempt to theorize what makes for successful propaganda music.

First, essential to propaganda music is the deployment of conventions that are both familiar and meaningful to its audience. By virtue of the fact that listeners are already familiar with the forms and stylistic elements of the music, they can focus more on what the music is seeking to express within its generic foundation. If listeners had to take the initial steps of comprehending and familiarizing themselves with the musical forms and stylistic elements, the message would fail to communicate with as much immediacy. The choice of which conventions to deploy takes on meaning to an audience that understands the political and social associations of those musical conventions. In other words, anyone familiar with punk's history would immediately associate crust-punk/dis-core style with radical, likely anarchist, politics. Thus lack of originality is not a bad thing in propaganda music, and too much originality would negatively affect propaganda music's efficacy.

Second, while intellectually convincing listeners is one aspect of propaganda music, distilling the message into something that is simple, provocative, and takes the listener into and along with it is crucial. If the distillation of the message to its most basic can be rendered as a point of epiphany at which, by virtue of the lyrical, musical, and dramatic momentum, the listener is made to feel that this distillation is the inevitable conclusion, then the propaganda music in question shall prove successful. Furthermore, except in instances of censorship and repression, propaganda music must deliver its message directly and without obfuscation rather than shrouding the message in mystery and ephemerality or rendering it through inference and implication. As Kirsten Patches described the qualities sought by Naked Aggression in their lyrics, "Words had to be in your face. No fancy words, no flowery language, no metaphor. It had to be bare bones."[37]

Third, the message requires reiteration on multiple levels to stick with its audience. As Barbara Mittler puts it in her study of the art and culture of the Chinese Great Proletarian Cultural Revolution (GPCR), "semantic overdetermination" was employed in the model operas of the GPCR such that their message was omnipresent and reiterated in music, lyrics, costumes, stage designs, and body movement.[38] Political punk bears a similarity in that albums amplify political messages in their artwork, lyrics, and stylistic choices. Moreover, the aesthetic of political punk was often one in which, as Kirsten Patches put it, "You sort of bash them over the head with these ideas against corporate globalization and anti-war."[39] Thus repetition, reiteration, and multiple enunciations of the same message on different artistic levels are a necessity and a virtue in propaganda music.

Fourth, provoking a visceral reaction from listeners must be achieved for propaganda music not to be perceived as forced or contrived. It is this visceral reaction that makes the listener feel intimately connected to the message and motivated to act on it rather than a passive or preached-to recipient. Therein resides the importance of the human voice as well as the felt power of performance and expressive nuance. While these three aspects can to some extent be measured empirically with musical analysis, they must also be understood as less tangible reactions only evident through a study of reception.

The Virtues of Well-Done Formulaic Simplicity

Perhaps the best way to begin to understand Aus-Rotten's music, its impact, and aesthetic debates within the punk scene over the value of crust-punk/dis-core is with zine reviews of the band's first two 7" records, 1993's *Anti-Imperialist* and 1994's *Fuck Nazi Sympathy*:

> This rules! Simple as fuck dischargy hardcore with dual trade-off singers. And classic Discharge type solos with bends and shit. The neat thing is that while the style is nothing original somehow they do lots of innovative things and it's like nothing I've heard before exactly. They just kick ass all around.[40]

> I could say that this is a third rate rehash of early UK punk with bad but relevant lyrics, but I won't. You should buy this to check out their Halloween costumes and try to figure out where the band's initials are in the logo.[41]

> [G]ood midtempo anarcho stuff—filled out well with dual guitars/vocals. Not really overflowing with originality, but it's hard not to sing along to a chorus like "Fuck Nazi Sympathy."[42]

> Anarcho-punk in the vein of early Discharge, Chaos UK, or maybe Abrasive Wheels or the Partisans. Grating powersaw guitar riffs and lots of singalong choruses makes me think Pittsburg picked up in '93 where England left off in '83.[43]

> This band smacks distinctly of DISCHARGE (except they're from Pittsburgh) but in a way they're even better in that their songs are more compact and there are two vocalists who scream back and forth together.[44]

What all these reviewers agreed on, whether they were enthusiastic exponents, derisive detractors, or somewhat ambivalent observers, was that Aus-Rotten's music was rooted in the stylistic formula of Discharge, maintained simplicity, and presented nothing profoundly original to punk. The song "Fuck Nazi Sympathy," transcribed in figure 2.4, is a salient example of the Discharge formula put to use.[45] Besides the overall bass-heavy, dark sonic atmosphere, the riffs retain a simplicity almost reminiscent of Motörhead. The verse riff simply alternates two power chords a tritone apart, and the chorus riff is a three-power-chord descent whose melodic contour and rhythmic arrivals help project the chanted refrain. The E♭ in the chorus riff indicates that bass and guitars have been down-tuned a semitone, thus darkening the sonic atmosphere. Moreover, forward momentum is slowed down in the chorus, with less rapid strumming by the bassist and two guitarists, and with the drummer suspending the kick-snare alternation in favor of a drum roll usually at the arrival of the third power chord of the riff. A similar effect of diminishing forward momentum is

Figure 2.4 Intro and verse and chorus riffs to Aus-Rotten, "Fuck Nazi Sympathy"

achieved in the bridge following the chorus as the guitar tracks ring out on a G♭ power chord followed by feedback while the bass and drums thunder away in D-beat drive. The verse riff has the relentless repetitive quality of Discharge, and each iteration of the riff is punctuated with a D-beat rhythm on the second power chord, both in the strumming pattern of the bass and guitars and in the audibly thumping kick drum. The repeated verse riff takes on an expansive, wall of sound quality as the sparse vocals articulate each line of the verse over two repetitions of the riff followed by two repetitions without vocals—frantic thrash would have made it through each verse in half the time by eschewing the riffs that leave out vocals. The chorus is but a three-word refrain repeated.

The lyrics themselves, only four lines plus a refrain, are more or less Discharge-esque slogans. While not sympathizing with Nazis would seem an obvious point, drawing a line in the sand within a punk scene where some might have personal inter-actions with white-supremacist skinheads was relevant considering punk's recent "dregs of the eighties" history. Moreover, each line admonishes its audience to take an active position. Most significant within these simple slogans is that in the fourth line: "Don't give them their freedom because they're not going to give you yours."[46] It is reiterated after the chorus refrain and constitutes a direct rebuke of the idea of extending free speech to fascists. This position was not necessarily shared by all oppo-nents of Nazis within punk, as some would advocate the right of anyone to express their belief so long as they do so peacefully. It points to a defining feature of Aus-Rotten's recordings: the presence of polemics that at times went against the tide of other political punk.

Other British anarcho-punk stylistic traits are also present on Aus-Rotten's first two 7"s. Dis-functional solos, perhaps even more melodically murky and timbrally distorted than Discharge's, and, as one reviewer remarked, "with bends and shit," ap-pear on "No Change, No Future, We're Lost," "Apathetic," and "Secret Police, Secret Army." "Brief but wicked leads" appear on "Vietnam Is Back '94." Militaristic drum-ming on the snare drum, reminiscent of Crass, can be heard on "Tuesday, May 18th, 1993" and "Vietnam Is Back '94." The tom-tom drum rolls combined with thundering bass of crust can be heard on "A.I.D.S.," and Aus-Rotten's drummer employs drum rolls on the snare drum or floor tom, not just as brief flourishes but functionally acting as drum beats, often with accents outlining a tresillo pattern.

Where our reviewers disagreed was in whether Aus-Rotten's formulaic simplicity made for powerful or boring listening, whether there was some small degree of innovation or expressive nuance that made these recordings somehow better than other similar examples, and whether the political enunciations were heartfelt and motivating or bland and flat. The positive reviewers justified their position in three respects. First, they believed that the formulaic simplicity was done well—that is, Aus-Rotten mastered the elements of dis-core style and deployed these conventions effectively and creatively, such that their music was not a mere rehash of their 1980s predecessors but a new and more powerful incarnation. As one reviewer quoted earlier put it, after noting the Discharge similarity, "in a way they're even better." Second, some reviewers cited specific examples of innovation or expressive nuance, such as the "dual trade-off singers" or the "more compact" nature of Aus-Rotten's songs. Third, how well the politics connected emotionally to the reviewers was justified mainly in *visceral* terms, such as "it's hard not to sing along to a chorus like 'Fuck Nazi Sympathy'" or, as a review from *Profane Existence* not quoted earlier put it, "Totally raw, the way it was meant to be."[47] The vocals were certainly one aspect that provoked this visceral quality, and the variety given by Dave Trenga's lower-pitched, more audible yells and guitarist Eric Goode's higher-pitched, more timbrally distorted screams and their deployment in back-and-forth vocal trades were part of what generated excitement and the feeling, to fans, of "sincerity." I would also add that Aus-Rotten incorporated the more frantic energy of early 1980s US hardcore into their dis-core framework to create a feeling of increased urgency.

While recognizing the mixed reviews Aus-Rotten's first two 7"s received, it is worth pointing out that the *Fuck Nazi Sympathy* 7" became one of the top-selling underground punk 7"s of the 1990s with 25,000 copies sold.[48] But Aus-Rotten's success at expressive nuance within formulaic simplicity can best be understood by close analysis of its 1996 LP *The System Works . . . For Them*, to which we now turn.

The System Works . . . For Them as Powerful Punk Propaganda

Dramatic improvement since I last heard these guys. Straight ahead, by-the-numbers political punk that's still a little oversimplified for my tastes but easily makes up for it in its anger and intensity. Reminiscent of the old Crass/Conflict records with the fold out sleeve with a book's worth of writing on everything from political prisoners, direct-action, vegetarianism. . . . Generic punk topics that *do* need addressing over and over again.[49]

Calls to action and revolution with straightforward powerful political punk from Pennsylvania—clear production and easily discernable lyrics make this accessible from a listening perspective. . . . The music may not be the most original but the amount of energy and effort that went in to this is a fucking inspiration.[50]

As these reviews of Aus-Rotten's 1996 *The System Works . . . For Them* LP indicate, despite the band's continued reliance on formulaic simplicity, the visceral reaction provoked by the sonic rendering of its political messages if anything surpassed its prior releases. The "dramatic improvement" of this LP over the band's first two 7"s can best be understood by delving into its expressive nuances in the context of its deployment of conventions.

The System Works . . . For Them opens with a Crass-style tape collage that lasts nearly three-and-a-half minutes, making clear the album's emphasis on its political message as we must wait over two minutes before the instruments enter underneath the found sounds. The choice of found sounds—audio clips from various sources that are usually not musical recordings, in this case fragments of political speeches—is highly significant within punk politics. Taken together, the audio clips are a polemic against pacifist philosophy and practice and a theoretical and practical justification for the use of violence to effect revolutionary change. Crass might inform the aesthetics, but Aus-Rotten here has taken the "peace" out of peace-punk. Significantly, the entrance of the instruments underscores a climactic moment in the audio collage in which social divisions and white supremacy in particular are identified as the greatest hurdle to the emergence of radical movements in the United States.

Simple as it may be, the instrumental buildup during the audio collage gives the album as a whole and the first song in particular a tremendous dramatic gravitas, as shown in table 2.1.[51] Reiteration, so key to the aesthetics of propaganda music, is pivotal in this process as the guitars strike a G power chord every two bars followed by seven beats of palm-muted eighth-note G's. The bass thumps away at these G's, aided by the thud of the kick drum every beat and the pulse of the hi-hat splash.

To describe this buildup as simply repetitive would be to miss the expressive nuances that give it its gravitas. First, while the left[52] guitar only attacks directly on (or, to be exact in micro-timing, slightly ahead of) the first beat of every bar, the right guitar adds an anacrusis to this attack just before the downbeat. After ten bars, the right guitar expands its anacrusis from one to three attacks, which start on the syncopated side of beat three and are aided by snare drum hits on the "and" of beats three and four every other bar. The seventeenth bar marks a change from the previous repetition, as the bass and guitars move up to an E♭ and stay on this pitch for two bars, with the right guitar playing this pitch up an octave in single sustained eighth-notes. This higher pitch is accented with a snare hit on each of its arrivals. The feeling of suspension brought about by dropping the consistent palm-muting is another example of disruption of the musical surface in punk. Over the next sixteen bars, the instruments alternate between this held E♭ for two bars followed by a return to the palm-muted G for two bars, though as the guitars palm-mute on G the bass adds tension by moving up to B♭. After the last two bars of E♭, as the bass and guitars land back on G, the drums switch from the previous constant beat on the kick drum to a standard medium tempo syncopated punk beat. After eight bars of this drum beat, the guitars cease palm-muting and instead strum with sustained attacks, raising the energy level. The music continues in this way for eight more bars and the volume of the instruments

Table 2.1 Instrumental buildup to Aus-Rotten, "The System Works . . . For Them" (blank spaces indicate a repetition of the music from the preceding space)

Bars	Drums	Left guitar	Right guitar	Bass
1–2	Kick drum every beat with open hi-hat in eighth notes	Strikes G power chord and then palm-mutes repeated G eighth-notes	Strikes G power chord with an anacrusis beforehand and then palm-mutes repeated G eighth-notes	Repeated G eighth notes
3–8				
9–10	Adds syncopated snare-drum hits on the "and" of beats three and four leading into downbeat of b. 9			
11–12			Expands anacrusis from one to three hits leading into downbeat of b. 11	
13–16				
17–18	Snare hit on beat one; no syncopated snare hits	Strikes and then strums E♭ power chord without palm-muting	Strikes E♭ power chord and plays single-note high E♭'s in the second bar	Moves up to E♭
19–20	No snare hit on beat one; return to syncopated snare hits	Back to palm-muted G's	Back to palm-muted G's	Back to G and then moves up to B♭ for the second bar
21–22	Snare hit on beat one; no syncopated snare hits	Strikes and then strums E♭ power chord without palm-muting	Strikes E♭ power chord and plays single-note high E♭'s in the second bar	Moves up to E♭
23–24	No snare hit on beat one; return to syncopated snare hits	Back to palm-muted G's	Back to palm-muted G's	Back to G and then moves up to B♭ for the second bar
25–26	Snare hit on beat one; no syncopated snare hits	Strikes and then strums E♭ power chord without palm-muting	Strikes E♭ power chord and plays single-note high E♭'s in the second bar	Moves up to E♭
27–28	No snare hit on beat one; return to syncopated snare hits	Back to palm-muted G's	Back to palm-muted G's	Back to G and then moves up to B♭ for the second bar
29–30	Snare hit on beat one; no syncopated snare hits	Strikes and then strums E♭ power chord without palm-muting	Strikes E♭ power chord and plays single-note high E♭'s in the second bar	Moves up to E♭
31–32	Changes to a medium-tempo punk beat with syncopated snare hits before and after beat three	Back to palm-muted G's	Back to palm-muted G's	Back to repeated G's
33–38				
39–40		Strums instead of palm-mutes G power chord	Strums instead of palm-mutes G power chord	
41–46				

is raised in a gradual crescendo. This dramatic buildup through crescendo comes to an accented end with a held-out G and the drums ceasing after a snare hit, thereby briefly suspending forward momentum before a drum-fill leads us into the first song of the album. It is these details of expressive nuance that make a fairly simple gradual buildup capable of provoking a visceral response and leading the listener into the political enunciations to come.

The album's title track, "The System Works . . . For Them," bursts forth following this build-up. Its verse riff, transcribed in figure 2.5, is at home in dis-core as well as more broadly in punk conventions, opening with three iterations of the safety-pin gesture followed by a punctuation of two power chords. When the vocals enter, this riff is presented three times with a pitch content that has been used since punk's beginnings—the "box riff," so called because when played on guitar or bass the roots make a box on the E and A strings.[53] But every fourth time the riff is given a slight variation, with the punctuation made with a low F and E♭, the latter an unusual pitch choice following a box riff and betraying the fact that the bass and guitars have been down-tuned a semitone.[54]

While this riff is deeply conventional to both dis-core in particular and punk as a whole, it is rendered in such a way as to amplify the dense lyrics, which challenge listeners on their culpability in the horrors of capitalism. Each line is made musically powerful by the punctuation that concludes it, with the constant pulse stream *disrupted* to make way for two snare hits in homorhythm with the other instruments' attacks, and joined by guitarist Eric Goode screaming "boy-cott." This word boils down the lengthy lyrics into a single invocation—another crucial trait of propaganda music.

The chorus plays a similar role to the "boy-cott" punctuation in concentrating the song's message by directly admonishing the imagined listeners for failure to live up to political punk's professed opposition to capitalism. In a dramatic change in texture from the verse, several musical elements co-conspire in the chorus to provide an uninhibited enunciation of the lyrics: the drummer does not use any cymbals and thus the chorus lacks the metallic splash so familiar in punk; G is the only pitch/power chord heard in the entire chorus; and the guitars mostly palm mute during the first iteration of the refrain before dropping out and giving way to slight feedback after hitting high and low G's at the beginning of the repetition of the refrain. Upon this repetition of the refrain, the drummer switches to what in crust parlance is often referred to as a "tribal beat," beating away at the floor tom with a tresillo rhythm. The declaimed vocals, which are yelled by both of Aus-Rotten's vocalists, match this

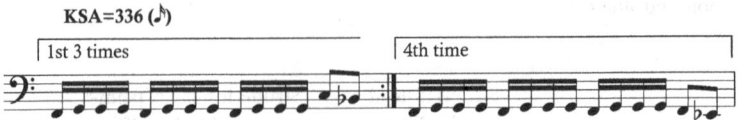

Figure 2.5 Aus-Rotten, "The System Works . . . For Them," verse riff

tresillo rhythm. Shown in figure 2.6, this rhythmically declaimed and collectively delivered chorus cannot help but conjure up the feel of a chant at a street protest, especially as the drummer bangs away at the physically and pitch-wise lowest pieces of the drum set, like feet stomping on pavement.

"The System Works . . . For Them" also marks a departure from Aus-Rotten's previously more sparse lyrics. It and many other songs on this album have the density of Crass's poetically written essays rather than the sloganeering of Discharge, even while continuing to offer boiled-down slogans perfect for sing-along crowd participation. As one *MaximumRockNRoll* review commented about a later Aus-Rotten album, "Their lyrics are long complex lessons."[55] Indeed, there is a greater political specificity on several songs on *The System Works . . . For Them*, such as "Poison Corporations," which lists particular corporations and pollutants responsible for environmental destruction; "No Justice, No Peace," which details the frame-ups of several political prisoners in the United States; and "Too Little, Too Late," which chronicles Rwandan genocide and the US government policies that ignore such atrocities and do little to aid the victims. This lyrical change is in part a solution to the problem of the popularity of sloganeering in punk that can generate significant crowd response but often little in the way of education or activity. Aus-Rotten addressed this very problem of the politics of proclamation on "The System Works . . . For Them" with lines such as "You hate these corporate killers but you fucking keep on paying, For the products you don't need."

More sophisticated and dense lyrics pose the problem of how to deliver them in a form that is intelligible and dramatically leads to their main point rather than drowns it in a sea of syllables. The verse punctuations and chorus refrain and texture on "The System Works . . . For Them" provide part of the answer. But more large-scale questions of form are also effectively addressed in this song. First, the verses, each

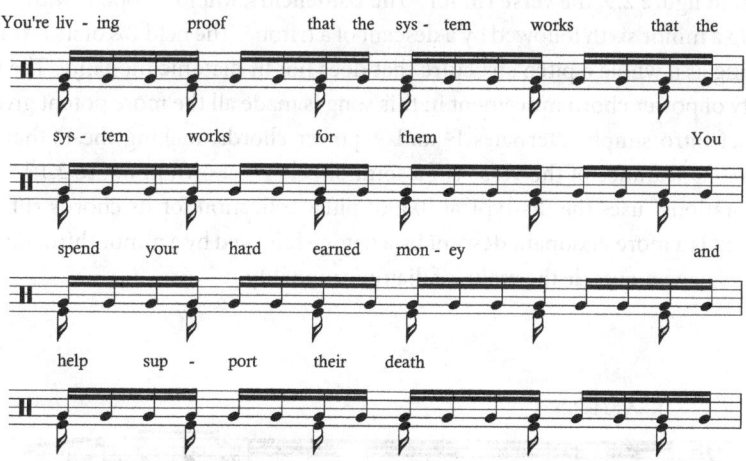

Figure 2.6 Aus-Rotten, "The System Works . . . For Them," chorus, drum reduction and vocals

with eleven lines of lyrics (on what would be the twelfth line, the band plays the riff without vocals), are formally subdivided into three sections by virtue of the riff structure: repetition followed by variation.[56] Second, in the third verse, lacking the "boycott" backing vocals, the left guitar switches from playing the riff with power chords to playing it up an octave in single notes, complete with the occasional feedback-drenched harmonic. This essentially doubles the power chord riff as a lead guitar part and ratchets up the song's intensity for the final verse. Thus, together with smaller nuances, a simple but effective large-scale formal plan renders the lengthy lyrical tirade more pointed and powerful, and gives the chorus refrain the aura of epiphany in the ongoing musical and semantic drama. In short, "The System Works . . . For Them" has all the elements of successful propaganda music. To further elucidate the makings of successful propaganda music, the musical poetics of crust-punk/dis-core, and the expressive nuances within Aus-Rotten's deployment of stylistic conventions, it is worth looking at aspects of several other songs on the same LP.

Dissonation of Riffs

As with Los Crudos, the pitch structures of Aus-Rotten's riffs were a *dissonation* of previous punk conventions by using tritones instead of perfect fifths or by departing from major or minor diatonic modality. One source of this change is Discharge, whose riffs often outlined tritones and employed a [0356] pitch structure. Salient examples of these Discharge-style riffs on *The System Works . . . For Them* appear on "Tedium" (figure 2.7) and "B.A.T.F." (figure 2.8), though the latter is rendered in a slower-paced punk rhythmic feel rather than metal-tinged.

Other riffs go further in dissonance than Discharge, whose tritone-based riffs did, after all, fit within the blues-riff conventions that rock in general draws from. As shown in figure 2.9, the verse riff for "The Battlefield's Still Red" opens with a brazen leap up a minor sixth followed by a descent of a tritone. The held B♭s of its refrain give the song as a whole a pitch structure that does not fit diatonic modality. The jarring quality of power chord movement in this song is made all the more potent given that its brief intro simply alternates F♯ and A power chords, making the F♮ that marks the first appearance of the verse riff a sonic shock. As shown in figure 2.10, "Poison Corporations" uses the dis-typical [0356] pitch collection for its chorus riff, but its verse riff is a more dissonant descent by a tritone followed by a minor third, thus decisively placing it outside the realm of diatonic modality.

KSA=346 (♪)

Figure 2.7 Aus-Rotten, "Tedium," verse riff

KSA=320 (♪)

Figure 2.8 Aus-Rotten, "B.A.T.F.," verse riff

KSA=372 (♪)

Figure 2.9 Aus-Rotten, "The Battlefield's Still Red"

KSA=424 (♪)

Figure 2.10 Aus-Rotten, "Poison Corporations," verse and chorus riffs

KSA=350 (♪)

Figure 2.11 Aus-Rotten, "No Justice, No Peace," verse riff

What is most striking about the pitch structures of Aus-Rotten riffs, however, it that they often *dissonate* what could have otherwise been a typical diatonic punk riff. As shown in figure 2.11, the verse riff of "No Justice, No Peace" starts with an ascent of power chords a major third apart. Anyone aurally familiar with punk might expect this to be the start of a box riff, with the C♯ and E power chords followed by B and G♯ power chords. By going instead to A♭ and then D, this riff defies those expectations and ends with two power chords a tritone apart. Subsequently, this riff is presented in retrograde, thereby opening with the tritone, in the section following the second chorus and accompanied by Crass-style militaristic drumming, as Dave Trenga eschews vocalizing and delivers something of a political speech.

The verse riff of "American Ethic," shown in figure 2.12, offers another example of riff dissonation. The E♭ power chord that begins the riff makes for a pungent tritone

Figure 2.12 Aus-Rotten, "American Ethic," verse riff

with the subsequent A power chord. This opening is a reverse (descending) safety pin gesture in a wide melodic leap—thus inverting another punk convention. Were it a D rather than an E♭ power chord opening this riff, its pitch-structure would fit within typical minor-mode 1980s hardcore riffs.

While melodic dissonance in Los Crudos's riffs served to ratchet up the frantic energy of hardcore, in Aus-Rotten's music this dissonation offers a sonic parallel to the lyrical contention that something is deeply wrong with the façade of American democracy. Indeed, the two best exemplars of dissonation on *The System Works . . . For Them* are in songs with exactly this political theme. "No Justice, No Peace" reveals the FBI's and the American justice system's frame-ups of Black and Native American revolutionaries such as Mumia Abu-Jamal, Leonard Peltier, the MOVE 9, and Dhoruba bin Wahad, and the dissonant A♭ sonically indicates the lyrics' contention that "Our judicial system's a fucking lie." The dissonant E♭ in "American Ethic" similarly serves to musically elucidate the lyrical critique of an American work ethic that justifies a blissful ignorance of the dependence of American living standards on Third World exploitation, environmental destruction, and US military domination, as well as the warped family and social relations such a blissful ignorance fosters.

One final example of dissonation illustrates the way that 1990s political punk took dissonance further to paint a bleak(er) picture of the world around it. The two dysfunctional guitar solos on *The System Works . . . For Them* are even more dissonant, more melodically meandering, and more distorted by pitch bends than on Discharge or even previous Aus-Rotten records. One such solo occurs on "The Battlefield's Still Red," a song about the continuing genocide in Rwanda and the absurdity that such a genocide can be allowed to continue after all that humanity knows about the historical realities of genocide and ethnic cleansing. Musically, the fast-moving and dissonant riff over which this solo is played offers little in the way of a harmonic foundation for a consonant solo.

The Thump and Thud of the Kick Drum

One tremendous asset to the performance on and recording of *The System Works . . . For Them* is that the crucial characteristic of the D-beat—the thump and thud of the kick drum—is prominent in the mix and delivered with a bass-heavy sonic punch. This kick-drum sound drives the forward momentum of the music, provokes that visceral feeling of power and urgency, contributes to the bass-heavy dark sonic

KSA=376 (♪)

Figure 2.13 Aus-Rotten, "When You Support These Fucking Bastards," verse riff (accents indicate heavy kick-drum hits)

atmosphere of the recording, and often punctuates the political enunciations of the lyrics. While the thump and thud is heard throughout the album, "The Battlefield's Still Red" and "When You Support These Fucking Bastards" are perhaps the best examples of its punch. On the former, the kick drum sometimes gives a D-beat rhythm to the second half of the verse riff and punctuates most of the held-out B♭ power chords on the chorus. On the latter, during the verse riff the kick drum outlines an accent pattern together with the pick strokes of the bass and guitars within what is a fairly simple and rhythmically straightforward three-power-chord riff, as shown in figure 2.13. During the chorus, the band uses the "stops" technique, in which all instruments give a series of unsustained attacks on one pitch or power chord while the vocals are delivered in the instrumental silence that follows these attacks. Here, the thump and thud is reduced to a singularity that punctuates each anguished cry from the three different vocalists.

A similar technique is employed following the second chorus of "Poison Corporations." The expressive power of this kick drum thump and thud on *The System Works . . . For Them* punctuates the album's lyrical tirades and makes us viscerally feel them in our guts, as the vibrations of the low-pitched punch energetically flow through our bodies.

Punktuation

The stops on "When You Support These Fucking Bastards" and "Poison Corporations" point to another feature that makes *The System Works . . . For Them* successful propaganda: the use of musical punctuation to hammer home messages. This punctuation comes in many forms, such as the two power chords that end the verse riff of the album's title track, which disrupt the musical surface and hardcore drumbeat pulse stream with homorhythmic attacks by the whole band, including the "boy-cott" vocals. Another example of a punctuation that disrupts the musical surface is the five accents on a C power chord that end the chorus riff to "American Ethic." "Poison Corporations" offers a different example of punctuation, in which most vocal lines of both verses and chorus are punctuated with a brief snare-drum roll. This song also features the strategic deployment of doubled vocals on specific words—"acid rain," "nuclear waste," "cash crops," "capitalist pigs," "McDonalds," "Imperialist," and "ruling class"—which serves both to amplify moments in the lyrics that ascribe specific blame

Figure 2.14 Aus-Rotten, "B.A.T.F.," bridge riff

for environmental destruction, and, musically and dramatically, to break the fast flow of syllabically dense lyrics. Finally, sections can function as larger-scale punctuations within the structure of a song, as does the bridge that follows each chorus on "B.A.T.F." The bridge's tritone-laden tresillo-rhythm riff, shown in figure 2.14, rhythmically disrupts the musical surface, and semantically and musically punctuates the chanted chorus it follows.

Boiled Down to a Chant

Like "The System Works . . . For Them," the chorus of "B.A.T.F."[57]—"A.T.F., A.T.F., we don't need the A.T.F."—could easily be a chant at a street protest, given its rhythmic declamation. The palm-muting of the guitars and lack of metallic splash from cymbals, which are absent on the chorus, make the doubled vocals more prominent in the mix. While other songs do not have that same chant quality, most songs on *The System Works . . . For Them* manage to boil down their message to a one-line refrain, brief slogans, or at least a poetically catchy chorus. "The Battlefield's Still Red" is one example of a one-line refrain that concentrates the song's protest against the Rwandan genocide. The chorus of "When You Support These Fucking Bastards" combines musical punctuation with a series of simple slogans:

> The starving are still hungry
> The suffering in pain
> The poor still have no money
> While the rich drink their champagne[58]

And "Poison Corporations" provides an example of a poetically catchy chorus giving a moral lesson:

> Poison corporations, they've sealed the planet's doom
> Thinking they could pay for whatever they consume
> What good is all their money when there's no one left to buy?[59]
> You can either try to stop them or you can watch our planet die

In all cases, the song's message is boiled down to its most simple at a dramatic high point in the musical structure, thus potentially acting as a moment of epiphany or bringing together the prior, denser lyrical tirade into a singular message.

Formal Design as Means to Intensity and Dramatic Momentum

As with most punk, Aus-Rotten's songs usually follow a verse-chorus structure, sometimes adding an intro or a bridge. It would be remiss, however, not to notice expressive nuances in formal design that give many of these songs dramatic gravitas through a sense of forward momentum that leads to moments of heightened intensity. The dramatic structure of the song "The System Works . . . For Them," and the instrumental introduction underneath a sound collage preceding it on the album, have already been described earlier. On "The Battlefield's Still Red," diagrammed in table 2.2, an alternation of two sustained power chords over a Crust "tribal beat" on the tom-toms allows Dave Trenga to emotionally introduce the song's subject matter. The D-beat drive of the first verse ratchets up the intensity with the fast-moving dissonant riff and syllabic density of its lyrics. On the chorus, the first three sustained power chords together with the switch by drummer Filthy Rich Bastard to single crash-cymbal accents, instead of the splashy pulse of the hi-hat, briefly slow down the

Table 2.2 Form outline of Aus-Rotten, "The Battlefield's Still Red"

Time/Section	Instrumental parts	Vocals
0:00–0:25 Intro	"Tribal" beat on tom-toms; guitars and bass alternate between F♯ and A	Dave Trenga enters after two alternations of F♯ and A
0:25–0:29 Transition	F♯ rings out while drums play a fill	No vocals
0:29–0:45 Verse 1	Verse riff (F up to D♭ and then down to G); D-beat drum pattern	Dave Trenga enters with rhythmically dense vocal delivery after four riffs
0:45–0:50 Refrain 1	Refrain riff (Four B♭ power chords repeated ringing out); drums accent on crash cymbal	Anguished scream of "The battlefield's still red!" on the fourth B♭ power chord
0:50–1:06 Verse 2	Same as Verse 1	After four verse riffs, a vocal trade (Dave Trenga, Eric Goode, Dave Trenga, third vocalist) with sparser vocals
1:06–1:12 Refrain 2	Same as Refrain 1	Same as Refrain 1
1:12–1:22 Verse 3	Same as Verse 1 but with a dis-functional guitar solo	No vocals
1:22–1:27 Refrain 3	Same as Refrain 1	No vocals
1:27–1:44 Verse 4	Same as Verse 1	New lyrics, but the same vocal delivery as Verse 1
1:44–1:49 Refrain 4	Same as Refrain 1	Same as Refrain 1
1:49–2:05 Verse 5	Same as Verse 1	Vocal trade (same as Verse 2)
2:05–2:11 Refrain 5	Same as Refrain 1	Same as Refrain 1

forward drive and draw greater attention to the anguished scream of the song's refrain by a third, unnamed vocalist. The second verse creates musical and dramatic variety with the first verse, with Dave Trenga and Eric Goode trading off yells and screams in Discharge-style vocal delivery, leaving two iterations of the riff vocal-free between each line of lyrics. From here we get a dis-functional solo followed by a third verse and a repetition of the second verse with choruses in between.

The significance that a simple choice of cymbal and/or other changes in rhythmic feel can take on is evident from the dramatic momentum of "When You Support These Fucking Bastards," diagrammed in table 2.3. The song's verse riff (figure 2.13) offers a contrast between the low-pitched E power chord and the move up the fret-board by a diminished seventh to a D♭ followed by a C power chord. The sonic contrast between the first and second half of the verse riff is furthered by the vocal trades that present a different vocalist on each half of the riff, with Dave Trenga's more audible yells on the first half and the more frantic screams of Eric Goode or a third vocalist on the second half. The drums and different rhythms also demarcate each half of the riff. On the first half, crash-cymbal accents and an audibly heavier thump and thud of the kick drum emphasize rhythmic groupings of four pulses rather than a

Table 2.3 Form outline of Verse 1 and Chorus 1 of Aus-Rotten, "When You Support These Fucking Bastards"

Power Chord	Drums	Vocals
E	Verse pattern 1: KSA = 376; heavy accents on crash cymbal and kick drum every four pulses	Dave Trenga (yells)
D♭/ C	Verse pattern 2: KSA = 376; open hi-hat and a less heavy kick-drum, creating the feel of a more continuous pulse stream	Eric Goode (screams)
E	Verse pattern 1	Dave Trenga (yells)
D♭/ C	Verse pattern 2	Third vocalist (screams)
E	Verse pattern 1	Dave Trenga (yells)
D♭/ C	Verse pattern 2	Eric Goode (screams)
E	Verse pattern 1	Dave Trenga (yells)
D♭/ C	Verse pattern 2 followed by a drum fill (mainly a snare drum roll) during the C power chord	Third vocalist (screams)
E	Verse pattern 3: KSA = 163; a slower punk-rock feel with splashy hi-hat	Dave Trenga (yells)
D♭/ C	Verse pattern 3 followed by drum fill (mainly a drum roll) that goes from snare drum to floor tom during the C power chord	Dave Trenga and Eric Goode (yells)
E	Single accent on kick drum and crash cymbal while guitars and bass ring out	Dave Trenga (yells)
E	Same as above	Eric Goode (screams)
E	Same as above	Dave Trenga (yells)
E	Same as above, but with a snare fill at the end	Eric Goode (screams)

constant pulse stream, and the standard hardcore strumming pattern of bass and guitars adds to this rhythmic emphasis. On the second half, the switch to continuous hits of the hi-hat and a less heavy hit of the kick drum, together with the more continuous strumming on bass and guitars, moves the emphasis to constant pulse and forward momentum rather than specific accents. Without transforming the riff's pitch structure, another change in musical texture and rhythm offers a dramatic lead-in to the chorus, as the new drum beat on the last line of each verse cuts the KSA in half while simultaneously maintaining forward momentum with a constant pulse on the hi-hat, hits on the kick drum, and brief fills mainly on the snare drum, all abetted by the constant strumming of the bass and guitars. The sloganeering chorus rendered musically with stops and that beautiful singular kick drum thud thus comes as a dramatic high point of the song.

"Poison Corporations" offers an example of dramatic gravitas brought about by the gradual buildup that begins the song, changes in drumming and riff structures and performance, the use of stops, and punctuation. The buildup at the beginning starts with constant strumming on a C power chord and a drumbeat of kick drum, snare drum, and tom-toms with no cymbals at 222 KSA. The right guitar is the first to depart from this constant C to play the full verse riff until the left guitar and bass join it with the full verse riff, thus making for a staggered entrance. After the transformation from constantly strummed C to the verse riff is complete, the drums leave the tom-toms for the metallic splash of hi-hat in a punk rock beat. After four iterations of the riff in punk-rock rhythm, the drums switch to a fast hardcore beat, thereby doubling the KSA to 424. Now we are ready for the ensuing lyrical onslaught of pointed facts about environmental devastation brought about by corporate drive for profit, punctuated by snare drum rolls. The chorus, boiling down the facts in the verse lyrics, is differentiated by a riff structure that is an overall melodic ascent higher on the fretboard than the descent of the verse riff. This differentiation is furthered by the drummer's switch to the crash cymbal. Following the first chorus and at the end of two iterations of the verse riff, pick slides by both guitars lead into the second verse vocals. The frantic fast pace and musical texture of "Poison Corporations" is broken with the kick-drum-accented stops after the second chorus, which makes for a dramatic highpoint in the song. Thus nuances such as switches in cymbals are what give Aus-Rotten songs their dramatic gravitas and intensity. Any accounting of form in punk music needs to pay attention to such details rather than accept the simplicity of verse-chorus structure as the be-all and end-all of musical structure.[60]

While Aus-Rotten's creative deployment of conventions facilitated the clear communication of its political message and that message's reinforcement through the political associations of the particular stylistic conventions it employed, it was the expressive nuances outlined previously that presented those stylistic conventions in such a way that compelled a visceral reaction. As one reviewer would put it about a subsequent Aus-Rotten album's success intellectually and viscerally, "it gets my blood pumping and my brain thinking, which is what classic punk must do," and thus constituted an "inspirational onslaught of angry as fuck anarcho crust punk."[61]

The Ubiquity of Crust-Punk/Dis-Core and the Problem with Sticking to Conventions

While at the dawn of the 1990s, commentary in punk zines lamented the lack of bands enunciating radical politics, as the decade wore on the sheer number of bands in the crust-punk/dis-core style, with the corresponding politics, became massive and perhaps overwhelming. The preponderance of bands of this style in the pages of zine record reviews was so great that even *Profane Existence*, the happy haven of crust, would ironically include a "DI$-SECTION" in the record reviews of its autumn 1994 issue with bands whose names began with "dis."[62] Of the seven records reviewed, only the one by Dissension received positive remarks. Three years later, the band Dissucks parodied the dis-name trend with its own moniker. A *Profane Existence* reviewer described them as a "new punk rock band from Philadelphia, PA, that have a blatant aversion to the trendy Discharge cloning running rampant these days."[63]

Before moving to a discussion of the problem of staleness that "Discharge cloning" resulted in, it is worth noting the achievements brought about by the ubiquity of crust-punk/dis-core bands. First, the style became so well-established and codified that simply hearing it even without reading the lyrics meant, for anyone in the punk scene, an immediate association of that sound with radical politics. This aural association was so pervasive that, when a band came along with political lyrics but without crust-punk/dis-core style, they were identified as an exception that proved the rule. A reviewer of the *Kill Kill Kill* EP by Anti-Flag, a band whose style is rooted in pop-punk and Clash-style British punk, wrote:

> With songs like "Kill the Rich," at first glance this record appears as though it would be a crust thing happening. But upon listening, I was thrown for a loop. There is a poppy-punk rock influence, but fortunately it has an edge, lacking the sugary glossiness of most of that stuff.[64]

Even as early as 1990, Lance Hahn of the pop-punk band Cringer would decry a problem experienced when touring: "People don't like melodic punk bands with political lyrics. It just doesn't work that way."[65]

The converse of the fact that it "just doesn't work that way" was that crust-punk/dis-core *did work* at denoting political position. This brings us to our second point about the virtues of convention: crust-punk/dis-core effected a stylistic distinction within the punk scene to musically delineate political bands from "apolitical" or right-wing bands. In the midst of pop-punk, straight-edge hardcore, drunk punk, emo, and other stylistic trends, crust-punk/dis-core demarcated the political wing of punk. It did so to such an extent that in the previous review, the musical "edge" heard on Anti-Flag's poppy-punk stylistically set it apart from "the sugary glossiness of most of that stuff" and thus enabled the band to sing convincingly about politics rather than love and break-ups, the usual fodder of pop-punk lyrics.

Finally, the vast array of crust-punk/dis-core bands meant that the problem of the lack of political bands at the dawn of the 1990s had been solved. But if Marx was right that history develops in spirals, then this solution led to a new problem: saturation and staleness. These issues are best understood by looking at the reception of a number of crust-punk/dis-core bands in zine record reviews. The response to Detestation, a band that included several veterans of the Portland anarcho-punk scene and attained significant notoriety in the late 1990s, is telling of an appreciation for successful deployment of the conventions of crust-punk/dis-core:

> Detestation is Kelly ex-Masskontrol and Defiance's new band, and this band pounds. Musically it's generic, Swedish sound hc [hardcore] (when I say generic, that is not always a negative comment), with female vocals that are comparable to Amy of Nausea fame.[66]

> Stylistically they draw from classic early 80's Scandinavian punk with a nod to Discharge. While the music is powerful, I feel it's Saira's vocals that put this band over the top.[67]

> They certainly are not the most original of bands, but their music is well done and their records are well constructed from look to lyrics.[68]

Notably, these reviewers readily identified Detestation's stylistic heritage, including the Scandinavian hardcore aspect, and recognized the band's lack of profound originality and, simultaneously, its success at creating good music within its conventional framework. For one reviewer, voice, in this case the screams of Saira, was the most potent element of Detestation's music.

Other bands would receive similar recognition for success while sticking to conventions. Deceived's *Smash Patriarchy* 7", for example, was described as "some above average old school crust that, while not advancing this genre's sound, does hold up quite well with others playing this type of music."[69] Distraught was labeled as "Brooklyn's Dis thrashers" who were musically "somewhere between the classic NYC anarchopunk sound of early Nausea with loads of next generation 'Discharge' type punk influences."[70] Other reviewers were less charitable to examples they considered to be mired by adherence to conventions. Misery's *Who's the Fool . . .* LP was described as a "competent crust record that's listenable but nothing to get excited about. It held my attention but it was exactly what I expected it to be, no surprises."[71] Anti-Product, a band who, in fairness, was quite young at the time, received the following responses:

> Crust with female and male vocals which is on the better side of the genre but still doesn't do anything for me. But like they said in the insert it's more about the politics of which this record is overflowing.[72]

> This band has the whole Crass format. Political punk that sounds a lot like Nausea. Lots of well-meaning lyrics about how the government is an evil thing. It's good if you're into this type of music, but for the most part it seemed too derivative and cliché.[73]

Significantly, even in criticisms of crust-punk/dis-core, the "well-meaning lyrics" and politics were considered its saving graces. The band Civil Disobedience provided the most strident example of this criticism. When asked in an interview about the "Discharge revival thing," they responded, "we support them, we agree with their messages, we just find the Discharge type repetition humorous. Personally we feel it's lacking creativity, but it is by no means wrong."[74]

Staleness, particularly in lyrical content, also ran the risk, for both band and audience, of losing a personal connection to the music's message. Interviewed by *Profane Existence*, Detestation responded to the interviewer's observation that the band's "new songs seem to be more commentary on day to day life rather than outright political statements":

KELLY: "I think that punk bands have pretty much covered all the bases as far as writing 'smash the state' lyrics, but . . . you can only write so many songs about burning cop cars."

SAIRA: "We just try to write songs that apply to our everyday life that we can actually live up to. 'Cause I don't personally go out and burn cop cars and government offices everyday, so I'm not going to write anything about it."

KELLY: "Some of those old songs are good, raw expressions of anger but, you know, sometimes it's kinda silly. . . . I'll read back some lyrics from old bands I was in and it's like . . . no one in [the band] Resist ever participated in a revolution. No one from [the band] Deprived lit a cop car on fire. I want to be able to stand behind everything I say. That to me is important, when people stand behind their shit."[75]

In this recognition of issues of staleness in crust-punk/dis-core style, we can see that the aesthetic values of propaganda music can easily become its detriments. Boiling down messages to simple slogans can become impersonal and clichéd. Relying on conventions to provide audiences with familiarity and meaning can produce boring music, both as a consequence of stylistic saturation and as individual failure to creatively deploy conventions. The Crass-style lettering, album covers depicting dead bodies, the familiar list of political subjects, and music—in short, the semantic over-determination of message—could begin to feel like beating a dead horse. And when all this happens, the listener response becomes a routine rather than visceral reaction.

Paths Out of Staleness

While recognizing the real problem of staleness in crust-punk/dis-core style, it is also important to point out that bands in this style, even ones relying on conventional formulas, did not all sound the same. The contrast between Detestation and Anti-Product, two important crust-punk bands of the late 1990s, is a salient example. Whereas the crust-punk on Anti-Product's first two 7" records owed a strong stylistic debt to Crass, particularly with the trebly guitars, Detestation's music was far more metal-inflected with its bass-heavy, dark sonic atmosphere, and had much more the feel of Discharge's repetitive regularity, especially given the prominence of the standard hardcore rhythm in strumming patterns, drumbeats, and even the rhythm of Saira's vocal delivery.

Beyond this stylistic variance, however, were two pathways out of the problems of staleness. First was the continual emergence of new bands and even local scenes of several bands who injected new energy into political punk, often by infusing it with the raw energy of early 1980s hardcore as well as with their own expressive nuances. A crop of Seattle bands in the late 1990s, with Whorehouse of Representatives as the standout, exemplified this phenomenon. Second was the presence of outliers who bore some relationship to crust-punk/dis-core, even if simply by virtue of being on the same record label and playing shows with bands of that style, but had a sound that was far more abnormal and quirky. Civil Disobedience provides the best exemplification of such stylistic outliers.

The wavelike nature of punk's history, with certain bands and local scenes reinvigorating the music at specific moments, was indicated in the following review of Whorehouse of Representatives' 1994 debut 7" record: "The Seattle punk scene seems to be going full blast right now and here's another great band making it happen. Very catchy, fast punk with female vocals and very insightful lyrics."[76] Reviews of the band's 1997 *Your Alcohol Taxes at Work* 7" indicated its stylistic location and suggested the expressive features that took its music out of routine political punk:

Aggressive punk music combining the Northwest anarchopunk style of bands like Defiance and Resist with European punk levels of complexity and angry female vocals with totally pissed off and well-written political lyrics.[77]

The music is mainly played at a fast tempo, with dual guitars buzzing away, and time changes along with breaks when needed. The lyrics reflect a common state of mind among the populace these days, which is one of despair and a feeling of no hope.[78]

Rightfully, neither of these reviewers pigeonholed Whorehouse of Representatives as being crust or dis-core, but situated them within regional stylistic trends ("Northwest anarchopunk") and identified specific features of their music, such as "angry female vocals," "time changes," and "European punk levels of complexity." There were some markers of crust-punk/dis-core in the band's music, as can be heard on their song "Greed is a Disease" from their split 7" with Brother Inferior.[79] As shown in figure 2.15, the verse riff repeats an inverted safety-pin gesture that descends from B♭ to A. The chorus riff outlines two tritones—D to G♯ and E♭ to A—that, taken together, do not fit within a singular diatonic mode.

As a whole, Whorehouse of Representatives lacked the metal inflection of crust-punk/dis-core and conveyed more the raw energy of early 1980s hardcore. The variability and nuance in its music were likely what resulted in such enthusiastic reviews at the height of staleness in political punk, with "Junkie," the opening track

Figure 2.15 Whorehouse of Representatives, "Greed Is a Disease," verse and chorus riffs

Figure 2.16 Whorehouse of Representatives, riffs from "Junkie"

of the *Your Alcohol Taxes at Work* 7", exemplifying the aforementioned musical traits, as shown in figure 2.16.[80] Starting at a slow tempo for punk, the introductory riff is notable for being played as single notes on the guitar and for its "lead guitar" quality, given the faster movement from one pitch to another. Expressive nuances such as the pitch bends by the bass and heavy double-pedaled kick-drum fill at the end of the riff further pull it out of punk routines. The song's intro as a whole is far from the usual repetition of the same riff, instead moving back and forth between palm-muted power chords and the opening "lead guitar" part when vocalist Michelle enters, with the guitars eventually moving to open strumming, the tempo speeding up, and the drummer offering quick flourishes of snare-drum rolls to ratchet up the intensity.

Following this intro, the verse riff takes us into the realm of blazing tempo hardcore, while the chorus slows the tempo down but maintains driving momentum with double hits on the kick drum. The right guitar track adds intensity by playing the chorus riff up an octave as single notes, like a lead guitar part. Rhythmic variation and punctuation is added to this chorus with the last iteration of the chorus riff played palm-muted in triplets, with the whole band homorhythmically matching the vocal delivery. A bridge before the last verse and chorus brings back the rhythmic feel of the song's intro, including the snare-drum roll flourishes. These frequent changes of tempo and riffs, the presence of lead guitar parts, and drum fills that add greater groove and momentum to typical hardcore and punk beats constitute the "European punk levels of complexity" that put Whorehouse of Representatives' music decisively outside the realm of stylistic staleness. It is also worth noting that while Whorehouse of Representatives' lyrics addressed many of the familiar political topics of crust-punk/dis-core, several of its songs took on a more personal tone, including "Junkie," which decries the effects of heroin addiction on addicts and addicts' friends alike. Furthermore, the band's very name, while political, was a departure from the more austere seriousness of crust-punk/dis-core band names (ausrotten is German for ex-terminate) and a move toward irony and even humor. Thus the perception of a more personal touch, particularly as embodied in the vocals, was a key part of what marked Whorehouse of Representatives as an innovative departure from routinization.

Even more innovative was the band Civil Disobedience, who went so far beyond routinization as to epitomize a quirky, abnormal approach to punk. Civil Disobedience politically fit into the crust-punk/dis-core scene—its *Invention Extinction* LP was on Profane Existence Records, and the band even moved from Michigan to the crust capital of Minneapolis[81]—but musically had little to do with its style. The following two reviews offer a beginning explanation of what made Civil Disobedience's music so unusual:

> With its roots coming from older, fast charge political punk of the early '80s, this lacks the metal influence of so much (for lack of better words) "crusty" music that seems so prevalent now. The difference is subtle but with their more quirky, brittle, and ultimately more creative qualities they manage to transcend much of the boring genericness of this style of punk. Aesthetically, there's nothing aston-ishingly new and innovative about this; bands have been playing this same stuff for over 15 years. But what sets this or any band apart for that matter is that intangible drive and passion that makes the music feel as though it comes from real people's lives and not from some fucking textbook.[82]

> This is THE shit. The guitar alternates between doing fast solo-esque (but not re-ally) notes and regular hardcore punk stuff while the bass keeps the general music moving. Then you've got cool as fuck trade off vocals. All this combined with wacky originality, a whole bunch of cool samples, political as fuck lyrics.[83]

The first review pointed to the fact that Civil Disobedience drew on a different breed of British political punk than crust/dis-core, namely the bouncy bass drive of Crass and the ska/reggae punk of Citizen Fish. Both reviewers pointed to the more intangible "visceral" feel of passion in the music as well as the band's quirkiness and "wacky originality." Indeed, Civil Disobedience's music seemed almost like a parody fit for a punk circus, matching its sarcastic lyrical approach often aimed at pointing out the insanity of late imperial America. This latter aspect is made clear through the choice of found sounds for its Crass-style sound collages on the band's *In a Few Hours of Madness* 7": commentary on the madness of war pointing to a doomsday scenario but told with the laughter of a lunatic. All this was worlds apart from the austere seriousness of crust-punk/dis-core.

"Manufactured Citizens," from the aforementioned 7" record, exemplifies Civil Disobedience's circus-like approach to political punk style.[84] The song's intro, transcribed in figure 2.17, features a syncopated bassline played with the so-called slap-bass technique, in which the bassist uses their non-fretboard hand to either slap the string against the fretboard with their thumb or pull the string outward with a non-thumb finger, resulting in the string hitting the fretboard and producing a popping, percussive sound. Funk bass player Larry Graham is generally credited with inventing the slap-bass technique, and it was used by several rock bands in the 1990s, most notably Primus, as part of a humor-laden style. This syncopated bassline is joined by the left guitar playing the "skank" syncopations of ska-punk and the drummer providing a disco-esque beat with rapid repetitive hits on the open hi-hat. Over this backdrop the right guitar plays a lead part—at first a harmonized alternation between A and B♭ emphasizing syncopation, then dropping the harmony and moving to rapid sixteenth notes that intensify the semitone alternation and ratchet up the level of carnival-esque punk style. Complete with the snarly vocals made all the more chaotic by zigzagging pitch inflections, this intro is an excellent exemplification of the quirky, wacky musical traits that make up Civil Disobedience's circus-crust style.

Following the intro, the verse riff puts the song more in the realm of fast peace-punk, but the right guitar continues with its parodistic-sounding lead guitar work emphasizing the previously established A to B♭ semitone motion, as shown in figure 2.18. The chorus, with its palm-muted riff shown in figure 2.19, is perhaps the most normatively punk part of the song, though the snarly vocal trades and chromatic ascent at the end of the chorus riff retain elements of quirkiness. Furthermore, the chorus riff's emphasis on the pitch and power chord E add a harmonic tension to the structure of the song. The creative absurdity of Civil Disobedience's music is a perfect fit for the lyrics of "Manufactured Citizens," which sardonically describe the "non-thought multitudes" who are "manufactured in the schools" to be "sold off in the marketplace" and "utilized in the factories" until "they're thrown away."[85]

While the propaganda music of Aus-Rotten and other bands like it was crucial to anchoring 1990s political punk with a sense of purpose and an urgency of action, the musical insanity of Civil Disobedience added humor to this mix, and new waves of political punk as exemplified by Whorehouse of Representatives reinvigorated political punk and provided it with a more personal touch. Problems of staleness

Figure 2.17 Civil Disobedience, "Manufactured Citizens," intro, bassline and lead guitar part

Figure 2.17 Continued

Figure 2.18 Civil Disobedience, "Manufactured Citizens," verse, bass and lead guitar

Figure 2.19 Civil Disobedience, "Manufactured Citizens," chorus riff

in crust-punk/dis-core style remained and perhaps could not be solved short of branching out to new musical territory, especially after a point of saturation was reached with the sheer number of bands in that style. But quirky outliers and fresh waves put crust-punk/dis-core within an atmosphere of greater diversity and musical creativity, allowing those imbibing the political message to take a breather from the more propagandistic. In this way, any account of punk styles is wise to consider the overall milieu they were part of and how different components of punk fulfilled different needs. It is to this latter point we now turn through a consideration of the music and role of several prominent 1990s political punk bands who did not play crust/dis-core style.

The Catchy Side of Political Punk

Concurrent with crust-punk, thrash, and extreme hardcore (see chapter 3), there were a number of political punk bands that rendered their messages with melody, often harking back to late-1970s punk or less ferocious hardcore, and that thereby cultivated a broader appeal than more abrasive and niche styles. A review of the 1996 *No Future No Hope* LP by the Portland band Defiance characterized both the style and value of such an approach:

> Defiance specializes in politically-astute, mid-to-fast-tempo powerchord punk with shouted vocals and choruses with more shouting. You've probably heard this kind of thing before, but it's extremely effective and highly listenable, and they get lots of brownie points for intelligence (covering topics like gay rights, the demoralizing aspects of work, rip-off punk acts that cash in)—in other words, tellin' it like it is.[86]

With tempos usually around 200 KSA and riffs that stayed within diatonic modality and often used box riff and [057] pitch structures typical of late-1970s punk, Defiance drew more from late-1970s punk style than crust or hardcore. The reviewer used "shouted vocals" to distinguish the definite melodic contours in Defiance's vocal lines from the screaming or timbrally distorted yelling of hardcore and crust-punk/dis-core, and the band's often catchy choruses gave its music the anthemic quality of early punk and hardcore. The melodic bass fills during power chords both harken back to late-1970s punk and add to the "catchiness" of the music.[87] Defiance shared with crust-punk/dis-core a reliance on familiar punk conventions, albeit different ones, and, in the earlier reviewer's opinion, did so in a way that was "extremely effective and highly listenable"—the latter an important trait of successful propaganda music. The reviewer also pointed out that Defiance's lyrics covered a somewhat broader range of topics than those typical of political punk, and credited the band with intelligently addressing these topics—likely meant to distinguish them from clichéd, uncreative lyrics by other bands. "Tellin' it like it is" suggests a more personal approach to political lyrics; many of Defiance's songs connected their political critiques to questions of personal integrity and life choices rather than political slogans or actions.

Another example of radical politics rendered with melody is the music of Anti-Flag, which, as recounted earlier in this chapter, surprised one reviewer who, expecting crust-punk given the band's lyrics, instead encountered its poppy-punk style. As can be heard on "You'd Do the Same," the opening song on its 1995 *Kill Kill Kill* 7", Anti-Flag, like Defiance, filled in their power chords with melodic motion in the bass, shown in figure 2.20, and its tempos were usually around 200 KSA.[88] As one reviewer of this 7" put it,

> This has all the elements of what I consider to be my favorite style of punk: lots of shouting and whoa-ohs in the background, fast guitar work (with some, but not too overpowering, 3 chord stuff—more technical sort of stuff), and a lot of variation in the song structures.[89]

Power chords: F#   F#   B   E

Figure 2.20 Anti-Flag, "You'd Do the Same," bass during intro

The "fast guitar work" along with the three-chord formulas point to the use of brief guitar solos and occasional lead guitar parts in Anti-Flag's music, as well as rhythmic punctuations. The "whoa-ohs" describes a typical trait of melodic punk heard in late-1970s bands such as the Misfits: melodic background vocals answering lead vocal lines with vocables. Anti-Flag's lead vocals were even more melodic and less timbrally distorted than those of Defiance, indicating their affinity with the pop-punk emanating from California at the time. Indeed, in contrast to the anguished screams of Aus-Rotten's "The Battlefield's Still Red," the refrain of Anti-Flag's "No More Dead" has a tearful melodic quality to it. As one reviewer summarized, "Anti-Flag put together some real fine tunes that utilize melody in the spirit of punk."[90]

Yet another band exemplifying catchy political punk was The Pist, who fused hardcore with Oi! and street-punk, both of which are characterized by slower tempos, diatonic, often major-mode riffs, and melodic vocals with catchy, sing-along choruses frequently thickened by background vocals.[91] Oi! in particular has strong associations with working-class skinhead culture in England. While The Pist did not cultivate their stylistic fusion with popularity ambitions in mind, Al Pist pointed out that "[i]t actually worked out well for us because we liked that music and it did get us a bigger audience I think because we had crusty kids at the shows, we had pop-punk kids, we had Oi! people, there were skinheads and straight-edgers and everything else."[92] Whereas several contingents of this audience would have likely tuned out crust-punk for reasons of stylistic preference, The Pist could communicate with them through its less pigeonholed and more polyglot style.

Furthermore, The Pist's style went along with a different approach to political lyrics that also resulted in a more inclusive audience. As the author and singer of these lyrics, Al Pist, explained to me:

> There were bands like Aus-Rotten who were very specific about what they were talking about. [And] bands like us who—I tried to speak in more general terms as opposed to this specific event or this specific person. I wanted to try to make it a little more inclusive so people who weren't familiar with the situation could get the general idea of what we're talking about as opposed to "this is how we feel about this specific incident"; it's more about "this is how we feel about this topic or this issue" and use examples to support that . . .
>
> I try to write things that people can relate to if they don't have the same frame of reference as me or if they don't have the same knowledge of a certain subject. . . .

You take something like an Aus-Rotten song, "Tuesday May 18, 1993," that's very specific. It's down to a specific date. It's great. I love that band. But that's not my style of writing. I don't like to mention specific people or events or things that may have an expiration date on them. I want it to kind of live on.[93]

Besides inclusivity, Al's lyrics also came from a more personal perspective based on issues that both lyricist and listener likely had direct experience with rather than issues like environmental destruction and Third World exploitation that required a more global view. "The Customer (Is Always Right)," for example, described the day-to-day experience of working customer service jobs in which you have to stomach constant mistreatment from customers; "Small Town Lies" decried the dilemma of thinking differently in a small-town America governed by ignorance; and "Great American Sportsman" rebuked the immorality of hunting culture. As Al Pist told me, "I was always more interested in personal politics, your day-to-day decisions, how you live your life."[94] The political effect of such an approach on The Pist's audience was described to me in this way by guitarist Bill Chamberlain: "People could see we lived by what we sang about. We wrote songs about what we believed and how we lived."[95]

Furthermore, many of The Pist's songs critiqued the punk scene itself, from macho violence ("New School"), and failure to live up to political sloganeering ("Do What You're Told"), to the growing attachment to punk as a fashion trend in the 1990s ("Alternative?"). Of particular significance given the Oi! inflections of The Pist's music (considering that Oi! is thought to be a working-class style of punk) was the song "Black and Blue Collar," which subjects working-class pride to the following critique:

> Here we are, just sheep in the flock
> Arranged neatly in line, just to punch the clock
> Compliments of the company, here's your early grave
> You set a fine example of the new American slave
> The working class pride of the working class multitudes
> Is the working class lie behind indentured servitude
> How much of our precious lives are going to waste?
> With all the fucking years that are spent in the workplace
> And blue collar pride is a fucking shame
> A capitalist's excuse just to play the system's game
> Possessed by your possessions, the mortgage and the bills
> The death we bought is slow, but we own it, and it kills[96]

Evident in these and other lyrics of The Pist was a greater poetic sensibility than most punk bands, with internal rhyme schemes, alliteration, and a greater significance placed on the sound and flow of the words.

Aiding the inclusivity and personal connection of their lyrics was Al Pist's voice, with its gruff but melodic quality rendering the lyrics easier to understand than is usually the case in punk. As Al explained:

Personally I like bands I can understand what they're saying so that's how I sing. You may not understand every word I'm saying. At least you can understand what the song is about and get the general message and maybe have something to sing along to, a chorus or whatever. That was kind of intentional. I'm limited too with my vocal ability; I can't scream like some of the screaming guys scream. You spend all this time writing music and recording it and going out and playing it, it's a shame when somebody can't understand what you're saying. That's one of the main criticisms of punk rock [by] people who aren't into it.[97]

The Pist, with their Oi!-inflected hardcore, more generalized, personal, and poetic lyrics, and audible, nonscreamed vocals, were able to connect more broadly within the punk scene than just to the cohort grouped around crust-punk/dis-core.

Naked Aggression

Asked to explain the music of Naked Aggression in an interview published in *Punk Planet* in early 1996, singer Kirsten Patches responded, "It's loud, fast, angry, and aggressive. At the same time it's melodic, meaning you can sing along with it. The tunes stick in your head. The lyrics are both political and personal."[98] Stylistically, Naked Aggression brought the raw anger of hardcore together with more nuanced grooves in their drumbeats and strumming rhythms, melody in the vocals, more complicated song structures that often heighten dramatic momentum, and occasional vocal harmonies and virtuosic guitar soloing indicating Kirsten Patches' and Phil Suchomel's classical music training.[99] Lyrically, while Naked Aggression addressed many of the familiar topics of political punk such as nuclear war, the Christian Right, and corporate globalization, the band also had a knack for voicing the personal frustrations of disaffected middle-class suburban American youth and raising these frustrations to a broader critique of capitalist society.

The song "Plastic World" concentrates many of these qualities.[100] As shown in figure 2.21, the instrumental section that opens it blasts out a hardcore-punk riff whose initial tresillo rhythmic pattern is punctuated by snare-drum hits followed by a "snare-on-the-floor" punk beat. "Snare-on-the-floor" is my invented term for when a punk drummer inverts the alternation of kick and snare drum of a typical punk beat so that the snare comes first, or "on the beat," making it a snare-kick alternation. The tresillo rhythm continues into the verses, but is rendered in single notes on the guitar rather than power chords. In the verses, the guitar and bass outline (in order) C♯-minor, F♯-minor, and B-major triads. In contrast to the snare accents and cymbal splash that open the song, the music for the verses takes on a despondent character owing to the different guitar timbre,[101] a drumbeat that eschews cymbals and emphasizes the tresillo rhythm with tom-tom and snare hits, and somber timbre and descending melodic contour in each line of vocals.

Figure 2.21   Riffs from Naked Aggression, "Plastic World"

This musical contrast is heightened in the chorus, which continues the tresillo rhythm but with power chords, the vocals melodically ascending, and the riff losing the previously prominent E for a [027] pitch structure that brightens the overall sonic atmosphere. The difference in sound serves to spotlight the change in the lyrics from despondent description to determined and unashamed acceptance of outcast status in a "plastic world." This embrace of living outside of consumerist culture was a common theme in Naked Aggression's music and brings together the feelings of alienated youth with a larger political perspective. Exemplifying the band's attitude toward the atomized suburban existence that was often the result of attaining the American dream, Phil Suchomel told an *MaximumRockNRoll* interviewer:

> So many people work their whole lives striving to attain this so-called dream and when they get it they find out it's a nightmare. Nothing unexpected happens in the suburbs. Everything is so routine. It's like reading the same book everyday for 40 years.
>
> It's like a Mr. Rogers neighborhood, it's not real. It only looks good from the outside. All those houses are filled with ignorant people who have no idea how bad third world conditions are, how the corporations they work for fuck up the rest of the world or about anything else outside their castles, expect maybe sports and other watered-down crap they see on T.V.[102]

In contrast to slower, more groove-oriented songs like "Plastic World" were songs in Naked Aggression's repertoire that follow a more straightforward hardcore-punk style with faster tempos and blaring riffs. But these hardcore-punk songs were structured to culminate in a distillation of the song's message at moments of heightened musical intensity, thereby exemplifying one aspect of propaganda music aesthetics. As shown in figure 2.22, on "Lies," after a brief introduction, the song's chorus is

Figure 2.22 Riffs from Naked Aggression, "Lies." Lyrics by Kirsten Patches / Naked Aggression, used with permission

presented with a riff that heightens the tension of its stepwise ascent by skips up a third for each anacrusis and punctuations of the word "lies" by background vocals, the crash cymbal, and the rhythmic arrivals in the riff. Following the definitively F-minor key of the chorus, the verse riff suggests D♭ major and opens up the texture with less overtly defined rhythmic accents. Each verse moves to an alternation between C and D♭ power chords that heightens the musical tension due to the semitone motion and suggests a transition back to F minor owing to the V and ♭VI harmonic implications. This alternation culminates with the C to D♭ alternation played homorhythmically by the whole band (including vocals) as short quarter notes on the words "The first step to re-si-stance is que-stio-ning what they are tel-ling you."

"Revolt," shown in figure 2.23, displays a similar process. After the arpeggiated guitar introduction, which allows the drums to gradually build the groove, the chorus offers rhythmically emphatic vocals in a call-and-response pattern between lead vocalist and group vocals, with the second syllable of the word "revolt" punctuated by

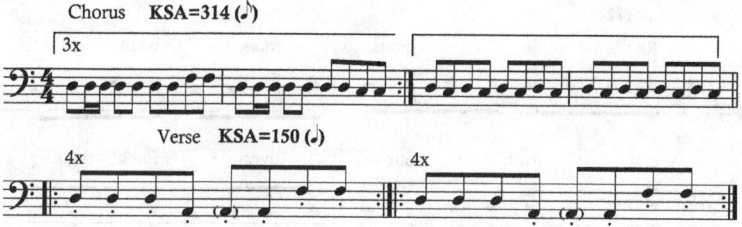

Figure 2.23 Chorus and verse riffs from Naked Aggression, "Revolt"

power chord motion. Naked Aggression heightens the energy at the end of this already high-octane chorus by increasing the rhythmic motion of the riff, rapidly alternating D and C power chords under an even-rhythm chant of the typical punk sentiment, "We must resist authority." The verses that follow (if verse is the right word here) use a similar strategy with a different musical feel. The KSA is cut in half, a tresillo-rhythm groove emerges, and the riff starts off more subdued by virtue of the palm-muted guitar. But in each verse, as the lyrics culminate in a repeated chant, the power chords ring out rather than being palm-muted on the pitch D that begins each bar, with the drums increasing in dynamics and activity for these chants. Thus each time the song's message is boiled down to its simplest and direct form, the music is brought to a peak of intensity. While this simplicity of message risked becoming cliché, and Naked Aggression was criticized for this in some record reviews,[103] the forward momentum leading to culmination in song structures, as well as expressive nuances such as slight variations in guitar strumming, are what made this simplicity effective as propaganda music.

Besides this reliance on simplicity and straightforward hardcore punk style, some songs delineated Naked Aggression from standard formulas by putting Phil Suchomel's and Kirsten Patches' backgrounds in classical music to use,[104] with "Religious Lies" providing one salient example. The refrain section, shown in figure 2.24, displays the band's propensity for cross-rhythmic groove, with its E-minor riff and vocal chant—"Re-li-gious fools want to con-trol our lives, fuck them!"—in a 3+3+3+3+2+2 rhythmic pattern.[105]

The verses, by contrast, take on an entirely different character than the emphatic accents of the refrain, as shown in figure 2.25. While the bass plays an F♯–D–E (i→♭VI→♭VII) progression accompanied by a drumbeat looser than that of the chorus and emphasizing the arrival of each new root, the guitar plays figuration betraying Phil Suchomel's training in classical guitar. Rather than yelling, Kirsten Patches uses a softer timbre that she would have cultivated in her choir days and delivers each vocal line with far more melodic motion than is the norm in punk (when punk vocalists do "sing," they usually just follow the root motion).

In this and prior examples, Naked Aggression used changes in key and distinctions between major and minor chords in a way far different from most punk bands, with different sections in contrasting keys, the guitar figuration providing clear major or

Figure 2.24 Naked Aggression, "Religious Lies," refrain riff

Figure 2.25 Naked Aggression, "Religious Lies," guitar and bass on the verse (first half)

minor thirds to chords, and even the use of functional V chords at the end of riffs (as on the refrain riff to "Religious Lies"). As shown in figure 2.26, the chorus of "Religious Lies" brings the two tonics of the song into direct contrast, moving back and forth between F♯ and E, though here it is E major owing to the continued use of G♯. This clear use of key changes and even the suggestion of dominant chords in Naked Aggression's music add to the catchy quality noted by reviewers and complicate the notion that their style was too simplistic. But since, aside from a few instances of guitar figuration, most of the band's music was rendered with power chords, the tonal centers of riff structures need to be examined more carefully to understand the use of keys in punk.

Finally, it is worth noting a pivotal aspect of the "matter" of Naked Aggression's music: Kirsten Patches' voice. Part of the genesis of Naked Aggression involved Phil hearing Kirsten yell at people and police during antiwar protests and recognizing that

Figure 2.26 Naked Aggression, "Religious Lies," chorus riff

while she had no prior experience singing in punk bands, the raw anger and vocal projection that emanated from her were perfect for a punk vocalist.[106] But this rawness and power could be combined or presented back-and-forth with Patches' alto choir voice and greater ability to sing on pitch than most punk vocalists to create something fairly unique. The combination of qualities in Naked Aggression's music, from the melody and yells in the vocals, song structures that heightened the delivery of messages through a process of culmination and distillation, greater use of more "groove"-oriented drumbeats (especially those using tresillo rhythms), to the occasional techniques borrowed from classical music, were what gave the band its broader appeal. As Patches described:

> Many different types of people of all ages attend our shows. There's a lot of punks of course, skaters, nerds, riot girls, straight edgers, teenagers, middle aged people, little kids.... All sorts of interesting people, many of whom are discontent with society at large.... There's a relentless and intense energy during the whole set that really blows my mind.[107]

"A bit harsh, but not to the point of being crust or grindcore"

To the aforementioned political punk bands with more melodic styles that maintained the energy of hardcore can be added Brother Inferior, a band from Tulsa, Oklahoma. Reception to their music is telling of the fine lines of stylistic distinction in punk and the importance of those who manage to straddle the boundaries. As one reviewer summed up, "They've learned their lessons well—combining solid, energetic and engaging 'traditional' hardcore with developed intelligent political commentary."[108] With Brother Inferior, it was more a matter of the various expressive nuances and contrasts in their music rather than particular innovative qualities that made them stand out in contrast to others playing "traditional" hardcore. This expressive nuance comes through in details such as the use of stops (where the instruments play a succession of brief accents followed by silence or the vocalist alone before returning to full punk band texture); the variety of tempos within songs and between songs; the use of riffs or bass fills with melodic catchiness; the occasional appearance of more complicated, single-note guitar parts rather than power chords; and skillful deployment of palm-muting and accents in just the right places. Moreover, singer Chad Malone's voice skirted a line between audible yelling and timbral distortion and thereby achieved a unique vocal timbre, capturing the personal, emotional character of hardcore rather than the more declarative quality of much crust. This vocal quality, together with the expressive nuances described earlier and instrumental timbres, made Brother Inferior immediately recognizable and distinct from other bands with a similar style. Thus with Brother Inferior, it was the skillful deployment and creative rendering of conventions that gave its political music the power to connect with its audiences.[109]

As the reviewer quoted earlier suggested, the band was also lauded for the "intelligent political commentary" of its lyrics, which often approached familiar political punk topics with greater depth and specificity than other political punk bands. A cogent example is the song "Ralph Reid," lambasting the then leader of the Christian Coalition. Given Brother Inferior's place of residence, fundamentalist Christianity was likely an issue they dealt with in a familiar and personal way.

Brother Inferior's appeal was perhaps best conveyed by a reviewer who described them as "Hardcore punk that sounds a bit harsh, but not to the point of being crust or grindcore."[110] Another reviewer was more specific with this musical delineation: "these guys play more raw punk rock with a driving mid-paced (well, actually fast but I avoid using the word to avoid confusion with grindcore bands that have redefined the word) beats, catchy riffs and yelling vocals."[111] Bands playing in the style of crust or grindcore could be easily pigeonholed and thus limited in their audience appeal to those who already listened to their style. As the number of crust and grindcore bands grew, they could be accused of being bland imitations relying on routinized formulas. Though its music was nothing profoundly innovative, Brother Inferior was immune to such criticisms, given the broader generic labels ascribed to it (hardcore or raw punk) and the universal approval the band received in record reviews.

Therein resides a broader lesson for the aesthetics of propaganda music: the danger of stylistic overdetermination and narrowness, and the potential of strongly coded musical styles to limit their appeal due to the (over)use of such codes. What kept 1990s political punk vibrant was the existence of many bands that did not rely on the codes of crust-punk/dis-core but instead skirted stylistic boundaries or simply excelled at taking a particular punk stylistic tradition and playing it well.

3
The Dystopian Sublime of Extreme Hardcore Punk

When Godzilla crushes Tokyo and is busy stomping on buildings, this is what he listens to on his walkman.

—Dan Fontaine, Review of His Hero Is Gone, *The Dead of Night in Eight Movements* 7"[1]

Energetic, thundering, brain-bruising chaos. Trillion m.p.h. concrete-crushing mayhem capable of reducing entire nations to cinder.

—Chris Dodge, Review of Assück / O.L.D. split 7"[2]

Long practiced in the art of jack-hammer thrash.

—Review of Capitalist Casualties, *Raised Ignorant* 7"[3]

Delivering 100-miles-a-minute blows to the ears with the finesse of a Boeing 747.

—Dropdead ad[4]

Seven paint-peeling, agonizing exercises in decibel corruption. Hyper speed, sonic smashing chock full of adolescent angst and unrelenting fury over our planet's sorry state.

—Chris Dodge, Review of Hellnation, *Suppression* 7"[5]

Fuck! 37 songs in less than 20 minutes. Musically, they punch a hole right through the sound barrier. This time around it's faster than a crusty on speed, more powerful than a skinhead's steel-toed kick, and able to leap tall emo kids in a single bound. Lyrically, they attack just about everything you love to hate. Cops, racists, homophobes, pro-lifers, military recruiters, rich people, bosses, gangs, and hippies all take a verbal beating from Ken and Co.

—Rob Coons, Review of Hellnation, *Your Chaos Days Are Numbered* LP[6]

BLLLEEEEAAAUUURRRRGGHHH! the record
A 41-band, 64 song 7" compilation (yes, it's a 7").

—Ad by Slap-A-Ham Records[7]

Rebel Music in the Triumphant Empire. David Pearson, Oxford University Press (2021). © Oxford University Press.
DOI: 10.1093/oso/9780197534885.003.0004.

The history of writing about music is full of attempts to invent metaphors describing the sounds we hear with visual imagery, actions, and in this case, nonmusical sounds (putting John Cage's aesthetic challenge aside for the moment). These attempts are always doomed to fail, given that no words or imagery can ever quite correlate with our aural experience of sound waves, but that will not stop us from continuing such attempts in a quest to make emotional and intellectual sense of the effects those sound waves have on us. The absurd lengths to which the previous quotes from record reviews and ads go in making metaphors to describe extreme hardcore (EHC) punk tell us something about the effect and techniques of this music. First, whether explained as Godzilla leveling Tokyo, "concrete-crushing mayhem capable of reducing entire nations to cinder," peeling paint, punching a hole in the sound barrier, or the "finesse of a Boeing 747," EHC constituted a sonic force aimed at aurally overwhelming us, and this force was felt to be violent, destructive, or an attack. Second, when it comes to technique, EHC exemplified speed in such a way that reviewers had to seek out new metaphors, such as "the art of jack-hammer thrash," for describing music faster than anything previously encountered even in punk.

Beyond particular affective dimensions and musical techniques, however, was the mere fact that this music provoked such absurd metaphors from reviewers. The word "absurd" here is not meant to ridicule these reviewers, but rather to point out the creativity and effort required to write a review of such sublime music. "Sublime" is the most appropriate word, given that the above metaphors convey a sense of awe verging on disbelief that people are capable of producing such intense, fast music. In what follows, I will first elucidate the musical values and techniques taken up by an increasing number of EHC bands in the 1990s by delving into musical details, drawing on the discourse about this style within punk zines, and noting aspects of the historical development of EHC. After building up an understanding of the style of this music, I will address its role within 1990s political punk of finding a musical form for presenting rage that could not be contained within even previous styles of punk and of taking the doomsday scenario presented by other punk and concentrating it into a musical dystopian sublime, with the latter perhaps best exemplified by the band His Hero Is Gone (HHIG). This analysis and interpretation shall also render notions of punk as merely a simplistic and unchanging genre to be profoundly wrong, given the cultivated techniques and complexities of a style that has continued to be a source of ongoing innovation.

The Musical Values and Techniques of Extreme Hardcore Punk

While previous analysis of bands such as Los Crudos and styles such as crust-punk/dis-core has demonstrated a trail towards transcending previous heights of intensity in punk, the EHC style was a cultivation of specific techniques and values, some of which were substantial departures from more straightforward hardcore styles. As such, even with a great range of diversity among bands and the development of a number of subgenres within EHC, it maintained a degree of stylistic coherence that can be identified by the use of specific techniques. Like all punk styles, EHC has a history, and in this case one that centers not just on the trans-Atlantic dialogue between British and US bands, but also on a cross-Pacific connection with Japanese bands and the impact of continental European thrash. Rather than a coherent narrative, however, this history is more about the simultaneous development of impulses toward extremes of tempo and timbre and the creation of new musical techniques to bring these impulses to fruition. At the dawn of the 1990s, these new techniques provided the musical resources necessary for the emergence of a common and coherent stylistic trend. For that reason, I address these questions of history within a description of the elements of EHC style, revisiting questions of the beginnings of this genre and its place within punk in the 1990s after elucidating its elements of style.[8]

The Blast Beat

Perhaps the most important trait necessary for a band to be considered EHC was the use of blast beats. As discussed in the introduction, with the turn to hardcore in the early 1980s, drummers generally stopped playing the kick drum quite as often within the overall pulse stream. The kick-snare alternation (KSA) was thus no longer a literal KSA, as the kick drum was often only played every four pulses and a cymbal, usually the hi-hat, filled the void. Thus, the beat would be kick and hi-hat / snare / hi-hat / snare. More frequent kick drum hits were used for the purpose of outlining accent patterns and providing punctuations within the overall pulse stream, and patterns such as the D-beat added rhythmic nuance. The less frequent use of the kick drum helped provide hardcore with some larger accent patterns and a sense of rhythmic groove, albeit one that departed from other rock grooves, within the constant pulse stream.

Within early 1980s hardcore, notably the music of D.R.I., are examples of moments in which drummers play a continuous KSA at extremely fast tempos. But in the latter half of the 1980s, several bands began to make what came to be called the blast beat a hallmark of their sound and the rhythmic foundation of entire songs or sections of songs rather than just brief flourishes. Within British punk-metal crossover, the generic label *grindcore* was used to describe a growing number of bands that took this approach, and Napalm Death and its drummer Mick Harris in particular are often credited with consolidating the blast beat.[9] US bands Siege, Infest, and Crossed Out are frequently heralded as early EHC bands,[10] and in the late 1980s these bands also cultivated the blast beat.

There are two basic approaches to the blast beat. The first is what has been described already: rapidly alternating between the kick drum and snare drum with a hi-hat or ride cymbal usually played along with the kick drum. This is basically a hardcore beat in which the pulse is completely filled in with kick and snare drum and the alternation between the two is sped up to the limits of what is physically possible. Both owing to the faster tempo (600–900 KSA) and the constant KSA, this blast beat is a qualitative rather than just a quantitative change that creates a new rhythmic feel or groove. Previous punk had almost always favored the hi-hat for the purpose of keeping the pulse. But in EHC, hits close to the center of the ride cymbal were often favored, likely due to the fact that the ting sound these hits create clarifies the pulse stream within the blast-beat blur. By contrast, the splashy, more sloppy sound of the open hi-hat would have the opposite effect (which is exactly why other punk styles favor it).

The second approach to the blast beat is to play the kick and snare drum at the same time along with a cymbal to create a continuous pulse stream with all drums sounding simultaneously rather than alternating. This converges all elements of the hardcore drumbeat into a singularity and creates an undifferentiated pulse stream. It is distinct from a drumroll by virtue of the fact that, rather than alternating limbs and allowing the drumsticks to bounce back onto the drum(s), the same limb is *hitting* the same drum repeatedly, thus diminishing differences in the angle and power of the hit on the drum. Although in this second approach the pulse stream is significantly slower than in that of the first approach's KSA, the simultaneous presentation of all elements of the drumbeat at once gives a profound *feeling of speed*.[11] Hereafter, I shall refer to the first approach as an *alternating kick and snare blast beat* (AKS blast beat) and call the second approach a *simultaneous kick and snare blast beat* (SKS blast beat). Examples of both approaches can be heard on the first three songs of Code 13's 1998 *A Part of America Died Today* 7". The first song, "Days of Rage," features an AKS blast beat, while the second and third songs, "The Die Is Cast" and "No One Is Innocent," make use of SKS blast beats.[12] The SKS blast beats generally have a crisper, more precise sound than the blur of AKS blast beats.

In either incarnation, the blast beat served the purpose of ratcheting up the tempo and the feeling of rapid intensity of hardcore. It went alongside an impulse toward even shorter song lengths, sometimes only a few seconds long, such as Code 13's "The Die Is Cast" (six seconds) or Dropdead's "Fucking Assholes Part 2" (three seconds). Not surprisingly, punk zine discourse on EHC valued speed and shortness, with praise heaped on bands perceived to have outdone prior achievements in these aspects. A 1990 Minnesota scene report in *MaximumRockNRoll*, for example, read, "DESTROY! are the undisputed fastest band in the upper midwest (or would at least like to think so)."[13] Comparing Dropdead to a famous professional racecar driver, a *MaximumRockNRoll* reviewer wrote that the band "races through 14 speedfests with more fury than Al Unser."[14] Within this praise for speed was a recognition of the technical mastery required, especially by drummers, to play blast beats with accuracy at fast tempos. An ad for Spazz's *La Revancha* LP, for example, described the band as "San Francisco's masters of high speed fury."[15] The sense of awe provoked by such speed was conveyed by statements like the following description of Phobia's *Enslaved* 7" in *Punk Planet*: "Spastic jackhammer snare drum activity splits the heaviness with speed."[16]

Praise for the brevity of song lengths that went along with speed is striking considering that from punk's beginning, its songs had been considered short by rock standards. A split 7" by Anal Cunt and 7 Minutes of Nausea was described by a *MaximumRockNRoll* reviewer as a "match made in heaven for noise mongers who like hearing a couple hundred songs (and I do use that word loosely) within a matter of minutes. [Anal Cunt] has gotten a zillion times faster and much sicker.... Satisfies the need for speed."[17] Agoraphobic Nosebleed's *Mobilize* 7" was described as "30 twenty second or less completely intense pneumatic thrashings from this Massachusetts band."[18] Emphasizing the awe provoked by packing numerous songs on a short record, a previously quoted review exclaimed, "Fuck! 37 songs in less than 20 minutes"[19] in response to Hellnation's *Your Chaos Days Are Numbered* LP. The brevity of blast-beat driven hardcore was emphasized most sardonically with the "41-band, 64 song 7" compilation" released by Slap-A-Ham Records titled *BLLLEEEEAAAUUURRRRGGHHH!*.[20] That this compilation was pressed on a 7" vinyl record rather than a 12" draws further attention to the brevity of the songs it contains. The technical mastery required to perform short songs at hyper speed challenges the notion that punk is entirely about lack of musical sophistication and can be performed by any amateur.

While the blast beat got its beginnings in hardcore punk, or at least punk-metal crossover, it was subsequently taken up by various genres of extreme metal.[21] An important distinction between the performance of blast beats in hardcore versus metal is that the latter made consistent use of double-bass-drum pedals for the purpose of greater precision, while in the former this was not a consistent feature. This distinction points to divergent musical values in the two genres. In metal, performance aims to make virtuosic technique seem effortless and render it with exact precision, and the use of double-bass-drum pedals aids in both.[22] In hardcore, performance generally openly displays the strenuous physical effort required, and thus seeing and even *hearing* the strain involved in playing a blast beat was valued. If you listen closely, you may notice that not every hit of the drum(s) in a blast beat in EHC is rendered with the same force, thus *differentiating* the constant pulse stream. The EHC drummers turn this physical necessity into a musical advantage by allowing their hits to get slightly weaker and then *re-attacking* the blast beat at a deliberate moment so as to create a larger accent pattern within the continuous pulse stream, usually every sixteen pulses or at arrival points within the music, such as the beginning of the riff or the start of a song section. These strong points of attack coincide with the drummer resetting the position of her/his limbs, usually by raising them slightly, to be able to exert greater physical force and as part of an overall cyclical body motion.[23]

The Dirge and Rhythmic Dichotomy

While there were short EHC songs that have only (or almost only) the rhythmic foundation of a blast beat, most EHC relied on frequent changes in groove (here understood simply as rhythmic feel) from blast beats to more normal hardcore drumbeats, mid-tempo punk beats, hardcore breakdowns (see chapter 1), and the much slower so-called *dirge* (see what follows), along with intricate, precise rhythmic statements such as stops or homorhythmic accents, the latter often in triplets or other rhythms that go against the prevailing pulse stream. These frequent changes in groove served the stylistic purpose of providing variation rather than only an undifferentiated pulse stream, the affective aim of generating different musical moods, and the technical result of challenging bands to be able to "turn on a dime" from one groove to another with accuracy. Furthermore, the EHC bands that were consistently recognized as the best of the style in the pages of punk zines generally had approaches to rhythm, groove, and the use of the drum set that gave them a unique rhythmic profile and set their music apart from the larger trend it is part of.

Before discussing the unique rhythmic profiles of several bands, it is crucial to comprehend the main dichotomy of groove in EHC: that between the blast beat and the dirge. The latter is characterized by what for punk are extremely slow tempos along with a darker, dirtier sonic atmosphere achieved through the use of the low-end of the guitar and bass fretboards, often with the instruments down-tuned; low-pitched, growled vocals; and less rhythmic density brought about by less frequent strumming and a lack of a strong constant pulse in the drums, with an emphasis instead on each rhythmic and melodic gesture and each single attack. The EHC bands that made greater or exclusive use of the dirge groove as opposed to the blast beat were often referred to as *sludgecore* to emphasize the type of (slow) motion in their music; "doom and gloom" was another descriptor used for dirge-driven music that conveys its mood. A good example of the dirge is the opening of Burned Up Bled Dry's "Yesterdays Sorrow" from their 1997 *Kill the Body . . . Kill the Soul . . . 7"* (see figure 3.1).[24]

The band builds the dirge first with the bass articulating the riff in single, held-out notes, with the whole band joining with a scream and crash cymbal. The singer's screams are sparse and each syllable lasts far longer than is normal for punk, and the rhythmic delivery of the vocals generally matches that of the instruments. The guitars and bass let each pitch/power chord ring out after their attacks rather than giving the usual fast strumming of punk. The only repeated attacks are reserved for the last, and lowest, power chord, and these are palm-muted to darken the sound and emphasize the singularity of each attack (the drummer adds to this effect with repeated hits on the floor tom). The drummer, for the most part, emphasizes the arrival of each new power chord with cymbal crashes and accents on the snare or kick drum. Motion into these accents is usually created with a kick-drum anacrusis, and the hi-hat marking

Figure 3.1 Dirge opening from Burned Up Bled Dry, "Yesterdays Sorrow"

the tempo is heard only faintly in the background. The dirge thus emphasizes each individual gesture as a singularity rather than the blurry forward momentum of the blast beat. In both technique and groove, the two constitute a dichotomy. Some EHC bands focused exclusively on either dirge or blast-beat grooves, while most emphasized blast-beat and fast-hardcore grooves, with the occasional dirge groove added for contrast.

The affect conveyed by the dirge is captured by several quotes from zine record reviews. One side of Misery's *Next Time 7"*, for example, was described as "a longer grinding tune with apocalyptic imagery and low end drone. This is pretty miserable music, in a good way."[25] Grinding was a common word used to describe dirge-driven music, and conveys the sense of churning slowness, with sounds that grate against the ears. A 1990 North California scene report in *MaximumRockNRoll*, for example, called the music of Asbestos Death "a slow grinding ear damage tunage."[26] A common visual metaphor for dirge is that of "trudging-through-mud."[27] While the dirge risked becoming too lacking in momentum if rendered without the proper sense of a succession of gestures,[28] it could be particularly powerful when combined in sudden back-and-forth contrasts with speed-driven beats. Ecstatic record reviews highlight the success of such an approach. In/Humanity, for example, was praised for its "manic, grinding experimental thrash that alternates between brutal dirges and extreme chaos."[29] Burned Up Bled Dry was valued by one reviewer for its "Good speedier songs with cohesive guitars and drums alternating with slower, resonating bouts . . . up there with my favorites in this music-for-the-world's-coming-conflagration-severe-pessimism-category-core."[30]

Burned Up Bled Dry's "Numbers" from their aforementioned 7" is a compelling example of the contrast between dirge and blast beat, as can be heard in the alternation between these two grooves after the beginning section of the song (see figure 3.2). The dirge here features only two attacks from the melodic instruments, with the semitone descent from D to C♯ aided by the drummer's move from the higher-pitched to lower-pitched tom-drums and the two vocalists reaching lower in their range for each growl, taking the music into the depths of doom and gloom. The tritone between the two guitars contributes to the sonic "sludge" by its muddy dissonance. The brief blast beat section that follows this dirge offers only two iterations of its riff before the return to the dirge, showcasing Burned Up Bled Dry's ability to "turn on a dime" from one groove to another. The less-than-a-minute-long song's rhythmic variance is heightened by the fact that this dirge/blast beat back-and-forth is preceded and followed by a section in a fast-paced hardcore rhythm emphasizing its riff's syncopation,

Figure 3.2 Dirge to blast beat alternation in Burned Up Bled Dry, "Numbers"

and then ended with a churning breakdown with palm-muted guitars followed by a final return to the blast beat.

The Intricacy and Variance of Groove and the Creation of Distinct Rhythmic Profiles

Burned Up Bled Dry's mastery of alternation from dirge to blast and other rhythmic grooves points to the importance of rhythmic variance in EHC and how such variance, along with rhythmic intricacy, created distinct rhythmic profiles for individual bands. Indeed, skillful changes in rhythmic groove were a crucial criterion by which reviewers separated the good from the bland. For example, one reviewer called Hiatus's *From Resignation to Revolt* LP, "a fucking symphony of tight, heavy thrash fueled by rage. By no means is this a generic grind band . . . it's highly technical, has amazing build ups, and the vocals are actually enunciated."[31] Emphasizing how changes in rhythmic groove keep those listening on the edge of their seat, another reviewer wrote, "Avulsion play a wicked and unpredictable sort of grindcore-thrash combination with four tracks that have so many changes of parts you're really left guessing what will come next."[32] Particular mixes of grooves and even musical styles are a key part of what gives EHC bands their distinct profiles. Monster X, for example, were an EHC band who also drew on late-1980s straight-edge hardcore, as the X in their name would suggest. As one reviewer put it, "On the one hand Monster X play crazy grinding music with totally fucked up and distorted vocals, but at the same time there is an '88 hardcore sound bleeding through the guitars."[33] Code 13 was described by the same reviewer as a "melting pot of hardcore" whose blast beats co-existed with crust-punk and even youth crew (another moniker for straight-edge hardcore style), the latter evident in the sing-along choruses.[34]

Dropdead, among the most highly regarded of 1990s EHC bands, had a rhythmic profile defined by what one reviewer called "pounding drums which switch from d-beat to blast beats."[35] While Dropdead's drummer Brian Mastrobuono rarely performed a d-beat rhythmic pattern, the heavy thump and thud of the kick drum during fast hardcore drumbeats is what gives rise to this descriptor. The song "I Will Stand" (transcribed in figure 3.3) from the band's 1998 self-titled LP exemplifies the band's rhythmic dichotomy, especially given that more or less the same riff is rendered with two different grooves.[36] The song is divided into two sections with a brief intro before each section and an outro without vocals. The first section is an excursion into blast beat extreme, with a KSA of 794. The second section, by contrast, uses a standard hardcore drumbeat, and the guitars and bass strum in a standard fast hardcore rhythm rather than the constant repeated strumming of the first section.

Audible within the blaring pulse stream of both sections are accents, usually on the crash cymbal, that mark the beginning of each riff iteration in the second section and the tritone motion of the riff during the first section, beginning with the words "To turn away from those traditions." These accents were one of the nuances Dropdead's

Figure 3.3 Dropdead, "I Will Stand." Lyrics by Bob Otis, used with permission

drummer provided that amplified melodic gestures and gave some sense of groove by accent patterns within the continuous pulse stream. Besides the contrast between blast beat and kick-drum-heavy hardcore in "I Will Stand," the intro that comes before each section demonstrates another aspect of Dropdead's rhythmic profile. Before the beat starts, each individual gesture of the riff is articulated and emphasized with powerful accents on kick drum and crash cymbal played homorhythmically with the guitars and bass, with the triplet rhythm that ends this intro contrasting with the subsequent duple pulse stream.

Hellnation, by contrast, favored more the rhythmic feel of a blur of speed. In their recordings, the drums sound more like a whirling roll, lacking the heavy kick-drum thud heard in Dropdead, but with cymbal crashes providing some larger accent pattern within the pulse stream. The hi-hat rather than the ride cymbal was favored by Hellnation's drummer Al (who also performed most of its vocals!). The band's vocal and guitar timbres emphasize the treble, unlike the bass-heavy sound of Dropdead, and its recording mixes tend to blend the instruments together, further contributing to the sonic blur. Hellnation's riffs often rapidly switch from one power chord to another and/or constantly strum in repetitive attacks with little rhythmic differentiation. Though its music has a greater proportion of blast beats than that of Dropdead, Hellnation occasionally gave a respite to the speed with either singular accents or a more bouncy-punk hardcore performed at slower tempos with a splashy hi-hat and diatonic pitch structures in the riffs. "Your a Joke" (transcribed in figure 3.4) from the 1998 *Tomorrow Will Be Worse* compilation exemplifies these qualities.[37] As Chris Dodge put it in a review of Hellnation, their "music ranges from head-bobbing,

Figure 3.4. Hellnation, "Your a Joke"

memorable hardcore to all out stench-thrash."[38] In "Your a Joke," the former quality can be heard for a brief moment when the second, notably diatonic, riff of the song is first presented and accompanied by a 312 KSA drumbeat with syncopation provided by the kick drum. As is evident from the lack of proportional tempos, EHC bands rarely played with a click track—to do so would violate the punk ethic of eschewing markers of polished professionalism.

Epitomizing the power violence end of the EHC spectrum (see later discussion for subgenre distinctions), Capitalist Casualties' blast beats were at a slightly slower tempo than the previous two bands analyzed. Consistently most audible from the drumset was the snare drum, which sounds much crisper than on Hellnation's recordings, likely owing to tightening the drum head, and thus possesses a more piercing quality and emphasizes the treble end of the recording mix. The guitar timbre added to the band's more trebly sound, as did Shawn's slightly snarled yells that sound full of saliva but less timbrally distorted than the vocals of Hellnation or Dropdead. Capitalist Casualties' drummer Max Ward favored the hi-hat over the ride cymbal, giving its music a more splashy, less precise feel, but he could also "turn on a dime" with precision either to enunciated accents or to different grooves, be they fast hardcore drumbeats that are slower than blast beats, more bouncy punk beats, or slower hardcore breakdowns. In contrast to the austere seriousness of Dropdead's sound, the intense yet slightly playful rhythms and timbres of Capitalist Casualties are fitting for its more tongue-in-cheek song titles. Summarizing the band as the "longest running purveyors of the original 'Power Violence' scene," Ken Sanderson wrote, "Their music repeated[ly] take[s] on an unparalleled complexity at extreme speed at the same time hammering with point blank lyrical directness ('Fuck the Christians,' 'Shut the Fuck Up,' 'Your Scene is Shit'). Manic drum throttling, harsh vocal blasting, shredding guitar oblivion."[39] These qualities, along with its dissonant riffs that were less jarring than Dropdead's, can be heard on Capitalist Casualties' "Extermination Through Labor" from their 1999 *Subdivisions in Ruin* LP, transcribed in figure 3.5.

Voicing the Inhuman(e)

While rhythm was perhaps the most defining feature of EHC, the vocal timbres cultivated in this style also separated it from other varieties of punk. "Cultivated" is the key word here, as EHC vocalists not only screamed their guts out but also manipulated their voices to achieve specific timbres. The two basic vocal timbres of EHC are (1) *high-pitched screams* that require engaging the abdominal cavity for projection and power and using the top and back of the throat to provide timbral distortion, and (2) *low-pitched growls* drawn from the back and bottom of the throat and from deep within the abdominal cavity—what I like to call "gut voice." Both techniques involve the engagement of the diaphragm and abdominal muscles and constriction of the throat in a way that would be frowned on by virtually any professional vocal teacher. The contrast between these two screaming styles can be heard on Code 13's

Figure 3.5 Capitalist Casualties, "Extermination Through Labor," riffs and drums

Figure 3.5 Continued

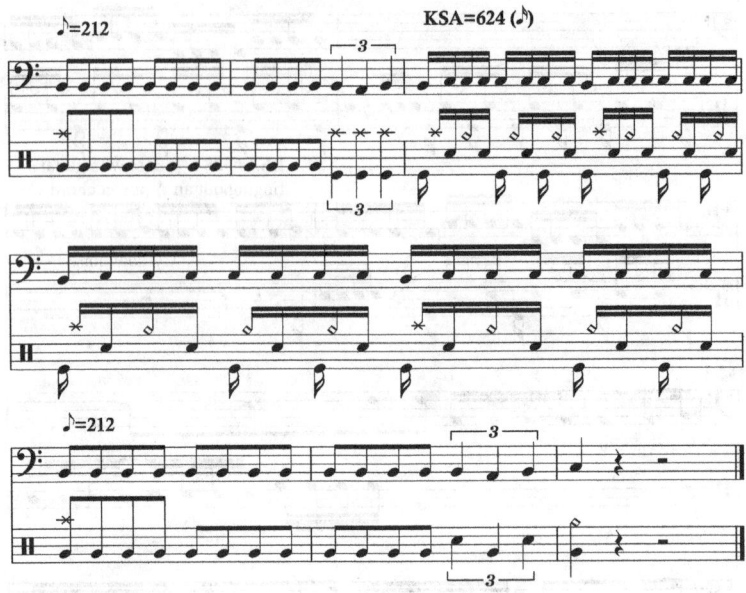

Figure 3.5 Continued

"Days of Rage." This dichotomy in vocal timbre is in some ways analogous to that between blast beat and dirge. The alternation between these two timbres was explained in zine record reviews variously as "a vocal style that ranges from demonic howls to deep chested growls"[40] or "vocals opting for the more screamy approach with the occasional growl thrown in for good taste."[41] While some vocalists performed with both timbres, others stuck with one or the other.

In either case, the clear physical strain and even contortion involved in producing such timbres and the high degree of distortion that results conveys a sense of *voicing the inhuman(e)*. Since much EHC was devoted to dystopian warnings of humanity's and the earth's downfall due to industrial capitalism, this inhuman quality was perfect for the "doom and gloom" of the lyrics. As a reviewer of Dropdead's 1998 LP put it, "Bob's raving screams . . . deliver urgent and sometimes grim lyrics dealing with man's doomed plight if we don't change our course of action."[42] Moreover, such screams expressed a rage that seemingly could not be contained even by the prior intensities achieved in punk. Their inhuman quality also situated the vocalists more as another element in the texture—almost another instrument—given the extreme level of timbral distortion on the voice. Many of the best EHC recordings blended the vocalists into the overall mix rather than setting them apart from and making them louder than the rest of the band, as is the norm in rock recordings.

Finally, these cultivated techniques are a pivotal part of what gives EHC its sublime power, as is most evident in the ecstatic responses to the band Hellnation. A review of their *Control* LP marveled at "a singer who had me checking the turntable speed on several occasions. I don't know how anyone can make their voice do that!"[43] Other reviewers credited Hellnation as "the first to take the high-pitched screech vocal style to another level"[44] and for "Great intelligent, pissed off lyrics sung with the highest grating vocals I can think of."[45] The awe and even disbelief expressed at such vocal timbres underscores the seemingly inhuman quality of vocals such as Hellnation's.

Riff Structures

While it would be problematic to overgeneralize about the riff structures of EHC given the ubiquity and diversity of bands in the style, it is worth pointing out that many used pitch structures that departed from diatonic modality and favored dissonant intervals. Dropdead, for example, favored tritones and [0134] pitch collections in their riffs. The former is evident on "I Will Stand" (figure 3.3). "Spirit Lies Broken" (figure 3.6) and "Us and Them" (figure 3.7) use both tritone-laden and [0134] pitch-collection riffs, along with Dropdead's signature dichotomy between blast beat and kick-drum-heavy fast hardcore.

Figure 3.6 Verse and chorus riffs from Dropdead, "Spirit Lies Broken"

Figure 3.7 Verse and chorus riffs from Dropdead, "Us and Them"

Besides containing dissonant intervals, many EHC riffs also shifted from one power chord to the next in a rapid motion analogous to the speed of blast beats, as is evident by the short duration that each individual power chord lasts in my riff transcriptions. The first riff during the blast-beat sections of Code 13's "Days of Rage" is one salient example (see figure 3.8). In addition to contributing to the overwhelming speed and intensity of EHC, such rapid shifts from one power chord to the next also betray the technical skill and precision required of those performing this music, with guitarists and bassists having to shift their fingers and hands up and down the fretboard and pick their strings with tremendous speed and in sync with the rapid movements of their fret hand.

Gesture

Given the often extremely fast constant pulse stream and highly distorted timbres of EHC, musical gestures, in the sense of musical statements that are short (i.e., shorter than a riff) but still a coherent statement, took on an importance in EHC greater than in other forms of punk. This facet has already been touched on in relation to the dirge, in which the forward momentum of pulse is dissipated or suspended in favor of successive individual musical gestures. The blast beat itself can be thought of as the reduction of a hardcore punk beat into a single gesture that is then repeated over and over.

The boiling down of musical ideas to short gestures is also evident in riff structures and vocal delivery. In Code 13's "Days of Rage," for example, the first riff during the blast-beat section of the song is a gesture of four power chords played in rapid succession. Whereas each individual power chord may be difficult to hear, the ascending and then descending melodic motion is what is most audible. Felix von Havoc's screams to this riff are also coherent gestures, usually with three distinct accented syllables matching the first three of the riff's four power chords, and a sense of rhythmic motion brought about by beginning each brief vocal line (or gesture) with the first power chord, ending it with the third power chord, and leaving the fourth power chord vocally empty.

The heavy accents that begin Dropdead's "I Will Stand" can similarly be thought of as a series of gestures that are then carried over as the riff for the rest of the song and made clear by the accent patterns of the drums. Another track telling of gesture in EHC is HHIG's "Headless/Heartless" (see figure 3.9). In the riff that comes after its brief intro, first played by two guitars, each new pitch/power chord can be felt as a new

AKS blast beat; KSA=704 (♪)

Figure 3.8 First riff during blast-beat section of Code 13's "Days of Rage"

Figure 3.9 Verse riff from His Hero Is Gone, "Headless/Heartless"

gesture, given the lack of continuous strumming. This effect is heightened when the drums enter with a fast hardcore beat while the guitars go on without continuously strumming. At the song's end, the riff is reduced to a semitone alternation between D and C♯ and taken into the territory of a sludgy dirge lacking the forward momentum of a fast pulse.

What these and other examples point to is how, within the thick, distorted texture and blaze of drumming in EHC, individual accents and gestures give the music a coherence as a succession of statements that emerge out of its overwhelming power and dizzying speed. Without such an emphasis on gesture with rhythm as its driving force, EHC would risk being heard, even by those familiar with punk music, as an incoherent wash of sound.

Genre Boundaries and EHC's Place in Punk

Since genres are defined not just by their musical style but also by their history, social setting, and perceived meanings, it is necessary to address these issues before moving to the aesthetic meanings of EHC. As was previously hinted, the 1990s wave of EHC had its harbingers in the 1980s, with the general impulse to intensify hardcore coming from continental European thrash bands like Lärm and Totalität and US fast hardcore bands like D.R.I., the so-called grindcore of England in the latter half of the 1980s, and pioneering US EHC bands Siege, Infest, and Crossed Out.

American EHC also looked to 1980s Japanese hardcore bands such as Gauze and G.I.S.M. and forged ongoing transnational links with its 1990s counterparts in Japan. Nearly all of the 1990s US EHC bands mentioned in this chapter went on successful tours of Japan, and some released split 7" records with Japanese bands. Hellnation even recorded a 7"—*Thrash or Die*—consisting entirely of covers of songs originally composed and recorded by eight different Japanese bands. The growing trend of EHC in the United States also generated an increasing American punk fascination with bands from Japan, particularly those transcending previous limits of technique and intensity; the band Melt Banana's popularity in the United States is perhaps the best indication of this fascination. Numerous Japanese EHC bands toured the United States in what were often the most anticipated performances in the American punk scene. The praise for Japan's copious number of such bands is best evident from *MaximumRockNRoll* 134 (July 1994), an "All Japan" issue featuring interviews with an array of Japanese bands. A common thread in these interviews was an affinity for the most intense hardcore. As the 1990s wore on, record reviews in *MaximumRockNRoll* indicated the growth of EHC as a global phenomenon. Thus EHC played a pivotal role in the globalization of punk with the US-Japan connection—and the fascination therein with experiencing the most intense and mind-blowing bands firsthand through live performances—as a pivotal progenitor.[46]

The affinities EHC has with extreme metal raises issues of genre distinction, genre subdivisions within EHC, and the politics of genre. Since extreme metal and EHC have some techniques in common (the blast beat, screamed and growled vocals, emphasis on a dark, low-pitched sonic atmosphere, and slow, grinding dirges), they were generally distinguished by the social scene they were part of—which record label released their recordings, where and to whom they performed, and what journalistic forms discussed their music—in addition to their lyrical subject matter. Further distinctions between EHC and extreme metal are outlined in the following review of Capitalist Casualties' *Disassembly Line* LP:

> This is the direction the whole Earache grind bullshit trend should have gone— fast, loud, tight, DIY and *pissed*. Instead, grind went the way of Morbid Angel in-stores and Grindcrusher tours.... The musicianship [of Capitalist Casualties] is killer: fast as fuck and tight as a wet knot, yet still heavy. The vocals are screamed with an anger [that] garblers like the singers for Carcass or Napalm Death couldn't emote if their royalty checks depended on them. The lyrics are ace too—angry with this bullshit world yet written in a personal tone of defiance and dignity that keeps well-worn subjects (nuclear power, Gulf War, etc.) from sounding trite or forced.[47]

Within this review, Joel of *Profane Existence* differentiated the adherence to DIY aesthetics by EHC bands from (his perception of) the quest for fame and royalty checks pursued by metal bands. Furthermore, Joel heard a greater authenticity in the form of anger and emotion in the screams of Capitalist Casualties than metal vocalists captured, even if they could employ the necessary techniques to produce intense screams. Finally, Capitalist Casualties addressed political topics that were pressing to the state of humanity, whereas 1990s extreme metal lyrics tended to deal with the occult and Satanic imagery. One more difference between the two genres was elucidated by a *MaximumRockNRoll* reviewer of Capitalist Casualties' *Subdivisions in Ruin* LP, who noted, "the recording and production is crisp and clear but still fucked just right."[48] While EHC needed clearer recordings than other punk due to the intricacies within its thick, distorted textures and blurs of speed, this clarity nevertheless required a lack of the all-out professional polish more common in extreme metal. "Clear but still fucked just right" recordings went along with the fact that EHC required greater technical prowess and precision from its musicians, but needed to execute such prowess and precision without making a "show" of virtuosity. As Rodel notes, metal-style virtuosic guitar solos, derided as "wanking" in punk zine discourse, were one genre-defining trait absent from most EHC.[49]

Besides the distinction between EHC and extreme metal, discourse in punk zines sometimes identified a number of subgenres within EHC with labels such as power violence, grindcore, sludgecore, and fastcore. Crust and thrash are also sometimes used as generic labels for EHC. While the markers of and boundaries between such subgenres are not entirely clear and vary depending on who is defining them, some basic sense of their differentiation can be gleaned. Sludgecore is the easiest to decipher, as it is music that emphasizes the slow-paced, dark and low-pitched, grinding dirge feel. Grindcore seems to be the most metal-inflected of EHC. Felix von Havoc identified "Napalm Death, Terrorizer, Assück, Agothocles, [and] early Carcass" as bands exemplifying grindcore and gave the following description of Florida-based Assück's *Anticapital* LP:

> [I]t blows away every other Grindcore record ever made except those by Napalm [Death] and Terrorizer with whom it stands as a monument to brutal Grind. Assück manages to combine the anger, fury and social commentary of a punk band with the musicianship and production quality of a Death Metal band[;] the result was a total assault of manic Grind power. This album rages from hyper speed to excruciating tense slow mosh parts back to whirlwind blasts.[50]

Power violence, on the other hand, is usually understood to be less metal-inflected than grindcore, with words like "manic" and "spastic" used to describe its embodiment of the cultivated sloppiness of punk aesthetics.[51] To make some broad generalizations, power violence was generally less bass-heavy, eschewed the low-pitched growl in favor of a more frantic-sounding scream, preferred the splashy hi-hat over the crisper ting of hits toward the center of the ride cymbal, and was more centered in California. Chris Dodge, bassist of Spazz, explained that "the term [power violence] actually came from Eric Wood who is in Man Is The Bastard and was in Neanderthal and Cyclops . . . he just came up with that phrase to describe what Neanderthal was playing." Dodge went on to explain, " 'Power Violence' stuck and it began to describe bands like Capitalist Casualties, Crossed Out, No Comment."[52] He summarized generic distinctions within EHC in this way:

> I would describe Crust as more straight forward angry hardcore like Extreme Noise Terror or something like that—more straight ahead, usually drunken, hardcore. Grind I would say is more metal-tinged. Power violence is more just blasts of speed. Everybody has their own opinion about where the lines are drawn.[53]

Aside from these distinctions based on musical style, Chris Dodge also heralded the lack of back stabbing, "shit-talking," or competition among power violence bands and made clear that, despite the moniker, power violence bands did not get physically violent at performances.[54]

While EHC generally eschewed the macho violence or misogyny of NYHC, it was nevertheless a rather male-dominated style within US punk.[55] For example, any survey of zine record reviews will indicate that there were far more crust-punk bands with women members than in EHC, where virtually none is apparent. Since EHC bands generally did not articulate or more blatantly act out patriarchal worldviews (in fact, many spoke out against patriarchy and Christian fundamentalism in their lyrics), the reasons for it being so male-dominated are less obvious, though some suggestions for this state of affairs can be made.

First, a musical technique like the low-pitched growl, while not an absolute requirement of the style, did effectively hinder the participation of most women due to physical differences. Second, EHC fit well within the male bonding involved in rock band culture, particularly in that the collective technical ability required by the style meant that many bands playing it were a tight group of friends who spent hours in the (often male) social space of band rehearsals. Indeed, many EHC bands came together as a group of male friends within small-town American environments rather than emerging out of larger, city-centered punk scenes which had greater participation by women, if nothing else due to the larger size of local urban scenes.[56] Finally, EHC bands often drew an antagonistic relationship between themselves and pop-punk and emo, two punk-derived genres with significant numbers of female fans. Hellnation titled one of their records *At War with Emo*, and an ad for a Capitalist Casualties record in *MaximumRockNRoll* described it as "The harshest shit in the Bay Area today! 8 fierce assaults of brutal intensity! No weak, tin-foil punk or songs about girls!"[57] While this ad was not necessarily intended as an advocation of macho domination and the distinctions from often apolitical emo and pop-punk have important implications for the enunciation of radical politics, the use of descriptors such as brutal, tough, and assault—words that generally connote male physical power—to describe EHC does nonetheless point to a more male-centric aesthetic to the style.

Nevertheless, I would caution against equating the degree to which a punk band plays a more hardcore style with masculinity. Doing so would fail to recognize that many women have been involved in creating and performing hardcore styles of punk, especially crust-punk. Furthermore, for many women punk musicians, finding a musical outlet that expressed anger and aggression was an act of empowerment, as is further discussed in chapter 4. Finally, less hardcore styles of punk could also express masculinity in their own ways. Pop-punk, the least hardcore of all punk styles, provides a perfect example, as bands in the genre usually enunciate a male-centric subjectivity, even if one at least projecting "sensitivity."[58]

What Did the Screams, Speed, and Sound Mean?

I think it's time for punk to be redefined, it's not just three chords, sound this way, and sing about this.... I mean, at the time when three chord punk was invented, that wasn't on the radio, and that sounded fucked-up compared to what was on the radio, so if that's what's on the radio now, then I think it's time to make it more strange, and I think that's what hardcore was supposed to mean in the first place. It doesn't mean you have to sound a certain way, but it just means taking things to a different level.

—Paul Burdette, drummer of His Hero Is Gone[59]

Punk music as a now decades-long tradition has been in a continual state of change, punctuated by the emergence of new approaches at various times in its history. One reason identified by Paul Burdette for this continual metamorphosis is underground punk's persistent need to stay out of the mainstream as previous incarnations of punk become part of that mainstream. As shall be further discussed in Chapter 5, as the 1990s wore on, "three-chord punk," or, more specifically, the pop-punk of bands such as Green Day, became a part of mainstream "alternative" culture. Its sounds were no longer shocking to the broader public and its musical language was no longer something that required being initiated into the underground punk scene to understand. EHC, by contrast, drew a boundary between itself and the larger public by virtue of its abrasive sounds and unintelligibility to anyone whose ears were not already immersed in hardcore. As Rodel claims,

[T]he development of extreme hardcore, a musical style that most non-punk fans (and even a fair number of punk fans . . .) find aesthetically unbearable, is an example of an attempt by punk to escape commodification by creating a style of music which, through its very aesthetics, is absolutely immune to appropriation."[60]

Stacy Thompson adds to this argument that EHC's immunity to appropriation was also brought about by its use of horrific imagery—album covers often portrayed piles of dead bodies as victims of starvation, war, or ethnic cleansing—and by choices of potentially offensive and sometimes vulgar band names, such as Anal Cunt, Assück, Dropdead, Hellnation, and Asshole Parade.[61] The EHC could keep not just the mainstream music industry away but also undesirable elements within the punk and hardcore scenes, as is suggested by the following review of Monster X:

Fuck! This is it! This is the new face of str8 edge.... Total grind to scare away the hordes of clean cut, kick boxing losers that have defaced that movement. How can you go wrong with a pro-legalization, pro-choice, anti-religion S.E. grind band.[62]

While this quest for immunity from mainstream appropriation was surely a factor in the turn to EHC, to argue that it was the primary impetus behind EHC risks reducing developments in musical style entirely to attempts to resist appropriation. It leaves out equally (if not more) important factors such as musical style as a means to express messages in songs, the desire of musicians to innovate rather than imitate prior punk, and the pleasure derived from playing and listening to such music. Furthermore, given that many prominent 1990s EHC bands got their start before the sudden mainstream popularity of alternative and then punk music in 1991 and

1994, respectively, the historical timeline does not support the notion that resisting commodification was the main impetus for EHC. A central thread throughout this book has been the importance of musical style in punk as a *mode of expression* that served the purpose of rendering messages in the most affectively powerful ways that musicians and audiences *enjoyed*. With EHC this is certainly the case. Enjoyment in particular has been evident in the numerous quotes from zine record reviewers ecstatically praising the speed and ferocity of their favorite EHC records.

Musicians' desire to innovate is evident from the greater levels of complexity achieved in and technical proficiency required to play EHC. This was spelled out in the following interview quote from Kenyon, one of the two bassists in the band Man Is The Bastard:

> I do listen to things like some obscure progressive and jazz fusion, more avant garde stuff. But I originally just listened to the typical Jimi Hendrix thing and then Venom and Metallica and all that stuff. For me, I use a more progressive style and musical ideas I've picked up . . . cuz I actually know my bass neck, music and music theory, so I just apply the two together. I use the heaviness of one, but with the expression of the other.[63]

Aside from being a fountain for creative innovation and listening pleasure, what was EHC a mode of expression *for*? The dichotomy between two basic types of lyrical themes in EHC is exemplified by Man Is The Bastard, whose music, as explained by Chris Dodge, was split between "totally intense songs about the atrocities of man" and "songs about really silly things," with the song "Gourmet Pez" exemplifying this latter trend.[64] The humor aesthetic was far more likely in the cultivated sloppiness of "spazzy" power violence rather than metal-tinged growly grindcore or slow-moving sludgecore. While the ferocity of EHC suggests seriousness, the absurdity of playing such fast music could also be taken as a musical joke, especially when vocalists rendered their screams with a sardonic snarl. As was suggested by numerous record reviewers, the band Charles Bronson perhaps best represents the humorous side of EHC, and its sarcasm was often put in service of critiquing the punk scene itself. One reviewer described Charles Bronson as "taking aim at the stupidity in the current scene and suburban life with a right-on sense of humor."[65] Another noted:

> With definitely more than a hint of caustic sarcasm they take all the appropriate shots at scene sacred cows. Victory Records (songs about Tony Victory and One Life Crew), drunk punks, phony hardcore and self-aggrandizing politicos all wind up in front of the firing squad on this record.[66]

Along with the snarled screams delivering the "caustic sarcasm" of its lyrics, other elements of Charles Bronson's sound helped to make its EHC style humorous. First, they rarely used the ting of the ride cymbal to keep the pulse; instead, a rather splashy-sounding hi-hat performed this function and contributed to a feel of cultivated sloppiness. Second, riffs in Charles Bronson generally stayed within diatonic modality and thus brightened its sound, with less of the jarring dissonance of tritones. Third, the overall sonic atmosphere of the band's music is far less dark, gloomy, and low-pitched than other EHC. Thus lyrics and musical style coconspired in Charles Bronson to make their power violence a sarcastic assault that draws attention to the absurdity of its speed.

In contrast to this EHC humorous aesthetic were the "totally intense songs about the atrocities of man." Stacy Thompson identifies a "conflict between the form and content" in such songs in which "the affect that each song must bear cannot be contained within its lyrics, and, consequently, the affect's charge overrides the lyrics and shapes the song into an inarticulate scream." As Thompson sees it, "During the rapid tempo parts, the guitar (or two guitars), bass guitar, and drums seem on the verge of outrunning one another and the singer."[67] To me, the operable word is "seem," as EHC bands possessed the greatest degree of technical precision in punk not just as individuals but also as a collective unit. Thus, the feeling that the music was on the verge of coming apart because what Thompson calls its content (lyrical subjects) demanded seemingly impossible musical techniques (form) was cultivated and controlled by the musicians. What Thompson points to is what I would call the *feeling of rage that cannot be contained* in EHC, in which its political enunciations necessitated a musical intensity *beyond* previous heights of punk rock ferocity. Perhaps the best way to understand this feeling of rage that cannot be contained is by listening to Code 13's "Days of Rage" while reading its lyrics:

> Restless nights and hate filled days
> Wanna set this town ablaze
> Twin Cities burns with frustration now
> Wanna see it burned to the ground
> Can I get a witness to the poverty and degradation?
> Decadence, corruption, oppression and desperation
> Pushed around, beaten down[;] Always get that run around
> I choose free will my mind is straight
> I can't escape the cruel hand of fate
> All that's left an empty shell
> Days of rage filled with hate
> Must destroy what can't be saved
> A shorter leash a smaller care
> Burning fire days of rage[68]

Joining message with musical style, the short emphatic gestures of the riffs, screams and growls, and the blast beat itself become exasperated cries seemingly out of breath and on the verge of physical collapse. This rage that cannot be contained was a fitting musical turn for punk in the neoliberal nineties. As discussed in chapter 1, the emergence of the United States as sole superpower following the Cold War facilitated the discursive dominance of the notion that there is no viable alternative to liberal demo-cratic capitalism, and the multicultural presidency of Bill Clinton and the Democratic Party's successful co-optation of many radical political movements blunted opposi-tion to the injustices of capitalism-imperialism. In attempting to come to terms with, for example, the human and environmental devastation taking place in the Third World which so many Americans remained willfully ignorant of, and in the absence of radical political movements that clearly pinpointed the sources of injustices in a way that resonated with a broader public, EHC bands sought out a sound that would express their exasperation and lack of hope in the power of people to transform the situation.

Dystopian Sublime

While this rage was directed at similar lyrical topics to those of crust-punk/dis-core—imperialist war, starvation, Third World exploitation, environmental devastation, an-imal cruelty and the meat industry, and the Christian Right—the lyrical poetics and musical style of EHC took this rage in the direction of a *dystopian sublime*. Use of the word "sublime" in music discourse has strong roots in late-Enlightenment aes-thetic thought and among the subsequent Romantic generation, with Beethoven's music often put forward as the paradigm for that which can inspire great awe by its beauty. Sublime music is generally understood to have some spiritual quality about it whose power transcends purely technical explanation—we are in awe of it because we cannot entirely explain its effects on us through purely rational means. While I have provided a detailed technical explanation for the style of EHC, I evoke the sublime to convey the awe this music provokes by its beauty (or, if you prefer, ugliness) that the above technical explanation cannot fully account for.

As Frédéric Claisse and Pierre Delvenne define it, dystopia is

> the depiction of a dark future based on the systematic amplification of current trends and features. It relates to a complex narrative posture that relies on the crit-ical observation of a threatening present that would lead to an apocalyptic future "if nothing were done." Yet, however inescapable this future may be described as, the very existence of such a narrative presupposes that the political community it tries to reach is actually able to do something to thwart it.[69]

This last point is expanded in Rob MacAlear's attempt to outline a rhetorical model of dystopia, which has great relevance for understanding EHC as a different kind of propaganda music than crust-punk/dis-core. As MacAlear puts it, dystopian fiction writers use "a 'fear appeal' in an attempt to persuade their readers of the necessity of intervention in the present to avoid the possible horrors of the future," and the rhet-oric of dystopia puts a "focus on ethical persuasion that encourages action in an audi-ence."[70] Thus, dystopian rhetoric relies not on hope but on "presenting a bleak future world."[71] Rather than elucidating the means to prevent the impending doomsday scenario, "dystopias are an attempt to intercede in history through a warning, and while they may model resistance within the text, they need not do so to argue for intervention."[72]

Within the political wave of 1990s punk, EHC's role was neither to provide detailed and informative political critiques (its songs were too short to do so) nor to elevate the spirit with rousing calls to action that invited audience participation (it lacked the catchy, melodic quality required to do so). Instead, EHC bands aimed to overwhelm our senses with their "doom and gloom" sounds in such a way that we are forced to confront, on a visceral level, the horrors of our society and their implications for the future. EHC thus represents the terrifying side of the sublime. If it were not so cumbersome, I would adopt the generic label "music-for-the-world's-coming-conflagration-severe-pessimism-category-core" put forward by a reviewer of a Burned Up Bled Dry record, as this label captures the spirit of this music.[73] Lyrics to the song "Bitter Fruit (The Seed)" by Dropdead offer one exemplification of EHC's rhetoric of fear:

> Today the future was decided
> by rich, arrogant fools
> Dogs of war who've condemned us to death
> with fevered dreams of consumption
> A fertile ground to plant the seed
> apocalypse disguised
> As the rain forests die
> and the oceans expire
> The fruit that we bear
> is diseased and defiled
> Offered up to the poor
> It's consumed by the child
> who inherits a future
> that fools have decided[74]

While dystopian EHC songs ascribed the lion's share of blame to the structures and chief architects of capitalism-imperialism, they also implicitly or explicitly condemned the broad American populace for its complacency and complicity. With Dropdead, for whom veganism was a central component of its politics, this came in the form of admonitions for buying the products of the meat and dairy industries and thereby contributing to the killing of animals and environmental destruction. His Hero Is Gone derided widespread submission to the present order through conformity, consumption, and willful ignorance as a significant cause of the contemporary near-dystopia their lyrics painted. The pithy lyrics to their song "Voluntary Amputation," for example, suggest that fascism would no longer require gestapo tactics because when it comes to "mind control devices," "We buy them on our own."[75]

Besides connecting the long-standing anticonformity ethos of punk to a larger political critique, HHIG's rhetoric of fear warned of the consequences of convenient new technologies that were so celebrated in the 1990s. For HHIG, widespread addiction to entertainment and communications technologies was a new form of mind control more effective than fascist dictatorship. In this regard there are affinities between HHIG and contemporary dystopian science fiction. In the latter, Keith Booker notes a transition from "optimistic visions of the possibilities inherent in technological progress" to "a dystopian turn in recent years with works (like the cyberpunk fiction of William Gibson and others) that show an attitude toward future technology that is ambivalent at best."[76]

The rhetoric of fear in EHC was embodied not just in song lyrics, but more powerfully in the *musical sounds themselves*. Rodel, who uses the term "apocalypticism" for the phenomenon I call dystopian sublime, connects this back to EHC's inability to be commodified. Quoting Adorno, she also points to the "positive" political role of this music:

> The apocalyptic aggression of extreme hardcore is more "positive" than the pleasantness of mass produced music, since in fomenting a crisis through the presentation of violent sounds extreme hardcore holds out the hope for real change, while mass-produced music "forsakes promises of future happiness in the name of a degraded utopia of the present."[77]

The Rhetoric of Fear in the Music of His Hero Is Gone

To conclude this chapter with an understanding of how the musical sounds of EHC embody dystopia, we turn now to analysis of the music of HHIG. That this band distilled the rhetoric of fear in its music to a greater degree than others in the same style is suggested by its reception. A telling description comes from a review of the *Fifteen Counts of Arson* LP, which stated, "Detuned guitars, gruff vocals, and misery lyrics define the sound."[78] Other reviews also connected sound with semantic content:

> Eight songs of killer punk rock, that just surges and spews with cerebral bursting anger. Deep howling vocals lyrically dealing with the downfall of humanity before our eyes. My favorite track "Epidemic" is a slow grinding number that just numbs the senses. After that, things take off into complete pandemonium more reminiscent of [the band] COPOUT.[79]

> Tense, churning rhythms that alternate between slow grind and fast hardcore. And the two vocalists unleash some of the most scathing screams around. The lyrics on this complement the music with a dark and depressing feel. They're all about battling against the different levels of confinement that we face everyday.[80]

One review even used the word "dystopia": "Lyrically this record has a political outlook that looks at the subjects with a feeling of helplessness and despair in a somewhat Dystopian sort of way."[81] For another reviewer, the band's dystopian outlook proved too devoid of hope: "My only criticism is that the words and imagery are so full of bleakness and despair."[82]

Aside from the connection between dystopian outlook and musical style, reception of HHIG also indicates an appreciation for their innovative approach and complex (by punk standards) compositions. Dan of *Profane Existence* differentiated HHIG from other EHC by virtue of the "roller coaster ride of musical experiences" they provided, by which he surely meant the tremendous variety of rhythmic grooves and sonic moods.[83] Another previously quoted review heralded HHIG for "pushing punk to another level," likely due to the greater complexity of their compositions, the technical prowess of the band's drummer, and the new timbres emanating from the guitars and bass.[84] One example of this complexity was the use of odd time signatures in some HHIG songs, such as the 7/8 of "Hand That Feeds," not coincidentally the seventh track on their *Fifteen Counts of Arson* LP.[85] Another was the alternation between a slow 12/8 or 6/8 groove to a triple-meter blast beat, as heard on both "Sin and Vice" and the latter half of "Carry On" on the band's *Monuments to Thieves* LP.[86] HHIG's "Enslavement Redefined" on their *The Plot Sickens* LP features multiple metrical approaches, starting in a 7/8 meter that alternates between a 2+2+3 and a 2+3+2 rhythmic division (as heard by the snare drum accents), moving briefly to 3/4, and then finishing in a triple-meter blast beat.[87] HHIG's technical abilities surpassed most EHC bands, as did its creativity in crafting songs with frequent changes in tempo, groove, and at times a more "through-composed" approach rather than a succession of repeated sections with only a few riffs. Thus HHIG was well positioned to deliver the dystopian sublime in such a compelling way that "in the Bay Area, their patches now outnumber Amebix."[88] As the metaphor that opened this chapter put it, "When Godzilla crushes Tokyo and is busy stomping on buildings, this is what he listens to on his walkman."[89]

A salient example of HHIG's rhetoric of fear can be heard on their song "Chain of Command" from their 1997 *Monuments to Thieves* LP. The ominous beginning to this track is created by building a power chord from the top down, with the two guitars and bass contributing one pitch at a time. The right guitar starts with a high C repeatedly and evenly picked, the left guitar then adds a G a perfect fourth below, and finally the bass enters with a C that becomes (down an octave) the beginning pitch of the first riff and tonic of the song. This opening riff (shown in figure 3.10), first played by the

Figure 3.10 First riff from His Hero Is Gone, "Chain of Command"

bass and accompanied by drums as the guitars continue their reiterations of C and G, wonderfully captures the dystopian mood by virtue of its powerfully accented alternation of an octave at the beginning followed by the minor-mode stepwise melodic descent from the higher C.[90] This riff's sonic descent into an aural abyss is made all the more potent by the move to a pungent F# after the G, which makes a tritone with the tonic C. Herein resides a crucial motivic gesture of "Chain of Command"—a descent by semitone. At the end of the song's intro, before the guitars join the bass by playing the riff and the vocals enter, both guitars perform a harmonic semitone—C and B by the right guitar and G and F# by the left guitar—dissonating their previous single notes and emphasizing the G to F# melodic motion in the first riff.

When the guitars do take up the first riff, HHIG captures the "doom and gloom" sonic atmosphere of sludge by employing C tuning, where the guitars and bass are tuned down a major third and their timbres are darkened by virtue of looser string tension and thicker strings. Moreover, the guitars render this riff not with power chords, but with single notes with the two guitars an octave apart, the left capturing the more piercing quality of a lead guitar but without the brightness it would have in normal tuning, and the right guitar providing the full-bodied timbre and powerful presence of the nickel-wound lower three strings. On the low (open string) C that begins the riff, bassist Carl Auge plays a power chord, thus strengthening the power and presence of the lowest pitch. Drummer Paul Burdette emphasizes the accents of each melodic gesture of the riff with cymbal and kick and snare drum accents, and uses drum rolls and fills that seem bent on a downward spiral by moving from the high-pitched snare to the low-pitched kick drum. Todd Burdette's vocals, though not quite the all-out low-pitched growl of sludge, do nonetheless stay within a low pitch range and seem to capture a mood of desperation pulled back from the verge of resignation by their sheer anger. All this is perfectly fitting for the song's lyrics decrying the American populace's blind conformity in pursuit of the American dream:

> Who holds the gun to your head and makes you lick
> The boot of the boss who would rather kick in
> Your fucking teeth than shed a tear of
> sympathy?
> We keep on licking
> They keep on kicking
> Keep making the pills
> How long will we swallow?
> How long will they feed?
> How long will we follow?
> How long will they lead?[91]

After this opening section of the song, the guitars drop out and the bass reduces the riff down to a tritone alternation between C and F#, each played for a bar as sixteenth notes. Here the drums contribute militaristic snare rolls to fit with the lyrical

Figure 3.11 End of second section from His Hero Is Gone, "Chain of Command"

Figure 3.12 Last riff from His Hero Is Gone, "Chain of Command"

admonishment of blind obedience to authority ("We keep on licking"), followed by brief, menacing rolls and accents on the floor tom. When the lyrics turn to their moment of distillation ("How long?"), the drums provide a more regular groove, though one still full of drum rolls, while the guitars enter with repeated attacks on the pitch G, forming a wonderfully dissonant minor ninth with the bass when it reaches up to F♯ (see figure 3.11). The right guitar eventually moves up an octave to provide a piercing timbre that seems to haunt our ears, especially as it harmonizes this G with an F♯ a semitone below it, further drawing out the implications of the semitone gesture so central to this song.

After this second section, the song seems to exhaust itself and the drums and bass lay out while the guitars provide dissonance and the noise of pick slides. A new riff, shown in figure 3.12, then enters that seems to sonically emphasize the despair of the lyrics through a gesture of melodic enclosure with one minor third after another a semitone apart.

The song's end dispenses with forward momentum and reduces "How long?" to a gesture of two anguished screams accompanied by two power chords built on the low C, buttressed by kick drum and crash cymbal, with first guitar noise and later the C power chord ringing out, filling in the three beats after this gesture. Here, lyrics and music come together in a rhetorical gesture condemning our own complicity in the march to dystopia. Left unspoken but thus all the more provocative in this rhetoric of fear is the implicit ending to this "how long": will we allow this state of affairs to continue?

4
Whose Rebellion was Punk in the 1990s?

With the transition from late-1970s punk to early-1980s hardcore, the US punk scene increasingly became the province of young suburban white males, both numerically and, perhaps more importantly, in its representations and constructions of subjectivity. There were of course exceptions to this trend—Bad Brains, widely acknowledged as the principal harbinger of hardcore musical style, was an all-Black band, and Latinos played an important role in the hardcore scene both in southern California and New York. But as Dewar MacLeod bluntly puts it, "Hardcore was white music."[1] Late-1970s punk has been recognized as a brief moment in rock's history in which women played far more prominent roles. As Lauraine Leblanc summarizes, "punk rock's disdain for virtuosity, its lyrical focus on topics other than male teenage sexual angst, and its focus on style allowed girls more access to the subculture's core than they had ever before enjoyed in any previous U.S. and British subculture."[2] But with the transition to hardcore, MacLeod notes, "boys and young men dominated the [hardcore] scene in every way, especially physically, as the pit where slamming occurred became a place where only the most fearless and physically fit dared to venture, and the rest of the audience was pushed to the edges."[3]

This state of affairs continued unabated through the 1980s. The rather macho NYHC scene and the increasing presence of far Right politics and Nazi skinheads in the later 1980s, described in chapter 1, made the punk scene even more white and male, with the threat and use of violence keeping many nonwhites and women out. One of the most significant aspects of punk in the 1990s United States is that this situation was increasingly challenged not just by the radical politics of the bands discussed in previous chapters but also by the vocal participation of gays, women, and immigrant and second-generation Latinos. The band Pansy Division sang about and celebrated gay sex with an in-your-face sense of humor, and the "queercore" category recognized the burgeoning presence of gay bands.[4] In the first half of the 1990s, Spitboy, an all-women hardcore band from the San Francisco Bay Area, blended hardcore manifestos, feminist political positions, and personal experience to challenge patriarchal mindsets within the punk scene and in the larger world. They also set a precedent by proving that women were more than capable of playing hardcore punk, and the 1990s crust-punk/dis-core explosion included numerous bands with women vocalists. Los Crudos became the first Spanish-language band to become popular in the US underground punk scene, and cultivated a following among the Latino residents of their Pilsen neighborhood in Chicago. This would mark the beginning of what has been arguably the most significant demographic shift in US punk

Rebel Music in the Triumphant Empire. David Pearson, Oxford University Press (2021). © Oxford University Press.
DOI: 10.1093/oso/9780197534885.003.0005.

since the early 1980s: Latinos are now a substantial presence in the scene across the country and currently there are dozens of US hardcore bands singing in Spanish.[5]

None of this happened, however, without struggle. While open hostility from politically reactionary audience members posed problems for gay, female, and nonwhite punk bands, perhaps the more difficult dilemma they confronted was the way in which the punk ethos of unity, egalitarianism, and individuality erased nonwhite cultural identities and papered over the very real social inequalities and power relations of US society that permeated punk no matter how much its DIY practices kept it underground and separate from the larger society. In what follows, I discuss the struggles that went on to open up space within the punk scene for and by those previously excluded. Moreover, I discuss how Latinos and women in particular transformed the politics of rebellion within 1990s punk by bringing deeply personal experiences with oppression into punk's political discourse.

Part 1
"Hispanisizing Punk"

Making a Scene Among Pilsen's Latino Immigrant Youth

The ferocious thrash style (described in chapter 1) that set Los Crudos apart from other punk bands; equally if not more important was their cultivation of a Latino audience. As Michelle Gonzales of Spitboy explained to me:

> I hate the word Hispanic, but in some ways Los Crudos is largely responsible for
> Hispanisizing punk. They did it in this really cool way. They were just like, "we're
> from this neighborhood, we play these shows, and we play for the community.
> Sometimes the punks from the community come out, and sometimes it's some-
> one's grandmother standing there watching us." That's how they started out.
> "We're from our community and we're gonna play [for] our community." Punk here
> [in the San Francisco Bay Area] isn't really like that. Punk is about "you gotta go to
> Gilman [a well-known punk venue], you gotta go to the show." You don't take it to
> the streets unless you know you're going to have a punk audience. I think because
> [Los Crudos] approached it [differently], that had a lot to do with how much they
> opened up punk to Latinos. Just singing in Spanish.[6]

Rather than focusing exclusively on the already existing underground punk scene, Los Crudos organized its own performances in their Chicago neighborhood of Pilsen. On the southwest side, Pilsen is a working-class neighborhood that has gone from one immigrant population to another since the mid-1800s, when it was populated by eastern European migrants. Mexicans began moving there in the 1920s in relatively low numbers. Beginning in 1960, the Mexican population grew rapidly, and by 1979

Pilsen was the second largest Mexican American community in the country. The 1990 census revealed that of its 46,000 residents, 88% were Latino and primarily of Mexican descent. Beyond the demographics, the immigrant residents of Pilsen created a strong sense of Mexican culture in their neighborhood by speaking Spanish to each other, opening and being the clientele at Mexican restaurants and stores, and painting wall murals with Mexican themes.[7] While most punk shows in Chicago at the time were in the suburbs, Los Crudos played in community centers and basements in Pilsen and reached out to youth in the neighborhood. This brought new Latino participants to the punk scene, as well as causing white youth to come to Pilsen for the performances.[8]

In an interview published in a 1993 issue of *MaximumRockNRoll*, Los Crudos singer Martín Sorrondeguy described the first punk show he put on in Pilsen at a community center called Casa Aztlan:

[I]t was kinda wild because like 300 people showed up, on 17th and Racine, which is a pretty gang-infested neighborhood. And the gang members were getting all freaked out and walking by with bats and I thought maybe something was going to happen, but they left everybody alone. A lot of white people came into the neighborhood to check out the show, but then a lot of local kids came out too, and you know it was kinda funny because at one point, there were all these cholos who walked in with their flannels and the bandanas, and they were like, "OK, how much is the show," and they all went into the show and were totally into it.[9]

This latter point highlights one of the reasons for the appeal in Pilsen and other neighborhoods like it of a Latino punk band with lyrics written and performed in Spanish. As Sorrondeguy explained to me:

Latinos are always being corralled into being a certain thing or being cornered into "this is what you are" and labeled. There's always a section of young kids that are like, "I don't want to be a cholo, I don't want to be a gangster, I'm not very fond of hip hop. I want something else." And this is something you found in LA and other places, and where kids were coming from generational gang families their parents were excited they were punk. Because it meant they were probably gonna live a little longer. Now a lot of the gang stuff in LA is sort of mixed into punk, so it's a little weird. In Chicago, we all come from gang neighborhoods. But we don't ever talk about that, because we don't want that entering our scene. We just don't want that, we've moved away from that. It became more popular because not all kids wanted to be the cholo, the stereotype.[10]

Latino punk thus provided another identity for immigrant and second-generation youth. And it was an identity that stood in defiance of the growing anti-immigrant legislation, repressive measures, and popular hysteria directed against Mexicans in particular and Latino immigrants in general during the 1990s. In 1994, for example, California's Proposition 187 barred undocumented immigrants from public services and required employers to report undocumented employees. Though it was never fully implemented, this was the first in a number of state laws imposing heavy restrictions on undocumented immigrants and taking aim at legal Mexican immigrants as well.[11] These repressive measures also fostered resistance, with massive student protests in California in the 1990s against Prop 187 and other similar legislation.[12]

Los Crudos's lyrics, screamed with a righteous anger, took aim at the increasing repression directed toward Latino immigrants as well as their exploitation and oppression in the economic and social structures of the United States. They situated all this within the context of US imperialist economic domination and political interventions in Latin America that frequently installed military dictatorships with death squads employed to stamp out dissent. Furthermore, they addressed problems within the Latino community, such as gang violence, as in the song "Las madres lloran" ("The mothers cry") and social divisions among immigrants from different countries, as in the song "La caída de Latino America" ("The Fall of Latino America"). One song indicative of Los Crudos's enunciation of the position of Latino immigrants in the United States is "Nos quieren como siempre" ("They Want Us As We Were"), which opens with the lyrics "Fuck your promises of integration and equality / It only happens when you find a way to take advantage of us" (English translation).

Beyond their semantic meaning, Los Crudos's lyrics were rendered musically with a rage and frenzied energy that resonated with many Latino and non-Latino youth, along with anyone who did not want to tread lightly or practice a politics of respectful opposition. In this regard, the band fused their political analysis and positions with the punk spirit of defiance that cared little about offending anyone—in this case, those who wished to keep Latino immigrants in a state of repression and exploitation. Los Crudos, for example, silk-screened patches and T-shirts with the words "Ilegal, y que?" ("Illegal, so what?"). Given that political opposition in the United States so frequently tapers its positions to fit within a discourse defined by the limitations of electoral politics, this deliberate destigmatizing of the "illegal immigrant" label presented a politics that asserted its own subjectivity and cared little about how mainstream white America would react.

This defiant stand would be especially important for the dilemmas confronting second-generation and immigrant Latino youth. As Sorrondeguy described this social group in a 1993 interview published in *MaximumRockNRoll*,

> They can't fit in, that's the thing, the whole point is that you can't fit in, it's very difficult because you can try to act as gringo as you want, but you know whether it be in the workforce, in the political field or whatever, you still look different so you'll never get to that level that they're at . . . let's be for real, why don't you just be proud of who you are, you know there's nothing wrong with supporting and helping your community, don't leave it behind and try to ignore it.[13]

In this respect Los Crudos's decision to sing in Spanish was a decidedly political act against assimilation and an affirmation of Latino identity, both within society at large and within the US punk scene in particular, which up until that point had for the most part lacked bands with lyrics in any language other than English.[14]

Moreover, while radical politics were increasingly the subject of punk lyrics in the 1990s, Los Crudos's lyrical concerns differed in some respects from those of crust-punk/dis-core. Asked by an interviewer for *Profane Existence* why the band did not address the common crust-punk topic of animal rights, Sorrondeguy responded, "I think it's totally out of context to sing about animal rights to people who are too poor to turn away something that's given to them."[15] In the same interview, Los Crudos noted the failure of political organizations such as Greenpeace and anti-war activists to reach out to the people in their neighborhood and considered it their purpose to fill this void.[16] Finally, while the propaganda punk of crust-punk/dis-core addressed topics that were by and large at a distance from the personal experience of those writing and singing the lyrics, Los Crudos addressed social problems they and their audience in Pilsen dealt with directly. To Uruguayan immigrant Martín Sorrondeguy, screaming about military dictatorship no doubt carried the weight of personal connection, given that his country of origin was ruled by a military dictatorship from 1973 to 1985. This is one reason Los Crudos was often described in the pages of punk zines with words like "authentic" and "sincere."[17]

With its self-conscious isolation as an "underground" scene, its emphasis on youthful energy, and its abrasive sounds, punk has often failed (on purpose) to generate broader support for its culture of rebellion. What is striking about Los Crudos is that they did manage to generate sympathy and support from adult Latino immigrants in Pilsen and from music scenes and political organizations that had little to do with punk. On the former point, many adult Latino immigrants supported the band for its political stances even if they did not enjoy its music. Moreover, given the prevalence of gang violence among youth in Chicago, adults often welcomed the punk culture Los Crudos was creating in Pilsen as a more positive and safer alternative for their children.[18] On the latter, in a 1994 interview in *HeartattaCk*, the band described playing a benefit concert for the Zapatista movement at St. Pius Church, where their ferocious thrash sounds shared the bill with a slew of folk bands. And Los Crudos received and responded to requests from various organizations not associated with the punk scene to perform at benefit concerts, including one for a Native American organization called the Women of All Red Nations (WARN).[19] Thus a Latino punk band was able to forge broader political and musical alliances than were the largely white crust-punk/dis-core and extreme hardcore bands described in previous chapters.

The Burgeoning of Latino Punk Throughout the United States

Los Crudos cultivated an underground punk scene within Pilsen that articulated a Latino and punk identity among a section of youth and enunciated a defiant political stand that resonated in the community. This would be significant in its own right, but Los Crudos also brought this identity and politics into the US punk scene more broadly. As such, it was a crucial harbinger of the growing participation in punk by Latino youth not just in Chicago and southern California but across the United States. In an interview published in 1999 after Los Crudos had broken up, Sorrondeguy described how the band went far beyond its intention of bringing punk to Pilsen:

> [O]ne of our main goals was to talk about the things we were experiencing, being from a different community. Where we come from is not a typically punk background or community—expressing our ideas in our language to young kids in our neighborhood. That was our main goal, and yeah, we did that and it went a lot further than we thought it would go
>
> . . .
>
> But a band singing in a different language and talking about things that are going on in a certain community, and then going to other areas and parts of the country where kids have never experienced anything like that with them, that was a very powerful thing.[20]

By the mid-1990s Los Crudos was heralded as one of the best hardcore punk bands in the United States, receiving ecstatic reviews and frequently making top ten records lists in the preeminent punk zines. It toured across the country and around the world, and its shows are still affectionately remembered for their energy and crowd involvement by many who attended. Alan O'Connor's study of punk record labels lists Los Crudos's self-titled LP as having sold 17,000 copies; considering the highest selling record on O'Connor's sample of underground punk records sold 25,000 copies, this number is significant.[21] While the exact reasons for the popularity of an all-Latino band with lyrics in Spanish within a still largely white punk scene are difficult to pinpoint, several factors stand out. First, the music of Los Crudos was and is widely acknowledged as among the best of 1990s US punk, and the stylistic elements elucidated in chapter 1—the dissonant pitch structures of its riffs and jarring shifts to different pitch material; the distorted timbre and frenzied energy of Sorrondeguy's voice that seemed to come from the heart and from the gut; and the blaring pace that did not need blast beats to achieve its furious speed—easily account for this popularity. Second, Los Crudos reinvigorated punk by bringing to it a new set of social experiences and a different subjective position than had previously been adequately represented in punk. Third, with the increasing commitment to radical politics in 1990s punk, the direct experiences with oppression that Los Crudos elucidated in its lyrics through specificity rather than generality offered something beyond the at times empty sloganeering of crust-punk/dis-core. As Sorrondeguy summed up:

> Initially I thought [Los Crudos] was just gonna be a neighborhood band; "we're never gonna go anywhere with this." Next thing you know our single got reviewed by *MaximumRockNRoll*. And all of a sudden I started getting letters from Russia, Italy, France. All these people started writing, and then we're being asked to play

Milwaukee, Madison, Minneapolis, Ohio, and it just started blowing up. If you saw us for the first time you didn't know what to expect. And then you were going, "what, oh my god, what is this?" I think there were sectors of the earlier punk scene that were around that were like, "why are you talking about this, why is this important?" Because we were invisible prior to that, and this is a new thing we were doing. Some people rejected it and some people were like, "alright, yes, this is it."

The Spanish-singing bands, in the beginning it was just Los Crudos, Huasipungo, and a few L.A. bands. And then it just became: it's okay to do that. It's okay to sing in a different language in a US context. And then all of a sudden within a few years all these other bands started happening. It just became this thing where it's common. Even Cleveland had Lucha Eterna. In Cleveland you wouldn't have seen that in the eighties. We were just going everywhere and doing what we were doing. I think we're gonna see more of it as the demographics change in certain cities.[22]

To understand why Los Crudos stood at the beginning of a larger trend of greater involvement by Latinos in US punk, some background on the growing Latino population in the United States is first necessary. While Latino involvement in US punk goes beyond youth of Mexican origin, Mexicans were and are the predominant nationality within this demographic shift and are the largest group of Latino immigrants in the United States today. Thus it makes most analytic sense to focus on Mexican migration to understand the burgeoning of Latino punk in the United States, though it should be understood that similar dynamics were at play with other Central and South American immigrants, such as Guatemalans, Salvadorans, Colombians, Peruvians, and Ecuadorians, without erasing the specific experience of particular migrants. Attempting to tease out the differences among these immigrants and in their processes of migration is beyond the scope of this book.

Mexican migration to the United States has undergone a number of shifts over the last century, though it has continued to supply a source of cheap labor employed in some of the most physically demanding jobs. Business interests have thus played an integral role in shaping immigration policy. In the 1920s, for example, the needs of agribusiness for cheap labor trumped anti-immigrant sentiment when it came to immigration law. During the Great Depression, hundreds of thousands of Mexican immigrants, whose labor was not in demand at the time, were rounded up and deported. After the Great Depression and beginning during World War II, with a new need for cheap labor, some Mexicans were allowed back in, and the Bracero Program, started in 1942, legalized a form of temporary contract labor. By 1960, a number of Mexican immigrant communities had been established, especially in the southwest, and included both permanent residents and braceros.[23]

Up until 1965, US immigration policy had been shaped by explicit racial exclusion and favored northern and western Europeans. The Immigration and Nationality Act of 1965 did away with this explicit discrimination and established a quota system. The Bracero Program was ended at the same time. These two policy changes combined had the effect of dramatically increasing the number of undocumented migrants from Mexico. With a quota limit on legal immigration and the continued need of US businesses for cheap labor, most of the millions of Mexicans coming to the United States for temporary work between 1965 and 1985 were then entering as undocumented immigrants.[24]

The next shift in immigration policy occurred in the mid-1980s. With the end, for the most part, of openly stated white supremacy in official politics following the civil rights movement, Reagan and the political establishment coded anti-immigrant rhetoric in the language of security and criminality. Undocumented immigrants crossing the US-Mexico border were portrayed as posing a security risk to US territory and were frequently dubbed as criminals. The result of this political rhetoric was the militarization of the US-Mexico border (which has only increased since then) and the Immigration Reform and Control Act of 1986 (IRCA). These measures had rather contradictory effects on Mexican migration, considering that their intention was to stop "illegal" immigration.[25]

Where they succeeded in their intent was in turning deserts along the US-Mexico border into graveyards for dehydrated migrants, thereby stopping "illegal" immigrants by killing them. But the tightening of the border also had the unintended consequence of causing many undocumented immigrants to stay in the United States, given the risks and costs of traveling back and forth between the United States and Mexico. Furthermore, the IRCA provided a pathway to permanent residency for many undocumented immigrants already residing in the United States, and 2.3 million Mexicans took advantage of this opportunity. This in turn caused many Mexican immigrants, now with legal status, to bring over immediate family members legally. It also had the unintended effect of increasing undocumented immigration: "having a newly legalized migrant in the family increased the probability of undocumented migrations by a factor of seven."[26] Considering the slump in the Mexican economy in the 1980s and the resultant difficulty of finding employment, that so many would take advantage of better job prospects in the United States is not surprising.

For the purposes of understanding Mexican involvement in US punk, several dynamics of this migration history stand out. One is that prior to the late 1980s, Mexican migration was mainly in the form of adult males coming to work temporarily and sending remittances back home. While certainly some settled in the United States and brought their families, with 1.3 million Mexicans migrants entering legally between 1965 and 1986, many more undocumented entered in largely circular migrations. One estimate is that from 1965 until 1986, "roughly 28.0 million Mexicans entered the United States as undocumented" while 23.4 million departed.[27] With the IRCA, many could bring their families over and settle in the United States permanently, and an increasing number of youth immigrated before working age. These young immigrants, as well as the children of families settling in the United States after the IRCA, provided the right age demographic for involvement in the punk scene.

Another important dynamic was the place of Mexican migrants in the US labor structure. Kerstin Gentsch and Douglas Massey demonstrate that Mexicans are still largely relegated to low-wage jobs to serve the needs of the post-industrial US economy for flexible, cheap labor. Furthermore, they conclude that there is little difference between the position of legal Mexican immigrants in the labor market and that of the undocumented, and that "the mobility prospects of Mexican migrants are dim, even for those having the legal right to live and work in the United States."[28] As Aihwa Ong demonstrates, through the workings of conscious policy and racial hierarchy, migrants to the United States are routinely slotted into specific economic and social positions based on their country of origin and perceived "race."[29] Contrary to the notion of capitalism providing equal opportunities for individual effort, the real invisible hand of capitalism has placed Mexican migrants in the most demanding jobs, earning low wages and lacking labor rights in order to serve the needs of the postindustrial US economy. The relegation of Mexican immigrants to a subordinate economic position is surely something that could have the effect of making some gravitate toward the rebellious culture and anticapitalist politics of punk.

While for the most part Mexican immigrants find themselves locked into a subordinate and exploited economic position, Robert Smith notes that cohort analysis reveals a small section with a limited degree of upward mobility, and given the settlement of whole families in the United States in recent decades, this is not surprising.[30] While this upward mobility is limited, considering that some resources would be necessary to participate in punk bands—such as purchasing cheap musical instruments, records, and a vehicle for touring—it is an important factor.

Finally, while Mexican migrants to the United States prior to 1990 overwhelmingly settled in California, Texas, and Illinois, since 1990 increasing percentages of Mexican migrants have settled in states across the Midwest and South, with North Carolina, Georgia, Colorado, and Arizona as standouts.[31] In New York City, there were only 35,000 to 40,000 Mexicans in 1980, but this increased to 100,000 in 1990, and to between 250,000 and 275,000 by 2000. This dramatic change represents both migration and births in the United states: from 1988 to 1996, the Mexican birthrate increased by 232%.[32] The reasons for the geographical dispersal of Mexicans throughout the United States in the 1990s include the growing political repression of Mexicans in California as well as changing labor needs in the US economy. Large cities central to the global economy such as New York needed immigrant labor in numerous service jobs, from cleaning offices and homes to taking care of children to food service; the construction industry required immigrant labor wherever the industry experienced boom cycles, such as in the run-up to the 1996 Olympics in Atlanta; and food production, from the fields to the slaughterhouses to the meatpacking plants, increasingly relied on immigrant labor in nonunionized employment.[33]

This dispersal of Mexican immigrants across the country meant there was potential for Latino punk to spread beyond Chicago and southern California; in a 1994 interview, Los Crudos described the increasing presence of Latinos at its performances across the country.[34] Latinos were a growing presence not just in the audience but also in bands. As demonstrated in the documentary *Beyond the Screams*, while Los Crudos, New York City's Huasipungo, and several southern California bands provided the only US-based punk with Spanish lyrics in the early 1990s, a growing roster of Latino punk bands began to emerge, including No Less and Sbitch in El Paso, Texas; Logical Nonsense in Santa Fe, New Mexico; and Youth Against in Chicago. Particularly noteworthy is the band Outraged from Watsonville, California, whose members were the children of farmworkers.[35] Lengua Armada, a DIY record label started by Los Crudos, served as an important means for releasing and distributing records by many of these new Spanish-language bands.

The burgeoning of Latino punk must also be put in the context of the struggles of the youth among the Latino immigrant population, who encountered increasing repression with laws such as Proposition 187, hostility to their language and culture, and the frustrated promises of upward mobility. For these Latino youth, punk was intimately tied to resistance, including the massive student protests in California against anti-immigrant legislation. Furthermore, the Zapatista uprising in Chiapas, Mexico, in which Indigenous peasants spearheaded an armed rebellion and constructed new, more egalitarian social relations and economic arrangements beginning in 1994, was a source of inspiration for Mexican youth in the United States, many of whom made common cause with it.[36] While street protests and Zapatista solidarity highlight direct practices of resistance, the growing popularity among Latino youth of punk, along with more mainstream rock bands enunciating radical politics such as Rage Against the Machine (whose vocalist Zack de la Rocha is Chicano), point to a larger mood of defiance. In this way, music can elucidate broader shifts in consciousness taking place in more everyday cultural practices—such as punk rock shows—that may not be fully evident from more singular and public events such as protests.[37] Furthermore, given the Latino appropriation of punk for constructing a youth culture and creating a forum for rebelling against the oppression Latino immigrants faced in the United States, antiquated notions of authentic musical practices being only those which were created in the homelands of migrants need to be rejected in favor of fully understanding the diverse cultural expressions of migrants.

Before moving to the challenges Latino participation faced in a largely white punk scene in which "colorblindness" constituted the main mode of antiracism, it is worth noting several transformative effects this Latino participation had on the US punk scene. First, it brought out the previously hidden history of prior Latino involvement in punk. *Beyond the Screams* was likely the first to document this history, but since then it has increasingly been brought to the surface. As Sorrondeguy told me,

[T]here's also this historical stuff that's coming out, you know, Freddie Alva wrote a piece about Latinos causing panic in the New York punk scene. It's a great piece because he basically talks about all the Latinos who were in New York punk that we didn't know about. Members of Antidote. Harry Flanagan is part Dominican. Who knew that? Of course the Miret brothers are Cuban.

. . . [Alice Bag] even talked to me about people who I didn't know were Latino. Like one of the early Go-Go's. Stuff like that I was like, "What? I didn't know that." I don't know that I would have ever known that Trudie was Argentine. That old punk girl who looks super amazing. What? I didn't know that.[38]

Second, Latino participants in US punk made increasing transnational connections with the punk scene in Mexico and in other Spanish-speaking countries. In this regard, Los Crudos described themselves as something of a guinea pig for US bands touring Mexico, as prior to their two tours throughout Mexico most US bands never went beyond Tijuana.[39] The band proved popular in Mexico, which had a punk scene going back to at least the 1980s. Dubbed cassettes of their first record sold at the famous El Chopo market in Mexico City, a crucial destination for, among other things, purchasing rock music recordings and serving as a hangout for Mexico City's substantial street punk crowd.[40] Third, as already stated, the burgeoning of Latino punk bands brought the issues confronting this population into the punk scene as a whole.

Finally, Latino punk opened up space for other social groups to engage punk in a way that foregrounded their identities and experiences rather than subsuming them within a more generalized, and by default white, punk culture. One example is that while carrying out research in San Francisco in the summer of 2015, I attended an entire show of Filipino punk bands who all openly talked about their cultural identity and history from the stage. Though it has little connection to the underground punk scene under examination here, Afro-Punk, an organization that has recently held sizable concerts in New York City, is a powerful proclamation of the possibility of fusing a punk ethos with Black identity and has brought historical involvement and ongoing engagement with punk aesthetics by Black musicians to the surface. The book *White Riot: Punk Rock and the Politics of Race* (2011) documents some of the myriad engagements with punk culture by people coming from different communities that has resulted in, for example, the Taqwacore created by Muslim punks.[41]

Punk's Shade of 1990s "Colorblindness"

While the impact of Latino participation on the punk scene was transformative, this did not occur without struggles, and its results were ambiguous. Among these struggles, first was with far Right opposition to Latino punk, such as the Nazi skinheads who heckled Los Crudos at a performance in St. Louis.[42] Were it not for the concerted efforts, recounted in chapter 1, to rid the punk scene of far Right and violent elements at the dawn of the 1990s, it is likely that this particular strand of opposition to Latino punk would have been far more emboldened, violent, and dangerous. Second was the casual racism of whites in the punk scene. In Chicago, Los Crudos was often referred to in conversations as "that spic band." The band responded to this with their only song sung in English, "That's Right, We're That Spic Band," an angry and sardonic anthem that calls out their casually racist detractors as closet Nazis.

The third and perhaps greatest challenge confronting Latinos in the punk scene was punk's particular shade of the "colorblind" ideology of the 1990s that imagined the United States as having gotten beyond its past of slavery, Jim Crow, lynching, and official segregation to a society in which only individual racists, rather than social structures enforcing white supremacy, posed a problem. In a 1998 article in

Punk Planet, Mimi Nguyen argued that while punk had addressed US foreign policy and economic injustices, and Riot Grrrl and queercore had brought the concerns of women and gays, respectively, into a more prominent position within the punk scene, "race" had yet to be substantially addressed. Moreover, while travel was a common topic in punk zines, this focus was limited to band tours and recreational travel and did not extend to migration and the experience of refugees. For Nguyen, at the heart of the problem was how the punk scene understood and opposed white supremacy as only avowed racists rather than a society-wide structure of oppression. In addition, punk values failed to acknowledge social differences within its own ranks.

On the former point, while opposition to Nazi skinheads, including a willingness to use violence against them, was one hallmark of the 1990s punk scene, identifying and opposing the structural, everyday functioning of white supremacy rather than people who blatantly espoused racist views was a substantial shortcoming of the punk scene. For example, Anti-Racist Action, an organization that many punks were involved in, focused on confronting avowed white-supremacist organizations and leaders rather than mobilizing against the more structural expressions of white supremacy, such as police brutality, mass incarceration, or anti-immigrant policies. On the latter point, Nguyen argued that while punks pride themselves on creating a unified culture among themselves, they failed to acknowledge social differences within their scene and instead practiced a "we're all punks" colorblindness. Furthermore, Nguyen noted "how problematic punk's 'rugged individualism' is for any expression of politics because of the ways it ducks the question of power." The punk ethos of unity, egalitarianism, and individuality thus resulted in a widespread backlash against any assertions of nonwhite cultural identity or demands to acknowledge the structural oppression of nonwhites, as is demonstrated in the numerous letters and columns published in punk zines expressing outrage at affirmative action or the purported "reverse racism" of the rap group Public Enemy.[43] In short, even if well intentioned, punk ideology in the 1990s did not have the capacity to analyze and oppose the actual functioning of white supremacy in the United States.

One prime indication of this incapacity was the ways in which the punk scene erased the identities and cultural backgrounds of Latinos involved in it. Sorrondeguy points out, "Everyone talks about Black Flag, but who talks about the first singer [Chavo] (who I thought was the best singer) being Puerto Rican? It's just not brought up."[44] As Sorrondeguy explained to me,

> When I've spoken to really old punks, like first wave punks—like I've talked to Alice Bag about this—she's like, "we just didn't talk about that." That came about later. We were all punk and that's what we rallied around, this idea that we were all punk and therefore we were all on the same playing field. I think that probably came over from the eighties as well. People took [the assertion of a nonwhite identity] as "you're separating," but no. There's a blanket or a cloak being thrown over us saying we're all this, and we're not all this . . . the truth behind it is that actually it was way more diverse than maybe people thought it was.[45]

Along those same lines, Michelle Gonzales, the Chicana drummer of Spitboy, described:

There were a lot more people of color hanging out at Blacklist [a punk space in San Francisco in the 1990s] than probably anywhere in the punk scene, but you didn't see them in the nineties 'cuz of the whole colorblind thing. You didn't see them. You might sort of register that they were a person of color, but you didn't talk about that. You couldn't have two identities, you just could be punk. You don't get to be punk and gay, you don't get to be punk and Mexican, you're just punk.[46]

In her memoir, Gonzales points out the absurd lengths to which punk colorblindness could be taken: "When we released our *Mi Cuerpo Es Mío* seven-inch, a Riot Grrrl from Olympia accused Spitboy of cultural appropriation [for having a Spanish title].... Apparently my body was invisible."[47]

Taína Asili, vocalist in the crust-punk band Anti-Product, described a constant disconnect between her Puerto Rican identity and her involvement in punk:

Performing at ABC No Rio [a punk venue in New York's Lower East Side] was interesting for me because my mother was born and raised in the Lower East Side and my grandmother still lived there. At that time it was a predominantly Latino community, particularly a lot of Puerto Ricans. I'm Puerto Rican. So I would have this connection to the Lower East Side. And yet ABC No Rio, with the exception of Huasipungo, felt like a very white space. And the punk scene in general on the East Coast seemed to be a very white space. And there seemed to be this obvious disconnection of the greater community [from ABC No Rio]. That was difficult for me. I felt like part of this [Puerto Rican] community in one way and part of this punk community in another way. And that's sort of a theme for the rest of my life in the punk scene. Feeling like I had to separate my punk self from my Latina self.[48]

When I asked Asili if she witnessed any attempts within the punk scene to connect with nonwhite people, she responded:

I think that Aus-Rotten was a good band that tried to—Dave [Trenga] in particular—was really important for talking about political prisoners and bringing more exposure to that. The history of the Black Panthers and the Young Lords. But I'm not sure that I can say that what I witnessed was really bridge-building with communities of color. People would talk about animal rights all day and I saw so much around animal rights. But talking about political prisoners and communities of color—I didn't see that much.[49]

Having joined Anti-Product and the punk scene as a teenager, Asili became more conscious of her own identity as the years went on and began asserting it from the stage. But when she did so, it was frequently met with a backlash. "When I would say, 'this song is going out to all the Latinos in the room,' people would get really angry. One woman even wrote a zine about how offended she was by my reverse-racism."[50] Toward the end of her time in Anti-Product, Asili relocated from upstate New York to Philadelphia. She did so specifically to be part of the movement to free political prisoner, former Black Panther, and radio journalist Mumia Abu-Jamal, who was born, raised, and sentenced to death row in Philadelphia, and to this end she worked closely with the radical Black organization MOVE. Asili also became involved in the then vibrant spoken word scene in Philadelphia, which was home to "amazing Black women poets" such as Jill Scott, Ursula Rucker, and Sonia Sanchez. In addition, she got to know the underground hip hop scene and sometimes performed alongside groups such as the revolutionary Black nationalist rap duo Dead Prez. All this amounted to closer connections between Asili and the Black and Latino communities in Philadelphia, and this, together with her interactions with Latino punks in California, resulted in further estrangement from the largely white punk scene.[51]

The growing conflict between Asili, on the one hand, and her bandmates in Anti-Product and the whiteness of the punk scene, on the other, even took on a musical dimension:

> My parents are Puerto Rican [and] are also musicians and dancers. So Puerto Rican music was integral to my childhood and an integral part of my musical passion that I also felt like I had to disconnect from. Also singing. I'm actually a really good singer, but I had to scream-sing [in Anti-Product].... Percussion was important to me, I was into hip-hop; I wanted to incorporate some other hip-hop rhythms [into Anti-Product's music]. My father was a conguero. I had a djembe and I wanted to incorporate the djembe into it. My band was really resistant.

Asili's djembe playing and spoken word, as well as rhythms outside of the usual kick and snare drum blare of punk, found their way onto several songs on Anti-Product's 1999 *The Deafening Silence of Grinding Gear* LP. Nevertheless, the full flowering of these elements of Asili's musical vocabulary would not take place until after she left Anti-Product and worked with the band Ricanstruction. Centered in New York and frequently performing at protests in Philadelphia, Ricanstruction was a Puerto Rican band that fused punk with Puerto Rican musical practices and hip-hop rhythms and vocal style. Prominent in their sound were clave patterns and an assortment of Latin percussion in addition to typical rock band instrumentation. Furthermore, in their lyrics, Ricanstruction foregrounded the Puerto Rican independence movement and the political thought and history of Black and Puerto Rican revolutionaries such as Malcolm X and Pedro Albizu Campos.[52]

Asili explained that whereas in Anti-Product there were "pieces of me that I had to let go of . . . in Ricanstruction I could be myself." But this musical fusion and foregrounding of Puerto Rican politics and identity were too much for the larger punk scene. As Asili lamented,

My white friends in the punk scene were like "that's not real punk." And I know Ricanstruction broke up because they felt like on the East Coast they just didn't have enough people within the punk scene supporting them, seeing them as real punks. When we embraced our full selves we weren't seen as legit punks.[53]

Confirming Asili's assessment is the following from a record review of Ricanstruction's *Liberation Day* CD in *Punk Planet*:

Well, in this band's bio (punk?), they want to come off as a NYC inner city latino hardcore act. Though the lyrics are of a political nature, the band sounds more like the red hot chili peppers. Not hardcore to me![54]

For both Asili and Michelle Gonzales, the conflict between their participation in punk and their growing self-awareness of their Latina identities ultimately proved too much to bear. They ceased their involvement in punk rather than continue to be subject to the colorblindness that erased their identities and cultures and to the hostility they encountered whenever they dared to assert those identities and cultures. As Gonzales explained to me,

Coming into a more self-aware consciousness about my Chicanisma, I could just really see that those two things [punk and Chicana identity] didn't work together in the late nineties. I just got sick of it and I was out of there. I slowly stopped going to shows.... People [in the punk scene] were really shocked [when I married a Mexican]. Clearly they don't understand me at all.... It just didn't feel like I could be fully who I was in the scene and have people really see me.[55]

For Asili, when she immersed herself in political work and cultural expressions other than punk while living in Philadelphia, she felt a sense of belonging to the communities she was part of. Simultaneously, she felt an increasing alienation from the punk scene:

So now leaving that community to go on tours [with Anti-Product], winding throughout the United States, it was predominantly a white punk scene; it just tugged on me in a way I couldn't tolerate anymore . . . I hit Oregon and I had a full out panic attack. And I went to an herbalist out there and she was like, "Listen lady, I don't know what you're going through, but you need to go home." [Anti-Product] had a huge following. I felt like there was a lot of women connecting to my work. I didn't want to leave. It weighed on my spirit and my body and my health and my well-being. We got to Berkeley, California and I stayed in a Chicano intentional community that night. I left the band and just being in that community I realized that as much as I loved my band I just couldn't do this anymore. I just had outgrown this band.[56]

Thus while the impact of Latino bands on the US punk scene described earlier in this chapter was significant, the results remained uneven and ambiguous. Several salient lessons emerge from this history. First, while immigrant and nonimmigrant Latino youth have creatively used an array of musical styles toward their own ends, conflict ensues particularly when this appropriation takes place on musical turf occupied by whites who feel threatened by the encroachment of Latinos onto "their" territory. This is not unlike the larger anti-immigrant hysteria in US society that hinges on the myth of immigrant free-loaders stealing jobs, tax money, and opportunities from white Americans, who—heaven forbid—might have to hear someone speak (or in this case sing) in Spanish. Second, the romanticization of punk's underground infrastructure, DIY ethos, and distance from mainstream society and culture as a measure of its resistance to the present social order that characterizes much recent scholarship on punk risks obfuscating the ways in which that very DIY, underground culture can easily reproduce the dominant social relations in US society. Finally, there are surely things to celebrate about the punk ethos of communal unity and celebration of individuality in a society characterized by conformity and blind obedience to authority. But this ethos takes shape in concrete social relationships and is ill-equipped to deal with structural conditions of oppression that create very real social and cultural differences which do not disappear when nonwhites take part in punk. Recognizing this contradiction between punk's championing of social alienation in American society and the different kinds of alienation white versus nonwhite punks confront, Mimi Nguyen summarized, "not all states of alienation are 'equal.' "[57]

Part 2

Not Just Boys' Fun

By the late 1980s, the increasing masculinity of the punk and hardcore scenes was reaching a breaking point as "female punks found themselves pushed out of active participation in the scene and moved into behind-the-scenes roles such as show organizers or band groupies."[58] This was one factor that led to the formation of Riot Grrrl, a music scene and political and cultural movement that, as Kristen Schilt describes it, "encouraged women and girls to take control of the means of cultural production and be a part of 'revolution girl-style now' through producing music and zines . . . that put their own personal experiences at the forefront."[59] Riot Grrrl created a network of chapters, often led by teenagers, that carved out space for girls and young women in underground music and fostered an unapologetic style of activism around both national political issues such as abortion rights and personal, day-to-day experiences of oppression. Music was central to this movement, and a variety of bands, such as Bikini Kill, Huggy Bear, Bratmobile, and Heavens to Betsy concocted styles that blended punk, indie-rock, indie-pop, and other styles. Performance practice was pivotal to Riot Grrrl, including writing provocative words on performers' skin, such as "slut," that drew attention to the objectification of women's bodies and the shaming of any expression of sexuality. While Riot Grrrl was not separatist per se, the movement did hold women-only meetings to construct safer spaces for conversation and empowerment, and Riot Grrrl bands often insisted that men move to the back of the room to allow women and girls to occupy the space in front of the stage and to be free from the violent moshing then ubiquitous at hardcore shows. For our purposes, one significant achievement of Riot Grrrl was subjecting the punk scene and other underground music scenes to a feminist critique and empowering women to create and participate in their own forms of underground music.[60]

While closely related to punk and drawing on punk for its musical style, stage theatrics, and DIY ethos, Riot Grrrl was in many ways a departure from the underground punk scene and the creation of something new, and thus will not be the focus of this study. However, preceding and concurrent with Riot Grrrl, but receiving little scholarly or journalistic attention, were an increasing participation of women in punk bands, challenges to male dominance within punk from within the scene, and the assertion of feminist politics in the punk scene. All this is evident in the existence and role of numerous women singers in crust-punk/dis-core bands, from Nausea in the late 1980s to Whorehouse of Representatives at the end of the 1990s. Particularly pioneering and epitomizing women's involvement in punk was the band Spitboy.

Spitboy

Formed by four women in the San Francisco Bay Area in 1990, Spitboy proved that women were more than capable of playing hardcore punk. The band spoke eloquently about the oppression of women in lyrics that both provided political analysis of the struggles over equality and reproductive rights women faced in the 1990s and voiced personal experiences of oppression and empowerment. As Michelle Gonzales, the band's drummer, put it to me about the band's formation:

Spitboy [was] a hardcore band. That was our thing. We wanted to be a band that we wanted to hear. We wanted women to play this kind of music, and we wanted to hear that, and it wasn't happening, so we were like, "that's the band we're gonna create."[61]

A northern California scene report in the April 1991 issue of *MaximumRockNRoll* described the impact of the band: "The best new local band award for this month goes to SPITBOY. They burst blood vessels."[62] A year later, the same zine indicated the unique vantage point Spitboy provided to the punk scene in the following review of the band's first 7":

I wasn't prepared for its absolute greatness. Musically, it's mid-tempo punk rock with angry/raw vocals. The lyrics reflect what it's like to be a woman in 20th century America and to deal with rape, sexism and fear of the streets daily. I think this record will encourage quite a few women to start bands of their own. Truly inspiring.[63]

While frustrations with the lack of women playing hardcore was one impetus for starting Spitboy, the band also consciously sought to put feminist politics in a more prominent position within the scene. Feminist texts prominent in the 1990s, such as Susan Faludi's *Backlash: The Undeclared War against American Women* (1991), along with the continued threats to reproductive rights from the Christian Right and the Clinton presidency's conciliatory policies to them, were equally motivators for Spitboy.[64] The very name Spitboy was inspired by the book *Daughters of Copper Woman* (1981) by Anne Cameron, which recounts an Eskimo creation myth in which a boy is created from the spit of a woman, thus inverting the Judeo-Christian patriarchal creation myth. As bassist Paula put it in a 1992 interview, in this story the woman's "gods speak down to her and tell her to believe in what she has and that it's part of her body and that what comes out of her body is natural," thus taking away the shame women are often socialized to feel about their body and its natural processes such as menstruation.[65]

High on Spitboy's agenda was communication with its audience. One crucial means by which this was achieved was consistently passing out lyrics sheets before the band performed so that, since the distorted guitar and yelled vocals often rendered words less than audible, the audience could read along and understand the message. As Gonzales put it in her memoir:

Spitboy had seen a couple of other bands pass out lyric sheets, but it wasn't a common practice. We later decided to pass out lyric sheets for every show, a practice that we continued overseas, even paying to have our lyrics translated into Spanish, German, and Italian. I loved seeing women at our shows at the front of the stage scanning the lyric sheet for the next song, nodding their heads and smiling as they read. In the end, reaching them and seeing their approval was what mattered most.[66]

Misogynist heckles that the band occasionally encountered during performances were confronted from the stage and turned into opportunities to communicate just what the effects of these heckles were on women. In a 1992 interview published in *MaximumRockNRoll*, the band recounted an incident at a show in Albuquerque, New Mexico, in which a male audience member yelled "spread your legs" and the entire band confronted it from the stage. The majority of people in attendance sided with the band, and the heckler was isolated and deflated. Gonzales described the emotional impact this incident had on the person who put on the show:

[H]e'd been putting shows on for years and [said] that this kind of shit happened all the time, that these people always come to shows and ruin things for everybody, start violent pits, start fights, start pushing people around. He said that no one had ever confronted it and he started crying. It was so amazing. It was his last show that he was putting on before he moved to New York and he just wanted to thank us because he felt that finally he'd reached people. That we'd reached so many people. Maybe not those guys but so many other people and it meant so much to him.[67]

This story epitomizes a central theme throughout this book: that punk is by no means a static music scene automatically beholden to rebellious politics, but a contested cultural domain in which the conscious struggles of its participants can transform the situation. Therein lies the importance of Spitboy in confronting patriarchy inside and outside the punk scene and providing a model for subsequent women in hardcore bands.

Spitboy accomplished this with some definite strategic thinking that differed in important ways from the Riot Grrrl movement. Furthermore, Spitboy and others were often frustrated with the fact that women punk and rock bands were frequently conflated with Riot Grrrl in the early 1990s due to the mainstream media attention the Riot Grrrl movement received, as well as with what they perceived as petty bickering from within the Riot Grrrl movement (mis)directed at bands who espoused feminist politics. One important difference between Spitboy and the Riot Grrrl movement was the use of the word "girl" (albeit reclaimed as grrrl). Gonzales explained to me, "if you were a feminist in the Bay Area [in the 1990s], you did not want to be called a girl. You wanted to be called a woman. It would have been a major paradigm shift to then call ourselves girls. We just were not willing to do it."[68] When Riot Grrrl began receiving national media attention, with stories on it published in "the *New York Times, Newsweek, Rolling Stone, Sassy, USA Today,* and *L.A. Weekly,*"[69] Spitboy and other women punk bands were often labeled as Riot Grrrl bands. Given their discomfort with the girl label—no matter how it was spelled—and strategic differences with the Riot Grrrl movement, Spitboy could not help but feel frustrated. As Gonzales succinctly summarized the band's feelings on repeatedly being asked in interviews if they were a Riot Grrrl band: "Not this fucking question again."[70]

Another point of difference was over the projections of sexuality on stage. Some members of Riot Grrrl bands, notably Kathleen Hanna of Bikini Kill, provocatively used their sexuality on stage to assert their own agency as women. In my interview with Gonzales, she enumerated the reasons Spitboy eschewed such an approach:

We were fans of most of the Riot Grrrl bands [such as] Bikini Kill. And I understand the idea of using one's sexuality for power, and I know that idea comes out of the sex worker movement, and all of that is really powerful and really important. But Spitboy approached things very differently. First of all we were not at all comfortable with using our sexuality. We did not want to be objectified at all. So much so that probably for those first years I rarely wore tank tops; I wore really baggy clothes [and we] kind of dressed boyish to protect ourselves. We were potentially opening ourselves up for ridicule or criticism. And one of the ways we protected ourselves was by being androgynous. And that just felt safer to us, because we didn't have that angle of using sexuality as power for a message. We were the total opposite. We were women. We didn't want to be objectified, we wanted to be treated the same as men. To some extent that meant looking kind of boyish, [but] not trying to be men in that business corporate Hillary Clinton sort of way. It was a uniform to reduce being up on a stage in front of people and people seeing us in this really sexual way, which made us feel vulnerable.

Probably a lot of it had to do with [the fact that] most of us have sexual abuse history. So we were like, "I don't want anyone to look at us sexually, period." We were in our twenties. We stomped around in our heavy boots and our armor. I liked Bikini Kill a lot, but it made me uncomfortable to see them and how sexual they were, just because it brought up so many uncomfortable memories for me. And I don't want to be seen as a girl, because for me, when I was in Spitboy, to be seen as a girl was to be seen as unprotected and vulnerable like when I was younger, and I was not going back to that.[71]

Another difference was over the questions of separatism. As previously mentioned, many Riot Grrrl bands insisted that men move to the back of the venue during their performances to allow women and girls to occupy the space in front of the stage and be free from macho violence. Furthermore, door prices for Riot Grrrl shows were sometimes higher for men to draw attention to the disparity in pay rates between men and women. Spitboy understood the importance of bringing attention to unequal pay rates and the need for women-only spaces to discuss experiences with patriarchy and empower women to feel comfortable speaking and taking charge. But the band had doubts about practices that potentially alienated male allies or espoused separatism. As Gonzales explained to me:

We didn't want to use the [separatist] approach, probably to a certain extent because we didn't want to have an antagonistic approach to men. Our message was so strong and feminist, but we wanted the message to be the message, and that was enough of an antagonistic relationship for us. Like many Riot Grrrls, we were all more or less heterosexual. Mostly we had boyfriends. It just didn't seem to make sense to us—and Bikini Kill somehow pulled this off—to be like "boys in the back" and totally be all sexual. It just seemed like mixed messages to me. And I didn't want to navigate a bunch of mixed messages. We got a lot of support from men in the Bay Area, and we didn't want it to be this antagonistic thing.

On the other hand, what [Bikini Kill] did was sort of ingenious because it really did get people thinking. It was another strategy, to say boys in the back, to get men to think about their privilege. It's not one that we would have ever taken, but it's one that I admire to a certain extent. We would have never been comfortable with it, and largely because there was a lot of mixed messages there. I don't like sending mixed messages; I like to keep things more clear. It seemed hard enough not to send a mixed message by being a feminist, because then people automatically think that you hate men because you're singing about women's issues. No, that's not it. Those things don't have to go together.[72]

Among 1990s punk bands with women members, Spitboy was by no means unique in eschewing both separatism and the use of sexuality on stage. Particularly within the political wing of 1990s punk, the emphasis was on communication with the entire audience, and the cultivated style of dress was often more androgynous or at least desexualized.

A final conflict worth mentioning between Spitboy and Riot Grrrl was the personal bickering that at times led to public attacks on political punk bands by some within the Riot Grrrl movement. In a November 1992 column in *MaximumRockNRoll*, Karin Gembus, the guitarist of Spitboy, derided as "high school social politics" calls emanating from within the Riot Grrrl movement for boycotts of the hardcore bands Born Against and Spitboy and the indie-rock band Nation of Ulysses due to political disagreements.[73] In extreme cases, the method of feminist critique cultivated by the Riot Grrrl movement could be carelessly carried out to jump to conclusions without adequate investigation. As recounted earlier in this chapter, Spitboy was accused of cultural appropriation over the title of their *Mi Cuerpo Es Mío 7"* by a Riot Grrrl zine writer. In this instance, Spitboy's conscious foregrounding of its drummer's Chicana identity through a Spanish title was misinterpreted by someone who, likely in misdirected self-righteousness, failed to investigate or simply ignored Gonzales's identity. While these incidents should not be taken as a representation of the Riot Grrrl movement as a whole, the tensions these incidents provoked exacerbated the split in strategy between it and Spitboy as well as women seeking to transform punk from the inside out more generally.

What Did Women's Participation in Punk Sound Like?

As with Latino punk, it would be wrong to attempt to correlate women's participation in 1990s punk with any particular style. While conspicuously absent from straight-edge hardcore—not surprising, considering the masculine ethos guiding this style—as well as from extreme hardcore punk and So-Cal punk (see chapter 5), women performed a variety of punk styles and were especially prominent as vocalists in crust-punk/dis-core bands. This latter fact, corroborated by zine record reviews which frequently called attention to and praised the presence of "female vocals," suggests that when women participated in bands, they tended to do so in the most explicitly political ones. Furthermore, the raging vocals enunciated by the women singers of Nausea, Detestation, and Whorehouse of Representatives call into question the notion that aggressive music must be interpreted as masculine. For women attracted to punk, the visceral espousal of anger in the music, especially though not only when coming from women, was often a point of attraction rather than perceived as an imposition of male power. When it did come from women performers, it could be especially empowering and connect to women audiences on an intense, perhaps even spiritual, level. As Michelle Luellen put it in an issue of the zine *HeartattaCk* devoted to women's voices and concerns, "The first time I heard Amy from Nausea sing, I thought I was going to die right there on the spot. She was my hero; I had never felt so personally connected to music in my life."[74]

While no one style of "female punk" existed in the 1990s, there are two ways in which women's participation affected the sounds produced. First was the way that songs dealing with personal experiences provoked a more visceral reaction, especially by way of the vocal delivery, than more impersonal propagandistic songs; this was similar to the effect Los Crudos and Sorrondeguy's vocals in particular had on audiences. Second was the construction of song forms that moved from a feeling of despair provoked by the violence and oppression faced by women, to a confrontation of that violence and oppression, to empowerment through the act of confrontation. These two features will be demonstrated through analysis of Spitboy's "The Threat" and Anti-Product's "The Power of Medusa." Before that analysis, however, it is worth describing in more general terms the style of Spitboy.

While Spitboy's style was an incarnation of hardcore unique to the band and did not usher in a stylistic "female punk" trend, it was nonetheless a crucial representation, in sound, of women performing hardcore and enunciating feminist politics. The following record reviews provide some indication of just what this representation sounded like:

> A record that makes you think, as well as dance. Angry, passionate and hopeful. Simple, straightforward punk with grooving bass moments, mixed and muddled screamed vocals.
>
> **—Ayn Imperato, Review of Spitboy, *True Self Revealed* LP[75]**

> Not fast enough to be thrash, not dissonant enough to be grindcore, too angry to be emo, is it a feminine Fugazi? No, it's SPITBOY! These four women convey a great deal of passion and frustration in these three midtempo songs dominated by screaming vocals.
>
> **—Jenn Hyman, Review of Spitboy, *Mi Cuerpo es Mío* 7"[76]**

> The well-thought out lyrics that deal mostly with sexism and life as an extremely empowered womyn in the 90's are backed up by angry, provocative vocals. The music is heavy yet melodic, and crusty around the edges, flexing more muscle than most Bay bands.
>
> **—A-ron, Review of Spitboy, Demo[77]**

As these reviews suggested, while Spitboy was definitively on the hardcore end of punk, this was not brought about by rapidity of tempo. Spitboy tended to favor tempos under 200 KSA and achieved a sense of "groove"—perhaps even inviting the possibility of dancing rather than moshing—by virtue of subtle syncopations, a driving hi-hat, and the locked together playing of drummer Michelle Gonzales and bassist Paula (and later bassist Dominique Davison). As Gonzales explained to me:

> Paula was just learning to play bass at the time [when Spitboy started]. One thing I loved about her bassline is that it was just super steady. Part of it was because she was just learning [to play bass] for that first record, but then she maintained that as her style. There was a certain steadiness to it that as a drummer is very good to play along with. Her and [guitarist] Karin would talk about [melodic intervals of] fifths a lot in terms of the basslines. That just sounded pretty to us. It was a higher register in the bass.[78]

Complementing this steady rhythm section with a greater propensity for groove than most punk bands were the often dissonant chords played by guitarist Karin Gembus. Unlike in most hardcore bands, Gembus did not just play power chords whose root matched the pitch played by the bass, but often constructed unique chords with dissonant harmonic intervals, as well as sometimes going into what might be considered lead guitar parts or cultivated noise. An excellent example of this dichotomy between the bass-and-drums groove—in this case in a 6/8 meter—and guitar noise and dissonant chords soaring over top is provided by the song "Fences" from the band's 1995 split LP with Los Crudos titled *Viviendo Aperamente / Roughly Living*. Gonzales attributes these guitar sounds to Gembus's appreciation for the music of Fugazi and other posthardcore bands grouped around Washington, DC's Dischord Records, who used similar techniques. Spitboy thus took inspiration from a mix of hardcore styles to come up with its own unique fusion. According to Gonzales, this was part of what distinguished them musically from the mostly male world of hardcore:

> We wanted to play hardcore, but we also had an ear for things that were somewhat melodic or pretty sounding even in a hardcore context. We didn't just want to be women playing dude music. We wanted to bring our own style to it. I don't want to say femininity, but just things as women that we valued or sounded nice to us.[79]

Finally, Adrienne Droogas's vocals were most often yelled but in such a way that the lyrics were more audible than other hardcore bands and contained a greater degree of pitch inflection. Furthermore, Droogas often built her vocal lines into screams that punctuated the music with angry intensity, but also occasionally sang more melodically. The range of musical experiences conveyed by vocal delivery is a key aspect of what makes their music sound more personal, heartfelt, and genuine—as though Droogas's choices between yells, screams, and singing were direct results of semantic meaning.

While Droogas was the principal voice of Spitboy and most of the band's lyrics were enunciated in the first-person singular, in many songs Droogas's voice was doubled by that of another member of the band. As Gonzales explained,

> The double vocals . . . we really did that because we were a very inclusive band. Adrienne was the lead singer, but if someone else wrote lyrics, that person sang on the song. That's just how we always did it. So if Karin is singing on a song, that's 'cuz Karin wrote that song. Sometimes she'll sing backup, but if she's doing the double line, it's 'cuz she wrote that song. I sang a lot because I wrote a little less than half the lyrics.[80]

One effect of these doubled vocals is that the subjective position, while often grammatically first-person, took on a collective identity and thereby articulated the lyrics as experiences common to women more generally.

While seeking to not just play "dude music" by personalizing hardcore, Spitboy also faced the dilemma of not wanting to sound like a stereotype of women playing hardcore. In her memoir, Gonzales recounts a moment in the recording studio when the band confronted the high-pitched sound of their own backing vocals on one song:

> It seemed like a terrible contradiction. We wanted to sound like women, but we didn't want to screech, we didn't want to grate, and knew of course that stereotypes about women were influencing how we felt. And without discussing it or planning, each of us knew what she had to do, lower her voice a register or two and deliver backing vocals that didn't sound like Edith Bunker from *All in the Family*. And even though I always felt a little bad about it, I know I sang my vocals in that same lower register whenever we played that song live thereafter.[81]

Thus for Spitboy, playing hardcore from a woman's perspective was in part a negotiation between the right mix of aggression and personal touch.

One exemplification of these stylistic features is the band's anthemic song "The Threat" from its 1991 self-titled 7". The lyrics describe the fear that rises when nightfall comes and women have to treat every shadow as a potential lurking attacker:

> Do you know what it is like to walk down the street at night?
> Do you know what it is like to feel the threat?
> The threat that fills the streets as the sun goes down?
> Threatening, threatening, threatening
>
> My aloneness has become an isolation
> An isolation that is nothing but fear
> Fear of who might be out there
> Fear of becoming the next statistic
>
> [Chorus]
> Streets that seem so safe at day

At night take on a meaning I've learned to hate
All the bushes, shadows, and people seem so
Threatening, threatening, threatening

Now my anger and fear has new meanings
As my power grows stronger with those who care
It's finally time to stop all the violence
Time for us to take back the night[82]

Though the lyrics start with an enunciation of fear, they move to a determination to "take back the night" from the men who use the cover of darkness to prey on women. As bassist Paula explained in a 1992 interview, in the band's music it was "really important not to get stuck in the role of a victim. The message has got to be empowering."[83]

This move from fear to empowerment occurs both on the lyrical and musical level. "The Threat" begins by mimicking a nervous heartbeat, with a succession of short-long attacks—played by the bass on its lowest pitch, E, and floor-tom and snare drum—in a cross-rhythm against the meter, as shown in figure 4.1. The guitar soars above this nervous heartbeat and Droogas asks, "Do you know what it is like to walk down the street at night?" Following this intro, the band turns to a driving, melodically descending riff at 150 KSA but full of rhythmic drive by virtue of the heavy but palm-muted attacks on the guitar, relentless hi-hat, and syncopated, anticipatory arrivals on G and E, as shown in figure 4.2. When the riff reaches E, Gembus bursts into one of her trademark dissonant guitar chords, forcing Droogas to intensify her yelling to be heard over the noise. Furthering this intensification is the fact that, while the vocals during the first half of each riff iteration are delivered mostly in quarter notes, the rhythmic density of the vocal delivery increases to eighth notes during the dissonant chord. As shown in figure 4.3, the chorus, during which the bass repeatedly plays E, offers a change in texture via a switch from hi-hat to ride cymbal and a lack of palm-muting by the guitar, with the right guitar playing more of a lead-guitar role by soaring up from B to a high A from which it descends.

Figure 4.1 Drums on the intro to Spitboy, "The Threat"

Figure 4.2 Verse riff on Spitboy, "The Threat"

Figure 4.3 Bass and right guitar track on the chorus of Spitboy, "The Threat"

Figure 4.4 Bassline and right guitar track on the bridge of Spitboy, "The Threat"

The transition from fear to empowerment occurs in the lyrics during the second verse, during which Droogas declares, "Now my anger and fear has new meanings as my power grows stronger with those who care." This transition in the lyrical narrative, however, is made clear musically by the subsequent bridge, shown in figure 4.4, during which the A that began the verse riff is repeated for eight bars, now as a major chord complete with melodic fills that highlight the major third, C♯. The effect of this major modality, the comparative lack of dissonance in Gembus's guitar chords, and drummer Gonzales moving from her "threatening drive" on the hi-hat to lighter attacks with the ting of the ride cymbal is to brighten the sonic atmosphere. This is furthered when, following this A-major chord, the band plays a progression from G to A up to E. Here, E sounds as an empowering arrival with the bass at its highest pitch in the whole song, rather than the harsh landing point that E was an octave lower during the verse riff. While the verse riff returns following this bridge, no new vocals are delivered over it, and the final chorus, which uses the same drumbeat as that heard underneath the A-major chord, becomes a moment of taking back personal control from the fear of walking at night. In this way, the sounds Spitboy created could take their listeners into the depths of patriarchal oppression while also suggesting a path of resistance, and claim the aggression of hardcore as a musical space in which women could also find their agency.

From Despair to Rage to Empowerment in Anti-Product's "The Power of Medusa"

Another example of women taking up space, asserting agency, and transforming the sounds of punk is provided by Anti-Product's final LP. When Taína Asili joined Anti-Product as a teenager, the band performed fairly typical crust-punk, though inflected with the bouncy basslines and drumbeats, brighter and lighter guitar timbres, and vocal trades of Crass's peace-punk. Its debut 7", released in 1996, provided staple songs with sloganeering lyrics covering the standard topics of crust-punk, such as war ("Dead Heroes, Dead Dreams," "War Is Prostitution," "Warfair,"), environmental destruction ("Utopian Wasteland"), and US imperialism ("Thanks a Lot"). But as Asili struggled with her band—who, besides her, were all men—to incorporate different rhythms, such as hip-hop and her own djembe playing, her spoken-word style of lyrics and vocal delivery, and a greater variety of musical moods, the band's music moved from a more propagandistic enunciation of political slogans to a more personal rage. As Asili told me:

> In my later years [in Anti-Product], the music certainly matched a more personal rage that I was feeling. So it was less of this fast upbeat feeling and more of an undertone of rage in the music and maybe more control in the rhythm. Stops were really important for us. And it had more crescendo and decrescendo. [The band] Submission Hold for me was very influential in breaking out of the box of musical styles in punk and feeling that we could incorporate more of the complex musical experience that I had. "Modern Day F-Word," "Power of Medusa"—all of the music was written to match the rage that I was feeling and also the pace of the poem.[84]

The result of these transformations can be heard on Anti-Product's final recording, 1999's *The Deafening Silence of Grinding Gears* LP. Most songs were built with more complex arrangements that feature changes in dynamics and rhythmic groove and greater use of rhythmic punctuations and "stops," where the whole band stops briefly after a single attack. The guitars and bass often play different parts rather than all following the same riff. And the variety of musical moods thus created allowed for unique song structures that follow the dramatic arc of the lyrics and vocal delivery and seem to give Asili an expressive freedom to soar above the instruments with a visceral emotional intensity. None of this was achieved without Asili's struggles with her own band, as she made clear:

> We have a song called "Modern Day F-Word" which is sort of this poem over music. I remember the band being like, "what is this? This isn't a punk song." But I was really into spoken word at that time and I really wanted to pull that into our music. And it ended up being one of the most popular songs that we ever wrote. Me taking up more space as a woman and talking about feminism in a more concrete way, in a way that was more personal to me, and to my experience, was challenging for the band. They didn't quite understand it. Eventually they would support it once they saw that it was well-received. I think maybe they were scared of how it would be

perceived by our audience. What ended up happening was many women started following our music more and many people of color started following our music more, and [my band] would see how meaningful that was to them so they would support it moving forward.[85]

Aside from "Modern Day F-Word," "The Power of Medusa" is another example of Asili's spoken-word style lyrics. The latter song expressed her personal experience as a young Puerto Rican woman confronting the constant media barrage of body images of white women with starvation-thin bodies that did not look like her own. Moreover, like Spitboy's "The Threat," the lyrics and musical structure move from despair to rage to empowerment. This musical process is discussed below in depth; before wading into that discussion, the form outline of "The Power of Medusa" provided in table 4.1 offers an entry point.

Table 4.1 Form outline of Anti-Product's "The Power of Medusa." Lyrics by Taína Asili, reproduced with permission

Time	Lyrics	Vocal Delivery	Band
0:00			Guitars and bass play intro riff in A minor (see figure 4.6) while drums provide atmospheric noise on the hi-hat; no firm beat is established.
0:15	I am searching for a likeness of my image. Desperately flipping through the glossy pages of a magazine.	Goes from spoken word to yelling; starts in a low register and moves to a higher register	Greater rhythmic density in the guitars; the drums outline the tresillo rhythm with the tom-toms
0:29	A firm gaze at the T.V. screen. Flickering scenes of long mindless bodies [at 0:36].	Continues yelling, raises in pitch, and intensifies the yelling on the word "bodies"	Drums enter with the principal beat of the song while guitars and bass ring out an A
0:36	Beautiful women (I am told) peering at my features in the holy mirror. My beauty is disguised by an opaque, white screen.	Intensifies the yelling and screams on the word "screen"	Guitars and bass re-enter with A-minor music (see figure 4.7)
0:55			Left guitar stops playing held-out notes and follows the rhythm of the drums and bass; the bass moves up an octave; the greater rhythmic density and heavier attacks by all instruments heighten the intensity

Table 4.1 Continued

Time	Lyrics	Vocal Delivery	Band
1:07	And so I hate . . . [repeated]	Vocal trade between Taína and Chris	Breakdown: guitars ring out on A while the bass keeps playing (back down an octave); drums drop out and come back in together with the guitars halfway through this section to build back up the intensity
1:20	And so I hate this insufficient shell that covers my soul. I hate my wild curly hair, my oddly colored skin, my large thighs and ass, bulging stomach, and awkward breasts.	Intensified yelling that verges on screaming; the rhythmic density and variety of the vocal delivery creates the effect of exasperation	Drums return to the principal drumbeat; return to A-minor music with the guitars more or less following the bassline
1:39	Their standards can't hold my (our) weight.	Doubled vocals	Guitars and bass drop out, leaving only the drums
1:45			Change to a major mode (see figure 4.8)
1:58	And so I am dropped. Falling into a pit full of a million hidden bodies that can't be shown.	Moves from spoken word to yelling to screaming	[continue previous section's music]
2:11	Below I hit hard. It all becomes clear. The spirits of the forgotten women enter my mouth and vibrate safely in my solid stomach. Carried away by my strong thighs. Hidden behind my almighty breasts. Guarded by the snakes that make up my hair. Fear of Medusa keeps the evil ones back. Because now they know that at any moment I could take one look at them	Mixture of spoken word, yelling, and screaming, switching from lower to higher vocal ranges, with a defined rhythmic contour and a tone of defiance	Drummer uses double-bass pedal to play sixteenth notes on the kick drum, keeps the hi-hat open, and adds cymbal crashes; return to A-minor music with guitars following bassline and the bass adding fills to intensify the forward momentum
2:49	And turn them all to stone.	Doubled vocals and a final scream on "stone"	Drums only with the original beat (no more double-bass pedal); guitars and bass drop out

Figure 4.5 Intro to Anti-Product, "The Power of Medusa"

As shown in figure 4.5, "The Power of Medusa" begins with a desolate introduction in A minor in which the guitars—in single notes rather than power chords—and bass alternate their singular attack on the tonic (with a fifth added by the right guitar after the first iteration). Semitone motion from the minor third to the second scale degree and back sets up a mood of despair. The lack of a drum beat in this introduction and little rhythmic density from the guitars and bass provide Asili with a spacious sonic atmosphere over which to begin her spoken word. As the song's introduction increases in intensity with heavier accents from the drums, Asili's "searching" vocals reach toward desperation by switching to a yelled vocal delivery in a higher vocal range.

Although the tempo of "The Power of Medusa," hovering around 150 beats per minute, is far slower than a typical punk song, when the drums enter underneath Asili's yelling, intensity and forward momentum manifest by way of the syncopated snare hits before and after beat three. The move from open hi-hat before and during beat one to a closed hi-hat thereafter makes beat two a powerful point of arrival and further intensifies the feeling of forward momentum. While the active bassline and palm-muted right guitar track match the rhythmic intensity of the drums, the left guitar track seems to sonically match the anguished despair of the vocals by virtue of playing single notes that ring out often for an entire bar. The left guitar outlines an A-minor triad as well as the semitone motion between the third and second scale degree heard in the intro. The combination of forward momentum by drums, bass, and right guitar on the one hand and a held cry by the left guitar (see figure 4.6) provides the perfect backdrop for Asili to intensify her voice from yelling to a scream as she confronts media images of idealized white beauty and compares them to her own body. Asili's final scream in this section on the word "screen" is answered by the left guitar moving to the same rhythm as the other instruments, the bass moving up an octave, and the band playing rhythmically tighter and slightly faster.

The apex of despair in the lyrics at which Asili announces the self-hatred provoked by her look in the mirror, however, demands that this forward momentum and rhythmic intensity be brought to a halt for the frustrated scream that accompanies the proclamation of "And so I hate." At this moment the drums and guitars drop out, leaving only the bass, now back down an octave, to accompany Asili's moment of frustration. Here the hardcore convention of a breakdown—in which the tempo is slowed down, often some instruments drop out, and the intensity is reduced (or modified) only to be brought back up again with the reentry of the full band and return to the previous tempo—is used to amplify the emotional breakdown taking place in the vocals. When the full band returns following the breakdown, Asili uses this renewal

Figure 4.6 A-minor music in Anti-Product, "The Power of Medusa"

Figure 4.7 Major-mode music in Anti-Product, "The Power of Medusa"

of intensity to enumerate the ways in which socialization to live up to white super-model beauty standards provokes self-hatred of her Puerto Rican female body. Here, she seems to trip over her own rapid vocal delivery in frustrated exasperation. But just as the song reaches its moment of greatest despair, an epiphany occurs in both lyrics and music: Asili's declaration that "Their standards can't hold my weight," rendered audible and all the more powerful by the departure of the guitars and bass from the musical texture.

Following this moment of epiphany that offers the first move away from despair and turns the rage into a confrontation with patriarchy and white supremacy, we are treated to a rare occurrence in punk: a key change, in this case from minor to major. While the tonic A remains emphasized as the opening note of the bass and guitar riffs in this new section, the composite of these two melodies (see figure 4.7) seems to center on the pitch F (a pitch that we have not heard in the song up to this point), effecting a shift to the F Lydian (major) mode. Whereas A minor had shrouded the first almost two minutes of the song in desolation and anguish, the song's overall tonic, A, suddenly becomes a bright beacon revealing the road forward when it is ensconced in a major mode. When Asili enters over this major-mode foundation, the lyrics indicate that she has fallen not into a pit of despair but into a revelation of "a million hidden bodies that can't be shown" in the glossy magazines and on the TV screen.

The final section of "The Power of Medusa," taking up less than a third of the song, returns to A minor, but gone is the anguished single-note cry of the left guitar track, and instead both guitars emulate the bassline, without any palm-muting. Combined with the thunderous rumbling of sixteenth notes on the kick drum via a double-bass drum pedal, intense attacks on the snare drum with little syncopation, a hi-hat now kept open, crashes on the cymbals, and more active bass fills, this A-minor material becomes not despair but defiance. In the lyrics of this final section, Asili's body parts and sense of self become not sources of shame but pillars of power buttressed by the "spirits of the forgotten women." She is thus able to confront the forces of patriarchy head on and win: "Because now they know that at any moment I could take one look at them and turn them all to stone." This final statement of empowerment is, like the first moment of confrontation, rendered all the more audible by virtue of the guitars and bass dropping out and the drummer returning to the original drumbeat with its syncopated snare hits. What makes this process of moving from anguish to empowerment all the more riveting is the visceral level on which Asili's voice reaches out to us and bares her soul through a mixture of vulnerable or declarative spoken word, anguished or determined yells, and screams that seem to possess the very power of Medusa to turn sources of the male gaze into stone.

The expressive efficacy of "The Power of Medusa" thus comes from a perfect combination of deeply personal and politically penetrating lyrics, Asili's delivery of those lyrics in a way that seems to come from the depths of her soul, and a song structure that flows out of and intensifies the poetic form and dramatic momentum of the lyrics. Whereas the propaganda aesthetic of crust-punk/dis-core offered musical declarations enunciated through the "us versus them" mentality of punk, "The Power of Medusa" takes a different approach. The conflicts it addresses take place not just on the terrain of oppressed versus oppressor, but also in the realm of inner struggle. This song thus brings to life a complex mix of emotions ranging from vulnerability to determination not found in most (male) punk. "The Power of Medusa" stands as a palpable indication of what could occur when women were able to bring their agency into the rage and politics of punk and stretch the boundaries of the punk rebellion to include their own personal experiences and, perhaps more importantly, the empowerment that comes from defying a society that instructs women in the proper ways to look, think, and act.

Fusion of Punk and Feminism?

To state what at this point should be rather obvious, Anti-Product's "Fear of Medusa" is a musical embodiment of the feminist principle that *the personal is political*. In the

1990s, with the so-called culture wars raging, and ongoing threats from the Christian Right and the politicians who supported it to restrict or take away women's reproductive rights, feminism and punk mixed together in a variety of ways. First, punk could be an attractive way for young women to challenge gender roles. Second, when women in bands took up the DIY mode of punk production, it not only enabled them greater artistic freedom than the commercial music industry would have, but also provided a means to acquire greater self-determination in a patriarchal society. Third, feminist politics were elucidated in the pages of punk zines and made available by bands via record inserts and information disseminated at shows. Finally, the defiant spirit of punk was sometimes brought into confrontations—such as street protests—with the Christian fundamentalists seeking to shame and criminalize the right to abortion.

Taína Asili provides a telling account of how punk allowed her as a teenager to reclaim her body:

> I was a young girl of color coming into my own coming from a really small town in upstate New York in a predominantly white community. The punk scene was a way for me to reclaim my body because [outside of the punk scene] I was constantly told that I wasn't beautiful, that I wasn't worthy of love and belonging in my brown woman body. Here was a scene where it was still predominantly white, but it was at least saying all of our bodies are beautiful, and if you don't like it . . .
>
> [Getting into punk] started out as a very rebellious reclamation of my body. If you don't like my brown skin, how about if my hair was purple? If you don't like the way I'm dressing, how about I rip up my stockings and put studs on my jacket? There was this sort of superficial reclamation that eventually went a lot deeper for me. [This was] my beginning introduction into feminist politics. In my undergrad years I ended up studying women's studies.[86]

While a sociological study of how punk identity allows some teenage girls to transgress gender roles is beyond the scope of this chapter,[87] Asili's personal experience points to the possibilities that the punk culture of rebellion could at least open up the space for defying the expectations of appearance forced on girls and young women.

Aside from embracing nonnormative physical appearances, punk and its DIY ethos in particular meant more than autonomous cultural production to women in punk bands. It could empower them to take up roles in musical production and everyday life that were usually dominated by men. In her memoir of her experience in Spitboy, Gonzales describes how "[t]ouring all on our own with no roadies, without anyone who wasn't in the band to help drive that first time around was hard, but it was important for us to know that we could."[88] This meant the band booked their own performances, dealt directly with the concert organizers when they performed at shows all across the country, and fixed their van when it broke down on the road. For

Gonzales and others, this DIY approach went hand in hand with an important aspect of 1990s feminism—women getting to know their own bodies:

> There was this great clinic here in Oakland where women could go and do a cervix exam on yourself. I did that. Who does that? There was the book *Our Bodies, Ourselves* [which] encouraged women to really be intimate with their bodies, to know where everything was and how it worked . . . in a way that didn't happen in the fifties.[89]

Feminist politics found a direct outlet in punk zines and in bands on tour, in their albums, and in interviews. The former is most palpably demonstrated in a series of columns beginning in *Profane Existence* 3 (April–May 1990) by Alicia non Grata titled *Take Back Your Life: A Womyn's Guide to Alternative and Natural Health Care*.[90] As the title suggests, by fusing punk's DIY ethos with new currents of feminist thought, this series provided the zine's readers with practical knowledge that women did not learn from their doctors. The latter was demonstrated by how Spitboy would often offer information on pro-choice, feminist, and women's health organizations, resources, and books to its audiences,[91] making punk a potential conduit to these organizations and the feminist movement more generally.

Finally, while mainstream pro-choice organizations often conveyed a sense of white middle-class respectability and concerned themselves with lobbying the Democratic Party, punk was one social force willing to confront anti-choice forces with uncensored defiance. Kirsten Patches of Naked Aggression described to me how her band brought punk—in spirit and physical presence—to pro-choice protests:

> In the nineties we would go to a punk rock picnic, play some kickball, then say, "Hey, everybody, there's some right-wing group that's protesting a doctor's house because he gives abortions. Let's go jump in our vans and cars and drive over there." We'd all drunkenly get in and drive across town and there'd just be waves of us jumping out of cars and vans to join the [pro-choice] picketers. And it would freak out everybody. Pro-choice people were freaked out [and] right-wing Christian people were freaked out because there's all these mohawks and crazy-looking people jumping out of vans to defend the doctor's house.[92]

Taking this punk pro-choice defiance from drunk and disorderly to politically determined resistance was a poster appearing in a 1993 issue of *Profane Existence* directed at Operation Rescue, a Christian fundamentalist organization that besieged abortion clinics across the United States in the 1990s. This poster featured a picture of a church with hands holding a Molotov cocktail and a lighter in the foreground and the slogan "Operation Rescue come to our town. We'll lock you in a church and burn the fucker down!"[93] Rumor has it that at a church Operation Rescue was using as a base of operations during one of its attempts to shut down an abortion clinic, copies of this poster were plastered inside the church overnight, giving the anti-choice activists who arrived the following morning a rude awakening.

Operation Rescue and others like it were subjected to a punk sardonic snarl in Naked Aggression's song "Killing Floor." Following some typical blues licks on the guitar, the band breaks into a heavy-swinging, slow-tempo twelve-bar blues with Kirsten Patches intoning the following words:

> There's this group around that calls themselves pro-life
> Well, instead they should call themselves pro-death
> Because by taking away our freedom of choice
> They are going to force many women who don't want to bear children
>   to the back alley
> And many women are going to die from these back alley abortions!
> But these people don't seem to care
> Operation Rescue, what do you want me to do?
> Shove a coat hanger up my cunt?[94]

For these last two lines, the band drops out and leaves Patches to sarcastically ask the first question and scream the second question. Subsequently, the band breaks into a frenzied, fast-paced punk twelve-bar blues with Patches yelling:

> I had an abortion in a back alley
> I had an abortion in a back alley
> I had an abortion in a back alley
> I had an abortion in a back alley
> Now I'm bleeding to death on the killing floor[95]

Aside from demonstrating Naked Aggression's punk appropriation of the blues for the expressive purpose of conveying the horror of back-alley abortions, this song also epitomizes the fusion of punk and pro-choice politics. The lyrics and music cut right to the point without requiring explanation or apologies—"telling it like it is" in the hardcore tradition.

Assessment

What effect did the influx of women and feminist politics into punk have on those involved in the scene? Did it diminish patriarchy within punk? It is difficult to answer these questions with any degree of precision, though some concrete evidence suggests a variety of results. At least within the burgeoning political wing of 1990s punk, feminist politics entered into the discussion in a way not seen in the 1980s. Virtually all of the bands whose music is analyzed in this study—including those consisting entirely of men—addressed the rise of the Christian Right and its attempts to reinforce patriarchy in their lyrics. Aus-Rotten in particular exemplified this transformation that occurred in the 1990s. While patriarchy was by and large absent as a subject in lyrics on its first two 7" records and on its first LP—*The System Works . . . For Them*, released in 1996—its two subsequent LPs, 1998's *. . . And Now Back to Our Programming* and 2001's *The Rotten Agenda*, made patriarchy a central concern in their lyrics.

Moreover, Aus-Rotten added Adrienne Droogas of Spitboy on vocals, initially only for one recorded song, but then to join the band on tour and play a more prominent role in it. As Droogas explained in an interview with Aus-Rotten published in *Profane Existence* in 2000, while the band had covered many crucial political topics, "I don't know if gender issues and sexism issues have been touched on as deeply and as personally as they need to be addressed."[96] One palpable result was a song on *The Rotten Agenda* LP titled "The Second Rape," which describes the humiliation women are forced to go through when they report being raped to the police and testify about it in court. While the song opens with statistics, audibly yelled by Dave Trenga, explaining how prevalent rape is in US society and analyzing how patriarchy functions within the very legal system that is supposed to punish rapists, it moves to a far more personalized depiction of what these statistics mean in human terms. When Droogas enters after Trenga, the rage is palpable in her voice as the statistics go from mere description to heart-wrenching. Aus-Rotten then uses the "trade-off" vocals technique common to crust-punk, with Trenga playing the role of a defense attorney at a rapist's trial, blaming and humiliating the rape survivor for what she wore and how she acted, while Droogas plays the role of the rape survivor testifying on the stand and having to defend herself against this public humiliation. Clearly this song would not have been possible nor had the same effect without Droogas joining the band.

Aside from feminism and opposition to the Christian Right prominently entering punk's politics, women in punk bands addressing these questions had a palpable effect on women in the audience. While Asili was hesitant to herald her work in Anti-Product as ushering in some nonpatriarchal punk utopia, she revealed:

> [C]onsistently most nights that we would play a lot of women would come up to me crying or just very emotional telling me that my music saved their life. Still to this day I get emails from people talking about how my music saved them from a difficult time or inspired them to get involved in social justice work that they're involved with to this day.
>
> I was seeing our audiences shift from a white boy sea of wildness to people really emotionally connecting. I would still see dancing, moshing, but there was also people really emotionally connecting. Instead of just this stereotype of what a punk dance looks like, people were actually dancing, making new moves—there was this body expression that was new. More women would come to our shows; more Latinos would come to our shows.

Writing in *HeartattaCk*, Christine Boarts, the force behind the zine *Slug and Lettuce*, described how, "When I was a younger punk—eager and ready to embrace the world of punk, there were a number of rad women around who were active in the scene: booking shows, playing in bands, being creative and artistic and serving as good role models."[97] Thus, for many young women getting involved in the punk scene in the 1990s, the existence of powerful women in prominent roles within the scene, who asserted their own experiences with and opposition to patriarchy and connected it to a larger analysis of patriarchy in society, played a transformative role.

Whatever progress was made on this front, however, remained uneven and ambiguous. It depended significantly on local punk scenes, with Kristi Fults pointing out in *HeartattaCk* how sexist comments from bands on stage were largely tolerated in the punk scene on the East Coast, whereas on the West Coast the audience would often shut down such comments.[98] Asili summed up Anti-Product's 1998 tour by saying, "So far we've played with 58 different bands on this tour and only six of them had women in them."[99] Furthermore, the notion of DIY punk as an underground haven divorced from the social relations of US society often deflected rather than opened up discussion of how patriarchy impacted the scene itself. As Allie Riot summed up in *HeartattaCk*, "In our liberated anti-racist, -classist, -sexist, -elitist, -homophobia scene, we fail to realize the difficulty of defying the . . . society we are produced from."[100] Nevertheless, patriarchy became at least a contested question within 1990s punk, with those passing through the scene experiencing empowered women and a feminist critique of both US society and the punk scene itself, whether or not they were transformed by this experience. Furthermore, women in 1990s punk have left us with a powerful sonic imprint of their struggles, as demonstrated in the previous analysis of songs by Spitboy and Anti-Product.

As with women's participation in punk, the 1990s wave of Latino punk bands had a mixed impact on the US punk scene. It undeniably opened up space for punk bands to sing in Spanish and other languages besides English in the US context. It opened up conversations, journalism, and scholarship about the history of Latino participation in punk, which had previously been virtually invisible. It forged connections between US punk bands and their counterparts throughout Latin America. It was the harbinger for other nonwhite identities to carve out their own expressions of punk in the United States, such as Taqwacore, Filipino punk, and Afro-punk. It gave voice to the sentiments of Latino youth who sought to defy the anti-immigrant policies and hysteria of the 1990s. Perhaps most significantly, it ushered in the now prevalent participation of Latinos in punk throughout the United States. Despite these accomplishments, Latinos in the 1990s US punk scene still had to contend with a "color-blind" racism that erased their identities and a backlash when they did dare to sing in Spanish or voice their own experiences with oppression. Thus Latino punk did not usher in an era of racism-free punk, but did at least open up conversations and carve out spaces for nonwhite participation.

The challenge to US punk's male- and white-centric subjective position in the 1990s is perhaps best embodied in the 1995 split LP featuring Los Crudos on one side and Spitboy on the other. As Gonzales describes in her memoir,

> The [LP's] title *Viviendo Aperamente*, or 'roughly living,' seemed to capture the content of the songs by both bands—Latino struggles and feminist struggles, living with such awareness was often abrasive, hard, rough. . . . In each other, Spitboy and Los Crudos found a band akin to the other, a band that was clear in message and resolute, charismatic, and endearing. It was a collaboration of message, sound, and mutual admiration.[101]

Demonstrating the indelible mark these two bands left on the punk scene, the following review of the *Viviendo Aperamente* LP published in *MaximumRockNRoll* makes a fitting conclusion for this chapter:

> *Absolutely fucking essential!* In your face passionate outrage and to-the-point lyrics dealing with issues of gender, race and the sour turns of society at large. Chicago's Los Crudos' eleven songs absolutely rip from the very beginning with totally overwhelming energy, stripped down hardcore and caustic Spanish-sung vocals. The final recordings from the Bay Area's now-disbanded Spitboy are their most powerful—heavy, lurching and rockin' mid-tempo rhythms layered through creative guitar work, hardcore vocal shouts, and occasional acoustic influences.[102]

5
Punk's Popularity Anxieties and the Introspective Aggression of So-Cal Punk

Concurrent with the underground political punk renaissance of the 1990s was the growing mainstream popularity of certain strands of punk. The rise of so-called alternative music heralded by Nirvana's 1991 *Nevermind* album opened the door to the music industry's second great awakening to punk, nearly two decades after several late-1970s British punk bands, such as the Sex Pistols and the Clash, had made their way onto major record labels and shocked society with their public displays of impropriety. By the mid-1990s, Green Day's "pop-punk" was scoring hit singles, Offspring's 1994 *Smash* album was on its way to becoming the then best-selling record on an independent label of all time, and a number of punk bands from the late 1970s were embarking on reunion tours and receiving mainstream press coverage. In short, punk was no longer limited to vinyl records on DIY labels, small dingy venues known mainly through photocopied flyers and word of mouth, and zines, but a part of mainstream American music and youth culture.

But it was not crust-punk, extreme hardcore, or any of the bands previously discussed that found their way into the public eye. Instead, late-1970s punk bands, punk-inflected alternative rock, pop-punk, and a new style called So-Cal punk were the beneficiaries of the burgeoning alternative culture industry. So-Cal punk bands tempered the speed and abrasiveness of 1980s hardcore with melodious vocals and even vocal harmonies. They sometimes added lead guitar parts, which were often performed with "octave chords" (explained later in this chapter), over hardcore riffs, as well as precisely played and rhythmically intricate palm-muting on guitars. So-Cal punk bands such as Bad Religion, NOFX, and Pennywise expanded the musical vocabulary of punk and wrote lyrics that dealt with the complexities of postmodern life, resulting in an aesthetic of introspective aggression.[1] Pop-punk, by contrast, used late-1970s punk rather than 1980s hardcore as the foundation for its musical style, and fused punk sensibility with catchy choruses and more personalized lyrics.

Most underground punk bands and zine writers looked at the mainstream success of some punk with suspicion at best, but more often than not with derision and disgust. Having spent the 1980s building an underground scene that prided itself on maintaining autonomous control of its cultural production, many within underground punk feared that the mainstream success of a few would dilute punk's ethos of

Rebel Music in the Triumphant Empire. David Pearson, Oxford University Press (2021). © Oxford University Press.
DOI: 10.1093/oso/9780197534885.003.0006.

rebellion and compromise its integrity. Indeed, the overwhelming response was pro-tection of the underground scene, and those within punk that signed contracts with major record labels or even became too popular on independent labels were cast out as traitors by those who insisted on adherence to a particular definition of DIY.

In the first part of this chapter, I will explore the rise of the alternative culture industry, its impact on punk, and the discourse of DIY authenticity that was asserted to defend punk against the incursions of the mainstream music industry. In the second part of this chapter, through reception history and musical analysis of NOFX's *The Decline*, I will elucidate the style of So-Cal punk. While this book is mainly concerned with under-ground political punk, So-Cal punk's popularity in the 1990s offers an important means to comprehend the broader appeal of punk to alienated suburban youth that formed a crucial context for the less popular but no less significant wing of political punk.

Part 1
Punk's Popularity Anxieties

Before the acrimonious debates about the sin of signing to a major label reached fever pitch in the pages of punk zines in the mid-1990s, a few punk or punk-inspired bands—especially Bad Religion and Fugazi—were provoking anxiety when their popularity began to outstrip the DIY underground from which they came. As early as August 1990, columns in *MaximumRockNRoll* responded with trepidation when Bad Religion began playing at larger, less DIY venues and with higher ticket prices.[2] A year later, this trepi-dation turned to outright criticism verging on scorn for fifteen-dollar ticket prices, alle-gations of "screwing over" concert promoters, and even the lack of punk propriety when band members supposedly acted like rock stars at a London concert at which, rumor has it, they complained of not being provided with enough towels.[3] Whether or not these rumors, or the allegations that Bad Religion was made to suffer when it went against the grain, were true—my point here is not to investigate the process of belief in the seemingly stranger than fiction London Towelgate scandal—the important thing is that they were the generator of a recipe for hate in a debate over DIY in the pre-eminent punk zine.

Much of the reason for the anxiety was that underground DIY punk had offered some means to screen participants and weed out the uncommitted—you had to seek underground punk out, read obscure zines and know punks, and order vinyl records through the mail to participate in the scene.[4] As Ben Weasel, singer of the Screeching Weasels, wrote in *MaximumRockNRoll* in January 1992, "With the suc-cess of bands like Fugazi and Bad Religion, a whole new crowd of people are coming to punk shows, but I get the feeling they're not getting much out of it outside of the entertainment."[5] Beginning with Bad Religion's 1988 *Suffer* LP, the band attracted a wider audience through its combination of 1980s hardcore with audible and melo-dious vocals, greater musical precision, cleaner-sounding recordings, and astute lyr-ical commentary on the conditions of suburban life in the American empire. Weasel's fear was that the catchiness and greater accessibility of this music and the thrill of the mosh pit at more professional venues would bring people into punk who were not committed to its ideals, politics, and underground network. At the same time, Weasel recognized the real dilemmas faced by bands like Bad Religion who became popular through independently released records and DIY touring: as their audiences grew larger, the DIY punk scene was no longer adequate for booking shows, promoting them widely, and securing venues big enough for the audience. But in turning to more professional venues and concert promoters, some worried that the fringe benefits of higher pay, nice hotel rooms, and a backstage area with good food and plentiful clean towels could potentially corrupt punk bands who came from DIY values.

The fears of a few thousand people showing up at Bad Religion and Fugazi shows would soon be eclipsed when Nirvana's single "Smells Like Teen Spirit," from their album *Nevermind*, reached number six on *Billboard*'s Hot 100 chart on 11 January 1992.[6] Though not punk per se, Nirvana drew on punk, metal, and indie-pop to create something that was dubbed grunge, and the band got its start on the large independent label Sub Pop and by playing shows in the DIY underground touring circuit.[7] In the autobiography of the So-Cal punk band NOFX, bassist and singer Fat Mike captures the impact of Nirvana's success:

> *Nevermind* was an extinction-level event in the music industry. L.A. hair metal was dead. Alternative, grunge, and punk took over. Even though NOFX wasn't on any record company's radar, curious kids flooded into record stores around the world to research Nirvana's punk influences, and some of them accidentally stumbled onto bands like ours. (It might have helped that our band name also started with "N.") The following years would turn out well for NOFX.[8]

As Fat Mike describes, Nirvana's *Nevermind* had two important effects for our purposes: it ushered in a sea change in popular culture, with alternative rock supplanting "hair metal" and prior mainstream rock more generally, and it drew attention to punk from a much wider audience.

In a 1996 article in *Punk Planet*, Paul Chan argues that the basis for the sea change in youth culture marked by the rise of alternative was in the new demographic—often called Generation X—that came of age in the 1990s. As Chan puts it, "the new alternative culture industry sought the money and minds of people born between the early 60's and the middle 70's—the kids of the baby boomers."[9] With many of their parents having participated to some degree in the movements of the 1960s, feminism, an embrace of individuality against conformity and obedience to authority, opposition to US wars abroad, gay rights, the politics of the civil rights movement, and a countercultural ethos were all values instilled in a portion of Generation X. Alternative music, with its rejection of rock star masculinity, espousal of alienation, and celebration of being different, was the product that spoke to these sentiments. As Chan defines it, alternative is "the creation of a set of signs, a body of sounds, and a set of sensibilities which would signify that difference *itself*."[10]

Not just a new style of music, but an entire industry developed around alternative, with major record labels and their subsidiaries, mainstream music magazines such as *Spin* and *Alternative Press,* and festival tours such as Lollapalooza constituting a field of cultural production around the new trend. The cable television station MTV—Music Television—played an important role in the propagation of alternative, prominently showcasing music videos by the first wave of grunge bands and those by subsequent incarnations of alternative music. Chan critiques this alternative music industry that "can not only sell an unimaginative and uniform product to a mass audience, but can do it deploying a paradoxical rhetoric thick with notions of 'difference' and 'noncon-formity.'"[11] Punk zines began running exposés on the workings of the alternative culture industry. *MaximumRockNRoll* ran ten pages of articles in its June 1994 issue which exposed, among other things, how independent record labels were often bought by, or set up as fronts for, the then "Big Six" major record labels to confer authenticity on the bands officially on those front independent labels, as well as the predatory venturing of A&R representatives into the underground punk scene.[12] The underground punk scene remained, for the most part, unimpressed with what they perceived as an inauthentic display of difference and anticonformity doled out by the alternative culture industry. This attitude toward mainstream alternative fans and their incursions into punk was immortalized in the always prescient lyrics of The Pist in a song titled "Alternative?":

What the fuck just happened? Where did you come from?
Something is happening here
I'm so glad to see our lifestyle watered down and mass produced
A pale reflection of the real thing

Can you understand what this movement is all about? No, you're just a
    consumer!
Am I seeing you or just a packaged product? I see a fucking liar!

When the so called alternative is happily accepted you can just blend
    right in
And rebellion's now a market, not a response to injustice, but you don't
    give a shit

If you need it all spelled out for you well maybe this just ain't for you
Your world has nothing to do with ours
Don't think you can buy respect, you gotta fucking earn it

We don't want to seem to be exclusive we want everyone involved
Everyone should be sincere if we are to evolve
With all the pathetic bullshit we are plagued with every day
We don't need no trendy assholes standing in the way

This might sound self-righteous, that just might be true
But we'll give fuckin credit where we think credit's due
Our respect goes out to those who choose to stand alone
And ignore the communal voices, you can think on your own

Don't you fucking listen to what anyone has to say
It's your fucking life, live it your own fucking way
Make your own decision, be yourself for once
Form your own opinions, tell everyone to shut the fuck up[13]

"I'm Telling Tim": Protectionism in the Face of Popularity

The attention alternative drew to punk provoked a crisis within the underground punk scene two years after Nirvana's breakout success. Fat Mike captures the onset of this crisis particularly well, and his description is worth quoting in full:

> By the time 1994 rolled around, Bad Religion had left [guitarist] Brett Gurewitz and Epitaph [Records] behind and signed to [major label] Atlantic Records. They were on the radio and the charts, and by the end of the year they released *Stranger Than Fiction*, which ultimately went gold.
>
> In February of '94, Green Day (who were on tour opening for Bad Religion at the time) released *Dookie*, and the punk scene went fucking apeshit. The album charted all over the world, won a Grammy, and has since been certified diamond (a feat achieved by only about a hundred or so albums in history). On April 8, 1994, the Offspring released *Smash*, which was the first Epitaph release to not only go gold but six times platinum, and which became known as the best-selling independent album of all time.
>
> In the 80's, punks were like the Freemasons or Skull and Bones. We had our own club, our own rituals. We could identify each other in public and, as far as straight society was concerned, we spoke a coded language. Punk allowed us to wear an outcast label as a badge of pride instead of a mark of shame. But suddenly our secret language was being decoded by the major labels. Our rituals were laid bare in the press. And the doors to our secret clubhouse were kicked open by MTV.[14]

When punk drew the media spotlight, robust record sales, and large concert audiences, many adherents to underground punk responded with disgust at the new crowds attracted by this mainstream success. They scrutinized the practices of punk bands, record labels, and festivals for their level (or lack) of DIY credentials, and they evaluated musical style negatively based on its potential for popular appeal. On the new crowds of teenagers drawn to punk, Jim Testa wrote about seeing Offspring perform after the success of *Smash* that "something about the spectacle of 3,000 instant punks—many of them so young that this had to be their first show—clamoring at this empty spectacle, so devoid of personality or feeling, really depressed me."[15] Will Dandy similarly described the spectacle he witnessed when Green Day performed at Lollapalooza:

They were so depressing to watch up there on the big stage with thousands of alternachicks singing along and swinging to the beat. Not to mention the fact that I felt like I was watching TV, not a show. It was scary. A big wall of speakers, everything just right, timed karate kicks and all that shit.... I wanted to cry and puke at the same time.[16]

Note here how easily DIY discourse can incorporate a masculine subjectivity as its measure of authenticity, with Dandy's critique of "alternachicks" "swinging to the beat" rather than moshing. Not unlike other male discourses of authenticity in music, DIY purity was defined and defended almost exclusively by men—just consider the gender of its advocates—and praised specific kinds of (male) aggression, subjective positions, and approved behaviors.[17]

The scrutiny which bands, record labels, and tours were subjected to is evident in the numerous letters published in *MaximumRockNRoll* that criticized bands and concerts for high admission prices, bouncers, and the sin of staying backstage before a performance, as well as in the ubiquitous question asked to bands interviewed by the zine about their position on signing to major record labels. While Felix von Havoc's review of Green Day's *39/Smooth* LP in a 1990 issue of *Profane Existence* proclaimed that "These guys turned down an offer from IRS records in order to stay on [L]ookout [Records], so you know they have some integrity,"[18] in 1994 the band became persona non grata in the underground punk scene. Their brand of pop-punk may previously have been acceptable stylistically, even receiving positive reviews from DIY stalwarts at *Profane Existence*,[19] but signing to a major label nailed the coffin shut on the band's underground credibility.

Coming in for harsh criticism was the Warped Tour, which, beginning in 1995, combined performances by So-Cal punk and pop-punk bands with professional skateboarding in a festival that traveled around the United States and Canada. Drawing an average of ten thousand on each stop after 2000, Warped relied on sponsorship from Vans, a skateboarding shoe company, to sustain the buses of punk bands and construction of stages.[20] Between the large teenage audience newly attracted to the more palatable side of punk sounds and the corporate sponsorship, Warped became the stage concert symbol of selling out in the eyes of underground punk. A 1999 issue of *Punk Planet* put the headline "The Warped Tour X-po$ed" on its cover and devoted ten pages of articles to revealing the ways in which, according to *Punk Planet* writers, Warped functioned as a conduit for marketing products to the consumer demographic of alternative-minded 11- to 25-year-olds.[21] In fairness to Warped, it also offered table space to social justice organizations at each stop on the tour, and I can personally attest to the fact that it proved favorable ground to "market" protests against the Iraq war to the teenage "demographic."

As Alan O'Connor explains in his study of DIY punk record labels, the late 1980s saw the emergence of what he calls commercial punk labels such as Epitaph, Lookout, and later Fat Wreck Chords. Whereas DIY punk record labels typically pressed between 1,000–3,000 copies of each release on vinyl, commercial punk labels had CDs and cassettes manufactured and expected to sell between 20,000–100,000 copies of each release, with some albums even going gold (selling over 500,000 copies). Commercial punk labels had offices and warehouses, a small staff, more professionalized promotion, and distribution in chain stores, and they made contracts with their bands. In contrast, DIY punk labels were run by one or two people from their homes, at most using a post office box for mail order, and, instead of making written contracts with bands, operated based on friendship, verbal agreements, and splitting the profits. Moreover, several DIY record labels were explicitly associated with radical politics. While the distinction between commercial and DIY punk labels was not absolute and some labels straddled the divide, as the 1990s wore on the distinction between the two became part of a wider split in the punk scene that carried over into performance practices and musical style, and that was embroiled in the ideological debate over what it meant to stay DIY.[22]

Epitaph Records in particular found itself in the crosshairs of this debate. Epitaph was started in the 1980s by Brett Gurewitz, guitarist of Bad Religion, to release albums by his own band, beginning with Bad Religion's 1988 *Suffer* album. It soon became the epicenter for the new style of So-Cal punk and stumbled upon popular success in the 1990s, with Offspring's *Smash* LP as its apex. Consequently, Gurewitz found himself needing to justify Epitaph's success in the pages of punk zines. In an interview in *Punk Planet* in 1994, Gurewitz described the spike in Epitaph's record sales as an unexpected surprise rather than being cultivated through marketing strategies. He claimed that it was up to the bands whether to make music videos, and that he only sent these videos to MTV—which served, among other things, as a key pillar of the alternative culture industry—at the bands' request, as "the bands will always be the boss, not me." According to Gurewitz, Offspring's commercial success came about not by design, but when, after the LA radio station K-ROQ started playing the band's single "Come Out and Play," audiences kept calling in to request the song, other radio stations followed suit, and then MTV put the video for the song in its rotation. While many in the underground punk scene deemed Epitaph no longer DIY due to its high record sales, polished recordings, and videos on MTV, Gurewitz insisted, "We're not a major label.... I turned down over twenty million dollars" from a major record label trying to purchase Epitaph as a subsidiary.[23]

Such justification would prove insufficient for DIY stalwarts. Total Chaos, a Los Angeles band playing music inspired by 1980s British hardcore anarcho-punk who had commanded respect from the underground political wing of punk, found its authenticity questioned when it released albums on Epitaph. A review of its 1994 *Pledge of Defiance* LP in the arbiter of anarcho-punk, *Profane Existence*, simply remarked "Epitaph??? Hmmm???"[24] In the subsequent issue of the zine, Total Chaos sought to justify signing to Epitaph by virtue of the record label's wider distribution. For the band, having their albums, now on CD rather than vinyl, sold in chain stores fulfilled a need for political hardcore punk reaching a broader audience. They praised Epitaph for being supportive of the band while on tour and not trying to simply profit off of their music—in effect arguing that Epitaph still adhered to DIY principles.[25]

DIY diehards disagreed: letters in the February 1997 issue of *MaximumRockNRoll* describe an attempt to organize an audience walk-out during a Total Chaos performance in New York City in protest over the band's association with Epitaph.[26]

Epitaph increasingly lost its credibility within the underground punk scene, with Dan of *Profane Existence* writing a column in 1995 describing the zine's rupture with Epitaph—it would no longer review records put out by the label or accept its paid advertisements.[27] Gurewitz's appearance on CNBC to discuss Epitaph's business efficiency would be the final nail in the coffin for many.[28] But business practices and sales figures were not the only battlegrounds on which DIY credibility was fought. Evaluations of musical style increasingly entered the acrimonious arguments over punk's newfound mainstream appeal. Bands with more melody and more polished recordings were accused of concocting their sounds in a search for profit, and So-Cal punk went from being praised for pursuing exciting new directions in style to being derided as bland, generic, and consumption-friendly for the teen market.

In terms of accusations of concocting sounds in pursuit of profit, Coffin Break's 1992 *Thirteen* LP received the following review: "There's a really disturbing, commercial feeling to the whole album. The edge has been replaced with way-too-typical college rock structures. And he sings . . . Give me the old, hoarse, off-key monotone anyday."[29] Note that the more melodious singing on this album is contrasted with authentic punk yelling, and the implication of the "commercial feeling" and "way-too-typical" structures is that this album was produced to covet commercial success. Bad Religion's *Recipe for Hate* LP—released in 1993 before the band signed to Atlantic Records—was criticized in *MaximumRockNRoll* for "its calculated eye on the 'alternative' mainstream marketplace," as it featured a cameo appearance by Eddie Vedder, the singer of popular alternative band Pearl Jam.[30]

A striking turning point in evaluations of So-Cal punk occurred in the pages of *MaximumRockNRoll* in 1994. Prior to that year, So-Cal punk bands on Epitaph Records tended to receive positive reviews. Offspring's 1989 self-titled LP was described as:

> A very loud release from this L.A. band whose music has a sound foundation of mid-tempo punk and garage rock with a heavy emphasis on a great raw guitar sound. The vocals work really well with the music and are sung with catchy rhythm. I found myself humming several songs from the record . . .[31]

The band's polished hardcore sound, catchy melodic vocal hooks, and even its social commentary continued to receive rave reviews up through its *Smash* LP:

> I intently studied the lyrics only to notice a pattern emerging: "there's no future, we're all living under the gun, in a fucked up world, which we created, even if we didn't think . . ." Speaking of firearms, about 1/3 of the songs are about, related to, or at least mention: guns. The production is in-fucking-credible and the power of the raw yet polished, strong melodic hardcore is soon to be a classic.[32]

In addition to this ecstatic review, the Offspring was featured on the cover of *MaximumRockNRoll*. The irony is that, for the underground punk scene, *Smash* would soon become a classic in a negative way—a symbol of "selling out."[33]

In the early 1990s, So-Cal punk was praised for both its innovative sounds and its more sophisticated rather than sloganeering critique of American society. Bad Religion's *No Control* LP, which was on seven of the eight "Top Fifteen" records lists in the February 1990 issue of *MaximumRockNRoll*, was reviewed as "post-modern, existentialist So-Cal punk."[34] NOFX's *The Longest Line* EP was praised for its "catchy song writing talent and flawless production" and "uncanny ability to put together perfect hooks and riffs."[35] And in a review of its *Wild Card* EP, Pennywise was described as "catchy like Bad Religion, these guys possess a wild rawness reminiscent of White Flag or the Didjits. Excellent beefy guitar, thumpy drums."[36]

But after 1994, such praise would be no more. The turnabout began with mild warnings, such as Tim Yohannan describing Pennywise's *Unknown Road* album as a formulaic imitation—"outside of slightly poppier playing, double bass drums and an occasionally squawky guitar lead, this is essentially the BAD RELIGION formula"— and hinting that NOFX "may be too tight for their own good."[37] Subsequently, So-Cal punk bands were almost always derided as being bland imitations of Bad Religion and NOFX. A reviewer of No Use For A Name's *Leche con Carne* LP gave favorable comments but asked, "What happened? Did Fat Mike put them through his secret 'Fat Records Clone Machine' that makes all bands sound like NOFX?"[38] Strung Out and Blout's split 7" was reviewed as "probably exactly what you'd expect of two new-ish SoCal punk bands. Both are mid to fast-paced and owe a great debt to Bad Religion. Octave chords galore. Not too much else."[39] *Profane Existence*, which was earlier to critique and even more dismissive of So-Cal punk, gave the following terse review of Pennywise's *Unknown Road*: "Is this Bad Religion?"[40] Reviewers for *Punk Planet*, the most prominent punk zine to continue giving positive reviews after the 1994 turning point, even felt compelled to answer criticisms of So-Cal punk's blandness. Will Dandy reviewed Pennywise's *About Time* album as "A bit slowed down and a lot more produced these guys come back with more melodic hardcore that half the world will say sounds exactly like Bad Religion and I'll argue with all of them that they're a lot different."[41]

Not only were the sounds of So-Cal punk derided, but its social critique, which had earlier been praised for its more existential approach and astuteness at questioning the conditions of American suburban life, was dismissed in zine reviews after 1994. Pennywise's *About Time* was mocked for its "urban angst/personal empowerment" songs.[42] Drunk in Public's *Tapped Out!* CD was similarly poked fun at as being "for the angst-ridden, skateboarding, cheesy guitar riff liking oppressed youth of today."[43] Undoubtedly as more So-Cal punk bands emerged, some were bland imitations of the style's progenitors and did not have the intellectual sophistication of Bad Religion or the sardonic wit of NOFX that made these two bands' lyrics speak eloquently to pressing social concerns on the minds of alienated suburban youth. But the vituperative criticism heaped on So-Cal punk bands beginning in 1994 was more about staking out an ideological position in which any punk band even associated with moving beyond the DIY underground scene needed to be excised for punk to maintain its purity and political efficacy. Indeed, exceptions could be made for So-Cal-style punk bands that did espouse radical politics, such as Propagandhi, as demonstrated by Steve Aoki's remark in *HeartattaCk* that "There are too many bands that follow the NOFX sound that turn me off, except for [the band] Propagandhi."[44] Epitomizing the connection between evaluation of musical style, performance and business practices, and DIY ideology is the following review of a twelve-band compilation put out by Fat Wreck Chords, which, after Epitaph, was the most prolific purveyor of So-Cal punk as well as pop-punk:

> Fourteen songs by (what they claim to be) 12 different bands. My claim is that there are only 3 bands. Actually, come to think of it, there is only one band, they just have faster and slower songs.... To further facilitate the cash flow they play music for mass consumption, lots of melody with little feeling or power. There's energy here, but it lacks the punch a real hardcore band would have. They play $15 shows on ten foot stages with little or no contact with kids. In some cases they go so far as to violate the DIY ethic itself, having some of their bands sign to majors.[45]

DIY as Ideology; Indies, Zines, and Shows as Ideological (Anti-)State Apparatuses

Why did signing to a major label or even getting too popular on an independent label spark such venom in the pages of punk zines? What was at stake? Answers to these questions reside in the fact that, by the 1990s, DIY was no longer just a way of putting out punk records when major labels would not and organizing shows that professional venues refused to book. It was now an ideology reinforced by a robust discourse that often connected DIY with anarchist philosophy and, like all ideologies, by rituals that interpellated individuals to ideology.[46] As Ben Weasel put it in the previously quoted article, "Although independent punk labels were probably mostly started because most punk bands couldn't get signed to majors, along with that came a radically different way of doing business."[47] What started as necessity became intrinsic to punk morality.

Moreover, a number of punk ideologues in the 1980s and 1990s viewed DIY as a crucial means by which to prevent its co-optation. Tim Yohannan of *MaximumRockNRoll* had a background in the counterculture of the 1960s, but argued that sixties counterculture had been successfully co-opted due to the fact that the means of cultural production and dissemination of protest folk and psychedelic rock remained in the hands of the corporate elite. Yohannan connected this with the fact that so many former hippies wound up working and living typical middle-class American jobs and lives.[48] As discussed in chapter 2, Crass, the preeminent progenitors of anarcho-punk, connected their DIY functioning as a band with their life in a commune outside of London and with anarchist philosophy. *Profane Existence* went the furthest in connecting punk practices with anarchist philosophy, seeing the potential threat punk could pose to capitalism as its creation of an alternative culture that maintained autonomy from the structures of the capitalist economy and state. In an article titled "Making Punk a Trend Again," the zine argued that the burgeoning popularity of punk, with the Sex Pistols on the cover of *Spin* magazine, "is quite the opposite of what punk means to us—punk is anti-establishment and the destruction of popular culture." While *Profane Existence* writers were not opposed to punk becoming popular numerically, they were adamant that "What should be opposed is corporate scumbag involvement in a counterculture we youths have built over the years *ourselves*."[49]

Maintaining distance from the mainstream music industry and "roughing it" on tour were thus viewed as crucial ways to reinforce DIY ideology and not succumb to the rock star ethos and all that it represented. The zine *HeartattaCk* was started in part to reassert DIY purity within hardcore, valuing "independence and self-determination." The zine's founder and editor, Kent McClard, announced in its inaugural issue that *HeartattaCk* would refuse to review or take ads for music on a major label or even with a barcode, stating that the barcode "symbolizes big business and the transformation of music from a form of expression into a commodity to be bought and sold."[50]

In a 1995 interview in *Profane Existence*, Kelly Halliburton, then playing bass in Defiance, a more melodic political punk band that probably could have pursued greater commercial success had it so desired, argued for the importance of DIY touring:

> [I]f you're travelling in a tour bus and stay in hotels, it dilutes a lot of the anger that's supposed to be there. If you're waking up every day often three hours of sleep on a hard floor . . . you know it's a drag but it comes with the territory. . . . I wouldn't trade this lifestyle for anything.[51]

Thus roughing it on tour was a crucial means by which to remain uncorrupted by the privileges proffered on bands with buses and hotel rooms.

Furthermore, eschewing rock star status meant maintaining an egalitarian connection between bands and audiences with minimal separation between the two. At the 1998 More Than Music punk festival in Columbus, Ohio, the grindcore band Assück took this so far as refusing to play on a stage that was several feet above the dance floor, as doing so would elevate the band, physically and symbolically, above the audience. Instead, the band performed at a house near the festival venue, where they were eye to eye with those in attendance.[52] In my experience, it was not uncommon in the latter half of the 1990s for punk bands to set up and perform on the dance floor rather than on stage, even at DIY venues with stages that were no more than two feet tall.

Thus what was at stake was not just a matter of business models, but an ideology and set of practices that sought autonomy from the cycle of capitalist marketing and consumption of music as an entertainment commodity. DIY as ideology and practice had constructed a means to control cultural production, dissemination, the integrity of the music's message, and even its reception. To underground punk, the impact of its music depended on this very autonomy and the dedication it fostered among audiences who embraced the music as something to be viscerally felt and critically thought about rather than simply enjoyed. As Adam Nathanson of the band Born Against explained, the "8,000 [records sold by his band] are going to leave more of an impact on music and people's thoughts than Trixter, or whoever else sold millions of records."[53] Moreover, the underground punk scene knew that even if what it enunciated to the world was truly rebellious and even politically radical, that could still be repackaged as a trend and commodity that diluted the very rebelliousness at the core of it. As Jeff Chan put it, "What is less visible and perhaps more frightening is the wholesale commodification of Punk—not simply the look, the attitude, or even the music, but the very idea of Punk."[54]

It was not just a matter of commodification, but also the defense of an alternative lifestyle predicated on individuality and egalitarianism that was threatened if the punk scene were to lose control over its practices to the mainstream music industry and consequently see that very individuality and egalitarianism corrupted. In short, the very identities and ways of life of participants in the punk scene were threatened by Green Day's record sales, Vans' sponsorship of the Warped Tour, and the Sex Pistols going on a reunion tour. Thus in 1992, as this threat first reared its head, Tim Yohannan placed a two-page spread in *MaximumRockNRoll* that read:

> In these confusing times where ideals can often become gray and fuzzy and everyone is so open-minded that they can't THINK at all . . . one thing is entirely clear to me. . . . PUNK has absolutely FUCKING nothing in common with corporate label$, with their $pirit-$ucking opportuni$m, or with their anti-democratic structure . . . or with the fuckhead bands that $ign with them. . . . So a big FUCK YOU and good riddance to the likes of Butthole Surfers Flipper Hole Nirvana L7 . . . and to all the "FANS", who, like the HIPPIES, can't see where this is all leading.[55]

Was It a Garden of Eden to Begin With?

I have peppered this exposition of the debate over DIY versus "selling out" with numerous quotes from zines in part to demonstrate the intensity of feelings involved. Some within the underground punk scene, however, questioned idealistic portrayals of DIY that painted the punk underground as a Garden of Eden shattered by the sin of a few bands eating the fruit offered by major record labels. Others viewed this mid-1990s crisis as a failure of punk to adapt to larger changes in US society. Still others wondered what the point of the whole debate was when there were far more pressing social concerns facing humanity.

Joel Schalit's 1997 article in *Punk Planet*, titled "Redistributing Cultural Goods Is Not the Same Thing as Redistributing Wealth and It Never Will Be: All Punk Commodities," argued that DIY was a response to marginalization and censorship during the economic downturn of the 1980s rather than a utopian, noncommodified cultural field. He stated that "As a result of being shut out of the production process of American popular music, punk intellectuals such as Jello Biafra and Tim Yohannan formulated an economic strategy by which they were able to construct their own artistic institutions and markets within which to create and disseminate their own music and literature."[56] While this economic strategy drew on 1960s social movement practices, it never fundamentally escaped capitalist production, with independent record labels still having their vinyl pressed at facilities which entered into the mode of labor exploitation of capitalism. As Schalit put it, "punk was co-opted because it lacks a coherent critique of capitalism. Instead of advocating the overthrow of capitalist relations of production, punk insists on reverting to an early form of capitalist development which emphasizes the necessity of the imagination, skills and hard work of the entrepreneur as opposed to the blindness and stupidity of the corporation and the bureaucrat."[57]

Schalit here points to an interpretive difference in critiques of capitalism that has bedeviled anticapitalists since the nineteenth century and reappears in punk's discourse on DIY. To understand this interpretive difference, it is worth pointing out how Stacy Thompson, in his own study of punk and the commodity form, interprets Marx. Thompson quotes Marx's description of the early appearance of commodity exchange, which reads:

> The sphere of circulation or commodity exchange, within whose boundaries the sale and purchase of labour-power goes on, is in fact a very Eden of the innate rights of man. It is the exclusive realm of Freedom, Equality, Property and Bentham. Freedom, because both buyer and seller of a commodity, let us say of labour-power, are determined only by their own free will. They contract as free persons, who are equal before the law. Their contract is the final result in which their joint will finds a common legal expression. Equality, because each enters into relation with the other, as with a simple owner of commodities, and they exchange equivalent for equivalent. Property, because each disposes only of what is his own. And Bentham, because each looks only to his own advantage.... [T]hey all work together to their mutual exchange, for the common weal, and in the common interest.[58]

Marx's description here could almost describe the DIY underground Garden of Eden. Thompson's interpretation is that, "For Marx, the commodity-form does not necessarily harbor radical inequalities; rather, the capitalist mode of production, as a more complex economic form based on the simpler form of the commodity, springs from inequalities rooted in the ownership of property-capital."[59] What Thompson misses here is that, for Marx, the transition from simple commodity exchange to capitalist production was not a radical negation of the former by the latter, but an extension of those very principles of Freedom, Equality, Property, and Bentham to the equal exchange of labor by people without property for wages from people with property. The commodity form is thus pregnant with the very social inequalities Thompson recognizes, and for Marx, small-scale commodity production and exchange inevitably result in the growth of capitalism, with its exploitation taking place within the bounds of individual freedom and formal equality—the original sins of capitalism. Marx's proposed solution was not a return to the Garden of Eden of small-scale commodity production and exchange. Instead, he argued for the exploited to take collective ownership of the means of production created by capitalism and move beyond formal equality between autonomous property-owning individuals and propertyless individuals who only own their own labor power. For Marx, the goal was a society based on collective voluntary association guided by the principle of "from each according to their abilities, to each according to their needs"—a radical *negation* of individual autonomy and formal equality. Thus punk's DIY discourse, which in practical terms sought to voluntarily restrain small-scale commodity production from turning into full-blown capitalist production, in some ways replayed nineteenth-century objections from anarchists to Marx's critique of capitalism.

Returning to the late twentieth century, Barry Shank connects punk DIY entrepreneurship with the neoliberal ideology and material reality taking hold in the United States and Britain during the 1980s and 1990s—notably the same time period and geographical locations in which underground punk developed:

> With creative destruction and insistent self-determination as core values, punk promised something very similar to the neoliberal belief in individualist freedom and entrepreneurial possibility, where the meritorious would be the victors. Although it may be surprising to think of it in this way, DIY was wholly in line with neoliberal assumptions.... DIY insisted that anyone could become a record producer, label owner, booking agent, critic, or publisher. This belief was a source of tremendous productive freedom within punk.... While many of punk's practitioners voiced an anticapitalist, or at least an anticorporate, rhetoric, the material base of the form did not escape the discipline of the market.[60]

Underground punk and neoliberalism are worlds apart politically, but ideologically they both trumpeted the autonomous individual as the unit of economic liberation and heralded creative entrepreneurial activity. Thus while underground punk opposed consumption as a mind-numbing activity performed by spectators without agency,[61] it still operated within capitalist commodity exchange and maintained continuity with bourgeois philosophy since the Enlightenment that privileges individual autonomy over collective liberatory strategies and practices. Moreover, in the new millennium DIY itself has been increasingly appropriated by both the music industry and hipster culture. The latter has adopted many of the practices of punk—such as shows in warehouses without sound permits or liquor licenses—but without the rebelliousness and certainly without punk's political convictions. In regard to the music industry, digital downloads and social media mean that major record labels and profitable concert venues shift the work and cost of promotion and recording onto musicians, waiting for bands to prove they can generate a sizable audience themselves before they are offered record contracts.[62]

Others noted that while punk could effectively shock mainstream sensibilities in the late 1970s, by the 1990s times had changed. As Bryan Alft put it in a 1998 *HeartattaCk* issue devoted to the state of DIY:

> Punk rock is old. It is simply a fact that after 20 years, any subculture becomes established to a point where it changes from new and contrary to a relatively accepted entity. I am not saying that punk rock cannot still be relevant and make a positive mark on this planet, but the shock value is more or less gone. Unfortunately, the popular culture "punk" of the nineties has made everything punk rock-related even more safe and digestible—as well as saleable. Tons of new kids discovered punk rock in these last few years. Hopefully, some will stay and discover the side of punk that has some value—the world that revolves around the Do-It-Yourself ethic and has no interest in Green Day or Earth Crisis.[63]

Alft here points to the power of a new cultural expression in its first incarnation to provoke extreme responses—positive and negative—that diminishes as that cultural expression becomes more familiar over time, and indeed, the history of music in the twentieth century is littered with examples of this dynamic.

Paul Chan, however, situates the conundrum as not mainly about punk itself. Instead, Chan draws attention to the ways in which punk failed to cohere a new strategy to confront changing conditions:

> Will the simple strategy of "kick the leper out of the village" suffice, when even the shared values and beliefs historically espoused by the Punk community are being packaged and sold for the consumption of anyone who craves a taste of the alternative anti-authoritarianism then and now? Obviously the answer is no.... But this speaks less of the ineffectiveness of the strategy, and more about its fundamental anachronisms. Things have drastically changed since punk's first incarnation in the late 70's. And the seeming lack of discussion about those societal changes (the emergence of multi-national capitalism, the collapse of alternative world-views such as communism, the debates concerning multi-culturalism, etc.) in relation to punk necessarily antiquates [punk's] strategies in confronting and combating powers which the community deems undesirable.[64]

With so many within punk fixated on the sin of selling out in the mid-1990s, others questioned this very fixation when what seemed far more important were the societal questions, some of which Chan mentions, that political punk addressed. For the all-women feminist hardcore band Spitboy, the debate over DIY seemed trite in comparison to its goal of confronting patriarchy inside and outside of the punk scene. Moreover, having experienced firsthand the imperfections, to put it mildly, of underground punk when it came to extending egalitarianism to women, the band considered adherence to DIY to be a far less accurate gauge of integrity than attitudes and behaviors towards women. As Michelle Gonzales explains, Spitboy continued to listen to Nirvana while touring DIY-style in their beat-up van, "choosing to somewhat ignore the major-label controversy, choosing to allow our taste in music to move forward with the times."[65] Kirsten Patches of Naked Aggression put her discomfort with the "gossipy" DIY debate bluntly when asked by *Punk Planet* to comment on punk bands on major labels: "This whole issue is another one of those self-righteous, finger pointing, who's holier than thou crusades. I really don't give a flying fuck about what band signs to what label or who distributes through what." She further admonished that, "There are many serious and urgent problems to be active and concerned about. Such as war, hunger, exploitation of workers, racism, sexism, the list goes on and on."[66] Less concerned with politics, NOFX would simply mock the ways in which the DIY debate constructed a rigid set of rules in a subculture supposedly about breaking all the rules in a song titled "I'm Telling Tim" that humorously referenced Tim Yohannan's role in enforcing these rules.[67]

Finally, it is worth noting that none of the underground political punk bands on which this study has focused attempted to bring their radical politics into the mainstream. Given the vitriolic level of debate on this question, such a strategy seems never to have even been considered, demonstrating the devotion to DIY within underground political punk. It was not until the new millennium that Anti-Flag, who played music more rooted in pop-punk but was a part of the political wing of 1990s punk, took this approach first by releasing albums on Fat Wreck Chords and performing at the Warped Tour and larger, less DIY venues and subsequently by signing to RCA Records, a major label. While all this meant Anti-Flag lost a more direct connection to its audiences, its political message and musical style did not change. On a personal note, when organizing antiwar protests in the early 2000s, of all the concert audiences I passed out flyers to, I always found Anti-Flag's audiences the most receptive and willing to get involved.[68]

Part 2

The Introspective Aggression of So-Cal Punk

While the rise of the alternative culture industry in the 1990s and its recognition of punk as a marketable product were parts of the reason pop-punk and So-Cal punk reached into the mainstream, the ability of these two styles to speak to the sentiments of the suburban youth who embraced them is surely also responsible for their newfound popularity. In what follows, I address just what made So-Cal punk resonate with a generation confronting the rise of neoliberalism and the digital era and the social instability these resulted in; the culture wars in which values associated with 1960s counterculture came under attack; and difficulties figuring out how to rebel without the certitude of an easy target (Reagan, Thatcher) or a viable alternative. While So-Cal punk is less overtly political than the music discussed in previous chapters, its very lack of overt certitude and tempering of aggression with introspection, together with its deployment of wit, rendered it capable of speaking to the complexities of what David Harvey dubbed the condition of postmodernity.[69] As always, lyrics alone only account for a portion of this capability. The musical style of So-Cal punk— those sentimental-sounding octave chords, melodic singing that still stays within the parameters of punk, addition of vocal harmonies and lead guitar parts to otherwise hardcore punk, intricate, precisely palm-muted guitar rhythms, and more polished recordings—is what provides it with an angry eloquence capable of addressing the complexities of postmodernity.

While pop-punk also captured some of this sentiment, it seems a bit too far afield from hardcore punk stylistically and too much of a mainstream success to merit much more attention here, given the focus of this book. Briefly, the rise of pop-punk was centered in Berkeley, California, with Lookout! Records and the venue 924 Gilman Street serving as the chief means of its dissemination on record and site of live performances, respectively. Pop-punk bands drew on the mostly three-chord, major-mode diatonicism prevalent in 1970s New York bands such as the Ramones, even copied their leather-jacket clad dress, and composed songs in verse-chorus formats, complete with catchy chorus vocal hooks familiar to all pop-rock. With a few exceptions, pop-punk bands' lyrics and posture eschewed the manifesto quality of hardcore, the spectacle of late-1970s British punk, and radical politics in favor of teenage-oriented themes such as social alienation, romantic relationships, and punk-rock-styled goofy behavior. The more easily palatable music and lyrics of pop-punk thus put it in a position to take advantage of the rise of alternative culture, which Green Day did when they moved beyond the underground pop-punk scene in Berkeley from which they came and signed to Reprise Records in 1994. Between Green Day continuing its career, and even taking a more political turn from the time of the George W. Bush administration on, and a number of other pop-punk bands entering the musical mainstream, pop-punk has had a firm place within American youth culture since the mid-1990s.[70]

So-Cal punk, on the other hand, never achieved quite that level of commercial success. The Offspring, something of a combination of So-Cal and pop-punk, along with Bad Religion, are the foremost stylistically So-Cal punk bands to achieve considerable commercial success on the roster of major record labels. Most other So-Cal punk bands operated just under the radar of the majors, but achieved substantial record sales on what O'Connor calls commercial punk labels, with NOFX's 1994 *Punk in Drublic* album eventually going gold.[71] As its moniker suggests, So-Cal punk's origins were in Los Angeles—more specifically its suburbs. In the Reagan era, these suburbs were an important bulwark of a right-wing resurgence demanding obedience to the guardians of the traditional family and moral order, along with the looming threat of nuclear war. The youth who were repulsed by this right-wing resurgence found one outlet in the abrasive sounds and raw anger of hardcore punk, which, as MacLeod's monograph and the documentary *American Hardcore* demonstrate, found fertile ground in that very suburban landscape surrounding L.A.[72]

But in the 1990s, youth frustrations with the idiocy of suburban life took on new dimensions. Traditional morality, Christian fundamentalism, and far Right politics were certainly still present, but teenagers were equally contending with the ramifications of 1960s counterculture among their parents, who may have been feminists or antiwar protesters and raised their children to question authority but failed to provide answers. Moreover, while the threat of nuclear devastation receded to the background after the Cold War was over, the new conundrums 1990s youth confronted were less cataclysmic but more confusing. The us-versus-them rhetoric that proved effective in 1980s hardcore would no longer suffice amid existential agonizing over what to do in a world with so many uncertainties about the future.

In this context, Bad Religion provided a means to musically examine rather than just express ire at these dilemmas. The band, whose members hailed from the L.A. suburbs, had been part of the early-1980s hardcore scene. After a hiatus during the mid-1980s, Bad Religion released *Suffer* in 1988, an album which modeled a new approach to making punk music. Fat Mike describes the effect of this sea change in punk style the first time he listened to the album while on tour in Europe, when the band the Yeastie Girlz played it for him:

> They dropped the cassette into the stereo and basically changed my life over the course of the ensuing 26 minutes and 14 seconds.... It was the best thing I'd ever heard. It was a style of melodic punk rock that walked the perfect line between pop and hardcore. I listened to the tape ten times that night. I thought that if I tried, maybe I could come close to writing something almost as good.[73]

While most songs on *Suffer* retained the fast tempos and blaring riffs of 1980s hardcore, singer Greg Graffin delivered his vocals with melody and a lack of timbral distortion, rendering the lyrics more audible than most punk, though the rapidity of vocal delivery hinders this audibility while conveying the urgency intrinsic to punk. Vocal harmonies, which came to be called "oozin aahhs" after the syllables with which they were delivered, were often added during choruses. The recording quality was far more clear and polished than most punk without quite reaching the standards of radio-friendly pop. Finally, Bad Religion frequently offered a fast-moving riff without vocals and then slowed down the harmonic motion of power chords when Graffin's vocals entered, thus turning a riff into a power-chord progression. The song "Do What You Want" captures these qualities, from the vocal harmonies that enter during the chorus to the way in which the power chords of the riff that precedes each verse are doubled in duration for the verses (see figure 5.1), while maintaining hardcore credibility by virtue of its tempo and short length of about one minute. Fittingly, the term "melodic hardcore" was the moniker first used to describe this innovative punk style.

Figure 5.1 Bad Religion, root motion in "Do What You Want"

Figure 5.2 Pennywise, "Dying to Know," verse riff

Two more elements became crucial markers of So-Cal punk style. First was the use of precise palm-muting by the guitars in alternation with openly strummed power chords, which created intricate combinations of trebly accents and driving, bass-heavy rumbles. Pennywise were the preeminent practitioners of this approach to palm-muting, as can be heard on riffs in their songs "Dying to Know" and "Perfect People," transcribed in figures 5.2 and 5.3, respectively. The latter song uses a palm-muted rhythm ubiquitous in So-Cal punk.

Second is the addition of lead guitar parts or contrapuntal lines—significant given that most punk music up to that point made no distinction between rhythm and lead guitar, with the guitar(s) and bass all playing the same riff. Lead guitar parts and counterpoint lines in So-Cal punk usually occur over power-chord progressions rather than riffs, as the latter are too fast and declarative to allow room for an additional melodic line. Thus, while Bad Religion rarely deployed lead guitar parts on *Suffer*, it

Figure 5.3 Pennywise, "Perfect People," verse riff (during second half of verse)

Figure 5.4 Octave-chord lead guitar part and chord root motion preceding and during the verses of NOFX, "Stickin' in My Eye"

opened the musical space necessary for their subsequent appearance by using power-chord progressions. Unlike in heavy metal, So-Cal punk usually delivered lead guitar parts not with single notes but with octave chords, in which the index finger holds down the A string while simultaneously silencing the D string and the ring finger holds down the G string two frets higher, thus making an octave. This makes for a lead guitar sound more akin to a power chord and too cumbersome to be played with the rapid virtuosity of heavy metal lead guitar parts, and, as will be explained later, creates a timbre crucial to the sentiments of So-Cal punk. NOFX's music exemplifies the use of octave-chord lead guitar parts and counterpoint, as demonstrated on "Stickin' in my Eye" and "You're Bleeding," respectively (see figures 5.4 and 5.5). Both have the effect of implying major or minor chords rather than simply thirdless power chords, and "You're Bleeding" showcases the possibilities for creating chromatic lines over a diatonic chord progression through octave-chord counterpoint.[74]

While octave chords, precise palm-muting, melodious vocals over hardcore riffs, vocal harmonies, and power-chord progressions had been introduced to punk prior to *Suffer*, So-Cal punk brought these techniques together and rendered them with its new ethos to signify a stylistic innovation. This new sound symbolized a more existential approach to punk that shrouded hardcore aggression in an introspective

Figure 5.5 Octave-chord counterpoint line and chord root motion during verses of NOFX, "You're Bleeding"

deluge often more intent on asking questions than providing clear-cut answers, or, alternatively, as in many NOFX songs, using humor to point out glaring contradictions in the social fabric or sometimes just to celebrate having fun. Whether it was with Fat Mike's wit or Greg Graffin's prolific vocabulary—he earned a PhD in zoology from Cornell University—So-Cal punk offered commentary with less certitude and more nuance than most prior punk. One song whose lyrics, by Brett Gurewitz, capture So-Cal punk's probing of the condition of postmodernity is Bad Religion's "21st Century (Digital Boy)," which includes following lines in its chorus:

> I don't know how to live but I got a lot of toys
> My daddy is a lazy middle-class intellectual
> My mommy's on Valium, she's so ineffectual
> Ain't life a mystery?[75]

Aside from the more existential approach, striking this song's lyrics is how a number of contradictory social maladies are brought together, from napalm fire to valium addiction to the spiritual emptiness of consumption in the digital era, that mires the observer in mystery instead of identifying clear-cut enemies. With the father figure in this song a "lazy middle-class intellectual" rather than a domineering authority figure demanding obedience, it would make little sense to yell or scream the lyrics. Likewise, while in the 1980s the technology that challenged humanity's existence was the nuclear bomb, here the digital toys that distract us demand from punk a different kind of confrontation. So-Cal punk style provided the sonic means by which to interrogate these postmodern conditions that defined the idiocy of suburban life.

The melodic vocals signified this need for introspection without entirely excising the anger required to guide that introspection if it were to facilitate rebellion. Vocal harmonies during choruses buttressed So-Cal punk with the gravitas of intense contemplation rather than the raw visceral power usually associated with punk. Intricate rhythms on the guitar rendered with intense palm-muting provided a different kind of intensity—brought about by precision and technique—to the introspection. Finally, the octave chord tempered punk's aggression with a sensitivity and sentimentality by virtue of its timbre. The combination of the bass-heavy, dark but soft sound of the nickel-wound A string and the more piercing, trebly timbre of the unwound G string of the guitar, rendered with full distortion, produced a seemingly ethereal yet simultaneously powerful effect (it is, after all, a power chord without the fifth). This quality is made all the more clear by the octave chord's association, and possible beginnings in, emo, short for emotional hardcore, a style that became prominent in Washington, DC, as hardcore bands rejected the masculinity and violence that embroiled that city's hardcore scene by the mid-1980s. In these ways, So-Cal punk could sonically enunciate a social critique that embraced emotional angst, despondency, intellectual contemplation, and wit along with anger, all of which were necessary for punk to come to terms with the social contradictions of the 1990s. To further elucidate the musical tactics of So-Cal punk, I turn now to an analysis of NOFX's *The Decline*.

The Idiocy of Suburban Life in the Midst of Social Decline

Hailing from Los Angeles and forming as a band in 1983, NOFX witnessed the final flowering of hardcore's initial incarnation and survived the gang violence that embroiled the L.A. hardcore scene in the 1980s. Wading through the stylistic diffusion of late-1980s punk, NOFX arrived at its signature sound after Bad Religion's *Suffer*, releasing albums on Epitaph Records beginning in 1989 with *S&M Airlines*. Its musicianship continued to improve and its style cohered as the years went on. Deciding not to sign to a major label, NOFX nevertheless became one of the most popular So-Cal punk bands, with its 1994 *Punk in Drublic* album—perhaps the apex of its stylistic development—eventually going gold. Unlike Bad Religion, NOFX often employed humor, wit, and that punk rock sneer of seeking to offend anyone and everything held sacred in society. Within and aside from this penchant for parody was often a sophisticated critique of middle-class American values and culture, which at times penetrated into the depths of despondency and tore the veil off of American triumphalism.[76]

For our purposes, *The Decline*, released in 1999, provides the most relevant example of NOFX's iteration of So-Cal punk and its social critique. As an eighteen-minute epic through-composed into different sections rather than a verse-chorus form, *The Decline* is structurally more akin to progressive rock, but its aggressive hardcore sounds and posture make clear its place within punk. Its lyrics, divided into various stories, declarations, and pessimistic commentary, are unified in their exploration of the idiocy of suburban life amid the decline of American civilization. In personalized accounts of gun violence perpetuated by NRA culture or prison sentences for recreational marijuana use; critiques of fundamentalist Christianity, the mind-numbing effects of consumer culture, the rise of debt, and addiction to antidepressants and pain pills; and tirades against the stupidity of the American populace, *The Decline* traverses the trail of "a losing battle" in which "the human existence is failing," resigning at the end to "admit defeat" and "live in decline." It thus constitutes a counter-narrative to the triumphant celebrations of liberal democratic capitalism so prevalent in the reigning discourse of the 1990s United States.

The realities of liberal democratic capitalist triumph were felt most painfully and palpably in the Third World countries undergoing IMF-dictated structural adjustment programs, which plunged their populations into dire poverty; in the mass migrations of rural populations to urban slums in the Third World and of people from the Third World to the United States and Europe in desperate search of employment; in the boom in the US prison population that targeted Black men in particular when, following deindustrialization, capitalism had little use for their labor and, after the end of official segregation and Jim Crow, the US power structure needed an officially color-blind enforcement of white supremacy; and in the war and subsequent sanctions that led to the deaths of hundreds of thousands of Iraqis in the 1990s.[77] While the malaise and maladies of the American middle class by no means compared to these experiences of poverty, dislocation, imprisonment, and violence, they were nevertheless an important indicator of the profound discontent and social dysfunction among those who were supposed to be beneficiaries of American empire. NOFX's *The Decline* is thus an important document of this discontent and dysfunction, and its deployment of the expressive devices of So-Cal punk constitutes a crucial avenue through which to understand the contours of social decline.

Before delving into nuances of musical expression, an explanation of the overall structure of *The Decline* is in order. *The Decline* is divided into different sections marked by changes in texture, rhythmic groove, musical style, and (rare for punk) key center. It follows a large-scale tonal plan, starting in A minor, frequently using F major as a related key, moving to E major during some middle sections, and ultimately landing on E minor for the over three minutes of outro that end *The Decline* in pessimism. The lengthy form outline in table 5.1 labels the different sections of *The Decline*, demarcates them by their musical tactics, and offers a starting point for connecting these musical tactics with the lyrics they enunciate.

In order to understand musical meaning in *The Decline*, perhaps the most helpful place to begin is at its end. The outro, represented in figure 5.6, repeats a trombone riff, which serves as an emblem of social decline, over music definitively in E minor by virtue of emphasis on the flatted sixth scale degree, C—brought out by semitone motion to the fifth scale degree—and the cadential ending in the guitar and bass that descends from the minor third, G, to F♯ before landing back on E to begin the phrase anew. The very appearance of a trombone in punk—though not entirely

Table 5.1 Form outline for NOFX's The Decline. Lyrics by Michael Burkett, reproduced with permission

Time	Section/Tempo	Music	Lyrics
0:00	Intro KSA = 364	Power chords on the bass followed by a hardcore punk riff played by the whole band; all in A minor	
0:38	A, stanza 1 KSA = 424	Fast hardcore punk rhythm with strident but melodic vocals over a nonrepetitious chord progression that ends with a chromatic descent	Where are all these stupid people from? And how did they get to be so dumb? Bred on purple mountain range Feed amber waves of grains To lesser human beings, zero feelings
1:00	A, bridge KSA = 424	Octave-chord lead guitar over a repeated A-minor chord with an ominous quality	
1:13	A, stanza 2 KSA = 424	Octave-lead guitar part continues, first over A and F chords and then over a transitional chord progression	Blame it on human nature, man's destiny Blame it on the greediocracy Fear of God, The fear of change, The fear of truth
1:31	A, stanza 3 KSA = 424	Repeated C–F–A♭ chord progression	Add the Bill of Rights, subtract the wrongs There's no answers Memorize and sing star spangled songs When the questions
1:48	A, conclusion BPM = 190, then KSA = 420	Palm-muted chords in C major, slower tempo, 12/8 meter, long-short subdivision, and a less angry vocal tone subduing the previous musical stridency	Aren't ever asked Is anybody learning from the past? We're living in united stagnation
1:53	Transition KSA = 420	Back to A minor and to a hardcore rhythm and tempo; alternation of new octave-chord riff with palm-muted guitars and tom-tom drumbeat	
2:02	B, stanza 1 KSA = 420	Mostly nonrepetitive chord progression; more sentimental sound achieved by less strident and occasionally harmonized lead vocals	Father what have I done? I took that .22 A gift to me from you To bed with me each night Kept it clean Polished it well Cherished every cartridge, every shell

Table 5.1 *Continued*

Time	Section/Tempo	Music	Lyrics
2:25	B, stanza 2 KSA = 420	A–F–G–A chord progression repeated twice with oozin aahh vocal harmonies the second time; drums move to the ting of the ride cymbal, creating a more ominous quality	Down, by the creek, under brush, under dirt There's a carcass of my second kill Down, by the park, under stone, under pine There's a carcass of my brother William
2:45	B, stanza 3 KSA = 420	The bass's driving, active part and the move from A minor to F major make this the moment of emotional release to come to terms with the tragedy in the lyrics	Brother where have you gone to? I swear, I never thought I could I see so many times They told me to shoot straight Don't pull the trigger, squeeze That will insure a kill A kill is what you want A kill is why we breed
3:03	C, instrumental introduction KSA = 300	The first respite from aggressive hardcore punk; fast-moving bass part alternating between a D pedal point in the high register and a chromatic descent in the low register, punctuated by drums and guitars at the end of each repetition	
3:19	C, stanza 1 KSA = 300	Drums enter with a slower (KSA = 300) but energetic punk rock beat and guitars enter with subdued octave-chord counterpoint; slurred, slow-moving, harmonized vocals	The Christians love their guns The church and NRA Pray for their salvations Prey on the lower faiths
3:32	C, stanza 2 KSA = 300	The band moves up a step with the pedal point going from D to E; vocals take on a more strident quality with faster rhythmic delivery	The story book's been read And every line believed Curriculum's been set Logic is a threat Reason searched and seized
3:45	Silence		
3:46	Interlude ♩ = 77	Melody on the bass in E major; reggae drums and guitar	
4:10	D, ritornello KSA = 424	E Major; fast hardcore punk rhythm with the drums using a double-bass pedal; an octave-chord lead guitar part over a chord progression	

(continued)

Table 5.1 *Continued*

Time	Section/ Tempo	Music	Lyrics
4:20	D, stanza 1 KSA = 424	Continues in E major; the music alternates between quieter guitars playing a chord progression with descending root motion and louder, blaring hardcore	Jerry spent some time in Michigan A twenty year vacation after all he had a dime A dime is worth a lot more in Detroit A dime in California A twenty dollar fine
4:39	D, ritornello	Similar to 4:39	
4:49	D, stanza 2 KSA = 424	More or less the same as at 4:20	Jerry only stayed a couple months It's hard to enjoy yourself while bleeding out the ass Asphyxiation is simple and fast It beats seventeen fun years of being someone's bitch
5:08	D, stanza 3 KSA = 424	Melodically descending nonrepetitive chord progression with octave-chords and vocal harmonies added	Don't think (Stay) Drink your wine (Home) Watch the fire burn (Be) His problems not mine (Safe) Just be that model citizen
5:27	Transition KSA = 424	Guitar riff generated from Ritornello D octave-chord part	
5:49	E, stanza 1 KSA = 212	Music based on Interlude 1 (reggae feel in E major); vocals sung by El Hefe with additional harmonies	I wish I had a schilling For every senseless killing I'd buy a government America's for sale And you can get a good deal on it And make a healthy profit
6:13	E, stanza 2 KSA = 212	Fat Mike returns to vocals; stanza 2 begins with palm-muted guitar; builds intensity by adding second guitar and with the drums moving to the tom-toms	Or maybe tear it apart You start with assumption That a million people are smart Smarter than one
6:29	E, conclusion KSA = 212	First entrance of trombone "decline" motif in E minor	
6:47	Transition ♪ = 220	Texture thins and then builds back up; breaks the typical duple division of punk by outlining rhythmic groups of 7–8–8–4	
7:17	F, intro	Only bass and vocals, recorded to sound from a distance	Serotonin's gone She gave up drifted away
7:26	F, stanza 1 ♩. = 170	Full band enters; vocals back to a normal volume; guitars are palm muted and lacking distortion; 12/8 meter with long-short subdivision; nonpunk, seemingly humorous music	Sara fled thought process gone She left her answering machine on The greeting left spoken sincere Messages no one will ever hear

Table 5.1 *Continued*

Time	Section/ Tempo	Music	Lyrics
7:48	F, stanza 2 ♩. = 170	Adds a lead guitar part played in single notes without distortion	Ten thousand messages a day A million more transmissions lay Victims of the laissez faire Ten thousand voices, a hundred guns A hundred decibels turns to one One bullet one empty head
8:08	F, conclusion KSA = 234	Distorted, non-palm-muted guitars; return to punk rhythm and tempo	Now with Serotonin gone
8:17	Transition KSA = 244	Descending power-chord riff from the end of section F, with lead-guitar alternating E and G♯ octave chords	
8:40	G, stanza 1 KSA = 244	Fast punk in an AB structure in which A is more subdued with an arpeggiated chord from the guitar, and B is more intense with distorted, strummed guitar chords and vocal harmonies	The man who used to speak performs a cute routine Feel a little patronized Don't feel bad. They found a way inside your head And you feel a bit misled It's not that they don't care
8:58	G, stanza 2 KSA = 244	Same as above	The television's put a thought inside your head Like a Barry Manilow jingle I'd like to teach the world to sing In perfect harmony A symphonic blank stare
9:13	G, conclusion KSA = 244	Repeats C to E chord motion punctuated by an E–D–C descent, under a vocal trade with the second singer yelling	It doesn't make you care (make you care) Not designed to make you care (make you care) They're betting you won't care (you won't care)
9:24	G, outro / transition KSA = 244	Guitar solo over nonrepetitive chord progression with an octave-chord counterpoint line	
9:38	Brief stop	Chord rings out and fades away	
9:43	H, intro ♩. = 114 / KSA = 684	Intensity raised with a fast-moving, virtuosic bass riff built from an E blues scale; the drums play a "two with three" subdivision (three hardcore duples within each beat of a 12/8 bar) while the guitars ring out one chord every bar	

(continued)

Table 5.1 *Continued*

Time	Section/ Tempo	Music	Lyrics
10:07	H, stanza 1 KSA = 472	Faster tempo, hardcore rhythm restores duple subdivision, and hardcore guitar riff under more intense vocals that verge on yelling	They'll place a wager on your greed a wager on your pride Why try to beat them when a million others tried?
10:16	H, stanza 2 KSA = 240, then KSA = 472	Two alternations between a slower punk rhythm that cuts the KSA in half and single notes ring out by the guitars, subduing the intensity for a despondent affect, with Eric Melvin yelling the lyrics, and then a return to the fast hardcore rhythm and blaring power chords with Fat Mike snarling the vocals	We are the whore Intellectually spayed We are the queer Dysfunctionally raised
10:32	H, outro KSA = 212	Second appearance of trombone "decline" motif	
10:49	Brief stop	Held E chord fading	
11:03	I, intro ♩ = 78	One guitar palm-mutes without distortion, eventually landing on G♯, with explosion sounds in the background	
11:33	I, intro' ♩ = 78	Drums enter with a reggae beat; bass plays a reggae-style "swell" effect, in E major with a twist at the end	
11:43	I, refrain 1 ♩ = 78	Same music as above; Fat Mike's vocal timbre is softer than normal, while Eric Melvin screams quietly in the background	One more pill to kill the pain One more pill to kill the pain One more pill to kill the pain Living through conformity
12:07	I, bridge ♩ = 78	Same music without vocals	
12:20	I, refrain 2 ♩ = 78	Same as I, refrain 1	One more prayer to keep me safe One more prayer to keep us warm One more prayer to keep us safe There's gonna be a better place
12:38	J, intro	The "safe" mood of I is interrupted by a series of accented guitar chords punctuated by hits on the crash cymbal	
12:47	J, stanza 1 KSA = 212	Major key (A or E tonal center); punk rhythmic feel with splashy cymbal	Lost the battle lost the war Lost the things worth living for Lost the will to win the fight One more pill to kill the pain
13:06	J, stanza 2 KSA = 212	Music intensified by palm-muting instead of open strumming from the guitars	The going gets tough the tough get debt Don't pay attention, pay the rent Next of kins pay for your sins A little faith should keep us safe

Table 5.1 *Continued*

Time	Section/ Tempo	Music	Lyrics
13:15	Transition	Punctuated accents on an A chord in a 3–3–3–3–2–2 rhythm	
13:17	K, intro KSA = 232	Minor key; octave-chord lead guitar part over one guitar palm muting and another guitar ringing out chords; punk rhythm continues	
13:36	K, stanza 1 KSA = 232	Vocals enter in a fragmented trade between Eric Melvin verging on screaming and Fat Mike distorting his voice in a sardonic yell; these vocals along with the fragmented lead guitar part give the music a frantic, anxious quality	Save us The human, existence Is failing resistance Essential the future Written off the odds are Astronomically against us Only moron and genius Would fight a losing battle Against the super ego When giving in is so damn comforting
13:57	K, stanza 2 KSA = 424	Drums and tempo switch to fast hardcore; nonrepetitive power-chord progression with an octave-chord counterpoint line; vocal trade ends and Fat Mike takes on a timbre both sardonic and despondent, which is occasionally harmonized	And so we go on with our lives We know the truth but prefer lies Lies are simple. Simple is bliss Why go against tradition when we can Admit defeat. Live in decline Be the victim of our own design With status quo built on suspect Why would anyone stick out their neck?
14:34	K, conclusion Varying tempo	Starts with palm-muted guitars hinting that a conclusion is near; the penultimate chords ring out, and the final chords are strummed without distortion and with the rest of the band going silent	Fellow members of club We've Got Ours I'd like to introduce you to our host He's got his and I've got mine Meet the decline
14:48	Transition KSA = 212	A single guitar palm mutes on C	
14:54	Outro KSA = 212	Trombone "decline" motif in E minor with the addition (and subtraction) of various layers, including octave-chord lead guitar part, vocals, keyboard, and chimes	
18:20	End	Faded to nothing	

out of the ordinary for NOFX, whose guitarist El Hefe plays trumpet in some of the band's songs—draws attention to the abnormality of its usage; it thus becomes a commanding musical voice when it is added to the typical punk band instrumentation. The trombone riff itself is an overall stepwise descent—albeit with octave displacement and a curve back up to D—that, in a minor key, encapsulates the pessimism with which *The Decline*'s lyrics end.[78]

Figure 5.6 transcribes the key elements of this decline motif, including the trombone riff, the chord roots, the octave-chord counterpoint, and the bass at its most active (heard most audibly in the conclusion to section E). The octave-chord counterpoint line offers a path out of pessimism when it reaches up to C, only to defer to despondency in the cadential movement from B to A with which it ends. Therein lies a palpable example of the octave chord's timbral elucidation of sensitivity and subjectivity as it cries out over the musical texture. Throughout the over three minutes of the outro, additional layers, including chimes, synthesizer, and guitarist Eric Melvin screaming the lyrics of section H's second stanza, are added and subtracted before the music finally fades to nothing. The minor-key melodic descent that blares out from the bell of the trombone at the conclusion of *The Decline* is far from the only signifier of social decline in this eighteen-minute punk epic, with numerous instances of

Figure 5.6 NOFX, *The Decline*, Decline motif

KSA=364 (♪)

Figure 5.7 NOFX, *The Decline*, intro, bass power chords

KSA=364 (♪)

[guitar & drum hits -   -]

[guitar & drum hits - - -   - -] [drum fill]

Figure 5.8 NOFX, *The Decline*, intro, hardcore riff

descending melodic motifs occurring along the way that foreshadow the pessimistic defeat heard in the outro.

The Decline's journey downhill to this valley of despair takes us along a range of musical experiences that lead to this inevitable conclusion, but offers moments of hope or at least refusal along the way. The sounds with which it opens (see figure 5.7)—the heaviness of power chords played *on the bass* accompanied only by drummer Erik Sandin keeping rapid time on the closed hi-hat—make clear the gravitas of what we are about to experience. Unlike much of NOFX's humor-driven repertoire, this is to be taken seriously. Following these power chords, the bass, soon to be joined by the full band, offers a riff that evokes the aggressive posture of 1980s hardcore (see figure 5.8). Moreover, both the bass power chords and this introductory riff demarcate the A minor territory within which *The Decline* begins, like the outro music prominently outlining motion from flatted sixth to fifth scale degree, and, in the riff, even (and unusually for punk) implying a major dominant chord to confirm the A-minor key with the G♯ and E harmony.

Following this introduction, section A keeps us in the realm of hardcore stridency, with Fat Mike's vocals entering with a sardonic tone that sums up the American populace with the questions, "Where are all these stupid people from? And how did they get to be so dumb?" and the description of "lesser human beings" with "zero feelings."

The fact that the music here (see figure 5.9), unlike in most punk, is a nonrepetitive chord progression tells us we are in for a punk epic which will take time to unfold, rather than a two-minute hardcore manifesto, and the chromatic descent from C down to A in the second half of the first stanza's chord progression is another melodic emblem of social decline.[79]

The bridge that follows this first stanza (see figure 5.10) further buttresses feelings of despair and danger with its ominous sounding octave-chord riff over an A-minor chord that refuses to budge until just before the second stanza. As in the outro, melodic motion up to C is forcibly brought down to A, confirming that the abyss humanity has fallen into cannot be climbed out of (here the rhythmic detail of playing C on the first pulse of the second bar and immediately moving back to A is significant).

In the transitional chord progression that ends the second stanza of section A, the timbre of the octave chords seems to bleed with an anguished sentimentality as Fat Mike's vocals confront the fears that grip the American populace in its state of decline. In the third stanza and conclusion of section A, when these vocals turn to ridicule the blind patriotism and unquestioning obedience that beget social stagnation, the music turns increasingly ironic, departing from hardcore punk to play a slower, long-short subdivision in a 12/8 meter and major key (see figure 5.11).

Figure 5.9 NOFX, *The Decline*, section A, stanza 1, chord progression root motion (0:38)

Figure 5.10 NOFX, *The Decline*, section A, bridge between stanza 1 and stanza 2 (1:00)

Figure 5.11 NOFX, *The Decline*, section A, conclusion (1:48)

Figure 5.12 NOFX, *The Decline*, transition from section A to section B (1:53)

Figure 5.13 NOFX, *The Decline*, section B, stanza 2, vocal harmonies (2:37)

The transition that brings us from section A to B (figure 5.12) brings us back into A minor by virtue of the chord progression that moves from A to E and the octave-chord riff emphasizing motion around the minor third. Its forward momentum is fragmented by the alternation of octave-chord riff, open chords, and the splash of the open hi-hat with palm-muted chords and tom-tom drums without cymbals.

Section B continues the hardcore aggression of the previous section but tempers it with the anguish of loss, as the lyrics, here a story told in the first person, decry the accidental shooting of the narrator's brother, made possible by an American gun culture that celebrates the thrill of the kill, and the sentimentality shown toward the instruments of death. Fat Mike's vocal tone is no longer sardonic, and the gravitas of the lyrics is buttressed by the vocal harmonies that accompany the second half of the second stanza (see figure 5.13)—the moment at which the thrill of hunting is replaced by the tragedy of taking a human life. Once again, A minor encloses us in an inescapable abyss of suffering by way of the Aeolian A–F–G–A (i–♭VI–♭VII–i) chord progression of the second stanza.

The third and final stanza, transcribed in figure 5.14, offers an emotional release to and reflection of the previous tragedy, moving to F major (which functions as a relative key to A minor in the context of *The Decline*). The moving bass line becomes a central voice in the musical texture here, able to carry the emotional weight of the moment.

Were *The Decline* to remain in the realm of blaring hardcore for its entire duration, besides risking musical monotony, it would not be able to address the breadth of social experiences it aims to. As shown in figure 5.15, section C offers the first respite from hardcore tempo and texture, slowing down to a punk rock groove with a thumping kick-drum. Here, intensity is created through a virtuosic bassline that jumps back and forth between a chromatic descent in its lower register and a pedal point in its upper

Figure 5.14 NOFX, *The Decline*, section B, stanza 3 (2:45)

Figure 5.15 NOFX, *The Decline*, section C, stanza 1 (3:19)

register, with subdued octave-chord counterpoint from the guitars. The move up a step for the second stanza—a familiar formula for increasing intensity at the end of pop and rock songs—offers a musical means to amplify the lyrical transition from a statement about the predatory nature of American Christianity to a frantic warning about the dire threat to reason posed by religious doctrine.

Following section C, a brief musical interlude furthers the respite from aggressive hardcore with reggae music—drenched in reverb and thus also suggesting dub—in E major. Since the late 1970s in England, reggae has served as a complementary musical mood to punk, played over the sound system in between bands at London punk shows, with British punk icons The Clash combining or contrasting reggae and punk in their "combat rock" from 1976 until their breakup in 1986.[80] Rancid, a band from Berkeley that rode the 1990s commercial popularity of punk to success, has continued that tradition with its own eclectic mix of pop-punk, reggae, ska, and hardcore. NOFX was no stranger to this tradition, using reggae on songs such as "Eat the Meak" and "Kill All the White Man," and in *The Decline* uses reggae as a musical release in between bouts of blaring hardcore.

Sections D through H continue the exposition of social decline through stories and commentary that play on two types of dramatic tension: between hope and resignation and between confronting reality and the euphoric delusion of ignorance and apathy. Section D plays to the latter dramatic tension, with the story in the lyrics in the first two stanzas about "Jerry" going to prison in Michigan for marijuana possession told alternately as a happy vacation (and, eventually, the escape of suicide) or a horrific prison experience. The delusion of a happy vacation is established musically

Figure 5.16 NOFX, *The Decline*, section D, ritornello (4:10)

Figure 5.17 NOFX, *The Decline*, section D, stepwise descent of bass during stanzas (4:20)

by continuing in the E-major key of the prior reggae interlude, rendered especially upbeat in the music of the introduction and bridge for section D—what I call section D's ritornello (transcribed in figure 5.16).

The dramatic tension in the lyrics is brought out in the first two stanzas by alternating between subdued guitars and vocals for the first and third lines and blaringly loud distortion and a more snarled vocal timbre for the second and fourth lines. Within the E-major euphoria, however, is the suggestion of social decline made by the stepwise descent of the bass (see figure 5.17). Ultimately the sarcasm of the third stanza, which offers the false solution of "Stay . . . Home . . . Be . . . Safe," proves that any attempt to seek out the safety of apathy and acquiescence is doomed to fail.

Section E plays on the dramatic tension between hope and resignation. Its first stanza cynically identifies the corporate corruption implicit in American politics ("America's for sale"). By using a reggae groove, it turns reggae not into a respite from the aggressive posture of hardcore but a means to sarcastically call attention to the illusion of escape. The second stanza of section E (figure 5.18), however, presents the first hint of hope and even faith in humanity, with the intensity of steadily palm-muted guitars providing forward momentum, and drummer Erik Sandin turning to a tom-tom driven beat that would be familiar to NOFX fans as signifying drive toward a conclusion (e.g., "Kill All the White Man"). Fat Mike's voice here takes on a declarative tone as he suggests the solution as being "maybe tear it [America] apart" and offers the hope "that a million people are smart, smarter than one." Yet this brief moment of optimism is met with the first appearance of the trombone "decline" motif, effectively canceling out hope.

KSA=212 (♪)

Drum Set

Begin Trombone
"Decline" motif
in E minor

Figure 5.18 NOFX, *The Decline*, section E, stanza 2 (6:13)

The transition between sections F and G (see figure 5.19) is perhaps the moment at which dramatic tension between hope and resignation reaches its apex, achieved not by any vocal enunciation of this tension but by playing on the contrast between the E-major key prominent in these middle sections of *The Decline* and the eventual E-minor ending already established by the previous appearance of the trombone "decline" motif. After Fat Mike finishes section F by marking the end of euphoria with the words "Now with Serotonin gone," guitars and bass play a power-chord riff definitively in E-minor, starting on the flatted sixth, C, and descending down to a resting point on E.

The melodic descent of this riff—another musical emblem of decline—is given dramatic emphasis by the syncopated arrivals of new power chords, punctuated by Erik Sandin's accents on the crash cymbal preceded by a kick-drum anacrusis. Yet after the first appearance of the descending riff, as the band rests on E, an octave-chord guitar

Figure 5.19 NOFX, *The Decline*, transition from section F to section G (8:17)

line enters with E for a bar followed by a syncopated anticipatory arrival on G# for the subsequent bar, brightening the sonic atmosphere by implying the key of E major. When this octave-chord line is played over the descending E-minor riff four times in a row, the effect is to juxtapose two diametrically opposed musical moods—hope and resignation—by the contradiction in key between the two melodic lines, made all the more potent by the G# appearing at the very moment the power-chord riff resigns itself to E in what, according to the internal logic of the power-chord riff, should be a tonic in E minor. This contradiction is made possible by the use of power chords for the riff, which, lacking a third, allow for an ambiguity of major or minor key.

Stanzas G and H, however, resolve this tension between hope and resignation definitively in favor of the latter. The lyrics of section G uncover the "symphonic blank stare" of millions of Americans "in perfect harmony" watching television programs "not designed to make you care." This critique of the apathy achieved when, to borrow a lyric from the band Propagandhi, we are "content to marinate in the plasma glow of the home entertainment prisons we commune before like dime-store shrines,"[81] is rendered with parody by the use of over-the-top, and thus ironic, euphoric background vocals. Section H, by contrast, eschews mockery in favor of gravitas followed by hardcore aggression. Its introduction (figure 5.20), a virtuosic bass riff with guitars alternating between E and D power chords allowed to ring out for dramatic effect and a drumbeat that marries a 12/8 meter with the fast kick-snare alternation of hardcore (effectively duple meter within the triple subdivision of each beat in 12/8), serves as an announcement that we are entering the terrain of seriousness and stridency.

Following this announcement, the drumbeat switches to a typical hardcore duple, and the blaring hardcore guitar riff (figure 5.21), along with Fat Mike's sardonic half-yelled, half-sung vocals, return to the aggressive hardcore posture of *The Decline*'s opening sections.

But having traversed the trail of social decline over ten minutes, the aggressive posture is now laden with a mounting pessimism. The lyrics here revoke the hint of hope heard in section E, declaring:

> They'll place a wager on your greed, a wager on your pride
> Why try to beat them when a million others tried?
> We are the whore, Intellectually spayed
> We are the queer, Dysfunctionally raised

Figure 5.20 NOFX, *The Decline*, section H, intro (9:43)

Figure 5.21 NOFX, *The Decline*, section H, stanza 1, riff (10:07)

These words call attention to the culpability of the American populace—not just those in power—in the process of social decline, as the greed and pride of this populace become a means by which to ensure their acquiescence. While the music of the first stanza of section H seethes with anger owing to its hardcore intensity, the second stanza alternates between resignation, with the bass accompanied by two octave-chord counterpoint lines, and blaring fast hardcore (see figure 5.22). The second appearance of the trombone "decline" motif that ends section H makes clear that resignation has triumphed.

Sections I through K serve as the final drive to the pessimistic conclusion. After a lone guitar wanderingly palm mutes single notes amid the sounds of explosions, section I returns to a reggae feel, with the swelling electronic effect of the bass providing a sonic analogue to the euphoria of "one more pill to kill the pain" and "one more prayer to keep us safe" (see figure 5.23). The bliss of prayers and pain pills is established by the E-major key, which had served a similar role in section D, and the bassline, of which its alternation between E and G♯ (with G♯ repeated by the guitar) is the same melodic line as that of the octave-chord line in the transition between sections F and

Figure 5.22 NOFX, *The Decline*, section H, stanza 2 (10:16)

G that had pointed toward optimism. In this way, what had been previously an emblem of hope is revealed as false by virtue of its use under lyrics calling attention to the falsity of escape. Once again, euphoria is set in tension with reality by virtue of Fat Mike calmly singing the lyrics while guitarist Eric Melvin screams them, but with Melvin's screams seemingly coming from a distance by virtue of the lower volume of these screams in the mix, as though the one confronting reality is treated as the voice of insanity to be muted.

The safe mood of section I is violently interrupted by distorted guitar chords accented by crash cymbal hits, though section J's first stanza continues the illusion of euphoria with major-key punk rock in which the lyrics admit defeat ("Lost the will to win the fight") but seek the sanctuary of prescription drugs ("One more pill to kill the pain"). Section J's second stanza continues the delusion ("The going gets tough the tough get debt") while simultaneously confronting the ramifications for subsequent generations ("Next of kins pay for your sins"). The severity of these ramifications is rendered sonically by austere palm-muted guitars rather than openly strummed chords.

As discussed previously, the potential catastrophe that 1980s hardcore confronted was nuclear war between the United States and the Soviet Union. Had the bombs been dropped, it would have been a quick death for many followed by the slow agony of nuclear fallout. The catastrophe that NOFX describes in *The Decline* reverses this sequence. It is a gradual process in which apathy and acquiescence in the face of mounting debt, a growing prison population, widespread addiction to pain medication and antidepressants, gun culture, comfort in Christianity's promise of an afterlife

Figure 5.23 NOFX, *The Decline*, section I, intro and stanza 1 (11:03)

for the obedient, and widespread stupidity in a culture of consumption drag us into an abyss from which we cannot climb out. This slowly developing catastrophe, however, still required a frantic sounding of the alarm. While *The Decline* as a whole serves this role, the beginning of section K intensifies this alarm. In the introduction and first stanza to section K, one guitar steadily palm mutes with intensity, while another provides an octave-chord lead guitar part emphasizing semitone motion and fragmented by its starts and stops, with both these guitar parts creating a nervous energy (see figure 5.24). Eric Melvin and Fat Mike's vocal trade-off, which splices each line of

Figure 5.24 NOFX, *The Decline*, section K, stanza 1 (beginning) (13:36)

lyrics between the two of them and sputters or screams the words out in brief bursts of rapid rhythmic delivery, amplifies the nervous energy of the guitars.

In the second and final stanzas of section K, the alarm has sounded but we have chosen to shut it off and sleep in. The turn from a slower punk rock beat to a fast hardcore beat with a KSA of 424 for the second stanza highlights the forward march of acquiescence. The tone of resignation is palpable in Fat Mike's voice, and the two octave-chord counterpoint lines confirm the key of A minor (again by implying a major dominant chord with the E and G♯ in the fourth bar), reaching C—the relative major of A minor—as their melodic apex, but always descending back down from it to signify that optimism cannot overcome decline. The use and foregrounding of not one but two octave-chord counterpoint lines for the final admission of defeat high-lights the timbral power of the octave chord to evoke anguish rather than just the anger promulgated by power chords (see figure 5.25).

While the lyrics of the concluding stanza of section K offer a final resignation to social decline, the music provides a synopsis of the tension between different keys that has set the stage for the two dramatic tensions—between confronting reality and the euphoric bliss of ignorance and apathy, and between hope and resignation—throughout *The Decline*. This concluding stanza is shown as a har-monic reduction in figure 5.26. It starts with palm-muted guitars, whose intense and intricate rhythms provide forward momentum and gravitas, in a IV–V–I ca-dential gesture landing on C. As the relative major of A minor and as the apex in the octave-chord counterpoint lines in the previous stanza, C provided a po-tential pathway out of pessimism. In this concluding stanza, however, the caden-tial arrival on C is soon canceled by motion back to A minor. The guitarists again employ the technique of moving their index finger one fret down to create a C power chord with the pitch B in the bass and then land on an A-minor chord that rings out as the band ceases its forward momentum. Fat Mike is left to sing the last lyrics accompanied only by one guitar, without distortion. This lone guitar

Figure 5.25 NOFX, *The Decline*, section K, stanza 2 (strumming patterns not notated) (13:57)

starts on an F major chord—recall that F has functioned as a closely related key to A minor earlier in *The Decline*—and then flattens the third to make an F-minor chord, effectively deflating any optimism F major might have offered. When Fat Mike finishes the last word—"decline"—a guitar steadily palm mutes on C in a drive toward the E-minor outro, thereby making C not a glimmer of hope but the VI of E minor. With this harmonic progression of the concluding stanza of lyrics evoking and resolving the harmonic and pitch contrasts heard throughout *The Decline*, any means of escaping the inevitability of social decline are foreclosed,

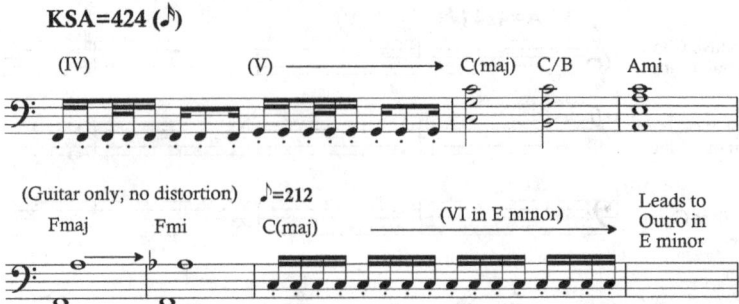

Figure 5.26 NOFX, *The Decline*, section K, concluding stanza (harmonic representation) (14:34)

and the trombone riff in E minor becomes the dystopia to which the previous musical drama was bound for.

Conclusion

Usually reserved for discussions of such music as late Beethoven string quartets and piano sonatas, the poetic language with which I have sought to describe and interpret NOFX's *The Decline* and other abrasive hardcore punk throughout this book may seem absurd to some. I offer two justifications. First, on a personal level, the visceral power of this music provokes that from me. Second, I believe that by approaching it in this way, by seeking meaning in musical sounds, even going so far as to give octave chords subjectivity, we can come to terms with what they tell us about the society we live in. Given that the 1990s went down in history as the moment of triumph of democratic capitalism, the dystopian critique of that very historical moment offered by *The Decline*, as well as by the extreme hardcore subgenre, offers a compelling counter-narrative that can be more audible if we understand its musical techniques and how they are assembled to sonically render the semantic meaning of song lyrics. In this way, punk music articulates an opposition to the triumphalism of American empire that will be missed if we only pay attention to the forms of opposition, such as protest movements, that are more traditionally used as the barometer for gauging social engagement and mass consciousness. In other words, yes, an octave-chord counterpoint line can tell us something important about the ways people think and feel.

NOFX's *The Decline* also provides an example of a kind of punk music that could achieve greater popularity within the cultural context of the 1990s. Grunge music and the alternative culture industry that sprung up in its wake opened the door for styles such as So-Cal punk to gain a broader hearing. NOFX was able to operate just below the mainstream music industry and slightly above the underground punk scene in part because its music had both melody and hardcore ferocity. Many in the punk scene, however, treated the DIY underground as an all-or-nothing proposition, excising not only those bands that signed to major labels, but also those, like NOFX, who became popular on large independent record labels. As an ideology of DIY authenticity was constructed to protect the punk scene from the alternative culture industry, the style of So-Cal punk became suspect. While DIY discourse is an important part of punk's history, as scholars we have an obligation to treat it critically and recognize that the more popular styles, such as So-Cal punk, are just as much a part of punk's history as are the more underground and overtly political styles.

Conclusion

From the battles to rid the punk scene of Nazi skinheads and the "dregs of the eighties," to the assertion of radical politics and construction of musical styles that served to enunciate these politics, to the efforts of women, Latinos, and gays to express their identities and struggles, to confronting the dilemma of mainstream commercial success, underground punk in the 1990s United States underwent a process of continual transformation. The impetus for this process of transformation was not just the larger changes in US society, but also and more importantly the conscious activity and agency of participants in the punk scene. It was the efforts of bands, zine writers, show organizers, and people taking part in the punk scene in various ways that reshaped 1990s punk as a culture of rebellion "behind enemy lines." These efforts created a coherent cultural force that rejected the triumphalism of an American empire emerging from its victory in the Cold War as the sole superpower, with its dominant position in globalized capitalism enforced by the most powerful military in human history.

While foregrounding the agency of people may seem an obvious point, scholarship on punk has too often concerned itself with finding some underlying essence to punk or interpreting it as a reaction to a particular historical conjuncture that, though flickering with intensity at its initiation, was bound to burn out. There is certainly an ethos to punk that has continued to inform its various incarnations over four decades as it has spread throughout the globe, but this ethos has continually been reshaped and molded to address the particular concerns of different punk scenes. And while punk scenes certainly responded to their historical moment, too much has been made of the spectacles of late-1970s punk rather than the sustained efforts of punk scenes around the world since then to engage with history on their own terms.

What this book has sought to do is provide a cultural history of a particular phase of US punk based on what anthropologist Clifford Geertz called "thick description" rather than overarching theoretical proclamations.[1] Certainly there are larger theoretical lessons to draw from my account, but I strove to take the theories put forward by punk musicians and zine writers, rather than academics, as the starting point for drawing these lessons and for narrating the thick description. My voice and the narrative I have constructed, of course, ultimately shaped this study, but hopefully with a respect for my subjects and in such a way that multiple interpretations are possible.

I consider musical style to be one crucial way to comprehend the agency of people and an artifact that can tell us something about the ways people think and feel. Understanding the timbres, riffs, drum beats, song structures, screams, yells, and vocal melodies of 1990s punk, especially when considered in contrast to prior and

Rebel Music in the Triumphant Empire. David Pearson, Oxford University Press (2021). © Oxford University Press.
DOI: 10.1093/oso/9780197534885.003.0007.

subsequent punk music, helps explain its particular enunciations of political rebellion, be they the dystopian sublime of extreme hardcore, the propaganda aesthetic of crust-punk/dis-core, or the feminist empowerment heard in women-led punk bands. By marrying empirical music analysis with hermeneutic discussion of musical meaning, my aim has been to highlight both the particular features that demarcate different punk styles and the expressive power of punk. Furthermore, this book should lay to rest notions of punk as merely simple, three-chord rock that any amateur can perform or as a postmodernist recycling of rock's past. What makes punk music fascinating are its continual innovations within an ongoing tradition and the expressive nuances of each of its many incarnations.

Finally, this book serves a more practical purpose. Musicians seeking to use their art to espouse radical politics and inspire their audiences to change their ways of thinking and acting confront many questions concerning the most effective strategies and tactics for doing so. These questions range from choices in musical style, production, dissemination, and performance, to how to interact with their audience and how to sustain their efforts in a society driven by commodity production and exchange. The rich legacy of how 1990s punk dealt with these dilemmas provides valuable lessons, positive and negative, that can be applied to answering those questions. To further that discussion, in what follows I attempt to provide a limited assessment of the successes and failures of 1990s US punk in constructing a culture of rebellion.

Punk Participation in Protest Movements

When the World Trade Organization (WTO), which negotiated trade agreements that greatly benefited US capitalist accumulation, met in Seattle beginning on 30 November 1999, it found itself the target of chaotic street protests involving tens of thousands of people. "Direct action" tactics blockaded streets and disrupted the WTO meetings, and various law enforcement agencies and the National Guard responded with repression, including copious use of pepper spray and tear gas and declarations of "no protest zones." The so-called Battle in Seattle marked the beginning of a series of powerful and militant protests against the institutions of global capitalism, such as the IMF and World Bank, which continued in the United States until repression and the post-9/11 political climate diminished their effectiveness. Often and somewhat erroneously referred to as the antiglobalization movement, these protests were no routine register of dissent, but chaotic affairs in which protesters aimed to disrupt or shut down meetings of global capitalist institutions in the face of police repression.

While punk music was by no means responsible for these protests, its impact on them is undeniable. As Corey Lyons of Aus-Rotten put it in an interview, "whenever you saw the news coverage of Seattle or Washington you always saw footage of the crusty kids and punk rockers getting arrested or getting sprayed with mace."[2] Indeed, those protesting as part of the anarchist black bloc, which played a driving role in direct action tactics and sometimes targeted corporate chain stores, such as McDonald's and Starbucks, for property destruction, often had developed their political consciousness in part by listening to punk as teenagers.[3] The willingness of some of these protesters to confront the violent repression of law enforcement was sometimes a result of the training—both political and physical—they received from the punk scene. The lyrics of bands such as Aus-Rotten and zines such as *Profane Existence* laid important foundations for critiquing the very institutions the protests against capitalist globalization were aimed at disrupting. Punk's history of confronting avowed white supremacists in its midst, as well as the practice of mosh pits, made participants in the punk scene no strangers to violence.

A personal anecdote provides an excellent example of the utility of a typical punk show experience as a means for protesting. At one of the antiglobalization protests I attended in Washington, DC, I witnessed a protester climb atop a five-foot-tall platform around a flag pole, rip down the American flag from the flag pole, and begin to burn it. Riot police then surrounded this protester as he stood atop the platform, pushing the surrounding crowd away in order to arrest the flag-burner. This protester responded by leaping off the platform, over the heads of the police, and into the arms of the surrounding crowd, where he quickly blended in and thereby escaped arrest. Anyone who has been to a punk show will recognize the above incident as strikingly similar to the act of stage diving from a five-foot-tall stage and into the welcoming arms of the audience.

The point of the above stories of punk and the protests against capitalist globalization is that they demonstrate the ways in which punk music served as a conduit to protest movements and organizations, and how the punk scene provided practical training in collective action, DIY activity, and (sometimes violent) confrontation, all of which were valuable skills for protest movements. While property destruction, direct action, and confrontations with riot police in Seattle and other similar protests are the more sensational examples, participants in the 1990s punk scene became involved in a variety of less historically visible but no less important efforts. Consistently mentioned in punk zines is the organization Food Not Bombs, which provided free vegetarian meals—using food that would have otherwise been thrown away—to homeless people, protesters, and anyone in need of a meal. Unlike most free meal programs, Food Not Bombs connected its activities to a critique of military spending and the fact that hunger today is not the result of a lack of food, but of a distribution system guided by profit rather than need. In many cities across the United States, punk scene participants were the driving force behind local Food Not Bombs chapters.[4]

Anti-Racist Action (ARA), discussed in chapter 1, was another organization marked by the involvement of punk scene participants. ARA's strength was in confronting manifestations of avowed white supremacists, often physically. One example of its efficacy was when, in 1995, ARA and others succeeded in shutting down a planned white-supremacist skinhead concert in St. Paul, Minnesota. Through intensive organizing efforts, including reaching out to residents of the neighborhood in which the concert was supposed to take place, four hundred protesters showed up as the concert was being set up. Fearing a violent confrontation, the mayor of St. Paul preemptively canceled the concert and had the police escort the white supremacists to safety as protesters threw rocks at them.[5] ARA's activities and the battles to expel Nazi skinheads from the punk scene have provided important lessons for combatting subsequent waves of organized white supremacists, including the "Alt Right" of the Trump era.

Punk participants also played active roles in the animal rights movement and in protests demanding the freedom of political prisoner Mumia Abu-Jamal. On the former, the 1999 Primate Freedom tour linked evening performances by Aus-Rotten and Anti-Product with daytime protest actions by antivivisection activists.[6] On the latter, Eric Goode of Aus-Rotten noted in a 2000 interview that "I didn't go down to the big Mumia demonstration in Philadelphia, but my friends who did came back and said there were all the punks with Aus-Rotten patches or Aus-Rotten shirts."[7]

Well before the "Battle in Seattle," participants in the punk scene were no strangers to confrontations with the authorities. On 16 November 1991, a legally permitted outdoor benefit concert featuring the bands Total Chaos, Dogma Mundista, and Resist and Exist at Hart Park in Orange County, California, was forcibly shut down by the police, who arrested and beat several of those in attendance, including performers. Proceeds from the concert were intended to benefit the struggle against the strip mining of Big Mountain, on Navajo land in Arizona.[8] This is only one of many punk shows shut down in a violent confrontation with police, though here the fact that the concert was connected to a protest movement is striking.

Another form of confrontation by punk participants was a willingness to publicly expose powerful officials. A salient example is when Madeleine Albright, then Secretary of State, was confronted at a CNN-broadcast town hall meeting in Columbus, Ohio, on 18 February 1998 by Jon Strange and other protesters. Strange, described as a "punk rock activist," disrupted the event by demanding Albright account for the hundreds of thousands of Iraqi civilians then dying due to US sanctions, as well as the recent US military bombings of Iraq. Strange's actions, buttressed by the stridency of punk sensibility, proved a media embarrassment for the Clinton administration.[9]

Outside of organized protests and public confrontations, there were likely many individual acts inspired by punk that remain mostly unrecorded in history. Martín Sorrondeguy recounted one striking individual act in my interview with him. Sorrondeguy described his surprise at the effect of a split record Los Crudos released with Manumission that was a benefit for the Western Shoshone Defense Project, an effort to prevent federal government encroachments on Native American land:

> When we did this record and put out all this information we were able to reach a whole new sector, and young people, because of that. It was weird because when we went out there [to Western Shoshone land], some kid was there because of that record. "Yeah, I got your record, I read about it, and I came out here." He was living in the middle of a desert. It was heavy. I think that's what punk did and it still does it.[10]

These and other stories like them point to the many ways that the political discourse and practical functioning of the punk scene provoked some people into political action and provided them with intellectual, organizational, and physical training crucial to their political activity. While it was only a minority of punk scene participants that went from music to political resistance, the 1990s political punk renaissance was nevertheless crucial to pushing this minority into action as well as to provoking a broader atmosphere of political debate. As Corey Lyons of Aus-Rotten summarized in an interview by *Profane Existence*, "If you look back at all the slogans thrown around in the punk scene, a lot of them can be traced back to the people sitting here right now. I think there are a lot of people, like Martín from Los Crudos or Jay Lee, that have really provoked a lot of reaction from their scene; they've challenged their scene to think."[11]

The Backlash

The tenacious minority within the punk scene who embraced radical politics and practiced what they preached faced a backlash as the 1990s wore on. Inside the punk scene, they were often criticized for being "PC"—politically correct—a label that continues to be used in the United States to admonish anyone who opposes white supremacy, patriarchy, and other oppressive institutions and social relations without engaging the content of their opposition. Those espousing radical politics had to constantly defend themselves against this labeling. For example, in a 1999 *HeartattaCk* article titled "ABC No Rio: A Volunteer's Story," Jen Hate devoted a substantial portion of her writing to refuting the notion that the venue ABC No Rio was run by "PC fascists."[12] In a 1998 interview by *Profane Existence*, Anti-Product explained the backlash they encountered for their politics. Vocalist Taína Asili described how while on tour, the band was heckled by people calling them "PC" or even yelling "fuck feminism." Guitarist and vocalist Chris Lawrence noted that aside from these taunts, "there are also times when people just leave because we talk about politics between our songs."[13]

The backlash against radical politics in punk during the later 1990s seems to be related to the rise of so-called drunk punk, also sometimes called "street punk," a subgenre that emphasized the drunk and disorderly side of punk and at times vociferously advocated being "apolitical." Interviewed in *MaximumRockNRoll* in 1994, the NYC drunk-punk band Public Nuisance distanced themselves from the political crust-punk band Nausea, whom they criticized for telling people what to do. Public Nuisance proclaimed that punk is about having fun, with beer being its common denominator.[14] In the mid-to-late 1990s, drunk-punk bands increasingly adorned the record reviews and advertisements in *MaximumRockNRoll*, most notably Blanks 77, the Quincy Punx, and the Casualties. The last band named their first 7" *40 Oz. Casualty* after their preferred source of inebriation, a forty-ounce bottle of cheap malt liquor. Drunk-punk style—its music and fashion—was summed up by a

MaximumRockNRoll reviewer who described Blanks 77's *Up the System* 10" as "Really simple formulaic snotty midtempo tunes from guys (and girl) with really spikey hair and lots of metal pyramids on their leather jacket[s]."[15]

Declarations against "PC" and the glorification of inebriation in drunk punk created antagonism against the radical political wing of punk and justified refusing to engage with its messages. The results of this growing antagonism are evident in the aforementioned interview with Anti-Product, in which *Profane Existence* asked, "Have you noticed that the punk scene in general has gotten a lot less politicized?" Chris Lawrence responded, "Yeah, especially back home where this anti-political thing seems to be growing really popular with all these 'street punk' bands."[16]

Crusties as the New Hippies

While involvement in protests and activism was an important achievement of 1990s punk, constructing an alternative lifestyle and attempting to live outside "the system" was considered equally as important. As Eric Goode of Aus-Rotten put it about being in a political punk band versus taking up a "normal" job, "I see this as being a part of an alternative lifestyle. . . . I would much rather live this lifestyle, play music, travel around and be happy doing what I am doing."[17] The content and efficacy of this alternative lifestyle construction, however, was increasingly questioned, especially when it mixed with or was subsumed in inebriation. In a 1996 *HeartattaCk* column, Felix von Havoc critiqued the focus on lifestyle change in political punk for its failure to transform the larger world:

> The level of political conviction in today's hardcore scene is very personal and life-style oriented. You may feel that by being a vegan, dumpster diving, squatter on the edge of society that you are living very close to your anti-capitalist and anti-system ideas. You may feel that boycotting products X, Y, and Z is doing major damage to the corporate system and bringing down major corporations to their knees. While you may have a lot of moral fiber and integrity, you are making virtually no difference in the big picture. Lifestyle-ism is a trap, a cop-out and a dead end. The lifestyle-ist winds up acting only to make themselves feel better and very little to change the world around them.[18]

When this lifestyle-ism became increasingly divorced from oppositional political activity, many of the ideologues of political punk felt compelled to demarcate themselves from the so-called crusties who embraced living outside of the system but mostly for the purpose of consuming drugs and alcohol. While the "crusty" moniker was derived from the musical style crust-punk, it was (and still is) used to describe people who dressed in dingy, mostly black, stitched-together clothes, were homeless or semi-homeless, often did not shower and grew their hair into tangled dreadlocks, and spent much of their time inebriated and/or high on drugs. Dan of *Profane*

Existence wrote in 1995 that those associated with the zine did not want to be called crusties because of "the well-earned negative reputation of those who consider themselves 'crusties'. That is, the people who stereotypically leach off the scene by pretending to be too broke to pay for shows or events, yet always seem to have money to be constantly drunk and stoned, and generally react violently/destructively when they don't get their way."[19]

The "well-earned negative reputation" of crusties had much to do with their sabotage of punk shows and gatherings intended to be centered on politics. In a 1996 *HeartattaCk* column, Adam described one such incident:

> Late June found this intrepid scribe in Eugene, Oregon for the **Resist and Exist Punk Gathering**. Hundreds of young people who've latched onto the music and aesthetics of the 80's anarcho punk movement flocked to Eugene for Resist and Exist. Unfortunately, it seems few of them are familiar with the sentiments of CRASS, Conflict, Subhumans, et al, because they turned the event into an utter disaster characterized by massive alcohol consumption and rampant alcoholism.[20]

Crusties in effect became the spoiled crop that crust-punk/dis-core reaped. They donned its fashion, made some of its lifestyle choices, and sometimes adopted a façade of its politics, but replaced its substance with substance abuse. As Felix von Havoc put it,

> [T]here is a good deal of difference between what was once called crust music and what is now called the "crustie" lifestyle. I'm sick of seeing good fast political hardcore and punk bands labeled as "crust." In the past few years I've grown particularly disenchanted with the crustie lifestyle and the kids who follow it . . . legions of crusties have opted for the romanticized alcoholic junkie loser stereotype. There is nothing rebellious about sitting around on the dole shooting dope, drinking malt liquor, and calling anyone who is doing anything constructive in the scene a "capitalist" or a "fascist." . . . Sorry folks, long matted hair, patched up dirty clothes, hard drugs, and being a social drop out make you only one thing, a HIPPIE.[21]

In punk discourse, "hippie" is one of the worst insults possible. Here, it points to how easily the emphasis, within 1990s political punk, on lifestyle change and dropping out of the system could be turned into a justification for and romanticization of the "alcoholic junkie loser."

Frustrations and Limitations

Given the backlash against political punk, and the growth of the "crusty" phenomenon, and the reality that only a minority of people within the punk scene took up and acted on radical politics, assessments of the effects of political punk by bands and in zines remained rather ambiguous. These assessments centered on the difference between a political movement and a cultural movement and the efficacy of projecting politics in the punk scene. On the one hand, writing in *HeartattaCk*, Bryan Alft, while recognizing how punk had introduced many people to radical ideas and motivated some to be involved in organizations such as Food Not Bombs and ARA, called attention to the limitations of a punk scene that sought to insulate itself from the outside world. Alft decried, "We are often so content to maintain an existence within a safe, closed community. We are very successful at communicating and debating ideas among ourselves, but we rarely reach people who are outside of the realm of punk."[22] On the other hand, the band In/Humanity pointed out the positive role of this insularity. Interviewed by *MaximumRockNRoll*, Paul of In/Humanity described punk as "a network that has to exist so the younger people coming up don't fall prey to racism, violence and don't believe in this shit that some people are trying to hand down." In the same interview, Chris of In/Humanity captured both the potential achievements of punk and its limitations, stating, "Punk rock won't change much in the world, but it will change people."[23] Both Alft and In/Humanity point to the difference between a cultural movement, whose main effect is on the people involved in it, versus a political movement, which has, as its aim, changing the world around it. Any fair assessment of punk should take this distinction into account.

Others questioned just how effective punk was in transforming the ideas and actions of participants in its cultural movement. Writing in *Punk Planet*, Jen Angel betrayed the fact that the minority within punk who took up its politics often subsequently left the punk scene: "I am frustrated by people who are politicized by punk and then once they gain their footing in the punk community they leave punk for elsewhere." She argued against this exodus, stating, "I don't think that trying to politicize a bunch of middle class white kids is pointless," and pointed out that the punk community provided a valuable space for such activity.[24] For Los Crudos, the resistance they encountered to their politics and assertion of Latino identity within punk was the very reason they felt compelled to continue their efforts, stating in a 1994 interview by *HeartattaCk*, "even within the punk scene I'd be really hesitant to say we're preaching to the converted because a lot of punks are fucked up."[25] But in the later 1990s, as the espousal of radical politics increasingly fell on deaf and drunk ears, many bands questioned the utility of their efforts. A reviewer of Aus-Rotten's 1998 . . . *And Now Back to Our Programming* LP observed that "Some of the lyrics seem really frustrated, like 'Is punk really doing shit??' and 'Are we helping anything?' "[26]

These questions concerning the efficacy of political enunciations and the limitations of a cultural movement were brought together in Felix von Havoc's discussion of a punk festival in Dayton, Ohio. The festival was organized as a benefit for Leonard Peltier, a Native American political prisoner in the United States, and featured some of the most prominent mid-1990s punk bands, such as Aus-Rotten, Los Crudos, Mankind?, and Code 13. Havoc wrote:

Martín of Crudos pointed out that if the event had been a march or rally in support of Leonard Peltier how many of the people at the show would have turned up? Maybe 1%? . . . From the positive perspective it shows the power of the ideas behind punk music that so many people showed up to lend their support to a man who has been wrongly imprisoned for most of our lifetimes. Realistically how many of these kids would have even heard of Leonard Peltier had it not been for punk bands and publications making his case known. . . . The sad truth though is that a lot of those in attendance probably still don't know who Peltier is. Most were there to party, period. The bands and the message seemed to take second place . . . it reminded me more of a crusty Woodstock than the Rock Against Racism shows of the 80's.[27]

The Visceral Impact Vibrates On

While the above ambiguous assessments point to real challenges in the efforts to make 1990s punk a culture of rebellion, its lasting impact on many is undeniable. As Taína Asili put it, "I'm still vegan, I'm still a feminist, I'm still working on issues around political prisoners and prisoner justice." She credited the punk scene with her initial exposure to these ideas and actions. Asili further commented that while she has continued performing music focused on social justice, she has yet (as of 2015) to find a powerful network like the punk scene for her current endeavors.[28]

While Asili left the punk scene, those I interviewed who still performed with their bands confirmed the palpable effect they had and continue to have. Describing Naked Aggression's recent tours, Kirsten Patches exclaimed,

The fact that we could still play shows twenty-five years later—that's crazy. We'll play a small town and fifty to a hundred people come out. That's shocking to me. We got invited to play Rebellion in the UK and we're pretty high up on the poster. I think we've had more of an effect than I realized. The fact that people still want to go to our shows and young kids are getting involved—that blows my mind. The hippie movement didn't even last that long goddammit. I guess [it's] because what we're singing about is still so relevant to what's happening to people now. I think we've had an impact because I'm still riding this wave. People are still asking for us.[29]

Al Pist noted similar experiences on The Pist's recent reunion performances:

It's been really nice especially doing these reunion shows when people come up to you and say, "Twenty years ago or ten years ago or five years ago when I first heard your stuff it really made me think about something a different way. I hadn't really thought about going vegetarian or vegan until I heard this song. It didn't hit me right away but the more I thought about it . . ."[30]

I believe that a part of what accounts for this continued impact of punk music on the way people think and live their lives has much to do with the visceral ways in which it connects to its listeners. The music becomes intrinsically connected to the ways people feel and to their sense of identity, and is intimately tied to memories of social experiences and camaraderie. For this reason, though probably most people touched by this music in the 1990s have little to do with punk today, something fundamental about their way of being in the world has been deeply impacted by punk music.

Punk in the New Millennium

Focusing on punk in the 1990s United States offered me an opportunity to delve into how a rebellious musical culture responded to a decade of transition from the end of the Cold War to the rise of globalization and the digital age. It might be surprising to some to find that punk was (and to some extent is) still disseminated on vinyl records and relied on an underground touring circuit made possible by letter writing and zines. In this way, punk pioneered an approach to networking now made easily possible with the Internet and with far less effort required. I have avoided discussing the impact of the Internet on punk, leaving it to other scholars, but a few words are in order.

For many veterans of the 1990s punk scene, the Internet seemed to negatively impact the underground network, since it did not require effort or dedication to communicate. In 2000, Adrienne Droogas complained that people no longer wrote letters, which had been common punk practice prior to online communication, and derided the Internet as "very impersonal."[31] In my interview with Kirsten Patches, she noted a shift in youth culture that broke down the personal communication so pivotal to the punk scene: "Now everyone can just be on Facebook on their handheld device. They don't have to communicate with other people. People are more captive to their own personal little fishbowl. The youth maybe don't look outward enough."[32] In these ways, the Internet substantially changed punk, diminishing the ethos of camaraderie created by the dedication and effort required to network by phone, mail, and personal connections.

The Internet was just one source of change for punk in the new millennium. Latino involvement in US punk has continued to grow since the 1990s, both numerically and geographically, and has opened up space for others from oppressed nationalities to participate more visibly and vocally in punk. The codification of musical style gave way to increasing musical fusions, between punk and nonpunk musical styles such as cumbia, and between different punk subgenres. A telling example of the latter is the political band Leftöver Crack, which fuses elements of crust-punk, extreme hardcore, So-Cal punk, pop-punk, and ska. Finally, the Bush administration in the 2000s provoked a broader array of punk bands, including the pop-punk band Green Day, to make oppositional politics far more central to their message.[33] These and other new developments would be fascinating avenues to pursue in future studies of punk.

In any event, the 1990s US punk scene left and will continue to leave its mark on subsequent and future incarnations of punk. It developed a more sophisticated political critique of US society that increasingly included the voices of women and Latinos and spoke to the postmodern conditions of life. It codified several musical styles as symbols of extra-musical meaning. And it further developed and reinforced an ideology around DIY as a defense mechanism against the incursions of the mainstream music industry into punk. In all this, what stand out are the conscious actions of those who pushed punk in one direction or another, often against inertia and opposition within both the underground punk scene and US society more broadly. It is these conscious actions that deserve our attention if we are to understand the transformative potential of music.

Notes

Introduction

1. Kirsten Patches, interview by author via Skype, 3 February 2016.
2. Ibid.; Liner notes, Naked Aggression, *Heard It All Before* CD (Corona, CA: SOS Records, 2005).
3. In recent years there have been attempts, in academic and activist circles, to replace the gendered terms "Latino" and "Latina" with terms such as Latin@ and Latinx. While I support these efforts to critique and transform the gendered divisions and male-domination inherent in many languages, including Spanish, at this point it seems far from settled as to which new terms will replace the old ones. The term "Latinx" has been critiqued for a variety of reasons, including the awkwardness of pronouncing a word ending in X in Spanish. Some insist that "Latino" can already be a nongendered term. Moreover, the vast majority of printed and spoken Spanish still uses the terms "Latino" and "Latina." Therefore, I use the terms "Latino," "Latina," "Latinos," and "Latinas" throughout this study and stick with "Latino/Latinos" as the terms to indicate a group of people of multiple genders. Perhaps after we have collectively settled how to deal with this dilemma, these terms can appropriately be replaced where they appear in this book. I hope my readers will understand that using the old, gendered terms does not imply any endorsement of their roots in patriarchal societies.
4. "LGBTQ" was not yet the more common term in the 1990s punk scene, so I use the word "gay" throughout this study to match the more common terminology of the time. Furthermore, the historical record provided by zines suggests that gay men were the main LGBTQ participants in 1990s punk, or at least "out" participants. "Homocore" and "queercore" were frequently used in the punk scene to denote bands with gay members.
5. For overviews of structural adjustment policies, corporate globalization, and the neoliberal turn in the world economy, see David Harvey, *A Brief History of Neoliberalism* (Oxford: Oxford University Press, 2007); and Saskia Sassen, *Globalization and Its Discontents* (New York: New Press, 1998).
6. Throughout this study, I use "white supremacy" in two ways. The first, which could be called the system of white supremacy, is to describe the normal functioning of US society, including economics, politics, social relations, and culture. By this I mean the fact that in all markers of social status, Black people and other nonwhite people face oppression, discrimination, and exploitation in varying degrees far worse than whites, and that this oppression is built into the structures of US society rather than being only a product of the conscious application of white supremacist ideology. This conception differs somewhat from the "white privilege" analysis that has become popular lately, which I believe does not go far enough in examining (and opposing) the power relations of white supremacy that generate white privilege. The second way I use "white supremacy," what could be called ideological white supremacy, is to refer to groups and individuals who overtly profess

white supremacist ideology, such as Nazi skinheads. Whenever I use "white supremacy" in this second way, I refer to specific white supremacist groups or individuals.

7. On the Clinton administration's policies in the 1990s, see Steven Schier, ed., *The Postmodern Presidency: Bill Clinton's Legacy in U.S. Politics* (Pittsburgh, PA: University of Pittsburgh Press, 2000) and Antonio de Velasco, *Centrist Rhetoric: The Production of Political Transcendence in the Clinton Presidency* (Lanham, MD: Lexington Books, 2010). On the oppression of Black people during this period, see Michelle Alexander, *The New Jim Crow: Mass Incarceration in the Age of Colorblindness* (New York: The New Press, 2012). On the Christian Right in the 1990s, see Sara Diamond, *Not by Politics Alone: The Enduring Influence of the Christian Right* (New York: Guilford Press, 1998). On anti-immigrant repression and hysteria, see chapter 4 of this book.

8. I use the term "political punk" to refer to punk bands whose politics were or are characterized by one shade or another of Leftist politics because this is the term the punk scene itself uses, and because it avoids a more cumbersome designation. This should not be taken to suggest that there are not also right-wing political punk bands, nor that bands who sing about personal relationships, getting drunk, or even about being "apolitical" are not also in some sense political.

9. David Ensminger, *The Politics of Punk: Protest and Revolt from the Streets* (Lanham, MD: Bowman & Littlefield, 2016), x–xi.

10. As Ensminger points out in opposition to Dunn's argument "that punk politics are essentially brokered at the local level," anarchist bands do espouse metatheory (Ensminger, *Politics of Punk*, 32).

11. Michelle Phillipov, "Haunted by the Spirit of '77: Punk Studies and the Persistence of Politics," *Continuum: Journal of Media and Cultural Studies* 20, no. 3 (September 2006), 386–87.

12. For accounts of the rise of '77 punk, see Tricia Henry, *Break All Rules! Punk Rock and the Making of a Style* (Ann Arbor: University of Michigan Research Press, 1989); Dick Hebdige, *Subculture: The Meaning of Style* (London and New York: Routledge, 1991 [1979]); and Dave Laing, *One Chord Wonders: Power and Meaning in Punk Rock* (Oakland, CA: PM Press, 2015 [1985]).

13. See Dewar MacLeod, *Kids of the Black Hole: Punk Rock in Postsuburban California* (Norman: University of Oklahoma Press, 2010), chapters 4 and 5 for a historical account of the transition to hardcore and the punk scene's attendant move to the suburbs in Los Angeles.

14. Raymond Patton, *Punk Crisis: The Global Punk Rock Revolution* (New York: Oxford University Press, 2018). For an account of punk's contributions to the fall of the Berlin Wall, see Tim Mohr, *Burning Down the Haus: Punk Rock, Revolution, and the Fall of the Berlin Wall* (Chapel Hill, NC: Algonquin Books, 2018).

15. David Easley, " 'It's Not My Imagination, I've Got A Gun On My Back!': Style and Sound in Early American Hardcore Punk, 1978–1983" (PhD Diss., Florida State University, 2011).

16. Kevin Dunn, *Global Punk: Resistance and Rebellion in Everyday Life* (New York: Bloomsbury Academic, 2016), 11.

17. Phillipov, "Haunted by the Spirit of '77," 388.

18. On Black Flag and the record label SST, started by Black Flag guitarist Greg Ginn, as poignant examples of DIY by necessity in the early 1980s hardcore punk scene, see MacLeod, *Kids of the Black Hole*, 93–95.

19. On pop-punk, see Stacy Thompson, *Punk Productions: Unfinished Business* (Albany: State University of New York Press, 2004), 71–77.
20. Dunn, *Global Punk*, 10–11.
21. Mark Spicer, "'Reggatta de Blanc': Analyzing Style in the Music of the Police," in Mark Spicer and John Covach, eds., *Sounding Out Pop: Analytical Essays in Popular Music* (Ann Arbor: University of Michigan Press, 2010), 136. Spicer's moniker for this musical gesture plays on the fact that the safety pin was ubiquitous in punk fashion, worn on clothes and pierced through skin.
22. I am clearly borrowing from set theory here, though I do not mean to imply inversional equivalency or any of the other theoretical baggage that goes along with set theory.
23. Sex Pistols, *Never Mind the Bollocks Here's the Sex Pistols* LP (London: Virgin Records, 1977).
24. NOFX with Jeff Alius, *NOFX: The Hepatitis Bathtub and Other Stories* (Boston: Da Capo Press, 2016), 123.
25. Ibid., 193.
26. This is corroborated by the transcriptions and analytic work of David Easley on early 1980s hardcore.
27. Minor Threat, *Complete Discography* CD (Washington, DC: Dischord Records, 1989). Given the inconsistency in and difficulty hearing strumming patterns in this recording, I have only notated the duration of each power chord in this example.
28. On zines, see Stephen Duncombe, *Notes from the Underground: Zines and the Politics of Alternative Culture* (London and New York: Verso, 1997).
29. Scene and show have now become standard parlance in rock and pop music.
30. As Phillipov puts it, "while the 'riot grrrl' movement of the 1990s has been theorized as a response to sexism within the punk scene, scholars still tend to situate the movement as part of the punk tradition—despite the fact that many of the riot grrrls themselves reject the 'punk' label, preferring instead to place their project within a variety of other musical and non-musical trajectories" (387).

Chapter 1

1. Martín Sorrondeguy, interview by author, San Francisco, California, 15 July 2015.
2. Frank Burkhard, Interview with Detestation, *HeartattaCk* 17 (Spring 1998), 26.
3. Martial Flaw, Interview with Civil Disobedience, *Profane Existence* 21 (January–February 1994), 16.
4. On the use of music as a recruitment tool by white-supremacist movements, see Urgo Corte and Bob Edwards, "White Power Music and the Mobilization of Racist Social Movements," *Music and Arts in Action* 1, no. 1 (2008): 4–20. See also Jonathan Pieslak, *Radicalism and Music: An Introduction to the Music Cultures of Al-Qa'ida, Racist Skinheads, Christian-Affiliated Radicalism, and Eco-Animal Rights Militants* (Middletown, CT: Wesleyan University Press, 2015), chapter 2. An excellent dramatization of this trend can be seen in the movie *This Is England*, directed by Shane Meadows (Warp Films, 2007).
5. Mark Andersen and Mark Jenkins, *Dance of Days: Two Decades of Punk in the Nation's Capital* (New York: Akashic Books, 2009), 266–67.
6. See, for example, the guest column by Dave Trenga, vocalist of Aus-Rotten, in *MaximumRockNRoll* 157 (June 1996) on the organized boycott of Eide's record store in

Pittsburgh because Eide's carried releases by Resistance Records, a white power record label. Issues of *MaximumRockNRoll* do not have page numbers, so they are cited without page numbers throughout.

7. Denver and Boulder, Colorado Scene Report, *Profane Existence* 3 (April–May 1990), 15.

8. Love and Rage, "Bay-Area Boneheads Bashed with Bottles, Boots, Brains and Brawn," *Profane Existence* 5 (August–September 1990), 4.

9. Interview with Lance Hahn of Cringer, *Profane Existence* 5 (August–September 1990), 25.

10. The news section of *Profane Existence* 11/12 (double issue, Autumn 1991), 5, for example, reported on an antiracist march of over three hundred people through East St. Paul, a neighborhood with a white-supremacist skinhead presence, organized by Anti-Racist Action with a security plan for self-defense in case of attack.

11. Martín Sorrondeguy, interview by author.

12. Frank Burkhard, Interview with Detestation, *HeartattaCk* 17 (Spring 1998), 24.

13. Al Pist, interview by author, Brooklyn, New York, 5 December 2015. M.D.C. is widely acknowledged as an important political hardcore band that started in the 1980s and continues to tour today. What the initials of their name stand for says much about their political edge: "Millions of Dead Cops."

14. *MaximumRockNRoll* 80 (January 1990).

15. Ken Sanderson, Review of Antischism, *Discography* CD, *MaximumRockNRoll* 145 (June 1995).

16. Alicia non Grata, Interview with Nausea, *MaximumRockNRoll* 82 (March 1990).

17. Thompson, *Punk Productions*, 54, 56–57. See Beth Lahickey, *All Ages: Reflections on Straight Edge* (Huntington Beach, CA: Revelation Books, 1997) for more on the straight edge movement and Felix von Havoc, Column, *HeartattaCk* 8 (November 1995), 30–31, for a punk critique of "jock bullshit" in the NYHC scene.

18. William Tsitsos, "Rules of Rebellion: Slam Dancing, Moshing, and the American Alternative Scene," *Popular Music* 18, no. 3 (October 1999), 404–6, quote on 410.

19. Thompson, *Punk Productions*, 58.

20. Admittedly, this characterization of NYHC is too negative, in part to help make sense of the perception within the punk scene of stagnation and violence. There were certainly plenty of exceptions to this characterization within NYHC style and culture, and we should be cautious about ascribing blame to NYHC bands for the violent state of affairs. One quality worth noting is that many straight-edge crews were among the first white youth to attend rap concerts and embrace hip-hop culture. Nevertheless, the macho violence in the scene that developed around the NYHC style precipitated a decisive split between subsequent bands based on this style and the wave of political punk this study is focused on. For an account of radical politics within the straight-edge hardcore scene of the 1990s, see Brian Peterson, *Burning Fight: The Nineties Hardcore Revolution in Ethics, Politics, Spirit, and Sound* (Huntington Beach, CA: Revelation Records Publishing, 2009).

21. The Pist, *Ideas Are Bulletproof* (Minneapolis, MN: Havoc Records, 1995). Lyrics by Al Ouimet, reproduced with permission. "New School" in this instance refers to New School Hardcore, which is what the 1990s musical descendants of NYHC were often called.

22. On the musical characteristics of the breakdown in early-1980s hardcore, see Easley. "Style and Sound in Early American Hardcore Punk," 4, 145–49.

23. Youth of Today, *Break Down the Walls* LP (New Haven, CT: Revelation Records, 1988; Original Release: Wishingwell Records, 1986).

24. Robert Walser, *Running with the Devil: Power, Gender, and Madness in Heavy Metal Music* (Hanover, NH: Wesleyan University Press, 1993), 46–48 discusses the importance of choices in mode in heavy metal, and notes that, "Most heavy metal is either Aeolian or Dorian, for example, although speed metal is usually Phrygian or Locrian; most pop songs are either major (Ionian) or Mixolydian" (46).

25. Interview with Citizens Arrest, *Profane Existence* 8 (January 1991), 26.

26. Interview with Fat Mike, *MaximumRockNRoll* 97 (June 1991).

27. Dan Sinker, Review of Bone, *Free to Think and Be 7"*, *Punk Planet* 23 (March–April 1998), 144.

28. Felix von Havoc, Review of Insted, *What We Believe* LP, *Profane Existence* 8 (January 1991), 30. "Pos-core" is another label sometimes given to straight-edge hardcore bands, and stems from the Bad Brains' advocating a "positive mental attitude."

29. MacLeod, *Kids of the Black Hole*, 103.

30. Ibid., 103. I am not so sure that Jello Biafra's stab at Zen fascism was intended to be irony.

31. Ibid., 103.

32. Reagan Youth, *Youth Anthems for the New Order* (New York: R Radical, 1984). Lyrics by Dave "Insurgent" Rubinstein, reproduced with the permission of Paul Bakija / Reagan Youth.

33. Reagan Youth, *Youth Anthems for the New Order*.

34. Brock Ruggles, "Not So Quiet on the Western Front: Punk Politics during the Conservative Ascendancy in the United States, 1980–2000" (PhD Diss., Arizona State University, 2008), 2.

35. In the language of abstract rights that pervades American political thought, the concept of "states' rights" has long served to obfuscate its concrete meaning: Southern states' right to maintain the slavery of Black people and, after the Civil War, to maintain policies of white supremacy such as Jim Crow segregation and sharecropping. Besides serving the purpose of obfuscation, "states' rights" also acts as a euphemism that the strongest social base for white supremacy in the United States understands perfectly well as championing its interests. On the masterly use of symbolism by the Reagan presidency, see Robert Dalleck, *Ronald Reagan: The Politics of Symbolism* (Cambridge, MA: Harvard University Press, 1984).

36. On Bill Clinton's "tough on crime" approach, mass incarceration policies, and cuts to social welfare, see Alexander, *The New Jim Crow*, 56–57.

37. Tim Yohannan, column, *MaximumRockNRoll* 80 (January 1990).

38. The classic text trumpeting American triumph in the Cold War as proof of capitalism's destiny to reign forever in its liberal democratic form is Francis Fukuyama, *The End of History and the Last Man* (New York: The Free Press, 1992).

39. Alicia non Grata, Interview with Nausea, *MaximumRockNRoll* 82 (March 1990). A.P.P.L.E. was a prominent peace-punk band in the 1980s.

40. Martín Sorrondeguy, interview by author. There were, of course, exceptions to this trend in the late 1980s, such as Positive Force in Washington, DC.

41. Kirsten Patches, interview by author.

42. Ibid.

43. Dan, column, *Profane Existence* 24 (January–March 1995), 48.

44. Taína Asili, interview by author via Skype, 6 August 2015.

45. Martín Sorrondeguy, interview by author.

46. Ibid.
47. Taína Asili, interview by author.
48. Michelle Gonzales, interview by author, Oakland, California, 7 July 2015.
49. Michelle Gonzales, *The Spitboy Rule: Tales of a Xicana in a Female Punk Band* (Oakland, CA: PM Press), 24.
50. Martín Sorrondeguy, interview by author.
51. Taína Asili, interview by author. "Patches" refer to cloth patches, usually with band logos, sown onto clothing.
52. Joel, "A New Punk Manifesto," reprinted in Profane Existence Collective, *Making Punk a Threat Again! The Best Cuts, 1989–1993* (Minneapolis: Loin Cloth Press, 1997), 34–35. Emphasis in original.
53. Kirsten Patches, interview by author.
54. Taína Asili, interview by author.
55. Bill Chamberlain, interview by author via telephone, 17 December 2015.
56. Al Pist, interview by author.
57. Kirsten Patches, interview by author.
58. Al Pist, interview by author.
59. "Why Minneapolis Is So Punk," *Profane Existence* 13 (early 1992), 18–19.
60. *Profane Existence* 23 (Autumn 1994), 15.
61. For more on Yohannan's views and how they shaped *MaximumRockNRoll*, see Scott Turner, "Maximizing Rock and Roll: An Interview with Tim Yohannon [sic]," in *Sounding Off: Music as Subversion/Resistance/Revolution*, ed. Fred Ho and Ronald Sakolsky (New York: Automedia, 1995), 181–94.
62. Jim Testa, "Trouble at ABC No Rio," *Punk Planet* 3 (November–December 1994), 50.
63. See its website, http://www.abcnorio.org/.
64. Alan O'Connor, *Punk Record Labels and the Struggle for Autonomy: The Emergence of DIY* (Lanham, MD: Rowman & Littlefield, 2008), 69.
65. Illinois Scene Report, *MaximumRockNRoll* 143 (June 1995), boldface in the original. "Politics" in this context refers to personality bickering within the punk scene.
66. Joel, column, *Profane Existence* 11/12 (double issue, Autumn 1991), 10.
67. Martín Sorrondeguy, interview by author.
68. "Emo" refers to emotional hardcore, in which lyrics dealt with personal issues, including heartbreak, and vocals and riffs featured much more melody than hardcore. See Eric Grubbs, *Post: A Look at the Influence of Post-Hardcore, 1985–2007* (Bloomington, IN: iUniverse, 2008).
69. On Fugazi, see Thompson, *Punk Productions*, 145–47. Also see Andersen and Jenkins.
70. Ruggles, "Not So Quiet on the Western Front," 223–24.
71. Felix von Havoc, column, *MaximumRockNRoll* 178 (March 1998).
72. Kirsten Patches, interview by author.
73. Jon Entropy, Review of Resist, *Ignorance Is Bliss* LP, Punk Planet 6 (March–April 1995), 79–80.
74. Bruce Baugh, "Prolegomena to Any Aesthetics of Rock Music," *Journal of Aesthetics and Art Criticism* 51, no. 1 (Winter 1993), 23, 24. For expositions of the role of body movement and dance in musical style and creation, see also Mark Butler, *Unlocking the Groove: Rhythm, Meter, and Musical Design in Electronic Dance Music* (Bloomington: Indiana University Press, 2006); Kyra Gaunt, *The Games Black Girls Play: Learning the Ropes from*

Double-Dutch to Hip-Hop (New York: New York University Press, 2006); Brian Harker, "Louis Armstrong, Eccentric Dance, and the Evolution of Jazz on the Eve of Swing," *Journal of the American Musicological Society* 61, no. 1 (2008): 67–121; and Tiger Roholt, *Groove: A Phenomenology of Rhythmic Nuance* (New York: Bloomsbury Academic, 2014).

75. Ken Sanderson, Review of Los Crudos / Manumission split 7", *MaximumRockNRoll* 132 (May 1994). A review by John in *Profane Existence* 24 (January–March 1995) similarly referred to the band as "Angry hardcore with a really raw sound reminiscent of early Italian and Spanish hardcore, though not as sloppy" (8).

76. The generic term "thrash" as used in punk is different from thrash-metal. Thrash is also probably the most ambiguous generic label within punk and is used to describe different stylistic trends by different people.

77. Ken Sanderson, Review of Los Crudos / Spitboy split LP, *MaximumRockNRoll* 151, part 1 (December 1995).

78. This and all subsequent Los Crudos songs analyzed in this study can be heard on Los Crudos, *Doble LP discografía* (San Francisco, CA: Maximum RockNRoll, 2014).

79. For example, in David Easley's analysis of early 1980s hardcore riffs, almost all riffs melodically fit within diatonic modality. The Dead Kennedys' "Religious Vomit" is a striking exception in its brazen use of a tritone. Easley, "Style and Sound in Early American Hardcore Punk."

80. See Table 1 in Walter Everett, "Making Sense of Rock's Tonal Systems," *Music Theory Online* 10, no. 4 (December 2004). This system, which is Everett's Type 5, also includes the triad-doubled minor-pentatonic system.

81. This is not to argue that Los Crudos was the first punk band to ever do this, but that it was not so common in 1980s hardcore, whereas it is quite ubiquitous in Los Crudos's riffs.

82. Since tonal centers are not always clear or are at least open to interpretation in music like this, I mainly focus on the choices of pitch material.

83. This statement is corroborated by the analytic work of David Easley.

84. As Easley points out, this motion up the fretboard in hardcore is a means of creating harmonic tension and subsequent release to a lower position on the fretboard within a musical style based on power-chord root motion rather than harmonic progression ("Style and Sound in Early American Hardcore Punk," 277). Minor Threat's "Straight Edge" (Example I.5 in the Introduction) is a perfect example of this phenomenon.

85. Given that strumming patterns vary in this song, I have only transcribed the duration of each power chord.

86. To the musicologists and music theorists reading this: yes, all the pitches of these two riffs could be derived from E♭ Phrygian, but do we really want to go there? And does that really make sense given the different tonal centers of the two riffs? In any event, this would be a shift to ♭II and back, which, as the last movement of Beethoven's op. 131 makes clear, can be a wonderfully jarring moment of the sublime. Thus any way we choose to analyze these riffs the effect is one of disruption.

87. The last half of the second and fourth lines of each verse, in which the syllables are declaimed in an even on-beat rhythm with the whole band homorhythmically aiding these accents, are exceptions.

88. The blast beat is explained in depth in chapter 3. For now, suffice it to say that in these instances the drummer plays constant, repeated hits on the same drums/cymbals rather than an alternation between different drums (i.e., kick and snare drum).

89. See Introduction, 23.
90. See, for example, Review of Crudos / Huasipungo split 7", *MaximumRockNRoll* 125 (October 1993).
91. Martín Sorrondeguy, interview by author.
92. Wedge was the drummer of thrash band 9 Shocks Terror and other Cleveland hardcore bands, and Sorrondeguy's reference to him was due to the fact that I grew up in Cleveland. Chris BCT put out cassette tapes of some of the European bands in question in the 1980s. Pushead was the vocalist of 1980s hardcore band Septic Death.
93. Martín Sorrondeguy, interview by author.
94. Steve Waksman, *This Ain't the Summer of Love: Conflict and Crossover in Heavy Metal and Punk* (Berkeley: University of California Press, 2009), 8.

Chapter 2

1. For this reason I do not use topic theory to analyze crust-punk/dis-core. Topic theory is excellent for analyzing musical "topics" that signify specific extra-musical ideas to listeners, such as horn calls in late-eighteenth-century symphonies signifying hunting. With the sole exception of the militaristic drumming described later in this chapter, crust-punk/dis-core style does not use anything resembling musical topics; there is no way to distinguish a crust-punk/dis-core song about environmental destruction versus one about war other than by the lyrics.
2. For overviews of structural adjustment policies, corporate globalization, and the neoliberal turn in the world economy, see Harvey, *A Brief History of Neoliberalism*; and Sassen.
3. Aus-Rotten, *The System Works . . . For Them* LP (New York: Tribal War Records, 1996).
4. On the legal case of Mumia Abu-Jamal, see Leonard Weinglass, *Race for Justice: Mumia Abu-Jamal's Fight Against the Death Penalty* (Monroe, ME: Common Courage, 1995).
5. Kirsten Patches, interview by author. Though Naked Aggression was not stylistically crust-punk/dis-core, its politics are quite similar to those of bands in that style.
6. Ibid. Patches is likely referring to the merging of several US banks.
7. Ibid.
8. Joel, "A New Punk Manifesto," reprinted in Profane Existence Collective, *Making Punk a Threat Again! The Best Cuts, 1989–1993* (Minneapolis: Loin Cloth Press, 1997), 34–35.
9. Alicia non Grata, Interview with Nausea, *MaximumRockNRoll* 82 (March 1990).
10. Ian Glasper, *The Day the Country Died: A History of Anarcho Punk, 1980–1984* (London: Cherry Red Books, 2006), 11 (quote), 13.
11. Ibid., 11, 14. To give a sense of Crass's popularity, its first five albums reached number one on the UK independent charts.
12. Thompson, *Punk Productions*, 84.
13. Glasper, *The Day the Country Died*, 8, 27.
14. Ibid., 16.
15. While there are parallels between the point I am making here and semiotic analysis, in this case signification only works for fans of punk who are familiar with its history, not with a broader public (with the possible exception of militaristic drumming). Thus an application of semiotic analysis to musical meaning within punk discourse is not the way I have chosen to interpret the meaning of punk musical styles.

16. Ibid., 13, 29. For a collection of the artwork of Crass, see Gee Vaucher, *Crass Art and Other Pre Post-Modernist Monsters* (Edinburgh, Scotland, and San Francisco, CA: AK Press, 1999).

17. As quoted in Glasper, *The Day the Country Died*, 17.

18. Thompson, *Punk Productions*, 85.

19. Glasper, *The Day the Country Died*, 14.

20. See Thompson, *Punk Productions*, 83–92, for a fuller discussion and assessment of Crass's DIY practices.

21. Waksman, *This Ain't the Summer of Love*, 147–49, quote on 147.

22. Ibid., 146, 161.

23. Ibid., 165, 168–69.

24. Ibid., 154–55.

25. I do not mean to imply any relationship to the Phil Spector "wall of sound" approach to studio recording—I am simply using wall of sound as a visceral description of the music.

26. Waksman's monograph elaborates on the distinctions between metal and punk throughout, and Walser, *Running with the Devil*, chapter 2, provides an exposition of the aesthetic values of metal music.

27. Tresillo rhythm connotes a dotted quarter note / dotted quarter note / quarter note rhythm or the same in rhythmic diminution, which creates a syncopated accent on the "and" of beat two.

28. See Walser, *Running with the Devil*, 53–54, for some theorization of the guitar solo in heavy metal along these lines.

29. Felix von Havoc, column, "Rise of Crust," *Profane Existence* 40 (Fall–Winter 2002), 9. Ian Glasper, *Trapped in a Scene: UK Hardcore, 1985–1989* (London: Cherry Red Books, 2009), also documents the rise of crust through accounts of some of the style's most seminal bands, including Amebix and Doom.

30. Havoc, "Rise of Crust," 9.

31. Ibid., 9. Havoc makes a precise distinction between crust and crust-core: "To me true crust is very metallic, like Hellbastard, Concrete Sox, Deviated Instinct or later Amebix. Crusty hardcore or Crust Core on the other hand is pretty much based in thrash and dis core such as Disrupt, Extreme Noise Terror, and Doom" (9). The more extreme hardcore variants of crust that use blast-beats will be explored further in part four of this chapter.

32. Ibid., 9.

33. Waksman, *Running with the Devil*, 170.

34. Havoc, "Rise of Crust," 9.

35. Some would argue for more finite generic distinctions between dis-core, crust, crust-punk, crust-core, etc. While these generic distinctions are real and relevant, my concern is to identify a broad swath of political bands with stylistic similarities and a music-as-propaganda aesthetic.

36. The main problem with studies of music as propaganda has been their adherence to the Western side of Cold War logic, with Arnold Perris's *Music as Propaganda: Art to Persuade, Art to Control* (Westport, CT: Greenwood, 1985) as a prime example in this regard. This Cold War mentality a priori assumes that all art in so-called totalitarian regimes is bland and that its artistic quality is tainted by political repression, as opposed to in the West, where little to no political repression of art is acknowledged (which can only be done by pretending Black people do not exist) and a fantasy of free individual artistic expression

reigns. Since, for classical music scholars, the music of Shostakovich punctures a hole in this simplistic and dubious narrative, great effort has been made to prove he was in truth a secret Soviet dissident (a contradiction in terms) who coded his music with messages of protest against the Soviet government. This great effort can only be successful by ignoring Shostakovich's enthusiasm for the Soviet regime as a young man, the prominent role he played as a cultural ambassador of the Soviet state throughout his career, and, most importantly for us, the way much of his post-1935 music was imbued with the aesthetic values of Socialist Realism.

37. Kirsten Patches, interview by author.
38. Barbara Mittler, "Cultural Revolution Model Works and the Politics of Modernization in China: An Analysis of *Taking Tiger Mountain by Strategy*," *The World of Music* 45, no. 2 (2003), 74. For a further exposition of the principle of semantic overdetermination, see Barbara Mittler, *A Continuous Revolution: Making Sense of Cultural Revolution Culture* (Cambridge, MA: Harvard University Asia Center, 2013).
39. Kirsten Patches, interview by author.
40. Will Dandy, Review of Aus-Rotten, *Fuck Nazi Sympathy 7*", *Punk Planet* 7 (May–June 1995), 68.
41. Yannick Lorain, Review of Aus-Rotten, *Fuck Nazi Sympathy 7*", *HeartattaCk* 2 (June 1994), 36.
42. Timojhen Mark, Review of Aus-Rotten, *Fuck Nazi Sympathy 7*", *MaximumRockNRoll* 133 (June 1994).
43. Felix von Havoc, Review of Aus-Rotten, *Anti-Imperialist 7*", *Profane Existence* 21 (January–February 1994), 20.
44. Jenn Hyman, Review of Aus-Rotten, *Anti-Imperialist 7*", *MaximumRockNRoll* 129 (February 1994).
45. Aus-Rotten, *Fuck Nazi Sympathy 7*" (Minneapolis, MN: Havoc Records, 1994).
46. Ibid.
47. Dan, Review of Aus-Rotten, *Fuck Nazi Sympathy 7*", *Profane Existence* 22 (Spring 1994), 20.
48. O'Connor, *Punk Record Labels and the Struggle for Autonomy*, 71.
49. Yannick Lorain, Review of Aus-Rotten, *The System Works . . . For Them LP*, *HeartattaCk* 13 (November 1996), 46.
50. Mick Krash, Review of Aus-Rotten, *The System Works . . . For Them LP*, *MaximumRockNRoll* 154 (March 1996). Note that in this and the previous review, political punk suffices to describe not just Aus-Rotten's lyrics but also its musical style, indicating that the crust-punk/dis-core formula immediately signified political punk.
51. This and all subsequent examples of Aus-Rotten's music can be heard on Aus-Rotten, *The System Works . . . For Them LP* (New York: Tribal War Records, 1996).
52. Left and right guitar tracks refer to what speaker each guitar comes out of on stereo or headphones.
53. Easley, "Style and Sound in Early American Hardcore Punk," 54–55.
54. E♭ in both the introduction and verse riff performs the function of dissonating the music by defying previous punk conventions in riff pitch structure.
55. Ty Smith, Review of Aus-Rotten, *And Now Back to Our Programming LP*, *MaximumRockNRoll* 193 (June 1999).
56. Easley, "Style and Sound in Early American Hardcore Punk," 63–68, notes something similar in his explanation of the repetition and change riff scheme.

57. "B.A.T.F." stands for the Bureau of Alcohol, Tobacco, and Firearms. The lyrics of this song were written in response to the B.A.T.F.'s standoff with the Branch Davidians, a religious sect, in 1993 in Waco, Texas. The standoff ended with a siege on the Branch Davidians' compound, led by the FBI, which resulted in the compound going up in flames and the deaths of dozens of those inside.

58. Aus-Rotten, *The System Works . . . For Them* LP (New York: Tribal War Records, 1996)..

59. Ibid.

60. Mark Spicer, in his "(Ac)cumulative Form in Pop-Rock Music," *Twentieth-Century Music* 1, no. 1 (March 2004), offers the following admonition along similar lines: "Unfortunately, as with harmony, it is often assumed that the formal structure of most average three- or four-minute pop-rock songs is trite and simplistic, consisting of not much more than a predictable strophic alternation of verses, refrains, and choruses (with the occasional introduction or bridge thrown in for good measure). If we examine pop-rock songs more closely, we can often find their composers employing techniques of considerable sophistication in order to create interesting and unique formal structures that transcend these predictable boundaries" (30).

61. Ty Smith, Review of Aus-Rotten, *And Now Back to Our Programming* LP, *MaximumRockNRoll* 193 (June 1999).

62. *Profane Existence* 23 (Autumn 1994), 28–29. Band names in punk have long been used to demarcate musical style, from the dis- and anti- prefixes, to the use of "youth" or "X" to denote straight-edge hardcore, to the "77" suffix signifying affinity with late-1970s Britpunk.

63. Dan, Review of Dissucks, *A Room with a View of a World Full of Shit* 7", *Profane Existence* 31, part 1 (Summer 1997), 46.

64. Mick Krash, Review of Anti-Flag, *Kill Kill Kill* EP, *MaximumRockNRoll* 147 (August 1995).

65. Interview with Lance Hahn of Cringer, *Profane Existence* 5 (August–September 1990), 26.

66. Nate Wilson, Review of Detestation/Substandard split 7", *HeartattaCk* 15 (June 1997).

67. Matt Average, Review of Detestation, *The Inhuman Condition* 7", *HeartattaCk* 16 (November 1997), 38.

68. Kent McClard, Review of Detestation, LP, *HeartattaCk* 18 (Summer 1998), 43.

69. Grey Kiser, Review of Deceived, *Smash Patriarchy* 7", *HeartattaCk* 12 (May 1996), 27.

70. Dan, Review of Distraught, s/t 7", *Profane Existence* 29/30 (Fall 1996), 72.

71. NN, Review of Misery, *Who's the Fool . . .* LP, *MaximumRockNRoll* 147 (August 1995).

72. Adi Tejada, Review of Anti-Product, *Big Business and the Government Are Both the Fucking Same* 7", *HeartattaCk* 18 (Summer 1998), 42.

73. Review of Anti-Product, *Dead Heroes, Dead Dreams* 7", *MaximumRockNRoll* 175 (December 1997).

74. Martial Flaw, Interview with Civil Disobedience, *Profane Existence* 21 (January–February 1994), 16.

75. Interview with Detestation, *Profane Existence* 31, part 1 (Summer 1997), 27.

76. Yagwie, Review of Whorehouse of Representatives, *It's a Corporate World After All* 7", *Profane Existence* 25 (Summer 1995), 79. Contemporary with Whorehouse of Representatives were a number of other political punk bands from Seattle such as No Class and Cease and Desist.

77. Dan, Review of Whorehouse of Representatives, *Your Alcohol Taxes at Work* 7", *Profane Existence* 29/30 (double issue, Fall 1996), 75–76.

78. Matt Average, Review of Whorehouse of Representatives, *Your Alcohol Taxes at Work* 7", *MaximumRockNRoll* 168 (May 1997).

79. Brother Inferior / Whorehouse of Representatives, split 7" (Minneapolis, MN: Profane Existence, 1998).

80. Whorehouse of Representatives, *Your Alcohol Taxes at Work* 7" (Seattle, WA: SABOTAGE: earth records, 1997).

81. Michigan Scene Report, *MaximumRockNRoll* 156, part 1 (May 1995).

82. Mick Krash, Review of Civil Disobedience, *Invention Extinction* LP, *MaximumRockNRoll* 169 (June 1997).

83. Will Dandy, Review of Civil Disobedience, *In a Few Hours of Madness* 7", *Punk Planet* 7 (May–June, 1995), 69.

84. Civil Disobedience, *In a Few Hours of Madness* 7" (Minneapolis, MN: Havoc Records, 1993).

85. Civil Disobedience, *In a Few Hours of Madness* 7" (Minneapolis, MN: Havoc Records, 1993).

86. Steve Spinali, Review of Defiance, *No Future No Hope* LP, *MaximumRockNRoll* 153 (February 1996).

87. These observations are based on Defiance, *No Future No Hope* LP (Mind Control, 1996).

88. Anti-Flag, *Kill Kill Kill* 7" (Pittsburg, PA: SelfServ Records / Ripe Records, 1995).

89. Kim Bae, Review of Anti-Flag, *Kill Kill Kill* 7", *Punk Planet* 15 (October–November, 1996), 90.

90. Kent McClard, Review of Anti-Flag, *Kill Kill Kill* 7", *HeartattaCk* 6 (May–June 1995) 20.

91. Aaron Genmill, Review of The Pist, *Ideas Are Bulletproof* CD, *Punk Planet* 9 (September—October 1995), 89, gives the following description: "This is above average Oi! influenced hardcore. Lots of fun, traditional, and fairly well thought out Anarchopunk lyrics. The songs are catchy, with a lot of cool bass hooks and memorable sing-a-long choruses."

92. Al Pist, interview by author.

93. Ibid.

94. Ibid.

95. Bill Chamberlain, interview by author.

96. The Pist, *Ideas Are Bulletproof* (Minneapolis, MN: Havoc Records, 1995). Lyrics by Al Ouimet, used with permission.

97. Al Pist, interview by author.

98. Interview with Naked Aggression, *Punk Planet* 11 (January–February 1996), 33.

99. There are several references to Beethoven's music in Naked Aggression's songs, including to Beethoven's Ninth Symphony in "Plastic World" and "Ode to a Fucked Up World." Kirsten Patches, interview by author.

100. This and subsequent Naked Aggression songs analyzed can be heard on the band's discography CD, *Heard It All Before* (Corona, CA: SOS Records, 2005).

101. Furthermore, whereas in the introduction/bridge the guitar rings out, in the verse the guitar clips the first note of each bar.

102. Interview with Naked Aggression, *MaximumRockNRoll* 107 (April 1992).

103. For example: "Punk as simplistic as fuck! Simplicity in itself isn't wrong at all, but in this case it's getting on my nerves after three songs. . . . This goes for the music and singing as well as for the political lyrics." Koji Motonishi, *HeartattaCk* 6 (May 1995), 24.

104. As recounted in the introduction, both were music majors at the University of Wisconsin-Madison before dropping out to devote themselves to Naked Aggression. Suchomel's background was in classical guitar, and Patches was a French horn player who had sung in choirs growing up and whose mother was a professional twentieth-century classical music singer.

105. Easley, "Style and Sound in Early American Hardcore Punk," 40–41, identifies this as a common rhythmic pattern in early hardcore riffs, especially at the end of song sections or longer riffs.

106. Kirsten Patches, interview by author; Interview with Naked Aggression, *MaximumRockNRoll* 107 (April 1992).

107. Interview with Naked Aggression, *Punk Planet* 11 (January–February 1996), 33.

108. Timojhen Mark, Review of Brother Inferior, *Anthems '94–'97* CD, *MaximumRockNRoll* 195 (August 1999).

109. These observations are based on listening to Brother Inferior, *Anthems '94–'97* CD (Tulsa, OK: Sensual Underground Ministries, 1997).

110. Jon Entropy, Review of Brother Inferior, *Bound and Gagged 7"*, *Punk Planet* 9 (September–October 1995), 79. See chapter 3 of this study for an explanation of grindcore.

111. Jon, Review of Brother Inferior, *Bound and Gagged 7"*, *Profane Existence* 26 (Autumn 1995), 39.

Chapter 3

1. *HeartattaCk* 12 (May 1996), 30. For the millennials reading this, a Sony Walkman was a small, portable, battery-powered cassette-tape player listened to with headphones.

2. *MaximumRockNRoll* 95 (April 1991).

3. *MaximumRockNRoll* 126 (November 1993).

4. *MaximumRockNRoll* 134 (July 1994).

5. *MaximumRockNRoll* 95 (April 1991).

6. *MaximumRockNRoll* 178 (March 1998).

7. *MaximumRockNRoll* 95 (April 1991).

8. Angela Rodel presents an outline of EHC style centered around the traits *short*, *fast*, and *loud*. While I am in basic agreement with her description, here I aim to deepen and provide greater specificity to our understanding of EHC style. See Angela Rodel, "Extreme Noise Terror: Punk Rock and the Aesthetics of Badness," in *Bad Music: The Music We Love to Hate*, edited by Christopher Washburne and Maiken Derno (New York: Routledge, 2004), 241–44.

9. Glasper, *Trapped in a Scene*, 11, 14; Derek Reddy, *The Evolution of Blast Beats* (Pembroke Pines, FL: World Music 4all Publications, 2007), 10. Napalm Death would move increasingly toward a metal style after its 1987 *Scum* LP (Glasper, *Trapped in a Scene*, 16–22).

10. See, for example, Matt Average, Review of Dropdead, *Hostile 7"*, *MaximumRockNRoll* 160 (September 1996).

11. It is also a wonderful reminder that all analytic categories inevitably run into phenomena that do not fit their parameters. In this instance, the lack of kick and snare alternation defies my analytic method for felt tempo in punk—KSA. *Feeling of speed* is a phrase I borrow from Shin of the band Gauze, who used it to distinguish his band's

approach from grindcore, and I believe this helpfully explains speed as an affect rather than just a matter of metronome measurements. Matt Average, Interview with Gauze, *MaximumRockNRoll* 167 (April 1997).

12. Code 13, *A Part of America Died Today 7"* (Minneapolis, MI: Havoc Records, 1998).
13. Minnesota Scene Report, *MaximumRockNRoll* 84 (May 1990).
14. Chris Dodge, Review of Dropdead / Rupture split 8", *MaximumRockNRoll* 119 (April 1993).
15. Ad, *MaximumRockNRoll* 160 (September, 1996).
16. Kevin Sanderson, Review of Phobia, *Enslaved 7"*, *Punk Planet* 19 (July–August, 1997), 139.
17. Review of Anal Cunt / 7 Minutes of Nausea split 7", *MaximumRockNRoll* 82 (February 1990).
18. Review of Agoraphobic Nosebleed, *Mobilize 7"*, *MaximumRockNRoll* 156, Part 1 (May 1995).
19. Rob Coons, Review of Hellnation, *Your Chaos Days Are Numbered* LP, *MaximumRockNRoll* 178 (March 1998).
20. See Ad by Slap-A-Ham Records, *MaximumRockNRoll* 95 (April 1991).
21. Roddy, 22, is in agreement with this assessment. Further adding to the back-and-forth between EHC and extreme metal is the fact that a number of EHC bands became metal bands, most notably Napalm Death.
22. See Walser, *Running with the Devil*, chapter 3, for a discussion of the ideology of virtuosity in metal.
23. These points come from my own visual observations of drummers and close listening to records.
24. Burned Up Bled Dry, *Kill the Body . . . Kill the Sou . . . 7"* (Tulsa, OK: Sensual Underground Ministries, 1997).
25. Steve Snyder, Review of Misery, *Next Time 7"*, *HeartattaCk* 15 (June 1997), 10.
26. North California Scene Report, *MaximumRockNRoll* 80 (January 1990).
27. Florida Scene Report, *MaximumRockNRoll* 193 (June 1999).
28. Another criterion for judging the success or failure of dirge is put forward by A. Noise in a Review of Gasp / Noothgrush split 7", *Profane Existence* 36 ([late] Summer 1998), 56. A. Noise calls this 7" "uninspired, boring, and soulless dirge category" and declares, "Dirge doesn't work when all you can do is bang, drone, and scream. It isn't that simple. You MUST groove and flow."
29. Beck Hamrick, Interview with In/humanity, *MaximumRockNRoll* 151, part 2 (December 1995).
30. Eric Furst, Review of Burned Up Bled Dry, *Kill the Body . . . Kill the Soul . . . 7"*, *HeartattaCk* 16 (November 1997), 37.
31. M. Flaw, Review of Hiatus, *From Resignation to Revolt* LP, *Profane Existence* 21 (January–February 1994), 21.
32. Dan, Review of Avulsion / Forced Expression split 7", *Profane Existence* 29/30 (Fall 1996), 70.
33. Kent McClard, Review of Monster X 7", *HeartattaCk* 12 (May 1996), 31.
34. Kent McClard, Review of Code 13, *A Part of America Died Today 7"*, *HeartattaCk* 18 (Summer 1998), 43.
35. Jon, Review of Dropdead s/t (1998) LP, *Profane Existence* 37 (1998), 72.
36. This and all subsequent examples of Dropdead's music can be heard on the band's self-titled LP (Providence, RI: Armageddon Label, 1998).

37. *Tomorrow Will Be Worse* four 7" records compilation (Covington, KY: Sound Pollution Records, 1997). The song title is given as it appears on the compilation.

38. Chris Dodge, Review of Hellnation, *People's Temple 7"*, *MaximumRockNRoll* 87 (August 1990).

39. Ken Sanderson, Review of Capitalist Casualties CD, *Punk Planet* 19 (July–August 97), 132.

40. Dan, Review of Avulsion / Forced Expression split 7", *Profane Existence* 29/30 (Fall 1996), 70.

41. Gabe, Review of Asshole Parade, s/t 7", *Profane Existence* 31, part 1 (Summer 1997), 43.

42. Jon, Review of Dropdead s/t (1998) LP, *Profane Existence* 37 (1998), 72.

43. Timojhen Mark, Review of Hellnation, *Control* LP, *MaximumRockNRoll* 138 (November 1994).

44. Max Ward, Review of Hellnation, *A Sound Like Shit* CD, *MaximumRockNRoll* 163 (December 1996).

45. Review of Hellnation, *Control* LP, *Profane Existence* 24 (January–March 1995), 10.

46. This ongoing US-Japan connection raises further questions of cultural differences, imperialist chauvinism, and exoticism within globalized punk. In her memoir of her experience in Spitboy, Michelle Gonzales identifies the band's tour of Japan as a pivotal turning point in her own understanding of her cultural differences with the other members of her band and the US punk scene more generally. The Japanese tour, unlike prior European excursions, brought out cultural differences between Spitboy and its American fellow travelers, on the one hand, and their Japanese counterparts on the other (see p. 124 in particular). These and other implications, along with the continued American praise for and obsession with Japanese hardcore for its musical intensity, would be fascinating topics for further study.

47. Joel, Review of Capitalist Casualties, *Disassembly Line* LP, *Profane Existence* 17 (October–November 1992), 16.

48. Tom Hopkins, Review of Capitalist Casualties, *Subdivisions in Ruin* LP, *MaximumRockNRoll* 192 (May 1999).

49. Rodel, "Extreme Noise Terror," 238–39.

50. Felix von Havoc, Column, *MaximumRockNRoll* 198 (November 1999).

51. Corroborating the "spazzy" feel of power violence as well as betraying the sometimes intricate subgenre distinctions in punk, Asshole Parade was described as "Fast and slow choppy sounding hardcore with raw vocals. This falls somewhere into what they call power violence, but not as spazzy as that." In Kerry, Review of Asshole Parade / Ansojuan split 7", *Profane Existence* 29/30 (Fall 1996).

52. "Power Violence with Chris Dodge of Spazz," Interview by Josh Hooter, *Punk Planet* 25 (May–June 1998), 50, 51.

53. Ibid., 51.

54. Ibid., 49, 50.

55. In Japan, by contrast, there were numerous EHC bands with women members during the 1990s.

56. His Hero Is Gone, for example, described growing up among blatant white supremacy and segregation in small towns in the South in Interview, *HeartattaCk* 14 (June 1997), 33.

57. Ad, *MaximumRockNRoll* 100, part 1 (September 1991).

58. On pop-punk, see Thompson, *Punk Productions*, 71–77.

59. Interview with His Hero Is Gone, *HeartattaCk* 14 (June 1997), 35.

60. Rodel, "Extreme Noise Terror," 242.

61. Thompson, *Punk Productions*, 100–101. Thompson uses "crust" to refer to what I call EHC.

62. Yannick Lorain, Review of Monster X, demo, *HeartattaCk* 2 (June 1994), 40.

63. Cornelius Neck, Interview with Man Is The Bastard, *MaximumRockNRoll* 118 (March 1993). The two bassists in this band and the far more intricate music the two bassists played—far beyond riffs—is an early example of the increasingly complex use of the bass in EHC and "noise" bands as the 1990s wore on and into the new millennium, with bassists employing greater use of harmonies rather than one pitch at a time.

64. "Power Violence with Chris Dodge of Spazz," Interview by Josh Hooter, *Punk Planet* 25 (May–June 1998), 49.

65. KS, Review of Charles Bronson / Spazz split 7", *MaximumRockNRoll* 154 (March 1996).

66. Mick Krash, Review of Charles Bronson / Ice Nine split 7", *MaximumRockNRoll* 165 (February 1997). Victory Records was the 1990s home of the new-school hardcore that descended from NYHC. From Cleveland, Ohio, the band One Life Crew was notorious in the punk scene for its right-wing lyrics, and the violence at their shows that was sometimes directed against people who expressed disagreement with their politics led to Victory Records dropping the band from its roster. "Pure Disgust," One Life Crew's song about Mexican immigrants in the United States, includes the words "Dirty fucking leaches, GET OUT."

67. Thompson, *Punk Productions*, 98.

68. Code 13, *A Part of America Died Today* 7" (Minneapolis, MI: Havoc Records, 1998).

69. Frédéric Claisse and Pierre Delvenne, "Building on Anticipation: Dystopia as Empowerment," *Current Sociology* 63, no. 2 (2015), 155–56.

70. Rob MacAlear, "The Value of Fear: Toward a Rhetorical Model of Dystopia," *Interdisciplinary Humanities* 27, no. 2 (2010), 24, 25.

71. Ibid., 26.

72. Ibid., 30.

73. Eric Furst, Review of Burned Up Bled Dry, *Kill the Body* 7", *HeartattaCk* 16 (November 1997), 37.

74. Dropdead, s/t LP (Providence, RI: Armageddon Label, 1998). Lyrics by Bob Otis, reproduced with permission.

75. His Hero Is Gone, *Fifteen Counts of Arson* LP (San Francisco, CA: Prank Records, 1996).

76. Keith Booker, *Dystopian Literature: A Theory and Research Guide* (Westport, CT: Greenwood Press, 1994), 7.

77. Rodel, "Extreme Noise Terror," 251.

78. Scott Yahtzee, Review of His Hero Is Gone, *Fifteen Counts of Arson* CD, *Punk Planet* 21 (November–December, 1997), 134.

79. Rob Coons, His Hero Is Gone, *The Dead of the Night in 8 Movements* 7", *MaximumRockNRoll* 157 (June 1996).

80. Rob Coons, His Hero Is Gone, *Fifteen Counts of Arson* LP, *MaximumRockNRoll* 167 (April 1997).

81. Dan, Review of His Hero Is Gone, *Fifteen Counts of Arson* LP, *Profane Existence* 31, part 1 (Summer 1997), 46.

82. Andy Darling, Review of His Hero Is Gone, *The Plot Sickens: Enslavement Redefined* LP, *MaximumRockNRoll* 199 (December 1999).

83. Dan, Review of His Hero Is Gone, *Fifteen Counts of Arson* LP, *Profane Existence* 31, part 1 (Summer 1997), 46.

84. Rob Coons, His Hero Is Gone, *Fifteen Counts of Arson* LP, *MaximumRockNRoll* 167 (April 1997).

85. His Hero Is Gone, *Fifteen Counts of Arson* LP (San Francisco, CA: Prank Records, 1996).

86. His Hero Is Gone, *Monuments to Thieves* LP (San Francisco, CA: Prank Records, 1997).

87. His Hero Is Gone, *The Plot Sickens: Enslavement Redefined* LP (Ottawa, ON: The Great American Steak Religion, 1998).

88. Review of His Hero Is Gone, *Monuments to Thieves* LP, *MaximumRockNRoll* 176 (January 1998).

89. Dan Fontaine, Review of His Hero Is Gone, *The Dead of Night in Eight Movements* 7", *HeartattaCk* 12 (May 1996), 30.

90. Without implying that members of HHIG were necessarily familiar with Baroque musical rhetoric, the affinity this riff possesses with the Baroque emblem of lament is nonetheless striking. On descending stepwise minor-key basslines and their rhetorical meaning in the Baroque era, see Ellen Rosand, "The Descending Tetrachord: An Emblem of Lament," *Musical Quarterly* 65, no. 3 (July 1979): 346–59.

91. His Hero Is Gone, *Monuments to Thieves* LP (San Francisco, CA: Prank Records, 1997). I have divided the lyrics to match up with how they fit metrically with riffs to make it easier to follow along.

Chapter 4

1. Macleod, *Kids of the Black Hole*, 131.

2. Lauraine Leblanc, *Pretty in Punk: Girls' Gender Resistance in a Boys' Subculture* (New Brunswick, NJ: Rutgers University Press, 2006 [1999]), 35–36, 44–48, quote on 48.

3. MacLeod, *Kids of the Black Hole*, 132–33.

4. On gay participation in punk and rock music more generally in the 1990s United States, see David Ciminelli, *Homocore: The Loud and Raucous Rise of Queer Rock* (Los Angeles: Alyson Books, 2005).

5. At the time of my interview with him (15 July 2015), Martín Sorrondeguy estimated that there were about sixty punk bands in the United States singing in Spanish.

6. Michelle Gonzales, interview by author.

7. Susan Grossman et al., "Pilsen and The Resurrection Project: Community Organization in a Latino Community," *Journal of Poverty* 4, no.1/2 (2000), 133–39.

8. Martín Sorrondeguy, interview by author.

9. Esneider, Interview with Los Crudos, *MaximumRockNRoll* 117 (February 1993). On Casa Aztlan, see http://blog.chicagohistory.org/index.php/2011/01/casa-aztlan/ (accessed 19 October 2016). "Cholo" is used somewhat differently in different contexts, but in the United States generally refers to non-Caribbean Latino, especially Mexican, immigrant, second-, or third-generation or Chicano youth who adopt the clothing and lifestyle of street gang members.

10. Martín Sorrondeguy, interview by author.

11. Mary Odem, "Subaltern Immigrants," *Interventions: International Journal of Postcolonial Studies* 10, no. 3 (2009), 375–78; Jorge Durand, Douglas Massey, and Emilio Parrado, "The New Era of Mexican Migration to the United States," *Journal of American History* 86, no. 2 (September, 1999), 531–36.

12. See, for example, "Thousands Protest Prop. 187 in L.A.," *San Jose Mercury News*, 3 November 1994, 3B.

13. Esneider, Interview with Los Crudos, *MaximumRockNRoll* 117 (February 1993).

14. Tod, Interview with Los Crudos, *Profane Existence* 17 (October—November 1992), 18.

15. Ibid.

16. Ibid., 19.

17. For example, record reviews of Los Crudos in *MaximumRockNRoll* 132 (May 1994) and 137 (October 1994) use the words "sincerity" and "heartfelt," respectively. Crust-punk/dis-core bands' general personal distance from their lyrical subjects should not, however, be used to dismiss the importance of their political critique. Indeed, one of the most significant things about propaganda punk of the 1990s is that so many bands from white, middle-class backgrounds felt compelled to speak out about US imperialism despite the fact that the social position they were born into benefited from it.

18. Martín Sorrondeguy, interview by author.

19. Interview with Los Crudos, *HeartattaCk* 2 (June 1994), 25.

20. Interview with Martín Sorrondeguy, *MaximumRockNRoll* 192 (May 1999).

21. O'Connor, *Punk Record Labels and the Struggle for Autonomy*, 71.

22. Martín Sorrondeguy, interview by author.

23. Odem, "Subaltern Immigrants," 362–68; Douglas Massey, Jorge Durand, and Nolan Malone, *Beyond Smoke and Mirrors: Mexican Immigration in an Era of Economic Integration* (New York: Russell Sage Foundation, 2002), 24–41.

24. Ibid.

25. Ibid.

26. Durand, Massey, and Parrado, "The New Era of Mexican Migration to the United States," 521–27, quote on 525; Robert Smith, *Mexican New York* (Berkeley: University of California Press, 2006), 22.

27. Massey, Durand, and Malone, *Beyond Smoke and Mirrors*, 45.

28. Kerstin Gentsch and Douglas Massey, "Labor Market Outcomes for Legal Mexican Immigrants Under the New Regime of Immigration Enforcement," *Social Science Quarterly* 92, no. 3 (September 2011), 875–93, quote on 891–92.

29. Aihwa Ong, "Cultural Citizenship as Subject-Making: Immigrants Negotiate Racial and Cultural Boundaries in the United States," *Current Anthropology* 37, no. 5 (December 1996), 742–45.

30. Robert Smith, "Mexicans: Social, Educational, Economic, and Political Problems and Prospects in New York," in *New Immigrants in New York*, ed. Nancy Foner (New York: Columbia University Press, 2001), 281.

31. Douglas Massey and Chiara Capoferro, "The Geographic Diversification of American Immigration," in *New Faces in New Places: The Changing Geography of American Immigration*, ed. Douglas Massey (New York: Russell Sage Foundation, 2008), 38.

32. Smith, "Mexicans: Social, Educational, Economic, and Political Problems and Prospects in New York," 276–77.

33. For overviews and case studies of these dynamics, see Douglas Massey, ed., *New Faces in New Places: The Changing Geography of American Immigration* (New York: Russell Sage Foundation, 2008); Arthur Murphy, Colleen Blanchard, and Jennifer Hill, eds., *Latino Workers in the Contemporary South* (Athens: University of Georgia Press, 2001).

34. Interview with Los Crudos, *HeartattaCk* 2 (June 1994), 27.

35. Martín Sorrondeguy, dir., *Más allá de los gritos / Beyond the Screams: A US Latino Hardcore Documentary* (Chicago: Lengua Armada, 1999).

36. Ibid.

37. One model for explicating changes in mass consciousness through musical preferences and style is Brian Ward, *Just My Soul Responding: Rhythm and Blues, Black Consciousness and Race Relations* (London: UCL Press, 1998).

38. Martín Sorrondeguy, interview by author. On the Latino involvement in New York hardcore, see Freddy Alva, "The Hispanic Impact on the Early New York Hardcore Scene," *noecho.net*, 5 May 2014 (http://www.noecho.net/features/the-hispanic-impact-on-the-early-new-york-hardcore-scene-by-freddy-alva, accessed 21 October 2016). Latino involvement in New York hardcore came principally from Puerto Ricans, Cubans, and Dominicans, and followed a different history than that being described here. Concerning the West Coast, Alice Bag, *Violence Girl: East L.A. Rage to Hollywood Stage, a Chicana Punk Story* (Port Townsend, WA: Feral House, 2011) is an excellent first-hand account by a prominent figure in early punk. For a scholarly account of the hidden history of Latino involvement in punk, see Michelle Habell-Pallán, "'Soy Punkera, ¿Y Que?': Sexuality, Translocality, and Punk in Los Angeles and Beyond," in *Rockin' Las Americas*, ed. Deborah Pacini Hernandez, Héctor Fernández L'Hoeste, and Eric Zolov (Pittsburgh: University of Pittsburgh Press, 2004), 160–78.

39. Interview with Los Crudos, *HeartattaCk* 2 (June 1994), 26.

40. Alan O'Connor, "Local Scenes and Dangerous Crossroads: Punk and Theories of Cultural Hybridity," *Popular Music* 21, no. 2 (May 2002), 231–32. On punk in Mexico City, see Kelley Tatro, "The Righteous and the Profane: Performing a Punk Solidarity in Mexico City" (PhD Diss., Duke University, 2013).

41. Stephen Duncombe and Maxwell Tremblay, eds., *White Riot: Punk Rock and the Politics of Race* (London and New York: Verso, 2011), part 6.

42. Interview with Los Crudos, *HeartattaCk* 2 (June 1994), 24.

43. Mimi Nguyen, "It's (Not) a White World: Looking for Race in Punk," *Punk Planet* 28 (November–December 1998), 80–83. This latter point comes both from Nguyen and my own reading of every issue of four prominent punk zines published in the 1990s. In my own interviews with Taína Asili, Michelle Gonzales, and Martín Sorrondeguy, all three suggested that punk's opposition to white supremacy was usually limited to outright Nazis.

44. Interview with Martín Sorrondeguy of Los Crudos, *MaximumRockNRoll* 192 (May 1999).

45. Martín Sorrondeguy, interview by author.

46. Michelle Gonzales, interview by author.

47. Gonzales, *The Spitboy Rule*, 86.

48. Taína Asili, interview by author.

49. Ibid.

50. Ibid.

51. Ibid.

52. Ricanstruction, *Liberation Day* CD (New York: CBGB Records, 1998).

53. Taína Asili, interview by author.

54. Nate Wilson, Review of Ricanstruction, *Liberation Day* CD, *Punk Planet* 27 (September–October 1998), 121.

55. Michelle Gonzales, interview by author.

56. Taína Asili, interview by author.

57. Mimi Nguyen, "It's (Not) a White World: Looking for Race in Punk," *Punk Planet* 28 (November–December 1998), 81.

58. Kristen Schilt, "'Riot Grrrl Is . . .': The Contestation over Meaning in a Music Scene," in *Music Scenes: Local, Translocal and Virtual*, ed. Andy Bennett and Richard Peterson (Nashville, TN: Vanderbilt University Press, 2004), 117.

59. Ibid., 115.

60. This summary draws on Sara Marcus, *Girls to the Front: The True Story of the Riot Grrrl Revolution* (New York: Harper Perennial, 2010).

61. Michelle Gonzales, interview by author.

62. Northern California Scene Report, *MaximumRockNRoll* 95 (April 1991).

63. Mike Millett, Review of Spitboy, self-titled 7", *MaximumRockNRoll* 108 (May 1992).

64. Michelle Gonzales, interview by author.

65. Interview with Spitboy, *MaximumRockNRoll* 108 (May 1992).

66. Gonzales, *The Spitboy Rule*, 24.

67. Interview with Spitboy, *MaximumRockNRoll* 108 (May 1992).

68. Michelle Gonzales, interview by author.

69. Marion Leonard, "Riot Grrrl," *Grove Music Online* (Oxford University Press), accessed 23 November, 2016, http://www.oxfordmusiconline.com/subscriber/article/grove/music/A2257186.

70. Michelle Gonzales, interview by author.

71. Ibid.

72. Ibid.

73. Karin Gembus, Column, *MaximumRockNRoll* 114 (November 1992).

74. Michelle Luellen, *HeartattaCk* 22, "Vuvaluation: A Women's Issue, Part 1" (May 1999). On a personal note and from the flipside of the gender divide, I still remember feeling like my mind was blown as a teenage boy the first time I heard Taína Asili scream on Anti-Product's song "Sexual Slavery"—hearing women articulate feminist critiques with such a feeling of raw anger certainly helped shape my own anti-patriarchy views and practices.

75. *MaximumRockNRoll* 120 (May 1993).

76. *MaximumRockNRoll* 133 (June 1994).

77. *Profane Existence* 14 (May–June 1992), 21. The comparison to other "Bay bands" is likely a swipe at the pop-punk style prominent in the Bay Area at the time.

78. Michelle Gonzales, interview by author.

79. Ibid.

80. Michelle Gonzales, interview by author.

81. Gonzales, *The Spitboy Rule*, 26–27.

82. Spitboy, Self-Titled 7" (Laytonville, CA: Lookout Records, 1991). Lyrics by Adrienne Stone (Adrienne Droogas), reproduced with permission.

83. Interview with Spitboy, *MaximumRockNRoll* 108 (May 1992).

84. Taína Asili, interview by author.

85. Ibid.

86. Taína Asili, interview by author.

87. See Leblanc's *Pretty in Punk* for a sociological study of street punk women and gender roles.

88. Gonzales, *The Spitboy Rule*, 53.

89. Michelle Gonzales, interview by author.

90. The word "womyn" was a feminist tactic aimed at overcoming the linguistic domination of men over wo*men*.

91. See, for example, the sidebar printed along with an interview with Spitboy in *MaximumRockNRoll* 108 (May 1992).

92. Kirsten Patches, interview by author.

93. *Profane Existence* 19/20 (double issue, summer 1993), 24–25.

94. Naked Aggression, *Heard It All Before* CD (Corona, CA: SOS Records, 2005). Lyrics by Kirsten Patches / Naked Aggression, used with permission.

95. Naked Aggression, *Heard It All Before* CD (Corona, CA: SOS Records, 2005).

96. Interview with Aus-Rotten, *Profane Existence* 38 (2000), 21.

97. Christine Boarts, Column, *HeartattaCk* 22, "Vulvaluation: A Women's Issue, Part 1" (May 1999).

98. Kristi Fults, Column, *HeartattaCk* 23, "Vulvaluation: A Women's Issue, Part 2" (August 1999).

99. Interview with Anti-Product, *Profane Existence* 36 (Late Summer 1998), 33.

100. Allie Riot, Column, *HeartattaCk* 23, "Vulvaluation: A Women's Issue, Part 2" (August 1999).

101. Gonzales, *The Spitboy Rule*, 117–18.

102. Kevin Sanderson, Review of Los Crudos / Spitboy, *Viviendo Aperamente* split LP, *MaximumRockNRoll* 151 part 1 (December 1995).

Chapter 5

1. I borrow the words and concept "introspective aggression" from Waksman, who uses "anger and introspection" to describe the aesthetic of early 1990s grunge music (*This Ain't the Summer of Love*, 301).

2. See Larry Livermore, Column, *MaximumRockNRoll* 87 (August 1990).

3. Larry Livermore, Column, *MaximumRockNRoll* 101 (October 1991).

4. Commitment has been an important value and lyrical theme in punk since at least the 1980s; see, for example, the 7 Seconds' song "Committed for Life."

5. Ben Weasel, "The Business of Punk Rock," *MaximumRockNRoll* 104 (January 1992).

6. http://www.billboard.com/charts/hot-100/1992-01-11, accessed 16 December 2016.

7. See Waksman, *This Ain't the Summer of Love*, 300–306 for an account of the emergence of grunge as a crossover between punk and metal.

8. NOFX with Jeff Alulis, *NOFX: The Hepatitis Bathtub and Other Stories* (Boston: Da Capo Press, 2016), 149.

9. Paul Chan, "The Kids Aren't Alright: Punk Identity and Difference in the Age of Multi-National Capitalism," *Punk Planet* 14 (August–September 1996), 78.

10. Ibid., 79.

11. Ibid., 79.

12. "Everything You Wanted to Know About Major Labels," *MaximumRockNRoll* 133 (June 1994).

13. The Pist, *Ideas Are Bulletproof* (Minneapolis, MN: Havoc Records, 1995). Lyrics by Al Ouimet, used with permission.

14. NOFX with Jeff Alulis, *NOFX*, 241.

15. Jim Testa, Column, *Punk Planet* 8 (July–August 1995), 14.

16. Will Dandy, Column, *Punk Planet* 8 (November–December 1994), 16. Note here how easily DIY discourse can incorporate a masculine subjectivity as its measure of authenticity, in contrast to "alternachicks" "swinging to the beat" rather than moshing.

17. On masculine discourses of authenticity in music, see Matthew Bannister, "Loaded": Indie Guitar Rock, Canonism, White Masculinities," *Popular Music* 25, no. 1 (January 2006): 77–95.

18. Felix von Havoc, Review of Green Day, *39/Smooth* LP, *Profane Existence* 5 (August–September, 1990), 35. At the time of this review, Lookout! Records had credibility as an independent label within underground punk.

19. In a review of the *Kerplunk!* LP, Criterion T wrote, "Green Day's simplistic pop-punk melodies and goofy . . . sing-along lyrics really grabbed my goat on their first album" (*Profane Existence* 14 (May–June 1992), 20). Criterion T's favorable review was, however, accompanied by a disclaimer from *Profane Existence* making clear that it did not represent the viewpoint of the zine.

20. Timothy Dowd, Kathleen Liddle, and Jenna Nelson, "Music Festivals as Scenes: Examples from Serious Music, Womyn's Music, and SkatePunk," in *Music Scenes: Local, Translocal and Virtual*, ed. Andy Bennett and Richard Peterson (Nashville, TN: Vanderbilt University Press, 2004), 158–63.

21. "The Warped Tour X-po$ed," *Punk Planet* 34 (November–December 1999), 74–83.

22. O'Connor, *Punk Record Labels and the Struggle for Autonomy*, ix–xi, 22–28. O'Connor's choices in terminology—commercial punk versus DIY punk—betray his own ideological position with regard to DIY.

23. Dan Sinker, Interview with Brett Gurewitz, *Punk Planet* 4 (November–December 1994), 28–31. Rancid, another Epitaph band, similarly justified the video for their song "Nihilism" appearing on MTV as luck rather than design. See Will Dandy, Interview with Lars [Rancid guitarist], *Punk Planet* 1 (May–June 1994), 32.

24. Manduke, Review of Total Chaos, *Pledge of Defiance* LP, *Profane Existence* 22 (Spring 1994), 22.

25. Interview with Total Chaos, *Profane Existence* 23 (Autumn 1994), 22–23.

26. See Letters, *MaximumRockNRoll* 165 (February 1997).

27. Dan, Column, *Profane Existence* 25 (Summer 1995), 57.

28. See, for example, columns in *MaximumRockNRoll* 158 (July 1996).

29. Dave Seifort, Review of Coffin Break, *Thirteen* LP, *MaximumRockNRoll* 116 (January 1993).

30. Mike Millett, Review of Bad Religion, *Recipe for Hate* LP, *MaximumRockNRoll* 124 (September 1993).

31. Review of Offspring, self-titled LP, *MaximumRockNRoll* 80 (January 1990).

32. Suzanne Bartchy, Offspring, *Smash* LP, *MaximumRockNRoll* 133 (June 1994).

33. It is worth noting that Offspring's mainstream success provoked an accusation of musical theft and a demand for financial compensation from Robbie Fields from the band Agent Orange. Fields claimed that in Offspring's first hit single, "Come Out and Play," the lead guitar part following the chorus was taken from the guitar solo in Agent Orange's 1980 recording of their song "Bloodstains." No lawsuit was ever filed, and Offspring denied this accusation. To my ears, the lead guitar part in "Come Out and Play" and the guitar solo in "Bloodstains" both use the same scale, and scales using augmented thirds surrounded by semitones were rare in punk, but there the similarity ends. Offspring may well have been inspired by Agent Orange's use of this scale, but they did not steal a guitar melody. For more on this incident, see Mike Boehm, "Offspring Lifted Key Guitar Riff, Publisher Says: Manager Denies 'Come Out and Play' Arabian Hook Is Agent Orange Creation," *Los Angeles Times* (4 April 1995).

34. Review of Bad Religion, *No Control* LP, *MaximumRockNRoll* 81 (February 1990).

35. Mike McNiel, Review of NOFX, *The Longest Line* EP, *MaximumRockNRoll* 109 (June 1992).

36. Michelle Haunold, Review of Pennywise, *Wild Card* EP *MaximumRockNRoll* 116 (January 1993).

37. Tim Yohannan, Review of Pennywise, *Unknown Road*, *MaximumRockNRoll* 125 (October 1993); Review of NOFX, *Don't Call Me White* 7", *MaximumRockNRoll* 135 (August 1994).

38. Review of No Use For A Name's *Leche con Carne* LP, *MaximumRockNRoll* 144 (May 1995). Fat Wreck Chords is the record label founded by NOFX's Fat Mike that released this album.

39. Brian Gathy, Review of Strung Out / Blout, split 7", *MaximumRockNRoll* 156, part 2 (May 1996).

40. Fishsticks, Review of Pennywise, *Unknown Road*, *Profane Existence* 21 (January–February 1994), 22.

41. Will Dandy, Review of Pennywise, *About Time*, *Punk Planet* 9 (September–October 1995), 85. The zine *Flipside* also refused to dismiss bands playing punk styles that garnered wider audiences.

42. Harvey Dent, Review of Pennywise, *About Time*, *MaximumRockNRoll* 147 (August 1995).

43. Marie Davenport, Review of Drunk in Public's *Tapped Out!* CD, *Punk Planet* 19 (July–August 1997), 133.

44. Steve Aoki, Review of Supergirls 7", *HeartattaCk* 14 (June 1997).

45. Brett Hall, Review of *Fat Music for Fat People* CD, *HeartattaCk* 7 (August 1995), 41.

46. Yes, I am invoking Louis Althusser, "Ideology and Ideological State Apparatuses," in *Lenin and Philosophy and Other Essays* (New York: Monthly Review Press, 2001), 85–126.

47. Ben Weasel, *MaximumRockNRoll* 104 (January 1992).

48. Turner, "Maximizing Rock and Roll."

49. "Making Punk a Trend Again," *Profane Existence* 13 (May–June 1992), 3. This article title deliberately inverts the *Profane Existence* slogan "making punk a threat again."

50. Kent McClard, *HeartattaCk* 1 (March 1994), 3. By contrast, the zine *Punk Planet* was founded in part to counter what its editor and writers felt was an increasingly narrow interpretation by *MaximumRockNRoll* and other authorities in the punk scene on what could rightfully be considered punk music and DIY practices.

51. Interview with Defiance, *Profane Existence* 26 (Autumn 1995), 34.

52. Josh Hooten, Interview with Steve Heritage of Assück, *Punk Planet* 27 (September–October 1998), 47.

53. Interview with the Young Pioneers, *Punk Planet* 23 (March–April 1998), 56. Adam Nathanson went on to be a part of the Young Pioneers after Born Against broke up. His choice of Trixter to make this point could not have been better, as Trixter was a glam-metal band that achieved brief commercial success at the same time Born Against was cultivating a following in the underground punk scene, but Trixter is for the most part forgotten about.

54. Chan, "The Kids Aren't Alright," 77. It will have to wait for the conclusion to critically evaluate just how well DIY ensured that punk's audiences stayed true to its message.

55. *MaximumRockNRoll* 108 (May 1992).

56. Joel Schalit, "Redistributing Cultural Goods in Not the Same Thing as Redistributing Wealth and It Never Will Be: All Punk Commodities," *Punk Planet* 17 (March–April 1997), 78.

57. Ibid., 79.

58. Karl Marx, *Capital*, vol. 1, trans. Ben Fowkes (New York: Penguin, 1990), 280, as quoted in Thompson, *Punk Productions*, 121.

59. Thompson, *Punk Productions*, 121.

60. Barry Shank, *The Political Force of Musical Beauty* (Durham, NC: Duke University Press, 2014), 176–77.

61. Among cultural studies scholars, it has become popular in recent decades to demonstrate how consumers can have agency in how they interpret entertainment. This is certainly a valid point, and the concept of the "resistant reader" was an important feminist intervention concerning agency—see for example, Janice Radway, *Reading the Romance: Women, Patriarchy, and Popular Literature* (Chapel Hill: University of North Carolina Press, 1984). However, overemphasis in the field of cultural studies on the agency of consumers risks making nuances principal over the overwhelming passivity consumer culture inculcates in the American populace, which punk correctly critiques. This is related to overarching tendencies within cultural studies to make the most out of any gesture that can be interpreted as "resistant" or "transgressive," in the wishful delusion that these gestures will amount to a radical challenge to oppressive institutions.

62. All too little critical discourse exists on both these phenomena, though Andrea Moore has provided an excellent critique of arts entrepreneurship in relation to the world of new classical music in her article "Neoliberalism and the Musical Entrepreneur," *Journal of the Society for American Music* 10, no. 1 (2010): 33–53.

63. Bryan Alft, Column, *HeartattaCk* 20 (November 1998).

64. Chan, "The Kids Aren't Alright," 77.

65. Gonzales, *The Spitboy Rule*, 91–92.

66. Interview with Naked Aggression, *Punk Planet* 11 (January–February 1996), 32, 33.

67. NOFX, *So Long and Thanks for All the Shoes* (Hollywood, CA: Epitaph Records, 1997).

68. While it is beyond the scope of this study, Rage Against The Machine (RATM) provides an important example of an "alternative" (broadly defined) band in the 1990s that espoused radical politics but disseminated them through the strategy of signing to a major label, having videos on MTV and songs on mainstream radio stations, and embarking on arena tours. Though RATM certainly attracted many fans not interested in their politics, they also inspired others not only to take up their ideas but also to get involved in political movements, such as the efforts to free political prisoner Mumia Abu-Jamal, support for the Zapatista rebellion in Chiapas, Mexico, and the protests largely by Chicano students against California's Proposition 187 and other anti-immigrant laws—in contrast to Kent McClard's dismissal of RATM as making money, not politics, in *HeartattaCk* 20 (November 1998). The point here is that for the underground punk scene, radical politics were bound up with DIY autonomy, and thus no matter what RATM said in their lyrics, how many benefit concerts they performed at, or how many of their fans got involved in political movements, they were part of the machine. Not coincidentally, RATM drew not just on anarchist philosophy but also on communist ideas and conceived of revolution more as a violent overthrow of the existing order rather than the building up of alternative countercultural spaces.

69. See David Harvey, *The Condition of Postmodernity: An Enquiry into the Origins of Cultural Change* (Oxford: Blackwell, 1989).

70. This brief summary draws on Thompson, *Punk Productions*, 71–77.

71. O'Connor, *Punk Record Labels and the Struggle for Autonomy*, 22.

72. MacLeod, *Kids of the Black Hole*.

73. NOFX with Jeff Alulis, *NOFX*, 103.

74. In "You're Bleeding," when Fat Mike's vocals enter during the verses, both rhythm and lead guitar play palm muted.

75. Bad Religion, *Against the Grain* (Hollywood, CA: Epitaph Records, 1990).

76. The best account of NOFX's history is provided in its autobiography, NOFX with Jeff Alulis, *NOFX*.

77. For elucidations of these realities, see Harvey, *A Brief History of Neoliberalism*; Sassen, *Globalization and Its Discontents*; Alexander, *The New Jim Crow*; and Anthony Arnove, ed., *Iraq under Siege: The Deadly Impact of Sanctions and War* (Cambridge, MA: South End Press, 2003).

78. Although it is unlikely Fat Mike is familiar with musical rhetoric in the Baroque era, the parallel between this trombone riff and the musical emblem of lament in Baroque opera is striking. On descending stepwise minor-key basslines and their rhetorical meaning in the Baroque era, see Ellen Rosand, "The Descending Tetrachord: An Emblem of Lament."

79. For the B in the sixth bar, the guitarists shift their index fingers down a fret but keep the upper voices of the previous C power chord, thus creating a C power chord over a B bass note (from the lowest pitch: B, G, C).

80. For an extended discussion of how the disparate styles of reggae and punk were fused together by late-70s UK bands such as the Clash and the Police, see Spicer, "'Reggatta de Blanc': Analyzing Style in the Music of the Police."

81. This line is from "Lotus Gait" on Propagandhi, *Failed States*, CD (Hollywood, CA: Epitaph Records, 2012).

Conclusion

1. Clifford Geertz, "Thick Description: Toward an Interpretive Theory of Culture," in *The Interpretation of Cultures* (New York: Basic Books, 1973), 3–30.

2. Interview with Aus-Rotten, *Profane Existence* 38 (Summer 2000), 24.

3. In his ethnography of direct action, David Graeber notes, "so many of the most active white anarchists seem to have been drawn in from an early experience of the punk scene." Graeber, *Direct Action: An Ethnography* (Oakland, CA: AK Press, 2009), 258.

4. On Food Not Bombs, see C. T. Butler and Keith McHenry, *Food Not Bombs* (Tucson, AZ: See Sharp Press, 2000). On punk involvement in Food Not Bombs, see, for example, Bryan Alft, Column, *HeartattaCk* 17 (Spring 1998); and Interview with Aus-Rotten, *Punk Planet* 8 (July–August 1995), 34.

5. News Section, *Profane Existence* 26 (Autumn 1995), 4.

6. Interview with Aus-Rotten, *Profane Existence* 38 (Summer 2000), 23; News Section, *MaximumRockNRoll* 188 (January 1999).

7. Interview with Aus-Rotten, *Profane Existence* 38 (Summer 2000), 24.

8. News Section, *MaximumRockNRoll* 105 (February 1992).

9. Dan Sinker, Interview with Jon Strange, *Punk Planet* 25 (May–June 1998), 34–37. On Iraqi civilian deaths due to US sanctions, see Arnove, *Iraq Under Siege*.

10. Martín Sorrondeguy, interview by author.

11. Interview with Aus-Rotten, *Profane Existence* 38 (Summer 2000), 24.

12. Jen Hate, "ABC No Rio: A Volunteer's Story," *HeartattaCk* 22 (May 1999).

13. Jon and Dan, Interview with Anti-Product, *Profane Existence* 36 (Summer 1998), 32–33.
14. Interview with Public Nuisance, *MaximumRockNRoll* 138 (November 1994).
15. Review of Blanks 77, *Up the System* 10", *MaximumRockNRoll* 129 (February 1994).
16. Jon and Dan, Interview with Anti-Product, *Profane Existence* 36 (Summer 1998), 33.
17. Interview with Aus-Rotten, *Profane Existence* 38 (Summer 2000), 22.
18. Felix von Havoc, Column, *HeartattaCk* 11 (May 1996), 24.
19. Dan, Column, *Profane Existence* 26 (Autumn 1995), 53.
20. Adam, Column, *HeartattaCk* 13 (November 1996), 14. Emphasis in the original.
21. Felix von Havoc, Column, *HeartattaCk* 9 (February 1996), 23.
22. Bryan Alft, Column, *HeartattaCk* 17 (Spring 1998), 17.
23. Interview with In/Humanity, *MaximumRockNRoll* 174 (November 1997).
24. Jen Angel, Column, *Punk Planet*, 17 (March–April 1997), 27.
25. Interview with Los Crudos, *HeartattaCk* 2 (June 1994).
26. Denver Dale, Review of Aus-Rotten, ... *And Now Back to Our Programming* LP, *HeartattaCk* 23 (August 1999).
27. Felix von Havoc, Column, *HeartattaCk* 6 (May–June 1995), 46–47.
28. Taína Asili, interview by author.
29. Kirsten Patches, interview by author.
30. Al Pist, interview by author.
31. Interview with Aus-Rotten, *Profane Existence* 38 (Summer 2000), 23.
32. Kirsten Patches, interview by author.
33. Green Day's 2004 *American Idiot* album, full of protest songs against the Iraq war and other policies of the George W. Bush administration, reached #1 on the Billboard 200 charts during three different weeks in 2004 and 2005. See http://www.billboard.com/articles/columns/chart-beat/7542053/green-day-earns-third-no-1-album-on-billboard-200-chart-with, accessed 20 April 2017. More recently, following Donald Trump's election to the presidency, Green Day incorporated an updated version of lyrics by the band M.D.C. into its performance at the 2016 American Music Awards: "No Trump, No KKK, No Fascist USA!"

Bibliography

Interviews by Author

Asili, Taína. Via Skype, 6 August 2015.
Chamberlain, Bill. Via telephone, 17 December 2015.
Gonzales, Michelle. Oakland, CA, 7 July 2015.
Patches, Kirsten. Via Skype, 3 February 2016.
Pist, Al. Brooklyn, NY, 5 December 2015.
Sorrondeguy, Martín. San Francisco, CA, 15 July 2015.

Zines

HeartattaCk. Goleta, CA.
MaximumRockNRoll. San Francisco, CA.
Profane Existence. Minneapolis, MN.
Punk Planet. Chicago, IL.

Discography

Anti-Flag. *Kill Kill Kill* 7". Pittsburg, PA: SelfServ Records / Ripe Records, 1995.
Anti-Product. *The Deafening Silence of Grinding Gears* LP. Portland, OR: Tribal War Records, 1999.
Anti-Product. Self-Titled 7". Conklin, NY: Obese Records, 1996.
Aus-Rotten. *The System Works . . . For Them* LP. New York: Tribal War Records, 1996.
Aus-Rotten. *Fuck Nazi Sympathy* 7". Minneapolis, MN: Havoc Records, 1994.
Bad Religion. *Against the Grain*. Hollywood, CA: Epitaph Records, 1990.
Bad Religion. *Suffer*. Hollywood, CA: Epitaph Records, 1988.
Brother Inferior. *Anthems '94–'97* CD. Tulsa, OK: Sensual Underground Ministries, 1997.
Brother Inferior / Whorehouse of Representatives split 7". Minneapolis, MN: Profane Existence, 1998.
Burned Up Bled Dry. *Kill the Body . . . Kill the Soul . . .* 7". Tulsa, OK: Sensual Underground Ministries, 1997.
Capitalist Casualties. *Subdivisions in Ruin* LP. Cotati, CA: Six Weeks Records, 1999.
Civil Disobedience. *In a Few Hours of Madness* 7". Minneapolis, MN: Havoc Records, 1993.
Code 13. *A Part of America Died Today* 7". Minneapolis, MN: Havoc Records, 1998.
Los Crudos. *Doble LP discografía*. San Francisco, CA: Maximum RockNRoll, 2014.
Los Crudos / Spitboy. *Viviendo Aperamente* (Roughly Living) LP. Goleta, CA: Ebullition Records, 1995.
Defiance. *No Future No Hope* LP. Mind Control, 1996.
Discharge. *Hear Nothing See Nothing Say Nothing* LP. Stoke-on-Trent, UK: Clay Records, 1982.
Dropdead. Self-Titled LP. Providence, RI: Armageddon Label, 1998.
His Hero Is Gone. *Monuments to Thieves* LP. San Francisco, CA: Prank Records, 1997.

His Hero Is Gone. *Fifteen Counts of Arson* LP. San Francisco, CA: Prank Records, 1996.

Mankind? *Won't You Join the Army Now So You Can Fight . . . and You Can Die! 7".* Meriden, CT: Eugene Records, 1993.

Minor Threat. *Complete Discography* CD. Washington, DC: Dischord Records, 1989.

Naked Aggression. *Heard It All Before* CD. Corona, CA: SOS Records, 2005.

NOFX. *The Decline.* San Francisco, CA: Fat Wreck Chords, 1999.

NOFX. *So Long and Thanks for All the Shoes.* Hollywood, CA: Epitaph Records, 1997.

NOFX. *White Trash, Two Heebs and a Bean.* Hollywood, CA: Epitaph Records, 1992.

Pennywise. *About Time.* Hollywood, CA: Epitaph Records, 1995.

Pennywise. *Unknown Road.* Hollywood, CA: Epitaph Records, 1993.

The Pist. *Ideas Are Bulletproof.* Minneapolis, MN: Havoc Records, 1995.

Reagan Youth. *Youth Anthems for the New Order.* New York: R Radical, 1984.

Ricanstruction. *Liberation Day* CD. New York: CBGB Records, 1998.

Sex Pistols. *Never Mind the Bollocks Here's the Sex Pistols* LP. London: Virgin Records, 1977.

Spitboy. *Self-Titled 7".* Laytonville, CA: Lookout Records, 1991.

Tomorrow Will Be Worse four 7" records compilation. Covington, KY: Sound Pollution Records, 1997.

Whorehouse of Representatives. *Your Alcohol Taxes at Work 7".* Seattle, WA: SABOTAGE: earth records, 1997.

Youth of Today. *Break Down the Walls* LP. New Haven, CT: Revelation Records, 1988. Original Release: Wishingwell Records, 1986.

Books, Journal Articles, and Documentaries

Alexander, Michelle. *The New Jim Crow: Mass Incarceration in the Age of Colorblindness.* New York: The New Press, 2012.

Althusser, Louis. "Ideology and Ideological State Apparatuses." In *Lenin and Philosophy and Other Essays,* 85–126. New York: Monthly Review Press, 2001.

Andersen, Mark, and Mark Jenkins. *Dance of Days: Two Decades of Punk in the Nation's Capital.* New York: Akashic Books, 2009.

Arnove, Anthony, ed. *Iraq Under Siege: The Deadly Impact of Sanctions and War.* Cambridge, MA: South End Press, 2003.

Bag, Alice. *Violence Girl: East L.A. Rage to Hollywood Stage, a Chicana Punk Story.* Port Townsend, WA: Feral House, 2011.

Bannister, Matthew. "'Loaded': Indie Guitar Rock, Canonism, White Masculinities." *Popular Music* 25, no. 1 (January 2006): 77–95.

Baugh, Bruce. "Prolegomena to Any Aesthetics of Rock Music." *Journal of Aesthetics and Art Criticism* 51, no. 1 (Winter 1993): 23–29.

Booker, Keith. *Dystopian Literature: A Theory and Research Guide.* Westport, CT: Greenwood Press, 1994.

Butler, C. T., and Keith McHenry. *Food Not Bombs.* Tucson, AZ: See Sharp Press, 2000.

Butler, Mark. *Unlocking the Groove: Rhythm, Meter, and Musical Design in Electronic Dance Music.* Bloomington: Indiana University Press, 2006.

Ciminelli, David. *Homocore: The Loud and Raucous Rise of Queer Rock.* Los Angeles: Alyson Books, 2005.

Claisse, Frédéric, and Pierre Delvenne. "Building on Anticipation: Dystopia as Empowerment." *Current Sociology* 63, no. 2 (2015): 155–69.

Corte, Urgo, and Bob Edwards. "White Power Music and the Mobilization of Racist Social Movements." *Music and Arts in Action* 1, no. 1 (2008): 4–20.

Dalleck, Robert. *Ronald Reagan: The Politics of Symbolism*. Cambridge, MA: Harvard University Press, 1984.

Davis, Mike. *City of Quartz: Excavating the Future in Los Angeles*. London and New York: Verso, 1991.

De Velasco, Antonio. *Centrist Rhetoric: The Production of Political Transcendence in the Clinton Presidency*. Lanham, MD: Lexington Books, 2010.

Diamond, Sara. *Not by Politics Alone: The Enduring Influence of the Christian Right*. New York: Guilford Press, 1998.

Dowd, Timothy, Kathleen Liddle, and Jenna Nelson. "Music Festivals as Scenes: Examples from Serious Music, Womyn's Music, and SkatePunk." In *Music Scenes: Local, Translocal and Virtual*, edited by Andy Bennett and Richard Peterson, 149–67. Nashville, TN: Vanderbilt University Press, 2004.

Duncombe, Stephen. *Notes from the Underground: Zines and the Politics of Alternative Culture*. London and New York: Verso, 1997.

Duncombe, Stephen, and Maxwell Tremblay, eds. *White Riot: Punk Rock and the Politics of Race*. London and New York: Verso, 2011.

Dunn, Kevin. *Global Punk: Resistance and Rebellion in Everyday Life*. New York: Bloomsbury Academic, 2016.

Durand, Jorge, Douglas S. Massey, and Emilio Parrado. "The New Era of Mexican Migration to the United States." *Journal of American History* 86, no. 2 (September 1999): 518–36.

Easley, David. "'It's Not My Imagination, I've Got A Gun On My Back!': Style and Sound in Early American Hardcore Punk, 1978–1983." PhD Diss., Florida State University, 2011.

Ensminger, David. *The Politics of Punk: Protest and Revolt from the Streets*. Lanham, MD: Bowman & Littlefield, 2016.

Everett, Walter. "Making Sense of Rock's Tonal Systems." *Music Theory Online* 10, no. 4 (December 2004). https://mtosmt.org/issues/mto.04.10.4/mto.04.10.4.w_everett.html

Fukuyama, Francis. *The End of History and the Last Man*. New York: The Free Press, 1992.

Gaunt, Kyra. *The Games Black Girls Play: Learning the Ropes from Double-Dutch to Hip-Hop*. New York: New York University Press, 2006.

Geertz, Clifford. "Thick Description: Toward an Interpretive Theory of Culture." In *The Interpretation of Cultures*, 3–30. New York: Basic Books, 1973.

Gentsch, Kerstin, and Douglas Massey. "Labor Market Outcomes for Legal Mexican Immigrants Under the New Regime of Immigration Enforcement." *Social Science Quarterly* 92, no. 3 (September 2011): 875–893.

Glasper, Ian. *Trapped in a Scene: UK Hardcore, 1985–1989*. London: Cherry Red Books, 2009.

Glasper, Ian. *The Day the Country Died: A History of Anarcho Punk, 1980–1984*. London: Cherry Red Books, 2006.

Gonzales, Michelle. *The Spitboy Rule: Tales of a Xicana in a Female Punk Band*. Oakland, CA: PM Press, 2016.

Goshert, John. "'Punk' After the Pistols: American Music, Economics, and Politics in the 1980s and 1990s." *Popular Music and Society* 24, no. 1 (January 2000): 85–106.

Graeber, David. *Direct Action: An Ethnography*. Oakland, CA: AK Press, 2009.

Grossman, Susan, et al. "Pilsen and The Resurrection Project: Community Organization in a Latino Community." *Journal of Poverty* 4, no. 1/2 (2000): 131–49.

Grubbs, Eric. *Post: A Look at the Influence of Post-Hardcore, 1985–2007*. Bloomington, IN: iUniverse, 2008.

Habell-Pallán, Michelle. "'Soy Punkera, ¿Y Qué?': Sexuality, Translocality, and Punk in Los Angeles and Beyond." In *Rockin' Las Américas: The Global Politics of Rock in Latin/o America*, edited by Deborah Pacini Hernandez, Héctor Fernández L'Hoeste, and Eric Zolov, 160–78. Pittsburgh: University of Pittsburgh Press. 2004.

Harker, Brian. "Louis Armstrong, Eccentric Dance, and the Evolution of Jazz on the Eve of Swing." *Journal of the American Musicological Society* 61, no. 1 (2008): 67–121.

Harvey, David. *A Brief History of Neoliberalism*. Oxford: Oxford University Press, 2005.

Harvey, David. *The Condition of Postmodernity: An Enquiry into the Origins of Cultural Change*. Oxford: Blackwell, 1989.

Hebdige, Dick. *Subculture: The Meaning of Style*. London and New York: Routledge, 1991 [1979].

Henry, Tricia. *Break All Rules! Punk Rock and the Making of a Style*. Ann Arbor: University of Michigan Research Press, 1989.

Lahickey, Beth. *All Ages: Reflections on Straight Edge*. Huntington Beach, CA: Revelation Books, 1997.

Laing, Dave. *One Chord Wonders: Power and Meaning in Punk Rock*. Oakland, CA: PM Press, 2015 [1985].

Leblanc, Lauraine. *Pretty in Punk: Girls' Gender Resistance in a Boys' Subculture*. New Brunswick, NJ: Rutgers University Press, 2006 [1999].

MacAlear, Rob. "The Value of Fear: Toward a Rhetorical Model of Dystopia." *Interdisciplinary Humanities* 27, no. 2 (2010): 24–42.

MacLeod, Dewar. *Kids of the Black Hole: Punk Rock in Postsuburban California*. Norman: University of Oklahoma Press, 2010.

Marcus, Sara. *Girls to the Front: The True Story of the Riot Grrrl Revolution*. New York: Harper Perennial, 2010.

Marx, Karl. *Capital*. Vol. 1. Translated by Ben Fowkes. New York: Penguin, 1990.

Massey, Douglas, ed. *New Faces in New Places: The Changing Geography of American Immigration*. New York: Russell Sage Foundation, 2008.

Massey, Douglas, Jorge Durand, and Nolan Malone. *Beyond Smoke and Mirrors: Mexican Immigration in an Era of Economic Integration*. New York: Russell Sage Foundation, 2002.

Mittler, Barbara. *A Continuous Revolution: Making Sense of Cultural Revolution Culture*. Cambridge, MA: Harvard University Asia Center, 2013.

Mittler, Barbara. "Cultural Revolution Model Works and the Politics of Modernization in China: An Analysis of *Taking Tiger Mountain by Strategy*." *The World of Music: Journal of the Department of Ethnomusicology, Otto-Friedrich University of Bamberg* 45, no. 2 (2003): 53–81.

Mohr, Tim. *Burning Down the Haus: Punk Rock, Revolution, and the Fall of the Berlin Wall*. Chapel Hill, NC: Algonquin Books, 2018.

Moore, Andrea. "Neoliberalism and the Musical Entrepreneur." *Journal of the Society for American Music* 10, no. 1 (2010): 33–53.

Murphy, Arthur, Colleen Blanchard, and Jennifer Hill, eds. *Latino Workers in the Contemporary South*. Athens: University of Georgia Press, 2001.

NOFX with Jeff Alulis. *NOFX: The Hepatitis Bathtub and Other Stories*. Boston: Da Capo Press, 2016.

O'Connor, Alan. *Punk Record Labels and the Struggle for Autonomy: The Emergence of DIY*. Lanham, MD: Rowman & Littlefield, 2008.

O'Connor, Alan. "Local Scenes and Dangerous Crossroads: Punk and Theories of Cultural Hybridity." *Popular Music* 21, no. 2 (May 2002): 225–36.

Odem, Mary. "Subaltern Immigrants." *Interventions: The International Journal of Postcolonial Studies* 10, no. 3 (2008): 359–80.

Ong, Aihwa. "Cultural Citizenship as Subject-Making: Immigrants Negotiate Racial and Cultural Boundaries in the United States." *Current Anthropology* 37, no. 5 (December 1996): 737–62.

Patton, Raymond. *Punk Crisis: The Global Punk Rock Revolution*. New York: Oxford University Press, 2018.

Perris, Arnold. *Music as Propaganda: Art to Persuade, Art to Control.* Westport, CT: Greenwood, 1985.

Peterson, Brian. *Burning Fight: The Nineties Hardcore Revolution in Ethics, Politics, Spirit, and Sound.* Huntington Beach, CA: Revelation Records Publishing, 2009.

Phillipov, Michelle. "Haunted by the Spirit of '77: Punk Studies and the Persistence of Politics." *Continuum: Journal of Media and Cultural Studies* 20, no. 3 (September 2006): 383–93.

Pieslak, Jonathan. *Radicalism and Music: An Introduction to the Music Cultures of Al-Qa'ida, Racist Skinheads, Christian-Affiliated Radicalism, and Eco-Animal Rights Militants.* Middletown, CT: Wesleyan University Press, 2015.

Profane Existence Collective. *Making Punk a Threat Again!* Minneapolis: Loin Cloth Press, 1997.

Rachman, Paul, dir. *American Hardcore: The History of American Punk Rock, 1980–1986.* Culver City, CA: Sony Pictures. 2006.

Radway, Janice. *Reading the Romance: Women, Patriarchy, and Popular Literature.* Chapel Hill: University of North Carolina Press, 1984.

Reddy, Derek. *The Evolution of Blast Beats.* Pembroke Pines, FL: World Music 4all Publications, 2007.

Rodel, Angela. "Extreme Noise Terror: Punk Rock and the Aesthetics of Badness." In *Bad Music: The Music We Love to Hate,* edited by Christopher Washburne and Maiken Derno, 235–56. New York: Routledge, 2004.

Roholt, Tiger. *Groove: A Phenomenology of Rhythmic Nuance.* New York: Bloomsbury Academic, 2014.

Rosand, Ellen. "The Descending Tetrachord: An Emblem of Lament." *Musical Quarterly* 65, no. 3 (July 1979): 346–59.

Ruggles, Brock. "Not So Quiet on the Western Front: Punk Politics During the Conservative Ascendancy in the United States, 1980–2000." PhD Diss., Arizona State University, 2008.

Sassen, Saskia. *Globalization and Its Discontents.* New York: New Press, 1998.

Schier, Steven, ed. *The Postmodern Presidency: Bill Clinton's Legacy in U.S. Politics.* Pittsburgh, PA: University of Pittsburgh Press, 2000.

Schilt, Kristen. "'Riot Grrrl Is . . .': The Contestation over Meaning in a Music Scene." In *Music Scenes: Local, Translocal and Virtual,* edited by Andy Bennett and Richard Peterson, 115–30. Nashville, TN: Vanderbilt University, 2004.

Shank, Barry. *The Political Force of Musical Beauty.* Durham, NC: Duke University Press, 2014.

Smith, Robert. *Mexican New York.* Berkeley: University of California Press, 2006.

Smith, Robert. "Mexicans: Social, Educational, Economic, and Political Problems and Prospects in New York." In *New Immigrants in New York,* edited by Nancy Foner, 275–300. New York: Columbia University Press, 2001.

Sorrondeguy, Martín, dir., *Más allá de los gritos / Beyond the Screams: A US Latino Hardcore Documentary.* Chicago: Lengua Armada, 1999.

Spicer, Mark. "(Ac)cumulative Form in Pop-Rock Music." *Twentieth-Century Music* 1, no. 1 (March 2004): 29–64.

Spicer, Mark. "'Reggatta de Blanc': Analyzing Style in the Music of the Police." In *Sounding Out Pop: Analytical Essays in Popular Music,* edited by Mark Spicer and John Covach, 124–53. Ann Arbor: University of Michigan Press, 2010.

Tatro, Kelley. "The Righteous and the Profane: Performing a Punk Solidarity in Mexico City." PhD Diss., Duke University, 2013.

Thompson, Stacy. *Punk Productions: Unfinished Business.* Albany: State University of New York Press, 2004.

Tsitsos, William. "Rules of Rebellion: Slamdancing, Moshing, and the American Alternative Scene." *Popular Music* 18, no. 3 (October 1999): 397–414.

Turner, Scott M. X. "Maximizing Rock and Roll: An Interview with Tim Yohannon [*sic*]." In *Sounding Off: Music as Subversion/Resistance/Revolution*, edited by Fred Ho and Ronald Sakolsky, 181–94. New York: Automedia, 1995.

Vaucher, Gee. *Crass Art and Other Pre Post-Modernist Monsters*. Edinburgh, Scotland, and San Francisco, CA: AK Press, 1999.

Waksman, Steve. *This Ain't the Summer of Love: Conflict and Crossover in Heavy Metal and Punk*. Berkeley: University of California Press, 2009.

Walser, Robert. *Running with the Devil: Power, Gender, and Madness in Heavy Metal Music*. Hanover, NH: Wesleyan University Press, 1993.

Ward, Brian. *Just My Soul Responding: Rhythm and Blues, Black Consciousness and Race Relations*. London: UCL Press, 1998.

Weinglass, Leonard. *Race for Justice: Mumia Abu-Jamal's Fight Against the Death Penalty*. Monroe, ME: Common Courage, 1995.

Index

Printed in the USA/Agawam, MA
March 15, 2022

790398.014